# The Economics of Foreign Exchange and Global Finance

Peijie Wang

# The Economics
# of Foreign Exchange
# and Global Finance

With 71 Figures and 75 Tables

 Springer

Professor Peijie Wang
Business School
University of Hull
Cottingham Road
Hull HU6 7RX
United Kingdom
p.wang@hull.ac.uk

Cataloging-in-Publication Data
Library of Congress Control Number: 2005927791

ISBN-10   3-540-21237-X Springer Berlin Heidelberg New York
ISBN-13   9783-540-21237-9 Springer Berlin Heidelberg New York

Springer is a part of Springer Science+Business Media

springeronline.com

© Springer Berlin · Heidelberg 2005
Printed in Germany

Hardcover-Design: design & production, Heidelberg

SPIN 11739296        88/3111-5  4  3  2  1  – Printed on acid-free paper

**To my beloved parents in the haven**
献给我最亲爱的父母

# Preface

The book is designed to integrate the theory of foreign exchange rate determination and the practice of global finance in a single volume, which demonstrates how theory guides practice, and practice motivates theory, in this important area of scholarly work and commercial operation in an era when the global market has become increasingly integrated.

The book presents all major subjects in international monetary theory, foreign exchange markets, international financial management and investment analysis. The book is relevant to real world problems in the sense that it provides guidance on how to solve policy issues as well as practical management tasks. This in turn helps the reader to gain an understanding of the theory and refines the framework.

Various topics are interlinked so the book adopts a systematic treatment of integrated materials relating different theories under various circumstances and combining theory with practice. The text examines issues in international monetary policy and financial management in a practical way, focusing on the identification of the factors and players in foreign exchange markets and the international finance arena.

The book can be used in graduate and advanced undergraduate programmes in international finance or global finance, international monetary economics, and international financial management. It can also be used as doctorate research methodology materials and by individual researchers interested in international finance or global finance, foreign exchange markets and foreign exchange rate determination, foreign exchange risk management, and international investment analysis.

Peijie Wang, May 2005

# Contents

# 1    Foreign Exchange Markets and Foreign Exchange Rates

A foreign exchange market is a market where a convertible currency is exchanged for another convertible currency or other convertible currencies. In the transaction or execution of conversion, one currency is considered domestic and the other is regarded as foreign, from a certain geographical or sovereign point of view, so is the term foreign exchange derived. Foreign exchange markets are not reserved for traders or finance professionals only but for almost everyone, from multinational corporations operating in several countries to tourists travelling across two currency zones. As long as national states or blocs of national states that adopt their own currencies exist, foreign exchange markets will persist to serve business, non-business, and sometimes, political needs of business firms, governments, individuals, and international organizations and institutions.

An exchange rate is the price of one currency in terms of another currency; it is the relative price of the two currencies. The initial and foremost roles of money are to function as a common measure of value and the media of exchange to facilitate the exchange of commodities of different attributes. When the values of commodities of different attributes are readily denominated by certain units of a currency or a kind of money circulated in a country or region, the relative price, or the ratio of values, of two commodities can be easily decided. The relative price of two commodities can be decided without the involvement of money, though less explicit. So, more important is the role of money as the media of exchange, for it is the bearer of commonly recognised value, exchangeable for many other commodities then or at a future time. Instead of barter trade where change of hands of two commodities is one transaction conducted at one place and at one time, people do not need to sell one commodity in exchange for another commodity or other commodities directly and immediately, but sell the commodity for certain units of a currency or a kind of money in which the value of the sold commodity is "stored" for future use.

In international trade, the situation is slightly different from that in domestic trade in that the value of one commodity is denominated in two or more currencies. In theory it is straightforward to derive the exchange rate between two currencies, which is simply the ratio of the units of one currency required to purchase, or obtained from selling, the commodity in one country or region to the units of the other currency required to purchase, or obtained from selling, the same commodity in the other country or region. Indeed, this is the idea of so called purchasing power parity, or PPP for abbreviation, an important theory and benchmark of studies in international finance. Unfortunately, this world is not a simple and carefree place. Different countries may not always produce identical products that possess the exactly same attributes, or some countries do not produce certain products at all, which leads to the needs of international trade on the one hand, and makes international comparison of commodities and consumptions difficult on the other hand. Then, transportation and physical movements of export goods incur additional costs, and governments of national states and trade blocs impose tariffs on imported goods that distort the total costs for the consumption of a wide range of commodities. Besides, national and regional borders prevent human beings, either as a factor of production or consumers, capital, technology, natural resources and other factors of production from moving freely between countries and regions, which further cause and enlarge differences in income, preference, culture, means of production and productivity, economic environments and development stages in different countries and regions. All of these influence exchange rates and are the determinants of exchange rates to varied extents. Theories incorporating one or more of these factors and determinants have been developed over the last few decades and will be gradually unfolded and examined in the later chapters of this book.

## 1.1    Foreign Exchange Rate Quotations and Arbitrage

Foreign exchange rates can be quoted as the number of units of the home or domestic currency per unit of the foreign currency, or as the number of the foreign currency units per domestic currency unit. Moreover, since more than one pairs of currencies are usually transacted on the foreign exchange market, the cross exchange rate or the cross rate arises. The cross rate refers to the exchange rate between two currencies, each of which has an exchange rate quote against a common currency. When there are discrepancies in different cross rate quotations arbitrage and arbitrage activities may take place.

### 1.1.1  Foreign Exchange Quotations

Foreign exchange rates can be quoted directly or indirectly. In a direct quotation, the exchange rate is expressed as the number of units of the home or domestic currency per unit of the foreign currency. An indirect quotation is one that the exchange rate is expressed as the number of the foreign currency units per domestic currency unit. For example, the exchange rate between the US dollar and the euro was quoted on September 19, 2003 in Frankfurt as €0.8788/\$ and \$1.1380/€. The former is a direct quotation and the latter is an indirect quotation, from the point of view of Germany or the euroland as the domestic country.

This book adopts direct quotations of foreign exchange rates in all the discussions where relative changes in currency values, e.g., appreciation and depreciation of a currency, are referred and relevant. Using direct quotations, an increase in the exchange rate indicates depreciation of the domestic currency or appreciation of the foreign currency, since one unit of foreign currency can purchase more units of the domestic currency. Similarly, a decrease in the exchange rate means that one unit of the foreign currency can purchase a smaller number of units of the domestic currency, so the domestic currency appreciates and the foreign currency depreciates. Table 1.1 is an example of foreign exchange rate quotations. Each of the rows shows the direct quotations for the country/region and each of the columns shows the indirect quotations for the country/region. e.g., the second to fourth cells in the first row tell how many units of the US dollar can be exchanged for one unit of the euro, the British pound and the Japanese yen respectively. These figures are direct quotations from the point of view of the US as the domestic country. The first, second and fourth cells in the third column report how many units of the US dollar, the euro and the Japanese yen are required respectively in exchange for one British pound. These figures are indirect quotations from the point of view of the UK as the domestic country.

**Table 1.1.** Foreign exchange rate quotations (September 19, 2003) – matrix illustration of direct and indirect quotes

|        | US$    | Euro€   | UK£    | JPN¥   |
|--------|--------|---------|--------|--------|
| US$    |        | 1.1380  | 1.6365 | 0.0088 |
| Euro€  | 0.8788 |         | 1.4373 | 0.0077 |
| UK£    | 0.6111 | 0.6956  |        | 0.0054 |
| JPN¥   | 113.97 | 129.80  | 186.51 |        |

## 1.1.2  Cross Rates and Arbitrage

It is common that more than two currencies are traded at the same time on the foreign exchange market. The cross exchange rate, or the cross rate, refers to the exchange rate between two currencies, each of which has an exchange rate quote against a common currency. e.g., if the common currency is the euro, and the exchange rates of the euro vis-à-vis the US dollar and the British pound are available at €0.8788/$ and €1.4373/£. Then the cross rate refers to the exchange rate between the US dollar and the British pound that should be equal to €1.4373/£ over €0.8788/$ or $1.6355/£. In the point of view of the euroland as the domestic country, this cross rate is the number of units of one foreign currency, which is the US dollar in this case, in terms of one unit of another foreign currency, which is the British pound. It can then be envisaged that there might be discrepancies between the direct or indirect quotes of the exchange rate and the cross rate for two currencies. In Table 1.1, it is shown that the exchange rate quote for the US dollar vis-à-vis the British pound is $1.6365/£ that is unequal to $1.6355 derived earlier from the cross rate calculation.

Such discrepancies give rise to so called triangular arbitrage, a risk free profitable opportunity for taking actions to deal with three currencies simultaneously. In the above case, one may sell £ for $, then sell $ for €, and finally sell € for £ to earn risk free profit. Suppose one has £1,000,000. In the first step, she exchanges £1,000,000 for $ at the rate of $1.6365/£, which gives her $1,636,500. In the second step, she sells $1,636,500 for € at the rate of €0.8788/$ and obtains €1,438,156. In the final step, she returns to her position in pounds by selling €1,438,156 for £ at the exchange rate of €1.4373/£, which renders her £1,000,596, a profit of £596 in excess of her initial £1,000,000.

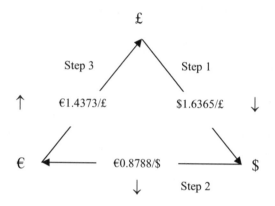

**Figure 1.1.** Arbitrage opportunity and process

However, such arbitrage opportunities rarely exist or are rarely exploitable for two primary reasons. Firstly, it is the bid-ask spread, i.e., the difference in buying and selling rates - a main transaction cost that was ignored in the above example and will be studied in the following section. Secondly, when such arbitrage opportunities do exist, they disappear quickly, due exactly to arbitrage itself. Figure 1.1 shows such a triangular arbitrage opportunity, the arbitrage process, and the elimination of the arbitrage opportunity and profit during the arbitrage process. The arrows indicate how the exchange rates may adjust to the arbitrage activity. In the first step, since there is increased demand for $ and increased supply of £, the exchange rate may fall from $1.6365/£ to a lower level. In the second step, the demand and supply analysis also suggests that the dollar euro exchange rate may fall below the initial €0.8788/$ level. So, quickly one will not be able to convert £1,000,000 for €1,438,156 but for a smaller amount of €. In the final step, demand for £ and supply of € increase, so one needs more € for a certain amount of £. The whole dynamic process indicates that the size of the arbitrage profit will soon be reduced. The process stops when the arbitrage profit is eliminated.

## 1.2   Foreign Exchange Transactions

Foreign exchange transactions involve buying and selling of one currency in exchange for another currency under various circumstances. There are inter-bank activity for foreign exchange, or the wholesale Forex business, and the retail Forex business for the clients of the banks. International commercial banks communicate with each other through, e.g., SWIFT, the Society for Worldwide Inter-bank Financial Telecommunications, to settle their Forex transactions. Transaction costs arise inevitably, regardless of wholesale or retail business, though the costs for the latter are usually higher than the former. In the following, we concentrate on the bid-ask spread, one of the primary transaction costs in dealing with foreign currencies, and its consequences regarding some seemingly existent arbitrage opportunities, such as the one we have studied earlier.

### 1.2.1  The Bid-Ask Spread

Banks such as Barclays and Citigroup, foreign exchange agencies such as Bureau de Change, and other international financial and banking institutions provide foreign exchange services and they provide foreign exchange services for a fee. A bank's bid quote (to buy) for a foreign currency will be less than its ask or offer quote (to sell) for the same foreign currency. This is the bid-ask spread. Table 1.2 and Table 1.3 exhibit the relevant trading information of euro and US dollar exchange rates vis-à-vis a range of other currencies on September 17, 2003. The source of both tables was the Financial Times. The fourth column of the tables shows bid-ask spreads or bid-offer spreads while the second column is the midpoint or an average of the bid and offer rates at the time when the market was closing. In Table 1.2, for example, the closing mid-point for the Norwegian kroner was 8.1873 and the bid-offer spread was 850-895 on the day. This information meant that the bid rate was NKr8.1850/€ and the offer rate was NKr8.1895/€; or the bank was ready to buy one euro for 8.1850 kroners from its customers and would sell one euro for 8.1895 kroners to its customers. Similarly, one can infer that, with a bid-offer spread of 154-206 and a mid-point rate of 4.5180, the bid rate for the Polish zloty was Zlt4.5154/€ and the offer rate was Zlt4.5206/€. That is, the bank would buy one euro with 4.5154 zloties from its customers and would sell one euro for 4.5206 zloties to its customers. Reading the table carefully, it is found that the bid-offer spread for the British pound vis-à-vis the euro and that for the US dollar vis-à-vis the euro were rather small at 006-009 and 235-239 respectively. We may conclude that large and frequently traded currencies would enjoy small bid-ask spreads while small and infrequently traded currencies would have large bid-ask spreads. It is because large, frequently traded currencies have lower volume-adjusted transaction costs, and small, infrequently traded currencies incur higher volume-adjusted transaction costs.

**Table 1.2.** Euro exchange rates vis-à-vis other currencies

| Sep 17 | | Closing mid-point | Change on day | Bid/offer spread | Day's mid high | low | One month Rate | %PA | Three months Rate | %PA | One year Rate | %PA |
|---|---|---|---|---|---|---|---|---|---|---|---|---|
| **Europe** | | | | | | | | | | | | |
| Czech Rep. | (Koruna) | 32.6950 | +0.0150 | 800 - 100 | 32.7890 | 32.6360 | 32.6918 | 0.1 | 32.6859 | 0.1 | 32.6658 | 0.1 |
| Denmark | (DKr) | 7.4282 | +0.0013 | 281 - 283 | 7.4440 | 7.4149 | 7.4284 | 0.0 | 7.4278 | 0.0 | 7.4313 | 0.0 |
| Hungary | (Forint) | 254.955 | +0.0850 | 700 - 210 | 255.590 | 254.600 | 256.5083 | -7.3 | 259.6231 | -7.3 | 271.4617 | -6.5 |
| Norway | (NKr) | 8.1873 | -0.0715 | 850 - 895 | 8.2799 | 8.1807 | 8.1909 | -0.5 | 8.1978 | -0.5 | 8.2439 | -0.7 |
| Poland | (Zloty) | 4.5180 | +0.0412 | 154 - 206 | 4.5387 | 4.4582 | 4.5297 | -3.1 | 4.5512 | -2.9 | 4.6321 | -2.5 |
| Romania | (Leu) | 38025.00 | +100.00 | 100 - 400 | 38040.0 | 37777.0 | - | - | - | - | - | - |
| Russia | (Rouble) | 34.4211 | +0.0628 | 093 - 328 | 34.4328 | 34.1937 | - | - | - | - | - | - |
| Slovakia | (Koruna) | 41.3400 | +0.0050 | 150 - 650 | 82.8884 | 41.2658 | 41.4813 | -4.1 | 41.7680 | -4.1 | 42.7075 | -3.3 |
| Slovenia | (Tolar) | 235.219 | -0.0390 | 059 - 378 | 235.378 | 235.059 | - | - | - | - | - | - |
| Sweden | (SKr) | 9.0585 | -0.0355 | 570 - 600 | 9.1017 | 9.0504 | 9.0646 | -0.8 | 9.0750 | -0.7 | 9.1329 | -0.8 |
| Switzerland | (SFr) | 1.5533 | -0.0024 | 530 - 535 | 1.5556 | 1.5481 | 1.5507 | 2.0 | 1.5457 | 2.0 | 1.5258 | 1.8 |
| Turkey | (Lira) | 1545650 | +8075 | 566 - 734 | 1548734 | 1527550 | - | - | - | - | - | - |
| UK | (£) | 0.7008 | -0.0034 | 006 - 009 | 0.7041 | 0.6989 | 0.7016 | -1.4 | 0.7034 | -1.5 | 0.7133 | -1.8 |
| **Americas** | | | | | | | | | | | | |
| Argentina | (Peso) | 3.2672 | +0.0359 | 638 - 705 | 3.2705 | 3.2189 | - | - | - | - | - | - |
| Brazil | (R$) | 3.2605 | +0.0130 | 582 - 627 | 3.2651 | 3.2378 | - | - | - | - | - | - |
| Canada | (C$) | 1.5363 | +0.0068 | 357 - 368 | 1.5391 | 1.5274 | 1.5372 | -0.7 | 1.5388 | -0.7 | 1.5458 | -0.6 |
| Mexico | (New Peso) | 12.2483 | -0.0028 | 405 - 561 | 12.2753 | 12.0992 | 12.2773 | -2.8 | 12.3485 | -3.3 | 12.7421 | -4.0 |
| Peru | (New Sol) | 3.9085 | +0.0165 | 075 - 095 | 3.9095 | 3.8749 | - | - | - | - | - | - |
| USA | ($) | 1.1237 | +0.0046 | 235 - 239 | 1.1239 | 1.1138 | 1.1227 | 1.1 | 1.1208 | 1.0 | 1.1128 | 1.0 |
| **Pacific/Middle East/Africa** | | | | | | | | | | | | |
| Australia | (A$) | 1.6926 | +0.0035 | 920 - 931 | 1.6931 | 1.6858 | 1.6965 | -2.8 | 1.7042 | -2.7 | 1.7423 | -2.9 |
| Hong Kong | (HK$) | 8.7643 | +0.0364 | 624 - 661 | 8.7661 | 8.6872 | 8.7559 | 1.2 | 8.7409 | 1.1 | 8.6863 | 0.9 |
| India | (Rs) | 51.6368 | +0.3283 | 192 - 544 | 51.6544 | 51.0620 | 51.6401 | -0.1 | 51.6234 | 0.1 | 51.7280 | -0.2 |
| Indonesia | (Rupiah) | 9520.55 | +53.39 | 605 - 505 | 9525.05 | 9426.10 | 9512.10 | 1.1 | 9495.85 | 1.0 | 9428.61 | 1.0 |
| Iran | (Rial) | 9366.04 | +27.57 | 325 - 883 | - | - | - | - | - | - | - | - |
| Israel | (Shk) | 5.0286 | +0.0085 | 220 - 351 | 5.0351 | 4.9998 | - | - | - | - | - | - |
| Japan | (Y) | 130.765 | +0.4570 | 719 - 811 | 130.811 | 129.340 | 130.5202 | 2.2 | 130.0497 | 2.2 | 127.8813 | 2.2 |
| Kuwait | (Kuwaiti D) | 0.3343 | +0.0010 | 341 - 345 | 0.3345 | 0.3318 | 0.3345 | -0.7 | 0.3348 | -0.6 | 0.3352 | -0.3 |
| Malaysia | (M$) | 4.2701 | +0.0177 | 693 - 708 | 4.2708 | 4.2330 | - | - | - | - | - | - |
| New Zealand | (NZ$) | 1.9291 | +0.0127 | 281 - 301 | 1.9301 | 1.9083 | 1.9340 | -3.0 | 1.9435 | -3.0 | 1.9906 | -3.2 |
| Philippines | (Peso) | 61.9440 | +0.3682 | 487 - 393 | 62.0393 | 61.2510 | 62.2045 | -5.0 | 62.7511 | -5.2 | 65.7800 | -6.2 |
| Saudi Arabia | (SR) | 4.2142 | +0.0171 | 132 - 152 | 4.2152 | 4.1773 | 4.2131 | 0.3 | 4.2103 | 0.4 | 4.2005 | 0.3 |
| Singapore | (S$) | 1.9719 | +0.0121 | 712 - 726 | 1.9726 | 1.9505 | 1.9694 | 1.5 | 1.9649 | 1.4 | 1.9457 | 1.3 |
| South Africa | (R) | 8.3041 | -0.1098 | 970 - 112 | 8.4012 | 8.2883 | 8.3628 | -8.5 | 8.4599 | -7.5 | 8.8624 | -6.7 |
| South Korea | (Won) | 1315.85 | +6.62 | 450 - 721 | 1317.21 | 1303.95 | 1318.00 | -2.0 | 1321.52 | -1.7 | 1333.86 | -1.4 |
| Taiwan | (T$) | 38.2957 | +0.1361 | 327 - 587 | 38.3587 | 37.9630 | 38.1410 | 4.8 | 37.8713 | 4.4 | 37.0940 | 3.1 |
| Thailand | (Bt) | 45.6728 | +0.3568 | 366 - 090 | 45.7090 | 45.1292 | 45.6210 | 1.4 | 45.5431 | 1.1 | 45.1928 | 1.1 |
| UAE | (Dirham) | 4.1273 | +0.0171 | 263 - 282 | 4.1282 | 4.0911 | 4.1238 | 1.0 | 4.1170 | 1.0 | 4.0897 | 0.9 |

Euro Locking Rates: Austrian Schilling 13.7603, Belgium/Luxembourg Franc 40.3399, Finnish Markka 5.94573, French Franc 6.55957, German Mark 1.95583, Greek Drachma 340.75, Irish Punt 0.787564, Italian Lira 1936.27, Netherlands Guilder 2.20371, Portuguese Escudo 200.482, Spanish Peseta 166.386. Bid/offer spreads in the Euro Spot table show only the last three decimal places. Bid, offer, mid spot rates and forward rates are derived from THE WM/REUTERS CLOSING SPOT and FORWARD RATE services. Some values are rounded by the F.T.

Source: the Financial Times

**Table 1.3.** US dollar exchange rates vis-à-vis other currencies

| Sep 17 | | Closing mid-point | Change on day | Bid/offer spread | Day's Mid high | low | One month Rate | %PA | Three months Rate | %PA | One year Rate | %PA | J.P. Morgan Index |
|---|---|---|---|---|---|---|---|---|---|---|---|---|---|
| **Europe** | | | | | | | | | | | | | |
| Czech Rep. | (Koruna) | 29.0958 | -0.1076 | 773 - 144 | 29.3200 | 29.0773 | 29.1188 | -0.9 | 29.1633 | -0.9 | 29.3533 | -0.9 | - |
| Denmark | (DKr) | 6.6105 | -0.0263 | 092 - 117 | 6.6677 | 6.6092 | 6.6166 | -1.1 | 6.6274 | -1.0 | 6.6778 | -1.0 | 107.4 |
| Hungary | (Forint) | 226.889 | -0.8670 | 622 - 156 | 229.060 | 226.622 | 228.474 | -8.4 | 231.644 | -8.4 | 243.934 | -7.5 | - |
| Norway | (NKr) | 7.2860 | -0.0942 | 827 - 893 | 7.4233 | 7.2827 | 7.2957 | -1.6 | 7.3143 | -1.6 | 7.4079 | -1.7 | 107.0 |
| Poland | (Zloty) | 4.0206 | +0.0201 | 176 - 237 | 4.0640 | 4.0005 | 4.0346 | -4.2 | 4.0607 | -4.0 | 4.1623 | -3.5 | - |
| Romania | (Leu) | 33839.1 | -51.3000 | 197 - 585 | 34062.0 | 33753.0 | - | - | - | - | - | - | - |
| Russia | (Rouble) | 30.6319 | -0.0712 | 269 - 369 | 30.6994 | 30.6269 | - | - | - | - | - | - | - |
| Slovakia | (Koruna) | 36.7892 | -0.1484 | 604 - 180 | 74.3260 | 36.7604 | 36.9477 | -5.2 | 37.2667 | -5.2 | 38.3767 | -4.3 | - |
| Slovenia | (Tolar) | 209.325 | -0.9050 | 220 - 430 | 211.000 | 209.220 | - | - | - | - | - | - | - |
| Sweden | (SKr) | 8.0613 | -0.0652 | 585 - 641 | 8.1590 | 8.0585 | 8.0739 | -1.9 | 8.097 | -1.8 | 8.2068 | -1.8 | 100.1 |
| Switzerland | (SFr) | 1.3822 | -0.0080 | 818 - 827 | 1.3944 | 1.3801 | 1.3811 | 1.0 | 1.3791 | 0.9 | 1.3711 | 0.8 | 107.7 |
| Turkey | (Lira) | 1375500 | +1500 | 000 - 000 | 1379500 | 1370000 | - | - | - | - | - | - | - |
| UK (0.6236)* | (£) | 1.6036 | +0.0145 | 035 - 036 | 1.6038 | 1.5863 | 1.6002 | 2.5 | 1.5935 | 2.5 | 1.5602 | 2.7 | 93.8 |
| Euro (0.8899)* | (€) | 1.1237 | +0.0046 | 235 - 239 | 1.1239 | 1.1138 | 1.1227 | 1.1 | 1.1208 | 1.0 | 1.1128 | 1.0 | 118.0 |
| SDR | - | 0.71740 | - | - | - | - | - | - | - | - | - | - | - |
| **Americas** | | | | | | | | | | | | | |
| Argentina | (Peso) | 2.9075 | +0.0200 | 050 - 100 | 2.9100 | 2.8900 | - | - | - | - | - | - | - |
| Brazil | (R$) | 2.9015 | -0.0005 | 000 - 030 | 2.9110 | 2.8980 | - | - | - | - | - | - | - |
| Canada | (C$) | 1.3672 | +0.0005 | 669 - 674 | 1.3741 | 1.3668 | 1.3693 | -1.8 | 1.3729 | -1.7 | 1.3891 | -1.6 | 107.9 |
| Mexico | (New Peso) | 10.9000 | -0.0477 | 950 - 050 | 10.9230 | 10.8630 | 10.9355 | -3.9 | 11.0177 | -4.3 | 11.45 | -5.0 | 85.5 |
| Peru | (New Sol) | 3.4783 | +0.0004 | 780 - 785 | 3.4785 | 3.4780 | - | - | - | - | - | - | - |
| USA | ($) | - | - | - | - | - | - | - | - | - | - | - | 97.5 |
| **Pacific/Middle East/Africa** | | | | | | | | | | | | | |
| Australia | (A$) | 1.5063 | -0.0030 | 060 - 065 | 1.5175 | 1.5053 | - | - | - | - | - | - | 110.2 |
| Hong Kong | (HK$) | 7.7995 | +0.0002 | 992 - 997 | 7.7997 | 7.7992 | 7.799 | 0.1 | 7.799 | 0.0 | 7.8055 | -0.1 | - |
| India | (Rs) | 45.9525 | +0.1025 | 450 - 600 | 45.9600 | 45.8000 | 45.9963 | -1.1 | 46.06 | -0.9 | 46.4825 | -1.2 | - |
| Indonesia | (Rupiah) | 8472.50 | +12.5000 | 000 - 000 | 8475.00 | 8455.00 | - | - | - | - | - | - | - |
| Iran | (Rial) | 8335.00 | -10.0000 | 400 - 600 | 8348.00 | 7942.00 | - | - | - | - | - | - | - |
| Israel | (Shk) | 4.4750 | -0.0110 | 700 - 800 | 4.4910 | 4.4700 | - | - | - | - | - | - | - |
| Japan | (Y) | 116.370 | -0.0750 | 350 - 390 | 116.520 | 116.010 | 116.255 | 1.2 | 116.035 | 1.2 | 114.915 | 1.3 | 89.6 |
| Kuwait | (Dinar) | 0.2975 | -0.0003 | 974 - 976 | 0.2980 | 0.2974 | 0.298 | -2.0 | 0.2987 | -1.6 | 0.3012 | -1.2 | - |
| Malaysia | (M$) | 3.8000 | - | 000 - 000 | 3.8000 | 3.8000 | - | - | - | - | - | - | - |
| New Zealand | (NZ$) | 1.7167 | +0.0042 | 161 - 173 | 1.7179 | 1.7053 | - | - | - | - | - | - | 122.6 |
| Philippines | (Peso) | 55.1250 | +0.1000 | 500 - 000 | 55.2000 | 54.8600 | 55.406 | -6.1 | 55.9885 | -6.3 | 59.1095 | -7.2 | - |
| Saudi Arabia | (SR) | 3.7503 | -0.0003 | 501 - 505 | 3.7505 | 3.7501 | 3.7526 | -0.7 | 3.7566 | -0.7 | 3.7746 | -0.6 | - |
| Singapore | (S$) | 1.7548 | +0.0035 | 545 - 551 | 1.7551 | 1.7477 | 1.7541 | 0.4 | 1.7531 | 0.4 | 1.7483 | 0.4 | 97.2 |
| South Africa | (R) | 7.3900 | -0.1287 | 850 - 950 | 7.5300 | 7.3850 | 7.4488 | -9.5 | 7.5482 | -8.6 | 7.9637 | -7.8 | - |
| South Korea | (Won) | 1171.00 | +1.0500 | 000 - 200 | 1172.00 | 1170.00 | 1173.95 | -3.0 | 1179.1 | -2.8 | 1198.6 | -2.4 | - |
| Taiwan | (T$) | 34.0800 | -0.0200 | 300 - 300 | 34.1300 | 34.0300 | 33.9725 | 3.8 | 33.79 | 3.4 | 33.3325 | 2.2 | 90.5 |
| Thailand | (Bt) | 40.6450 | +0.1500 | 200 - 700 | 40.6700 | 40.4400 | 40.635 | 0.3 | 40.635 | 0.1 | 40.61 | 0.1 | - |
| U A E | (Dirham) | 3.6729 | - | 727 - 731 | 3.6731 | 3.6727 | 3.6731 | -0.1 | 3.6733 | 0.0 | 3.6749 | -0.1 | - |

*The closing mid-point rates for the Euro and £ are shown in brackets. The other figures in both rows are in the reciprocal form in line with market convention. †Floating rate now shown for Argentina. ‡ Official rate set by Malaysian government. The WM/Reuters rate for the valuation of capital assets is 3.80 MYR/USD. Bid/offer spreads in the Dollar Spot table show only the last three decimal places. J.P. Morgan nominal indices Mar 4 : Base average 2000 = 100. Bid, offer, mid spot rates and forward rates in both this and the pound table are derived from the WM/REUTERS 4pm (London time) CLOSING SPOT and FORWARD RATE services. Some values are rounded by the F.T. The exchange rates printed in this table are also available on the Internet at http://www.FT.com.

Source: the Financial Times

For comparison purposes bid-ask spreads can also be calculated and provided in percentage as follows:

$$Bid - sak\ spread\ in\ percentage = \frac{ask\ rate - bid\ rate}{ask\ rate} \qquad (1.1)$$

Applying this formula to the previous cases of the Norwegian kroner, the Polish zloty, the British pound and the US dollar, the percentage bid-ask spreads of the four currencies in terms of their euro exchange rates are:

Norwegian kroner: (8.1895 – 8.1850)/8.1895 = 0.055%
Polish zloty: (4.5206 – 4.5154)/4.5206 = 0.115%
British pound: (0.7009 – 0.7006)/0.7009 = 0.043%
US dollar: (1.1239 – 1.1235)/1.1239 = 0.036%

It can be observed that the bid-ask spread of the Polish zloty is about 3 times of that for the British pound or the US dollar. The Norwegian kroner, though a small currency and even smaller than the Polish zloty, experiences more trading activity in the west and, consequently, enjoys a small bid-ask spread. The British pound and the US dollar are among the largest and most frequently traded currencies, so their bid-ask spreads are very small.

## 1.2.2 Transaction Costs and Arbitrage Opportunities

Many discrepancies in foreign exchange rate quotations cannot be exploited due to bid-ask spreads. These can be the discrepancies in triangular cross rate quotations, and can be the discrepancies involving just two currencies, when the exchange rates are quoted at different places or by different banks.

For example, suppose that the euro and the US dollar exchange rate is quoted directly in New York as 1.1235-39 and quoted directly in Paris as 0.8897-900, does any arbitrage opportunity exist? For comparison we have to find out whether there are discrepancies in the quotations in the two places. We can either change the direct quotations in Paris to indirect quotations, or change the direct quotations in New York to indirect quotations. Let us try the former. The bid rate for the euro is 1/0.8900 = $1.1236/€ and the ask rate for the euro is 1/0.8897 = $1.1240/€. There are obviously discrepancies in the quotations in Paris and New York but there are no exploitable arbitrage opportunities. Suppose one exchanges €1,000 for the US dollar in Paris, and then converts the US dollar back to the euro in New York. In Paris, she obtains $1,123.6 from selling the euro; but to buy one euro, she needs to pay $1.1239 in New York. So in the end, the transactions return her €9997, which is a loss of €3. One may try all the other possibilities but it is certain no arbitrage opportunities can be found in this case.

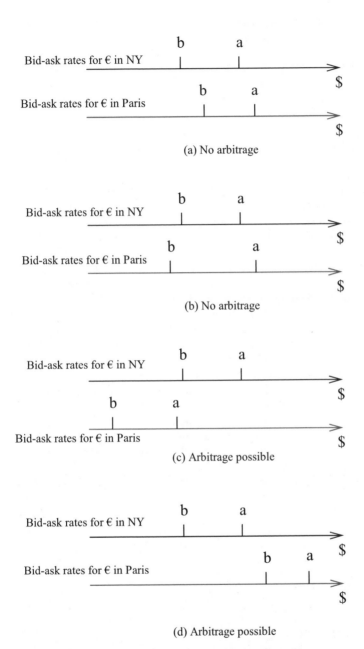

**Figure 1.2.** Bid-ask spread and arbitrage

For arbitrage opportunities to exist and be exploitable, the bid-ask spread must be "skewed" in the two locations and skewed to a fairly large extent. That is, keeping the quotations in New York unchanged, the ask rate for the euro in Paris must be lower than $1.1235/€, the bid rate for the euro in New York; or the bid rate for the euro in Paris must be higher than $1.1239/€, the ask rate for the euro in New York. Figure 2 demonstrate a few situations in which there may or may not exist exploitable arbitrage opportunities. So, the following indirect quotations in Paris would have provided arbitrage opportunities: 1.1242-46 (direct quote is 0.8892-95) and 1.1207-12 (direct quote is 0.8919-23). With the first quote, one could have exchanged €1,000 for $1,1242 in Paris, and then sold the US dollar for the euro at the ask rate of $1.1239/€ in New York, resulting in €1,000.27, a very thin profit of €0.27. Or one could have exchanged $1,000 for €889.76 (=$1,000/$1.1239/€) in New York, and then converted the euro for the dollar at the bid rate of $1.1242/€ in Paris, resulting in $1,000.27, an equally very thin profit of $0.27, or a 0.027% relative return. With the second quote, one could have exchanged $1,000 for €891.90 (=$1,000/$1.1212/€) in Paris, and then converted the euro to the US dollar at the bid rate of $1.1235/€ in New York, resulting in $1002.05, a small profit of $2.05. One can try, with the second quote, to start with €1,000 in New York, and the result would be a €2.05 profit.

From the above analysis we can conclude that discrepancies in quotations can be exploited to make arbitrage profit only when the bid rate in the first place is higher that the ask rate in the second place, or the ask rate in the first place is lower that the bid rate in the second place. As such situations do not happen often, arbitrage opportunities arising from the discrepancies in quotations at different places or banks rarely exist. Even if exploitable arbitrage opportunities do exist, the profit margin is usually rather thin.

The large the bid-ask spread, the less probable that a discrepancy like (c) or (d) in Figure 2 would come up. Therefore, it is not a large bid-ask spread itself, but its consequence, that prevents the discrepancy in the quotations from being an exploitable arbitrage opportunity.

Now let us revisit the triangular cross rate case and incorporate bid-ask spreads for these exchange rate quotations. The case is shown in Figure 3, where the bid-ask spread is provided next to its relevant exchange rate quote. We still suppose one uses £1,000,000 to exploit possible arbitrage opportunities. In the first step, she exchanges £1,000,000 for $ at the rate of $1.6363/£, which gives her $1,636,300. In the second step, she sells $1,636,300 for € at the rate of €0.8786/$ and obtains €1,437,653. In the final step, she returns to her position in pounds by selling €1,437,653 for £ at the exchange rate of €1.4377/£, which renders her £999,967, a loss of £33 from her initial £1,000,000. So, arbitrage profits are eliminated by the bid-ask spreads and arbitrage opportunities do not exist. However, if the bid-ask spread of the sterling and dollar exchange rate were smaller at 1.6364-66, the chain of transactions would have brought her a profit of £29 in this case. Therefore, bid-ask spreads eliminate many seemingly existent triangular arbitrage opportunities based on discrepancies in cross rate calculations that ignore bid-ask spreads and use mid-point exchange rates.

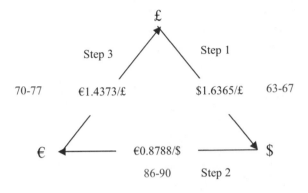

**Figure 1.3.** Bid-ask spreads and triangular arbitrage

## 1.3 Spot and Forward Exchange Rates

A spot exchange rate is quoted for immediate delivery of the purchased currency, or the currency is delivered "on the spot" (usually within three working days). A forward exchange rate is the rate agreed today for delivery of the currency at a future time. Typically the future date is one month, three months and one year ahead. In this book, we use S to stand for the spot exchange rate or spot rate, and F for the forward exchange rate or forward rate.

Table 1.2 and Table 1.3 also list forward rate quotations. There are two ways of forward rate quotations. One is the outright rate that is quoted in exactly the same way as the spot rate is quoted. The first column under the title of one month, three months and one year provides such quotes of forward exchange rates. e.g., in Table 1.3, the spot exchange rate of the US dollar against the euro was closed at $1.2108/€ on December 3, 2003, the one month forward rate was $1.2097/€, the three month forward rate was $1.2078/€ and the one year forward rats was $1.2001/€ on that day. The other is the discount to the spot rate, expressed in annualised percentages. The second column under the title of one month, three months and one year provides such quotes of forward exchange rates. Using the same forward rates, for example, the one month forward rate of $1.2097/€ represents an annualised discount of 1.1% to the spot rate of $1.2108/€, being calculated as 12×(1.2108-1.2097)/1.2108 = 1.1%; similarly the one year forward rate of $1.2001/€ represents a discount of 0.9% to the spot rate of $1.2108/€, derived as (1.2108-1.2001)/1.2108. In addition, swap rates may be used in forward rate quotations as well. A swap rate is the discount of the forward rate to the spot rate in an absolute term. e.g., the three month swap rate was 0.003, with an outright quote of the forward rate being $1.2078 and a spot rate of $1.2108/€.

**Table 1.4.** US dollar exchange rates vis-à-vis other currencies
- December 17 versus September 17

| Dec 17 | | Closing mid-point | Change on day | Bid/offer spread | Day's Mid | | One month | | Three months | | One year | | J.P. Morgan Index |
|---|---|---|---|---|---|---|---|---|---|---|---|---|---|
| | | | | | high | low | Rate | %PA | Rate | %PA | Rate | %PA | |
| **Europe** | | | | | | | | | | | | | |
| Czech Rep. | (Koruna) | 26.1571 | -0.0643 | 407 - 734 | 26.3150 | 26.1030 | 26.177 | -0.9 | 26.2158 | -0.9 | 26.3971 | -0.9 | - |
| Denmark | (DKr) | 6.0113 | -0.0227 | 102 - 124 | 6.0518 | 6.0078 | 6.0169 | -1.1 | 6.0274 | -1.1 | 6.0706 | -1.0 | 109.0 |
| Hungary | (Forint) | 212.959 | -0.9880 | 630 - 289 | 214.650 | 212.630 | 215.259 | -13.0 | 218.814 | -11.0 | 233.244 | -9.5 | - |
| Norway | (NKr) | 6.7190 | +0.0513 | 169 - 211 | 6.7211 | 6.6376 | 6.7284 | -1.7 | 6.7425 | -1.4 | 6.8014 | -1.2 | 109.9 |
| Poland | (Zloty) | 3.7509 | -0.0248 | 484 - 534 | 3.7860 | 3.7484 | 3.7653 | -4.6 | 3.7917 | -4.3 | 3.9119 | -4.3 | - |
| Romania | (Leu) | 32852.8 | -117.00 | 353 - 702 | 33036.0 | 32783.0 | - | - | - | - | - | - | - |
| Russia | (Rouble) | 29.2580 | +0.0085 | 530 - 630 | 29.2739 | 29.2530 | - | - | - | - | - | - | - |
| Slovakia | (Koruna) | 33.2566 | -0.1389 | 310 - 822 | 33.5510 | 33.2310 | 33.3981 | -5.1 | 33.6591 | -4.8 | 34.5881 | -4.0 | - |
| Slovenia | (Tolar) | 191.225 | -0.7150 | 140 - 310 | 192.500 | 191.110 | - | - | - | - | - | - | - |
| Sweden | (SKr) | 7.2945 | -0.0321 | 923 - 966 | 7.3325 | 7.2909 | 7.306 | -1.9 | 7.3258 | -1.7 | 7.4035 | -1.5 | 103.1 |
| Switzerland | (SFr) | 1.2551 | -0.0041 | 547 - 555 | 1.2638 | 1.2544 | 1.2541 | 1.0 | 1.2523 | 0.9 | 1.2438 | 0.9 | 110.4 |
| Turkey | (Lira) | 1429500 | -1500 | 000 - 000 | 1438000 | 1427000 | - | - | - | - | - | - | - |
| UK (0.5676)* | (£) | 1.7618 | +0.0120 | 617 - 620 | 1.7628 | 1.7497 | 1.7575 | 2.9 | 1.7494 | 2.8 | 1.7124 | 2.8 | 96.8 |
| Euro (0.8077)* | (€) | 1.2381 | +0.0049 | 379 - 383 | 1.2388 | 1.2294 | 1.237 | 1.1 | 1.235 | 1.0 | 1.2268 | 0.9 | 124.1 |
| SDR | - | 0.67870 | - | - | - | - | - | - | - | - | - | - | - |
| **Americas** | | | | | | | | | | | | | |
| Argentina | (Peso) | 2.9675 | -0.0050 | 650 - 700 | 2.9720 | 2.9650 | - | - | - | - | - | - | - |
| Brazil | (R$) | 2.9335 | +0.0020 | 320 - 350 | 2.9460 | 2.9312 | - | - | - | - | - | - | - |
| Canada | (C$) | 1.3246 | +0.0065 | 245 - 247 | 1.3360 | 1.3240 | 1.3267 | -1.9 | 1.3299 | -1.6 | 1.3421 | -1.3 | 110.4 |
| Mexico | (New Peso) | 11.2670 | -0.0650 | 655 - 685 | 11.2800 | 11.2385 | 11.3178 | -5.4 | 11.4115 | -5.1 | 11.874 | -5.4 | 81.1 |
| Peru | (New Sol) | 3.4706 | +0.0001 | 705 - 708 | 3.4803 | 3.4705 | - | - | - | - | - | - | - |
| USA | ($) | - | - | - | - | - | - | - | - | - | - | - | 93.4 |
| **Pacific/Middle East/Africa** | | | | | | | | | | | | | |
| Australia | (A$) | 1.3487 | +0.0053 | 486 - 488 | 1.3526 | 1.3444 | - | - | - | - | - | - | 118.2 |
| Hong Kong | (HK$) | 7.7633 | +0.0004 | 627 - 638 | 7.7647 | 7.7627 | 7.7584 | 0.8 | 7.7463 | 0.9 | 7.7168 | 0.6 | - |
| India | (Rs) | 45.5100 | -0.0200 | 700 - 500 | 45.5500 | 45.4700 | 45.495 | 0.4 | 45.4875 | 0.2 | 45.6562 | -0.3 | - |
| Indonesia | (Rupiah) | 8492.50 | +11.00 | 000 - 500 | 8495.00 | 8482.00 | - | - | - | - | - | - | - |
| Iran | (Rial) | 8312.00 | - | 100 - 300 | - | - | - | - | - | - | - | - | - |
| Israel | (Shk) | 4.3830 | +0.0190 | 780 - 880 | 4.3890 | 4.3700 | - | - | - | - | - | - | - |
| Japan | (Y) | 107.350 | -0.2650 | 320 - 380 | 107.860 | 107.280 | 107.24 | 1.2 | 107.035 | 1.2 | 105.88 | 1.4 | 94.2 |
| Kuwait | (Dinar) | 0.2945 | -0.0002 | 944 - 946 | 0.2947 | 0.2943 | 0.2948 | -1.2 | 0.2955 | -1.4 | 0.2992 | -1.6 | - |
| Malaysia | (M$) | 3.8000 | - | 000 - 000 | 3.8000 | 3.8000 | - | - | - | - | - | - | - |
| New Zealand | (NZ$) | 1.5424 | +0.0055 | 408 - 439 | 1.5461 | 1.5361 | - | - | - | - | - | - | 129.0 |
| Philippines | (Peso) | 55.4300 | -0.0550 | 600 - 000 | 55.5100 | 55.3600 | 55.752 | -7.0 | 56.37 | -6.8 | 59.5195 | -7.4 | - |
| Saudi Arabia | (SR) | 3.7503 | - | 501 - 505 | 3.7505 | 3.7501 | 3.7512 | -0.3 | 3.7536 | -0.3 | 3.7658 | -0.4 | - |
| Singapore | (S$) | 1.7104 | +0.0051 | 100 - 107 | 1.7109 | 1.7065 | 1.7096 | 0.5 | 1.7087 | 0.4 | 1.705 | 0.3 | 95.7 |
| South Africa | (R) | 6.5012 | +0.1437 | 985 - 040 | 6.5370 | 6.3800 | 6.545 | -8.1 | 6.6227 | -7.5 | 6.9587 | -7.0 | - |
| South Korea | (Won) | 1188.65 | -2.8500 | 860 - 870 | 1190.50 | 1187.40 | 1192.35 | -3.7 | 1197.95 | -3.1 | 1216.9 | -2.4 | - |
| Taiwan | (T$) | 33.9750 | -0.0400 | 300 - 200 | 34.0200 | 33.9300 | 33.94 | 1.2 | 33.85 | 1.5 | 33.455 | 1.5 | 87.1 |
| Thailand | (Bt) | 39.6500 | -0.0100 | 000 - 000 | 39.7000 | 39.6000 | 39.655 | -0.2 | 39.675 | -0.3 | 39.7 | -0.1 | - |
| U A E | (Dirham) | 3.6729 | - | 727 - 731 | 3.6731 | 3.6727 | 3.673 | 0.0 | 3.6734 | -0.1 | 3.6756 | -0.1 | - |

*The closing mid-point rates for the Euro and £ are shown in brackets. The other figures in both rows are in the reciprocal form in line with market convention. †Floating rate now shown for Argentina. ‡ Official rate set by Malaysian government. The WM/Reuters rate for the valuation of capital assets is 3.80 MYR/USD. Bid/offer spreads in the Dollar Spot table show only the last three decimal places. J.P. Morgan nominal indices Dec 12 : Base average 2000 = 100. Bid, offer, mid spot rates and forward rates in both this and the pound table are derived from the WM/REUTERS 4pm (London time) CLOSING SPOT and FORWARD RATE services. Some values are rounded by the F.T.

Source: the Financial Times

While forward discounts are used in the quotations of forward rates, it is the forward premium that is adopted in research in international finance as an important concept and term. Formally, the forward premium is defined as:

$$\frac{F_{0,T} - S_0}{S_0} \qquad (1.2)$$

where $F_{0,T}$ is the forward exchange rate contracted at time 0 and matures at time T, and $S_0$ is the spot exchange rate at the time the forward contract is made. Equation (1.2) becomes a forward discount if a minus sign is put before the formula. There exists a relationship between the forward premium and interest rate differentials in the two countries, which will be discussed later. However, prior to studying the relationship formally, it can be envisaged that the spot exchange rates at future times are expected to be on average equal to their corresponding forward exchange rates. If future spot exchange rates are on average equal to their corresponding forward exchange rates exactly, then the forward exchange rate is an unbiased predictor of the future spot exchange rate and no arbitrage profit can be systematically made over time through trading on the forward market. Less likely, If future spot exchange rates are equal to their corresponding forward exchange rates exactly, then the forward exchange rate is a precise and perfect predictor of the future spot exchange rate and no arbitrage profit can be made at any times through trading on the forward market. For the purpose of comparing future spot exchange rates with their corresponding forward exchange rates, Table 1.4 provides additional information on US dollar exchange rates vis-à-vis a range of other currencies on December 17, 2003, three months after the information in Table 1.3 is made available. Comparing the three months forward exchange rates in Table 1.3 and the spot exchange rates in Table 1.4, it is obvious that these forward exchange rates are not precise predictor of their respective future spot exchange rates. Nevertheless, we are not sure, based on the information contained in these two tables, whether forward exchange rates are unbiased predictor of future spot exchange rates - we need more information to reach a conclusion, only possibly.

## 1.4 Effective Exchange Rates

The above presented and analysed exchange rates are bilateral, i.e., they are the exchange rates between two currencies. An effective exchange rate is a measure of the value of a currency against a trade-weighted 'basket' of other currencies, relative to a base date. It is calculated as a weighted geometric average, expressed in the form of an index.

$$E_i = \prod_{j=1}^{m} \left( S_{i,j} \right)^{w_{i,j}} \tag{1.3}$$

where $E_i$ is the effective exchange rate of country $i$, $S_{i,j}$ is the bilateral exchange rate between countries $i$ and $j$, $m$ is the number of countries with noteworthy trade with county $i$, and $w_{i,j}$ is the weight allocated to the bilateral exchange rate involving the currency of country $j$, its derivation to be discussed in the following. As the bilateral exchange rates in equation (3.1) are nominal, in contrast to real exchange rates that are price level - or inflation - adjusted, the effective exchange rate presented by equation (3.1) is also known as the nominal exchange rate.

The weights, or trade weights, in the effective exchange rate formula are designed to measure, for an individual country, the relative importance of each of the other countries as a competitor to its manufacturing sector. In the case of the UK, the trade weights reflect aggregated trade flows in manufactured goods for the period 1989 to 1991 and cover 21 countries. The base date for the index is 1990, and is set at 100.

The weight for each country is derived from three components. Using the UK as an example again, the weight of the US dollar in the sterling index is derived, considering: (1) US competition in the UK domestic market, (2) UK competition in the US domestic market and, (3) Competition between US and UK manufactured goods in third country markets.

Table 1.5 provides the trade weights information of G7 countries' effective exchange rate indexes. These effective exchange rate indexes are available in the International Financial Statistics, a monthly publication of the International Monetary Fund (IMF). It can be observed that geography is still an important factor for trade weights and the choice of trading partners, liked or disliked. In the sterling effective exchange rate index, Germany accounts for 16.49%, the EU for 69.96% and euro area countries for 64.82%, while the US accounts for 16.49. In the US dollar effective exchange rate index, Canada accounts for 25.09%, the EU accounts for 41.19% and euro area countries for 29.80%. The trade weight of the US in the Canadian dollar effective exchange rate index that is 82.39% is by far the largest.

The new nominal effective exchange rate for the euro is calculated by the European Central Bank (ECB). It is based on the weighted averages of bilateral euro exchange rates of 11 euro area countries against 13 major trading partners before January 1, 2001, and 12 euro area countries against 12 major trading partners after January 1, 2001 when Greece joined the euro. The index is set to 100 for the first quarter of 1999. These weights, based on 1995-97 manufactured goods trade and capturing third market effects, are: US dollar 25.05%, Pound sterling 24.26%, Japanese yen 15.01%, Swiss franc 8.84%, Swedish krona 6.23%, Korean won 4.91%, Hong Kong dollar 3.90%, Danish krone 3.50%, Singapore dollar 3.50%, Canadian dollar 1.96%, Norwegian krone 1.70%, and Australian dollar 1.13%.

The effective exchange rate is an artificial index in the sense that it is based on a specific base period. Thus, this rate does not indicate the absolute level of competitiveness of any country, just as price indices do not show actual price levels. However, the effective exchange rate can be used to measure the relative changes in international competitiveness during a certain period of time. An increase (a decrease) in the effective exchange rate of a currency in a certain period indicates the currency has depreciated (appreciated) against the basket of currencies.

**Table 1.5.** Trade weights in G7 effective exchange rates (derived from 1989-1991 trade flows)

|  | US | Japan | Germany | France | UK | Italy | Canada |
|---|---|---|---|---|---|---|---|
| Australia | 0.67 | 1.42 | 0.19 | 0.13 | 0.48 | 0.17 | 0.15 |
| Austria | 0.56 | 0.96 | 6.01 | 1.31 | 1.19 | 2.78 | 0.21 |
| Belgium | 2.12 | 1.88 | 7.35 | 8.38 | 5.39 | 4.50 | 0.46 |
| Canada | 25.09 | 3.19 | 0.78 | 0.76 | 1.38 | 0.76 | — |
| Denmark | 0.47 | 0.51 | 1.71 | 0.78 | 1.38 | 0.72 | 0.12 |
| Finland | 0.59 | 0.61 | 1.34 | 0.78 | 1.41 | 0.77 | 0.21 |
| France | 5.84 | 4.63 | 16.29 | — | 12.59 | 18.60 | 1.57 |
| Germany | 11.50 | 13.69 | — | 28.56 | 22.49 | 29.48 | 2.81 |
| Greece | 0.13 | 0.19 | 0.59 | 0.35 | 0.31 | 0.85 | 0.03 |
| Italy | 4.56 | 3.79 | 12.99 | 14.38 | 8.27 | — | 1.21 |
| Japan | 30.29 | — | 7.08 | 4.20 | 7.00 | 4.45 | 5.95 |
| Netherlands | 2.23 | 2.07 | 7.36 | 4.88 | 5.71 | 3.53 | 0.66 |
| New Zealand | 0.25 | 0.61 | 0.07 | 0.04 | 0.21 | 0.08 | 0.07 |
| Norway | 0.47 | 0.47 | 0.90 | 0.50 | 1.19 | 0.52 | 0.14 |
| Portugal | 0.23 | 0.18 | 0.85 | 1.00 | 0.84 | 0.64 | 0.06 |
| Ireland | 0.70 | 0.45 | 0.77 | 0.81 | 3.08 | 0.60 | 0.15 |
| Spain | 1.47 | 1.39 | 4.46 | 7.00 | 3.85 | 5.92 | 0.32 |
| Sweden | 1.88 | 1.48 | 3.28 | 1.85 | 3.45 | 2.02 | 0.61 |
| Switzerland | 2.03 | 2.40 | 6.45 | 4.07 | 3.27 | 4.96 | 0.43 |
| UK | 8.91 | 6.67 | 11.07 | 10.87 | — | 9.23 | 2.45 |
| US | — | 53.40 | 10.48 | 9.34 | 16.49 | 9.43 | 82.39 |

Source: IMF

International competitiveness is affected not only by the exchange rate but also by domestic and foreign price movements. For example, even when the nominal effective exchange rate of the Canadian dollar remains unchanged, the relative competitiveness of Canadian goods increases when the inflation rate of the rival exporting countries surpasses that of Canada. The idea has led to the construction of real effective exchange rates. The real effective exchange rate is an indicator designed to take into account the inflation differentials between countries. Each of the bilateral exchange rates is adjusted by the price indices of the two countries during the period, leading to the real exchange rate, which will be addressed later. Real bilateral exchange rates replace nominal bilateral exchange rates in the effective exchange rate formula, equation (1.3), to derive real effective exchange rates.

## 1.5 Other Currency Markets

In addition to spot and forward exchange markets, foreign currencies are also traded on currency derivatives markets in the forms of currency futures, currency options, currency swaps, and so on. The market for forward foreign exchange is also a derivatives market, since forward foreign exchange is a derivative of the spot foreign exchange. However, given that forwards are so common and widely used in foreign exchange transactions, with a trading volume far exceeding that in any other currency derivatives market, forward foreign exchange deserves a separate and special treatment as has been discussed earlier and will be further examined later.

A currency futures contact specifies that one currency will be exchanged for another at a specified time in the future at a pre-specified price, which is the exchange rate. Futures are standardised contracts trading on organised exchanges with daily resettlement through a clearinghouse. A margin account is set with an initial margin, and to be maintained above the maintenance margin. Forward contracts usually lack these features.

An option gives the holder the right, but involves no obligation, to buy or sell a given quantity of an asset in the future at a pre-determined price. There are two types of options. A call option gives the holder the right, but involves no obligation, to buy a given quantity of an asset at a time in the future at a pre-determined price. A put option gives the holder the right, but involves no obligation, to sell a given quantity of an asset at a time in the future at a pre-determined price. A currency option gives the holder the right, but involves no obligation, to buy or sell a given quantity of a currency in the future at a pre-determined price, which is the exchange rate. Currency options can be traded on an organised exchange and over-the-counter (OTC).

In a swap, two counterparties agree to a contractual arrangement to exchange cash flows at periodic intervals. When cash flows from a swap are denominated in two or more currencies, the swap is a cross-currency interest rate swap, or a currency swap. Chapter 10 to Chapter 12 study currency derivatives in detail.

# 2 Exchange Rate Regimes and International Monetary Systems

One must have knowledge in foreign exchange rate regimes and foreign exchange rate arrangements to better understand foreign exchange rate behaviour, since the choice of foreign exchange rate regimes can influence or determine how the exchange rate between two currencies moves and fluctuates on foreign exchange markets. For example, if an arrangement is made for a currency which fixes the currency's exchange rate against the US dollar, then there is little sense to study the market force for the sake of exchange rate determination for the currency.

This chapter examines various foreign exchange regimes in international monetary systems and discusses their features. A brief review of the history of international monetary systems is also provided in the chapter, since the past lessons from the international monetary history can be helpful to the foreign exchange rate regime decision, the implementation of foreign exchange policies and the attainment of policy objectives.

## 2.1 Exchange Rate Regimes

The exchange rate can be totally flexible or completely free to float on the foreign exchange market on the one hand, and fixed or pegged to one of the major currencies or a basket of currencies on the other hand. Between these two extremes, there can be a few types of exchange rate arrangements and combinations. The IMF has classified the prevailing exchange rate regimes into eight categories. They are: Exchange Arrangements with No Separate Legal Tender, Currency Board Arrangements, Conventional Fixed Peg Arrangements, Pegged Exchange Rates within Horizontal Bands, Crawling Pegs, Exchange Rates within Crawling Bands, Managed Floating with No Predetermined Path for the Exchange Rate, and Independent Floating.

This classification system ranks exchange rate regimes on the basis of the degree of flexibility of the arrangement or a formal or informal commitment to a given exchange rate path. The classification emphasises the implications of the choice of exchange rate regimes to the independence of monetary policy. However, it must be stressed that absolute independence of monetary policy from exchange rate policy does not exist under any exchange rate regimes. Monetary policy decisions are taken in conjunction with a country's external positions one way or another, with or without explicitly imposed foreign exchange rate policy constraints. Table 2.1 presents information regarding exchange rate arrangements of IMF member countries or regions. It is based on members' actual, de facto regimes, as classified by the IMF as of April 30, 2003, which may differ from their officially announced arrangements.

Under independent floating, the exchange rate is market determined. The regime is also called free floating or clean floating. Foreign exchange intervention, if any, does not aim at establishing a level for the exchange rate; rather, it aims at moderating the rate of change and preventing undue fluctuations in the exchange rate. Monetary policy is, in principle, independent of exchange rate policy with an independent floating exchange rate regime.

Managed floating that is sometimes called dirty floating, or managed floating with no predetermined path for the exchange rate in full, has a lower degree of flexibility, compared with independent floating. The monetary authority influences exchange rate movements through active, direct or indirect intervention to counter the long-term trend of the exchange rate without specifying a predetermined exchange rate path or without having a specific exchange rate target. Indicators for managing the exchange rate are broadly judgmental. e.g., through balance of payments positions, international reserves, parallel market developments, and adjustments may not be automatic.

The IMF distinguishes "tightly managed floating" where intervention takes the form of very tight monitoring that generally results in a stable exchange rate without having a clear exchange rate path from "other managed floating" where the exchange rate is influenced in a more ad hoc fashion. The former intervenes with the aim of permitting authorities an extra degree of flexibility in deciding the tactics to achieve a desired path, while the latter lacks such an aim in managing the exchange rate.

Under the arrangement of exchange rates within crawling bands, the currency is maintained within certain fluctuation margins of at least ±1% around a central rate, which is adjusted periodically at a fixed rate or in response to changes in selective quantitative indicators. The degree of flexibility of the exchange rate is a function of the band width. Bands can be either symmetric around the crawling central rate or asymmetric with different upper and lower bands. The commitment to maintaining the exchange rate within the band imposes constraints on monetary policy, the narrower the band, the lower degree of independence monetary policy possesses.

Conventional fixed peg arrangements are exchange rate regimes where a country formally or de facto pegs its currency at a fixed rate to another currency or a basket of currencies, where the basket is formed from the currencies of major trading or financial partners and weights reflect the geographical distribution of trade, services, or capital flows, or the SDR. The monetary authority can adjust the level of the exchange rate, although relatively infrequently. There is no commitment to keep the parity irrevocably. The exchange rate may fluctuate within a narrow

**Table 2.1.** Exchange rate arrangements

| Exchange rate regime (number of countries/ regions) | Country/region |
|---|---|
| Exchange arrangements with no separate legal tender (41) | *Another currency as legal tender:*<br>Ecuador; El Salvador; Kiribati; Marshall Islands; Micronesia; Palau; Panama; San Marino; Timor-Leste<br>*ECCU:*<br>Antigua and Barbuda; Dominica; Grenada; St. Kitts and Nevis; St. Lucia; St. Vincent and the Grenadines<br>*CFA franc zone WAEMU:*<br>Benin; Burkina Faso; Côte d'Ivoire; Guinea-Bissau; Mali; Niger; Senegal; Togo<br>*CFA franc zone CAEMC:*<br>Cameroon; Central African Rep.; Chad; Congo, Rep. of; Equatorial Guinea; Gabon |
| Currency board arrangements (7) | Bosnia and Herzegovina; Brunei Darussalam; Bulgaria; Hong Kong SAR; Djibouti; Estonia; Lithuania |
| Conventional fixed peg arrangements (42) | *Against a single currency* (33):<br>Aruba; Bahamas, The; Bahrain; Bangladesh; Barbados; Belize; Bhutan; Cape Verde; China; Comoros; Eritea; Guinea; Jordan; Kuwait; Lebanon; Lesotho; Macedonia, FYR; Malaysia; Maldives; Namibia; Nepal; Netherlands Antilles; Oman; Qatar; Saudi Arabia; Suriname; Swaziland; Syrian Arab Republic; Turkmenistan; Ukraine; United Arab Emirates; Venezuela; Zimbabwe<br>*Against a composite* (9):<br>Botswana; Fiji; Latvia; Libya; Malta; Morocco; Samoa; Seychelles; Vanuatu |
| Pegged exchange rates within horizontal bands (5) | *Within a cooperative arrangement ERM II* (1):<br>Denmark<br>*Other band arrangements* (4):<br>Cyprus; Hungary; Sudan; Tonga |
| Crawling pegs (5) | Bolivia, Costa Rica; Nicaragua; Solomon Islands; Tunisia |
| Exchange rates within crawling bands (5) | Belarus; Honduras; Israel; Romania; Slovenia |
| Managed floating with no pre- announced path for the exchange rate (46) | Afghanistan; Algeria; Angola; Argentina; Azerbaijan; Burundi; Cambodia; Croatia; Czech Rep.; Dominican Rep.; Egypt; Ethiopia; Gambia, The; Ghana; Guatemala; Guyana; Haiti; India; Indonesia; Iran, I.R. of; Iraq; Jamaica; Kazakhstan; Kenya; Kyrgyz Republic; Lao PDR; Mauritania; Mauritius; Moldova; Mongolia; Myanmar; Nigeria; Pakistan; Paraguay; Russian Federation; Rwanda; São Tomé and Príncipe; Serbia and Montenegro; Singapore; Slovak Rep.; Tajikistan; Thailand; Trinidad and Tobago; Uzbekistan; Vietnam; Zambia |
| Independent floating (36) | Albania; Armenia; Australia; Brazil; Canada; Chile; Colombia; Congo, Dem. Rep. of; Georgia; Iceland; Japan; Korea; Liberia; Madagascar; Malawi; Mexico; Mozambique; New Zealand; Norway; Papua New Guinea; Peru; Philippines, The; Poland; Sierra Leone; Somalia; South Africa; Sri Lanka; Sweden; Switzerland; Tanzania; Turkey; Uganda; United Kingdom; United States; Uruguay; Yemen, Rep. of |

Source: IMF

margin of less than ±1% around a central rate or the maximum and minimum value of the exchange rate may remain within a narrow margin of 2% for at least three months. The monetary authority stands ready to keep the fixed parity through direct intervention, e.g., via sale or purchase of foreign exchange on the foreign exchange market, or indirect intervention, e.g., via aggressive use of interest rate policy, imposition of foreign exchange regulations or exercise of moral suasion that constrains foreign exchange activity, or through intervention by other public institutions. Flexibility of monetary policy is limited, but traditional central banking functions are still possible.

Non-fixed pegs do not peg the currency to another currency or a basket of currencies and are in general more flexible than fixed pegs. Under pegged exchange rates within horizontal bands, the value of the currency is maintained within certain margins of fluctuation of at least ±1% around a formal or a de facto fixed central rate. It also includes the arrangements of the countries in the exchange rate mechanism (ERM) of the European Monetary System (EMS), which was replaced with the ERM II on January 1, 1999. Though the Deutsch mark was the currency to which the other currencies of the EMS pegged, it was not pre-arranged to be the anchor currency – it performed the role due to its strength. So, the EMS was not a conventional fixed peg arrangement. There is a limited degree of monetary policy discretion, with the degree of discretion depending on the band width.

Under crawling pegs, the currency is adjusted periodically in small amounts at a fixed rate or in response to changes in selective quantitative indicators, such as past inflation differentials vis-à-vis major trading partners and differentials between the target inflation and expected inflation in major trading partners. The rate of crawl can be set to generate inflation-adjusted changes in the currency in retrospect, or set at a pre-announced fixed rate or below the projected inflation differentials, which is forward looking. The commitment to maintaining crawling pegs imposes constraints on monetary policy.

Currency Boards are monetary regimes based on an explicit legislative commitment to exchanging the domestic currency for a specified foreign currency at a fixed exchange rate. The domestic currency is issued only against foreign exchange and that remains fully backed by foreign assets, eliminating traditional central bank functions, such as monetary control and lenders of last resort, and leaving little scope for discretionary monetary policy. Some flexibility may still be afforded, depending on how strict the rules of the boards are. In the case of Hong Kong, although it operates a currency board system, the monetary authority can still be, and is regarded to have a role of, lenders of last resort, because it is backed by the People's Republic with enormous assets and foreign reserves.

There are two types exchange arrangements with no separate legal tender. One is formal dollarisation where the currency of another country circulates as the sole legal tender. The other is shared legal tender where members belonging to a monetary currency union share the same legal tender. Members of the currency union also share domestic monetary policy with each other, e.g., monetary policy of the ECB is jointly determined by its member states and may have impact in the whole euro area. Smaller states may benefit from being part of the currency union in the sense of effective control over domestic monetary policy. e.g., although the Netherlands and Belgium could have operated their own domestic monetary policy under an independent floating exchange rate regime before the single currency, they hardly enjoyed monetary policy independence of their own and had any influence on German monetary policy that not only impacted but also determined Dutch and Belgian monetary policy. With the single currency and the ECB, the two countries have some say in the euro area monetary policy.

## 2.2   A Brief History of International Monetary Systems

With the rise of international trade in the second half of the 19th century, the establishment of international monetary systems became practically necessary. The industrial revolution, starting in Britain and soon spreading to Germany, France, America and other western countries, took place and got an accelerating momentum earlier in the same century at a time that witnessed so many famous inventors and engineers whose names are still influential in our everyday life now: James Watt (1736-1819), Isambard Kingdom Brunel (1767-1849), Werner von Siemens (1816-1892), Gottlieb Daimler (1834-1900), Karl Benz (1844-1929), and Rudolf Diesel (1858-1913), to mention a few. The industrial revolution greatly increased productivity through inventions and the use of engines in production, and later, in mass production. A substantial portion of manufactured goods had to find foreign markets. Consumption and production were no longer confined within national borders. Consequently and subsequently, international trading rules and methods of settlements took their initial shape at the time, and continued to evolve over time.

The history of international monetary systems can be divided into five periods: The classical gold standard (1875-1914), interim instability (1914-1943), the Bretton Woods system (1944-1971), the collapse of the Bretton Woods system (1971-1973), and the recent float (1973- ). These systems are introduced and discussed in the following.

*Classical Gold Standard* (1875-1914). The starting point of the classical gold standard is not clear-cut, which can be as early as 1820s when the UK first adopted the gold standard, or in the 1870s when most western powers followed. Yet, no matter how the beginning of the gold standard period was decided, the emergence of the gold standard was a response to the rise of international trade at the time, brought about to a great extent by the industrial revolution. The gold standard is a fixed exchange rate regime. Nations on the gold standard pegged their currencies to gold, and then the exchange rate between two currencies was fixed in terms of a specific amount of gold. For example, if the US dollar was pegged to gold at $1 = 1/30 oz of gold and the sterling was pegged to gold at £1 = 1/6 oz of gold, then the exchange rate of sterling vis-à-vis the US dollar was fixed at $5/£. Maintenance of the exchange rate involved the buying and selling of gold at that price.

The gold standard was featured by its price-specie-flow mechanism, an automatic adjustment mechanism for maintaining trade balance, where specie was gold coins. It worked as follows: a balance of payments surplus (deficit) led to a gold inflow (outflow); gold inflow (outflow) led to higher (lower) prices which reduced surplus (deficit). Moreover, exchange rates under the gold standard were highly stable, which helped conduct and promote international trade.

*Interim instability* (1914-1944). This period covered two world wars and the Great Depression. By early 20$^{th}$ century, the supply of minted gold was very limited relative to the rapid expansion of the economy in the last few decades, and the growth of international trade was held back because there were insufficient monetary reserves. The situation deteriorated quickly in World War I, during which many countries abandoned the gold standard, because it prevented them from printing more money as a means of paying the expenses of the war. This money printing process led to higher inflation during and immediately after the war, and increases in inflation rates naturally differed among countries. Consequently, a fixed exchange rate regime implemented through the gold standard was neither desirable nor workable.

Attempt was made to restore the gold standard because of a highly instable international trade environment following the abandonment of the regime. This led to a brief spell of the gold exchange standard between 1925 and 1931, in which only the US and the UK were pegged to gold, while other countries held gold, US dollar or sterling reserves. This temporary international monetary system and order was soon torn down by the Great Depression, since a fixed exchange rate arrangement appeared to amplify the extent of recessions and unemployment in the time of economic contraction. The lack of international co-ordination and commitment to maintaining a trustworthy international monetary and trading system resulted in a dreadful situation where countries adopted tactics of competitive depreciation of their currencies to gain comparative advantages in international trade. These, coupled with protectionist economic policies, were very harmful to the world economy as a whole. The foreign exchange market was extremely volatile as a consequence.

*The Bretton Woods system* (1946-1971). Concerns in exchange rate instability and disorders in international monetary systems and trade continued to deepen in World War II. Negotiations started as early as in 1942 to establish a credible international monetary system after the war. In July 1944, 44 nations gathered at Bretton Woods, New Hampshire to hold a conference that gave birth to a post war international monetary system named after the conference venue. Two international institutions, the International Monetary Fund and the World Bank, were created at the Bretton Woods conference. The Bretton Woods system was a fully negotiated international monetary system and order intended to govern currency relations among sovereign states. It was designed to combine binding legal obligations with multilateral decision-making processes conducted through an international institution, the IMF.

Under the Bretton Woods system, the US dollar was valued at $35 per ounce of gold. The commitment by the US to redeem international dollar holdings at the rate of $35 per ounce laid down the central foundation of the Bretton Woods system. The US dollar was the numeraire of the system, the standard to which other currencies were pegged. Consequently, the US did not have the entitlement to set the exchange rate between the US dollar and other currencies. Changing the value of the US dollar in terms of gold has no real effect, because the values of other currencies were pegged to the dollar. The US dollar had special position in system and was the $n^{th}$ currency - if there are n currencies, then there are only n-1 bilateral exchange rates to be pegged.

The Bretton Woods system was a kind of gold exchange standard. Upon entering the IMF, a country submitted a par value of its currency expressed in terms of gold or in terms of the US dollar using the weight of gold in effect on July 1, 1944, which was $35 per ounce of gold. By signing the agreement, member countries submitted their exchange rates to international disciplines. All exchange transactions between member countries were to be effected at a rate that diverged not more than 1% from the par values of the respective currencies. A member country could change the par value of its currency only to correct a fundamental disequilibrium in its balance of payments, and only after consulting with the IMF. In case when the IMF objected a change, but the member devalued its currency, then that member was ineligible to use IMF's resources. There would be no objection to a change if the cumulative change was less than 10% of the par value. forbids members to restrict current account balances. Members were obligated to maintain currency convertibility for current account transactions to facilitate trade but convertibility was not required for capital account transactions.

*The collapse of the Bretton Woods system* (1971-1973). At the launch of the Bretton Woods system, the US Federal Reserve held three quarters of all central bank gold in the world and the US was the only dominant force enjoying global monetary supremacy; while the economic and financial fortunes of Europe and Japan had been largely ruined by the war. However, ultimately the US dollar was not gold. The system would continue to work properly while the mass of US dollars circulating in the rest of the world was backed by gold held in the US but would cease functioning vice versa. With economic recovery taking momentum gradually in Europe and Japan, there was an increasing need for international liquidity in the form of US dollars to facilitate growth in international trade. This could only lead to outflows of US dollars under the Bretton Woods system. In 1959, the problem of dollar overhang, the amount of US dollars in international circulation in excess of gold reserves held by the US Federal Reserve, surfaced for the first time. Shortly before that in 1958, Europe's currencies returned to convertibility, which also contributed to the diminished desire to obtain and accumulate reserves in the form of US dollars. Before 1958, less than 10% of US balance of payments deficits had been financed by calls on the US gold stock, with the rest being financed by US dollars. During the next decade however, almost two thirds of US balance of payments deficits were transferred to the rest of the world in the form of gold, mostly to Europe. The gravity of the problem was first revealed by Triffin (1960) in what was later known as the Triffin dilemma. He argues that, the gold exchange standard of the Bretton Woods is fundamentally flawed by its reliance on the pledge of convertibility of the US dollar into gold. The Bretton Woods system had to rely on US deficits to avert a world liquidity shortage. The resulting erosion of US reserves was bound in time to undermine confidence in the continued convertibility of US dollars. Therefore, the Bretton Woods system and the countries in the system confronted a dilemma. To stop speculation against the dollar, US deficits would have to cease, which would deepen the liquidity problem. To solve the liquidity problem, US deficits would have to continue, which would bring about a confidence problem for the continued convertibility of US dollars. In the 1960s, dollar overhang began to grow larger and larger as a result of increased capital outflow induced by higher returns abroad, military commitments, and the Vietnam War. By 1963, the US gold reserve held at Manhattan barely covered liabilities to foreign central banks, the gold coverage had fallen to 55% by 1970, and to 22% by 1971. Thus, from 1963, had the foreign central banks tried to convert their dollar reserves into gold, the US would have been forced to abandon gold convertibility. The Bretton Woods system was clearly under grim strain and the collapse of the system was just a matter of time.

America's domestic problems also contributed to the collapse of the Bretton Woods system. In the 1960s, the US economy experienced higher inflation, higher unemployment and lower growth relative to, most notably, Japan and Germany. The US dollar appeared to be overvalued and the speculation on the devaluation of the US dollar continued to grow and accelerate. On August 15, 1971, the US president Nixon announced in a Sunday evening televised address that the convertibility of the US dollar into gold was suspended. In response to the crisis, international monetary negotiations were undertaken within the framework of the Group 10 in a meeting at the Smithsonian Institution in Washington DC. The agreement was then formalised by the IMF to be known as the Smithsonian Agreement, which was a temporary regime. The Smithsonian Agreement made following currency realignments: the Japanese yen appreciated 17%, the Deutsch mark 13.5 %, the British pound 9%, and the French franc 9%. The US dollar devalued to $38 per ounce from $35 per ounce. The boundaries for exchange rate fluctuations were widened from ±1% to ±2¼% of the central rates after currency realignment. This devaluation of the US dollar had no significance because the US dollar remained inconvertible. One and a half years later, with the second devaluation of the US dollar in February 1973 to $42.22 per ounce, and after new waves of speculation against a realigned structure of par values negotiated in the Smithsonian Agreement, the currencies of all the industrial countries were set free to float independently. Both the par value system and the gold exchange standard, the two central elements of the postwar monetary regime, came to an end. The Bretton Woods system finally and officially collapsed.

*The recent float* (1973-). In February 1973, the official boundaries for the more widely traded currencies were eliminated and the floating exchange rate system came into effect. The gold standard became obsolete and the values of a range of currencies were to be determined by the market. Under this regime, for those countries that have chosen to float their currencies independently, foreign exchange intervention, if any, does not aim at establishing a level for the exchange rate but aims at moderating the rate of change and preventing undue fluctuations in the exchange rate. As having seen in the previous section, most industrialised countries have adopted independent floating, but the present international monetary system is a mixture of several kinds of exchange rate arrangements operating in parallel at the same time. It is because the world is no longer dominated by America or America with its western partners doing international trade and business. International trading rules, international monetary systems and orders suitable for industrialised countries or benefiting industrialised countries alone cannot be applied to developing countries without being challenged for reasonable amendments and adjustments.

## 2.3  The European Single Currency

The European single currency, the euro, is a milestone in the history of international monetary systems. After World War II, most western economies adopted the Bretton Woods system, which paved the way for international monetary stability and established the supremacy of the US dollar. As shown and discussed earlier, the weaknesses and problems inherited with the Bretton Woods system surfaced to limelight in the 1960s. Between 1968 and 1969 foreign exchange market turbulence led to the depreciation of the French franc and the appreciation of the German mark, threatening the stability of other European currencies and the system of common prices set up under the European common agricultural policy. In this context, the Barre report proposed greater coordination of economic policies and closer monetary cooperation within Western Europe in February 1969. At the summit in The Hague in December the same year, the heads of state and government of Western Europe decided to create an economic and monetary union (EMU), an official goal of European integration. Headed by the Prime Minister of Luxembourg, Pierre Werner, A working group (the Werner group) was given the task of drawing up a report on how this goal might be reached by 1980. The Werner group submitted its final report in October 1970. It envisaged the achievement of full economic and monetary union within ten years according to a three-stage plan. The ultimate goal was to achieve full liberalisation of capital movements, the irrevocable fixing of parities among national currencies and the replacement of national currencies with a European single currency. The report also recommended that the coordination of economic policies be strengthened and guidelines for national budgetary policies drawn up.

The project to create the European Monetary System (EMS) started in 1979 when members of the European Union organised the European Monetary System to link their currencies to prevent large fluctuations in exchange rates and counter inflation among member states. The EMS was based on the concept of fixed, but adjustable exchange rates. The currencies of all the Member States, except the UK, participated in the exchange rate mechanism (ERM). Exchange rates were based on central rates against the ECU, the European unit of accounts, which was a weighted average of the participating currencies. A grid of bilateral rates was calculated on the basis of these central rates expressed in ECUs, and currency fluctuations had to be contained within a band of 2.25% either side of the bilateral rates, except the Italian lira, which was allowed to fluctuate within a band of 6%.

The report of the Delors Committee of April 1989 set to achieve EMU in three stages. The first stage was to step up cooperation framework between European central banks, the second stage was focused on the progressive transfer of decision-making on monetary policy to supranational institutions and the establishment of a European System of Central Banks (ESCB), and in the third stage, the national currencies would have their convergence rates irrevocably fixed and would be replaced by the European single currency. The European Council in Madrid adopted the Delors report in June 1989 as a basis for its work and decided to implement the first of these stages from July 1, 1990, when capital movements in the Community would be liberalised completely. The Council then decided to convene an intergovernmental conference to prepare the amendments to the Treaty of Rome, which was signed on March 25, 1957 and established the European Economic Community (EEC), in view of the development of EMU. Approved by the European Council of December 1991, the amendments proposed by the intergovernmental conference were incorporated in the Treaty on European Union, best known as the Maastricht Treaty, which was signed at Maastricht, the Netherlands on February 7, 1992 and entered into force on November 1, 1993. The Treaty's EMU project was based on the general outline of the Delors report but differed from it on some significant points. In particular, the second stage was delayed until January 1994 and some objectives for the second stage, e.g., the transfer of responsibilities for monetary policy to a supranational body, were excluded or trimmed down.

The first stage of EMU began on July 1, 1990 and ended on December 1, 1993 when the process of the single market was completed. The second stage of EMU began on January 1, 1994 and ended on December 31, 1998. An important monetary institution, the European Monetary Institute (EMI) and the predecessor of the European Central Bank, was established at Frankfurt. The tasks of the EMI were to strengthen cooperation between the national central banks and the coordination of Member States' monetary policies, and to carry out the necessary preparatory work for the establishment of the European System of Central Banks (ESCB), which was to conduct the single monetary policy from the beginning of the third stage, and for the introduction of the single currency. On May 31, 1995, the European Commission Green Paper was drawn on the practical arrangements for the introduction of the single currency. The European Council, meeting in Madrid on December 15 and 16, 1995, confirmed that the third stage of EMU would commence on January 1, 1999, in accordance with the convergence criteria, timetable, protocols and procedures laid down in the Treaty establishing the European Community. The European Council considered that the name of the currency had to be the same in all the official languages of the European Union, taking into account the existence of different alphabets, being simple and to symbolise Europe. The European Council therefore decided that, as of the start of stage three, the name given to the European currency would be "euro". This name was meant as a full name, not as a prefix to be attached to the national currency names.

In order to be able to participate in the euro area, each Member State must satisfy four criteria. (a) Price stability: The inflation rate of a given Member State must not exceed by more than 1½ percentage points that of the three best-performing Member States in terms of price stability during the year preceding the examination of the situation in that Member State. (b) Government finances: The ratio of the annual government deficit to GDP must not exceed 3% at the end of the preceding financial year. If this is not the case, the ratio must have declined substantially and continuously and reached a level close to 3% or, alternatively, must remain close to 3% while representing only an exceptional and temporary excess. The ratio of gross government debt to GDP must not exceed 60% at the end of the preceding financial year. If this is not the case, the ratio must have sufficiently diminished and must be approaching the reference value at a satisfactory pace. (c) Exchange rates: The Member State must have participated in the exchange-rate mechanism of the European monetary system without any break during the two years preceding the examination of the situation and without severe tensions. In addition, it must not have devalued its currency on its own initiative during the same period. (d) Long-term interest rates: The nominal long-term interest rate must not exceed by more than 2 percentage points that of, at most, the three best-performing Member States in terms of price stability. The period taken into consideration is the year preceding the examination of the situation in the Member State concerned.

To clarify the process of introducing the single currency, the European Council adopted the scenario for the changeover to the single currency, which was based on the draft prepared at its request by the Council, in consultation with the Commission and the EMI. The reference scenario comprised three successive phases that take account of users' capacity to adjust. Phase A was the launch of Economic and Monetary Union. On May 1 and 2, 1998 the Council, meeting at the level of the Heads of State or Government, designated, in accordance with the procedure laid down by the Treaty, the Member States which had achieved a sufficient degree of convergence to participate in EMU. Data for 1997 formed the basis of this "transition examination". In May 1998 the Council announced the bilateral parities between participating currencies. Phase B was effective start of Economic and Monetary Union. Phase B, and with it the third stage of EMU, began on January 1, 1999 with the irrevocable fixing of conversion rates among currencies of participating countries and against the euro. This phase has a three-year duration. From this point on, the euro became a currency in its own right and its external value was that of the official ECU basket, which ceased to exist. The ESCB, which was established on July 1, 1988 and composed of the European Central Bank (ECB) and the national central banks, become operational to formulate and implement monetary and exchange-rate policy in euros. Large-value payment systems started to operate in euros and new issues of public debt to be denominated in euros. However, the euro remained a book currency only, notes and coins in circulation were still denominated in the national currencies. Phase C was general introduction of the single currency. On January 1, 2002, euro notes and coins started to circulate alongside national notes and coins; national notes and coins were gradually withdrawn.

The start of the third stage of EMU on January 1, 1999 marked the effective beginning of economic and monetary union. It was from this date that the ECU ceased to be a basket of currencies and became a currency in its own right, in the form of the euro. In economic terms, the implementation of EMU increased convergence of policies, with reinforced multilateral surveillance and an obligation on the euro-area Member States to avoid excessive government deficits. In monetary terms, the implementation of EMU gave birth to a single monetary policy managed by ESCB consisting of the ECB and the national central banks. Finally, most importantly and symbolically, the implementation of EMU introduced the euro as the single currency of the participating countries in Europe.

The irrevocably fixed conversion rates between the euro and the currencies of the Member States adopting the euro were determined and adopted on 31 December 1998. As regards Greece, which adopted the single currency on 1st January 2001, the Council fixed the conversion rate of the Greek drachma on 19 June 2000. The conversion rates are presented in Table 2.2.

**Table 2.2.** Conversion rates of the euro and national currencies

| 1 euro = | Exchange rate | Former national currency |
|---|---|---|
| - | 40,3399 | Belgian francs |
| - | 1,95583 | German marks |
| - | 340,750 | Greek drachmas* |
| - | 166,386 | Spanish pesetas |
| - | 6,55957 | French francs |
| - | 0,787564 | Irish pounds |
| - | 1936,27 | Italian lire |
| - | 40,3399 | Luxembourg francs |
| - | 2,20371 | Dutch guilders |
| - | 13,7603 | Austrian schillings |
| - | 200,482 | Portuguese escudos |
| - | 5,94573 | Finnish marks |

* applicable from 1st January 2001
Source: ECB

Currently three European Union members, Denmark, the UK, and Sweden, do not adopt the euro. These member states are euro zone "pre-ins" while the adopting countries are euro zone "ins". A new exchange rate mechanism (ERM II) has been set up to guarantee monetary stability and solidarity between the euro and the national currencies of the "pre-ins".

It is worthwhile mentioning that the euro is not the first single currency in monetary history. The United States experienced some kind of currency unification on its territory since its independence from the Unite Kingdom in the 18th century. In 221 BC, Qin Shi Huang (first emperor of the Qin dynasty) unified the currencies and other measurement systems in the then alleged central domain of all lands, where hundreds of states and duchies existed, which were reduced to seven larger states by the time of Qin Shi Huang's unification. A unified currency, together with other unified measurement systems, has played important roles in holding this vast land together for over two millenniums almost continuously. Presently, there are a few currency unions in operation, e.g., East Caribbean Currency Union (ECCU) and Western Africa Economic and Monetary Union (WAEMU). Some other single currencies have been proposed and their feasibility has been examined as well. Although it is not sure whether these exercises, experiments and discussions may lead to the implementation of a single currency in the area concerned, there is no doubt that a currency area must be large enough so that the internal economic activity within the area is substantially greater than the external economic activity conducted with the outside world to reduce costs and inconvenience. A size of the United States, the People's Republic and the European Union can be appropriate and feasible in this sense, which, though, does not rule out the functioning of a small number, and only a small number, of special currencies, such as the Swiss franc.

# 3    International Parity Conditions

International trade or exchange of goods and services across borders gives rise to international settlement with payments being made in different currencies. Discrepancies may arise as a consequence when the settlement is executed in one currency as against the other currency. Moreover, economic conditions and changes in economic conditions in different countries may take effect on the value of goods measured in different currencies and the relative values and opportunity costs of these currencies. International parities are concerned with the relationships between the values of two or more currencies and the respective economic conditions in these countries, and the way in which these relationships respond to the changing economic conditions in these countries. International parities are important since they establish relative currency values and their evolution in terms of economic circumstances, and cross border arbitrage may be possible when they are violated.

This chapter studies three international parity conditions: purchasing power parity (PPP), covered interest rate parity (CIRP), and uncovered interest rate parity (UIRP) or the international Fisher effect (IFE). The relationships between these parities are also examined and discussed. PPP is concerned with the relative values or the exchange rate of two currencies and the prices in the two countries. CIRP identifies the relationships between the spot exchange rate, the forward exchange rate, and the interest rates in the two countries. IFE establishes the relationship between changes in the exchange rate and the interest rate differential in the two countries, exploiting the relationship between the interest rate differentials and the inflation differentials.

## 3.1   Purchasing Power Parity

Purchasing power parity is a theory about exchange rate determination based on a plain idea that the two currencies involved in the calculation of the exchange rate have the same purchasing power for the same good sold in the two countries. Simply put, it is the law of one good, one price. In international finance, PPP means that the same goods or basket of goods should sell at the same price in different countries when measured in a common currency, in absence of transactions costs.

There are two versions of PPP. One is absolute PPP and the other is relative PPP. The former studies the exchange rate for the two currencies in terms of the absolute prices for the same basket of goods in the two countries, and the latter examines how the exchange rate changes over time in response to changes in the price levels in the two countries.

### 3.1.1 Absolute Purchasing Power Parity

Absolute PPP is best described by the law of one good, one price. It is the application of the law of one good, one price in international finance which states that the same goods or basket of goods should sell at the same price in different countries when measured in a common currency, in absence of transactions costs, i.e.:

$$P_h = S \times P_f \qquad (3.1)$$

where $P_h$ is the price for a good or basket of goods in the domestic or home country, $P_f$ is the price for the same good or basket of goods in the foreign country, and $S$ is the exchange rate expressed as the units of the home currency per foreign currency unit. Equation (3.1) indicates that the exchange rate is the ratio of the prices for the same goods in the two countries:

$$S = \frac{P_h}{P_f} \qquad (3.2)$$

For example, if the price of a basket of apples is \$3 in the US and the price of a basket of same apples is £2 in the UK, then according to PPP, the direct quote of the exchange rate in the US must be $S = P_h/P_f = \$3/£2 = \$1.5/£$, and the direct quote of the exchange rate in the UK must be $S = P_h/P_f = £2/\$3 = £0.6667/\$$. Suppose the exchange rate departs from \$1.5/£, one might be able to make profit by buying apples in the UK (US) and transporting the apples to the US (UK) for sale. Let us examine what may happen, assuming that the basket of apples still sells at £2 in the UK and \$3 in the US, but the exchange rate is \$1.6/£ instead. Measured in the US dollar as the common currency, the price of the basket of apples is \$3 in the US but \$3.2 (£2×\$1.6/£) in the UK; and measured in the British pound as the common currency, the price of the basket of apples is £2 in the UK but £1.875 (\$3/\$1.6/£) in the US. The law of one good one price, or absolute PPP, is violated, and consequently, there might be arbitrage opportunities for cross border trade activities. In this case, the pound is over valued and the dollar is under valued, or the same apples are cheaper in the US than in the UK. Therefore, it is profitable to export the apples from the US to the UK, e.g.:

Step1:    Buy 10 baskets of apples for \$30 in the US;
Step 2:   Transport the apples to the UK for sale for £20;

Step 3:   Exchange the pound for the dollar at the exchange rate of $1.6/£, resulting in $32.

The profit from this trade activity is $2 or the profit margin is 6.7% [(32-30)/30], ignoring the transportation cost and other transaction costs. Obviously, there can be no profit if the transportation cost is equal to or higher than $2 per 10 baskets.

We can infer two implications from the above example. Absolute PPP is a *sufficient* condition for no arbitrage in international trade and finance, but it is not a *necessary* condition. Upholding of absolute PPP guarantees the elimination of arbitrage, while a violation of absolute PPP may or may not give rise to arbitrage opportunities, depending on the level of associated costs in the international trading process. Let examine a second example:

Suppose that the price of a Mini Cooper is €1,200 in France and S = €1.4/£, then the price of the same Mini Cooper in the UK should be $P_f = P_h/S =$ €1,200/(€1.4/£) =£857. We ask three questions. (a) If instead the Mini Cooper is sold for £950 in the UK, what may happen? (b) If HM Customs and Excise of the UK levies an import duty of 20% on manufactured goods, does arbitrage still exist? (c) If the importer incurs a 15% cost to cover transportation, administrative and other fees, does arbitrage still exist? We discuss these three questions in the following.

(a)      It is cheaper to buy the car in France. Therefore, it is profitable to import the cars from France and sale them in the UK, e.g.:

Step1:   Buy 100 Mini Cooper cars in France for 100×€1,200 = €120,000;

Step 2:   Transport the cars to the UK for sale for 100×£950 = £95,000;

Step 3:   Exchange the pound for the euro at the exchange rate of €1.4/£, resulting in €133,000.

The profit from this trade activity is €13,000 and the profit margin is 10.8% [(133,000-120,000)/120,000]. Arbitrage will take place. The price of Mini Cooper will rise in France and fall in the UK until the arbitrage opportunity is wiped out.

(b)      Now the cost for a Mini Cooper in the UK through this exporting channel will be €1,200/€1.4/£×120% = £1028.57, higher than £950, the price of a Mini Cooper currently prevailing in the UK. So, it is not profitable to import Mini Cooper from France in this case.

(c)      Now the cost for a Mini Cooper in the UK through this exporting channel will be €1,200/€1.4/£×115% = £985.71, higher than £950, the price of a

Mini Cooper currently prevailing in the UK. So, it is not profitable to import Mini Cooper from France in this case.

From the above example, it is observed that transaction costs, such as transportation, taxes and tariffs, commission charges, prevent seemingly existed arbitrage opportunities from materialising. Therefore, there would be no arbitrage opportunities while in the meantime the law of one price does not hold in two countries, if the countries are geographically distant, and/or are not engaged in or committed to free trade. The prices for the same goods remain distorted in the two countries, since it is not profitable to exploit the difference.

Having studied PPP theory and examined the above cases, it might be interesting to present the well publicised big Mac standard of *The Economist* in the following, and reflect on what the figures in Table 3.1 suggest.

However, research does not rely on evidence from one or two examples, but from many that can be representative. In the case of PPP, it means that a substantial number of goods should be included in the comparison of the relative prices of goods in the two countries in concern, in relation to the exchange rate. In this regard, research on PPP usually adopts the weighted average of the prices for a basket of goods, in the form of the consumer price index (CPI) or other kinds of price indices, rather than the prices of individual goods, in empirical investigations at specific times or during certain time periods. Equation (3.2) then becomes:

$$S_t = \frac{P_{h,t}}{P_{f,t}} = \frac{\sum_{i=1}^{N_h} w_h^i p_{h,t}^i}{\sum_{i=1}^{N_f} w_f^i p_{f,t}^i} \tag{3.3}$$

where $S_t$ is the exchange rate at $t$, $P_{h,t}$ is the price level at $t$ in the home country, $P_{f,t}$ is the price level at $t$ in the foreign country, $p_{h,t}^i$ is the price for the $i^{th}$ good at time $t$ in the home country, $w_h^i$ is the weight of the $i^{th}$ good in the price index in the home country, $N_h$ is total number of goods included in the price index in the home country, $p_{f,t}^i$ is the price for the $i^{th}$ good at time $t$ in the foreign country, $w_f^i$ is the weight of the $i^{th}$ good in the price index in the foreign country, and $N_f$ is total number of goods included in the price index in the foreign country. Ideally, $N_h = N_f$ and $w_h^i = w_f^i$ for same, if not identical, goods for verifying the parity conditions, i.e., the weight for the same good in the price index is the same and the number and types of goods included in the price index are the same in the all countries under investigation. But these are usually not the case and, consequently, a divergence from equation (3.3) is not necessarily a rejection of PPP. Issues related to empirical tests of PPP will be dealt with in Section 3.1.4. It is worthwhile pointing out that a logarithm version of equation (3.3):

$$s_t = p_{h,t} - p_{f,t} \tag{3.4}$$

is typically used in empirical research, where $s_t = Ln(S_t)$, $p_{h,t} = Ln(P_{h,t})$ and $p_{f,t} = Ln(P_{f,t})$.

**Table 3.1**. The Big Mac Standard of the Economist

| The golden-arches standard | Big Mac prices | | Implied PPP* of the dollar | Actual $ exchange rate 25/04/00 | Under(−)/over (+) valuation against the dollar, % |
|---|---|---|---|---|---|
| | in local currency | in dollars | | | |
| United States† | $2.51 | 2.51 | − | − | − |
| Argentina | Peso2.50 | 2.50 | 1.00 | 1.00 | 0 |
| Australia | A$2.59 | 1.54 | 1.03 | 1.68 | -38 |
| Brazil | Real2.95 | 1.65 | 1.18 | 1.79 | -34 |
| Britain | £1.90 | 3.00 | 1.32‡ | 1.58‡ | +20 |
| Canada | C$2.85 | 1.94 | 1.14 | 1.47 | -23 |
| Chile | Peso1,260 | 2.45 | 502 | 514 | -2 |
| China | Yuan9.90 | 1.20 | 3.94 | 8.28 | -52 |
| Czech Rep | Koruna54.37 | 1.39 | 21.7 | 39.1 | -45 |
| Denmark | DKr24.75 | 3.08 | 9.86 | 8.04 | +23 |
| Euro area | €2.56 | 2.37 | 0.98§ | 0.93§ | -5 |
| France | FFr18.50 | 2.62 | 7.37 | 7.07 | +4 |
| Germany | DM4.99 | 2.37 | 1.99 | 2.11 | -6 |
| Italy | Lire4,500 | 2.16 | 1,793 | 2,088 | -14 |
| Spain | Pta375 | 2.09 | 149 | 179 | -17 |
| Hong Kong | HK$10.20 | 1.31 | 4.06 | 7.79 | -48 |
| Hungary | Forint339 | 1.21 | 135 | 279 | -52 |
| Indonesia | Rupiah14,500 | 1.83 | 5,777 | 7,945 | -27 |
| Israel | Shekel14.5 | 3.58 | 5.78 | 4.05 | +43 |
| Japan | ¥294 | 2.78 | 117 | 106 | +11 |
| Malaysia | M$4.52 | 1.19 | 1.80 | 3.80 | -53 |
| Mexico | Peso20.90 | 2.22 | 8.33 | 9.41 | -11 |
| New Zealand | NZ$3.40 | 1.69 | 1.35 | 2.01 | -33 |
| Poland | Zloty5.50 | 1.28 | 2.19 | 4.30 | -49 |
| Russia | Rouble39.50 | 1.39 | 15.7 | 28.5 | -45 |
| Singapore | S$3.20 | 1.88 | 1.27 | 1.70 | -25 |
| South Africa | Rand9.00 | 1.34 | 3.59 | 6.72 | -47 |
| South Korea | Won3,000 | 2.71 | 1,195 | 1,108 | +8 |
| Sweden | SKr24.00 | 2.71 | 9.56 | 8.84 | +8 |
| Switzerland | SFr5.90 | 3.48 | 2.35 | 1.70 | +39 |
| Taiwan | NT$70.00 | 2.29 | 27.9 | 30.6 | -9 |
| Thailand | Baht55.00 | 1.45 | 21.9 | 38.0 | -42 |

*Purchasing-power parity: local price divided by price in United States  †Average of New York, Chicago, San Francisco and Atlanta  ‡Dollars per pound  §Dollars per euro
Sources: McDonald's; The Economist

Source: The Economist

## 3.1.2 Real Exchange Rates

Having studied absolute PPP, we can progress to introduce the concept of the real exchange rate.

The real exchange rate is the exchange rate adjusted by the price levels in the two countries, defined as follows:

$$Q = S \times \frac{P_f}{P_h} \tag{3.5}$$

where $Q$ is real exchange rate. Real exchange rates are one if absolute PPP holds. Home or domestic currencies are over valued if $Q < 1$ and are under valued if $Q > 1$. Foreign currencies are under valued if $Q < 1$ and are over valued if $Q > 1$.

A logarithm version of the real exchange rate is:

$$q = s - (p_h - p_f) \tag{3.6}$$

where $q = Ln(Q)$, $s = Ln(S)$, $p_h = Ln(P_h)$ and $p_f = Ln(P_f)$. The real exchange rate in logarithms is zero when absolute PPP holds. Home or domestic currencies are over valued if $q$ is negative and are under valued if $q$ is positive. Foreign currencies are under valued if $q$ is negative and are over valued if $q$ is positive.

The real exchange rate is a useful concept and simple means to gauge the strength of currencies. For example, in the above Mini case, the real exchange rate of the euro vis-à-vis the pound in France is:

$$Q = S \times \frac{P_f}{P_h} = €1.4/£ \times \frac{£950}{€1200} = 1.1083 > 1.$$

So, the euro is under valued and the pound is over valued if Mini Cooper cars are the only goods traded between France and the UK. From the view of the UK as the domestic country, the real exchange rate of the pound against the euro in the UK is:

$$Q = S \times \frac{P_f}{P_h} = £0.7143/€ \times \frac{€1200}{£950} = 0.9023 < 1,$$

which indicates again that the pound is over valued and the euro is under valued.

Since the real exchange rate is the exchange rate adjusted by the price levels of the two countries, it is absolute PPP in a different expression. Tests for the validity of absolute PPP are equivalent to testing whether the real exchange rate is one. Many empirical studies adopt this line of enquiry.

### 3.1.3 Relative Purchasing Power Parity

Unless it is in a one-good case where absolute PPP can be exactly checked, examinations of PPP involve aggregate price levels in the two countries. Aggregate price levels are merely index numbers that provide a good indication of changes in price levels over time but have little meaning about their absolute value at a specific time. For example, a statement such as "the US CPI is 135 in the fourth quarter of 1998" itself does not tell us whether the price level is high a low. So, aggregate price levels must have a base year, at which the price level is set to be 100 and against which the size of increase or decrease can be measured. e.g., if the base year is 1990 in the above case, then a CPI of 135 means that the price level at that time is 35 percent higher than that in 1990. That is, in the fourth quarter of 1998, one can use \$135 to purchase goods that are only worth \$100 in 1990. In other words, the purchasing power of \$135 in the fourth quarter of 1998 is equal to the purchasing power of \$100 in 1990.

With the above considerations, it is logical to introduce a relative version of PPP. Relative PPP examines the relationship between changes in exchange rates and changes in the aggregate price levels in the two countries involved. Taking log differences of the absolute PPP equation yields:

$$\Delta s_t \approx \Delta p_{h,t} - \Delta p_{f,t} = \pi_{h,t} - \pi_{f,t} \qquad (3.7)$$

where $\Delta s_t = \ln(S_t) - \ln(S_{t-1})$ is the (percentage) change in exchange rates in the period $t$-1 to $t$; $\pi_{h,t} = \Delta p_{h,t} = \ln(P_{f,t}) - \ln(P_{f,t-1})$ is the (percentage) change in the price levels, or the inflation rate, in the domestic country in the same period; and $\pi_{f,t} = \Delta p_{f,t} = \ln(P_{f,t}) - \ln(P_{f,t-1})$ is the (percentage) change in the price levels, or the inflation rate, in the foreign country in the same period. Price indices, usually consumer price indices (CPI), are used for the measurement of inflation.

Relative PPP establishes an evolution path for exchange rate changes, which is a consequence of relative price developments in the two countries. Suppose absolute PPP holds at time $t$-1 and relative PPP holds in the period $t$-1 to $t$, then absolute PPP holds at time $t$ also. The size of the change in the exchange rate reflects the relative purchasing power gain of one of the two currencies, or the relative purchasing power loss of the other currency, to the right extent when relative PPP holds. However, if absolute PPP does not hold at time $t$-1 but relative PPP holds in the period $t$-1 to $t$, then absolute PPP does not hold at time $t$ either, even if the exchange rate has adjusted to reflect correctly the relative purchasing power gain or loss during this period. This exposes a problem with relative PPP: it is possible that absolute PPP or PPP in its original form does not hold at any times while rela-

tive PPP holds at all times. One of the reasons for adopt relative PPP is that absolute PPP is difficult, if not impossible, to be tested and verified in empirical research. But test results from relative PPP cannot substitute those for absolute PPP.
Confirmation of relative PPP does not necessarily lead to the conclusion that the
two currencies have the right purchasing power with the given exchange rate –
parity may or may not exist.

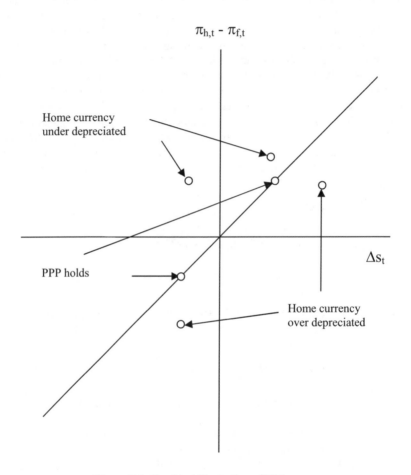

**Figure 3.1.** Graphical illustration of PPP

Relative PPP indicates that: (a) the domestic currency will depreciate if inflation in the domestic country is higher than that in the foreign country, and (b) the
domestic currency will depreciate to the extent equal to the inflation differential
between the two countries. For example, if inflation in the US was 2% and infla-

tion in Japan was 0% in 2000, the yen should have appreciated by 2% vis-à-vis the dollar in the same period, according to relative PPP.

Figure 3.1 is a graphical illustration of relative PPP. Points on the 45 degree line indicate that changes in the exchange rate are equal to the two countries' inflation differentials and relative PPP holds. A point to the right of the 45 degree line means that the home currency is over depreciated. It can be that an increase in the exchange rate is greater than the inflation differential between the home country and the foreign country, e.g., $\Delta s_t = 2\%$, $\pi_{h,t} = 3\%$ and $\pi_{f,t} = 2\%$; or an increase in the exchange rate while the domestic inflation is lower than the foreign inflation, e.g., $\Delta s_t = 1\%$, $\pi_{h,t} = 1\%$ and $\pi_{f,t} = 2\%$; and so on. A point to the left of the 45 degree line suggests that the home currency does not depreciate enough to reflect the inflation differential between the two countries in the period.

### 3.1.4 Empirical Tests and Evidence on PPP

There is a huge body of literature on the study of the validity of PPP. These studies feature different sample periods, different currencies, different specifications, and different estimation methods. The majority of these studies are backed up by contemporarily popular econometric models. This section attempts to present, analyse and explain the empirical evidence in and verdict on PPP in an intuitive way, avoiding technical econometric jargons whenever possible.

With regard to the coverage of recent empirical research, while the currencies investigated differ, the majority of studies focus on bilateral exchange rates of industrialised countries against the US dollar. Frequently examined sample periods are the era of flexible exchange rates that began in the 1970s, though there are studies where the sample period covers two centuries. The price indices used are also different, with the most commonly employed for research being the consumer price index (CPI), followed by the wholesale price index (WPI), producer price index (PPI) and the gross domestic product (GDP) deflator.

Results and findings from the empirical literature are broadly mixed. In the following, we briefly review some of the representative studies in the area, which traces the evolution of the research, covering static tests of PPP based on linear regressions of exchange rates on relative prices, unit root tests on the stationarity of real exchange rates, cointegration tests on the comovement between the nominal exchange rate and relative prices, and panel data tests on the convergence to PPP using cross country data.

#### Regression Tests of PPP

In the mid 1970s, the conventional tests of PPP involved the use of regression analysis, that is, to test the coefficient restrictions imposed by PPP. Frenkel (1978) runs regression[1] for the monthly dollar-pound, franc-dollar and franc-pound exchange rates over the period of February 1921 to May 1925 during which exchange rates were flexible. His results are generally supportive of the PPP hypothesis in both the absolute and relative versions. However, Frenkel (1981) uses data from the recent float for the dollar-pound, dollar-franc and dollar-mark exchange rates and finds that PPP is not supported by the data. Similar results are reported by Krugman (1978) for both the inter-war and the recent float.

## Stationarity of Real Exchange Rates

In the early 1980s, with the development of econometric techniques, a further test of PPP shifts attention to examine the time series properties of real exchange rates. Studies at this stage take into account the non-stationarity of variables. A means of testing for PPP in a framework that allows for non-stationarity is to define the real exchange rate and to test if this series is non-stationary. If the null hypothesis of a unit root or non-stationarity cannot be rejected, then the real exchange rate contains a unit root and does not revert to its mean value, indicating, consequently, that PPP does not hold in the long-run. In determining whether a variable follows a non-stationary process, the unit root test is one of the commonly employed econometric methods. With this method, many previous studies have reported that non-stationarity cannot be rejected for the real exchange rate series in the floating period, for example, Adler and Lehmann (1983), Darby (1983), Hakkio (1984), Meese and Rogoff (1988), and Baillie and McMahon (1989). Consequently, these studies reject the notion of long-run PPP, implying that shocks have a permanent effect on the level of the real exchange rate, while changes are unpredictable, and that there is little or no tendency for nominal exchange rates and prices to adjust in such a way as to promote PPP.

While most of the empirical evidence does not reject the unit root hypothesis for real exchange rates for most countries in the post Bretton Woods era and reject the notion of long-run PPP, there are nevertheless a smaller number of studies that are in favour of PPP. For example, using monthly data between September 1975 and May 1981, Cumby and Obstfeld (1984) reject the non-stationarity hypothesis for the real exchange rate between the US dollar and the Canadian dollar. Abuaf and Jorion (1990) examine the real exchange rates of 10 industrialised countries for the recent floating period and the period between 1900 and 1972 and find mean-reversion in the real exchange rate.

However, doubts were raised at this stage of the debate over the power of standard tests. Given the phenomenal volatility of floating exchange rates, it can be very hard to distinguish between slow mean reverting and a non-stationary the real exchange rate, especially for the post Bretton Woods data, since the current floating exchange rate period is too short to assess accurately the validity of PPP. Froot and Rogoff (1994) calculated that, if PPP deviations damp sufficiently slow, sup-

---

[1] The regression equation is $s_t = \alpha + \beta(p_{h,t} - p_{f,t}) + v_t$, to test the restrictions $\alpha = 0$ and $\beta = 1$. PPP in the form of equation (3.4) is confirmed when $\alpha = 0$ and $\beta = 1$.

pose that the half life of PPP deviations is three years, then it may require 76 years for one to be able to reject reliably the existence of a unit root in real exchange rates. With a longer half life, even longer data would be required. Put it differently, PPP deviations can be slow to reverse, and conventional econometric techniques have low power to identify stationary but persistent dynamics. Therefore, it is argued that the reason that most previous studies fail to reject a unit root in real exchange rate time series is probably to the poor power of the tests employed rather than the evidence against long-run PPP.

One of the approaches to address the low power problem is to expand the sample period. Frankel (1986), using 116 years (1869-1984) of annual data for dollar-pound real exchange rate, is able to reject the unit root hypothesis for the whole period between 1869 and 1984, but is unable to reject the hypothesis using data from 1945 to 1984. He finds that PPP deviations have an annual decay rate of 14 percent and a half life of 4.6 years. The long horizon data sets are also employed by several studies during the 1990s, with a variety of different approaches, and almost invariably tend to find evidence of mean reversion in the real exchange rate. Diebold et al (1991), for example, look at the data during the Gold Standard era, with shortest data spanning 74 years and longest 123 years, and are able to reject the unit root hypothesis by adopting the fraction integration model. They find that PPP holds in the long-run for each of the currencies and the typical half life of a shock to parity is approximately three years. Similarly, non-stationarity is rejected by Grilli and Kaminsky (1991) for the time period between 1885 and 1986 and by Glen (1992) for the period spanning 1900 and 1987. Employing two centuries' annual exchange rate data, Lothian and Taylor (1996) find strong evidence of mean reversion with an estimated half life being 4.7 years for the dollar-pound exchange rate and 2.5 years for the franc-pound exchange rate. Hence, based on studies using long historical data sets, Lothian (1998) concludes that real exchange rates contain economically important mean-reverting components and that, as a result, PPP is still a useful approximation. Moreover, Lothian (1998) shows that the difficulty in finding evidence of PPP with the US dollar as the numerator currency is primarily the result of the 1979-1982 period during which the US dollar first strongly depreciated and then strongly appreciated.

Although the above long time span based studies do find the mean reversion of real exchange rate, they have ignored changes in exchange rate regimes. It is not clear whether the findings based on long time period data confirm simply the presence of parity reversion in the pre modern floating period or show its presence over the recent float as well. In addition, it is also argued that tests of unit roots in the real exchange rate preclude the coefficients, that is, the construction of the real exchange rate implicitly restricts the coefficients corresponding to the domestic and foreign price levels as -1 and 1. Due to measurement errors as well as trade barriers, the exchange rate may not move one by one with price levels as implied by PPP. In this regard, the recently developed cointegration methodology offers a more appropriate econometric test means for this kind of relationship.

### Comovement Between the Nominal Exchange Rate and Relative Price Levels

If two or more variables, such as the exchange rate and the corresponding price levels, are cointegrated, then in the long-run these variables will settle down together in a unique way, without wandering away far apart. Therefore the implication of long-run PPP is generally interpreted as the comovement of the nominal exchange rate and the relative price levels between the two countries in concern over time.

The early application of the cointegration approach to testing for PPP is based on the Engle and Granger (1987) two-step procedure. Taylor (1988), Enders (1988), Mark (1990) and Patel (1990), among others, carried out investigations in this framework for the recent floating period; whereas Kim (1990) employs data sets spanning most of the 20$^{th}$ century. In general, the empirical tests adopting the Engle-Granger two-step procedure generally fail to observe long-run tendencies for nominal exchange rates and relative prices to settle down on an equilibrium track.

The above Engle-Granger procedure based tests have been criticised by a number of more recent studies, for example, MacDonald (1993), Cheung and Lai (1993), Cochrane and DeFina (1995), who have argued that the failure to find a cointegration relationship between the exchange rate and relative prices may be due to the econometric method used, rather than the absence of a long-run relationship. These studies advocate the use of then newly emerged multivariate cointegration methodology of Johansen (1988) and Johansen and Juselius (1990), commonly known as the Johansen procedure. This maximum likelihood based approach allows testing for PPP in a trivariate framework and avoids some drawbacks of the Engle-Granger two-step regression procedure.

Adopting the Johansen procedure, MacDonald (1993) tests for a long-run relationship between exchange rates and relative prices for five bilateral US dollar exchange rates against the Canadian dollar, the French franc, the German mark, the Japanese yen and the British pound, and also tests for the proportionality of the exchange rate with respect to relative prices, using post Bretton Woods data from January 1974 to June 1990. He classifies the distinction between what he calls the weak-form PPP and the strong-from PPP. The weak-form PPP requires deviations from a linear combination of exchange rates and national price levels be stationary; while the strong-form PPP additionally requires the degree one homogeneity of the exchange rate with respect to the relative prices in the two countries. He reports that the weak-form PPP receives robust support from the data, whilst the strong-form PPP is given practically no support. In other words, there is a long-run relationship between a number of bilateral US dollar exchange rates and their corresponding relative prices, but the proportionality of the exchange rate to the relative prices fail to be established. Similar research is also followed by Cheung and Lai (1993), Cochrane and DeFina (1995), Kugler and Lenz (1993), and Pippenger (1993), among others. Overall, their evidence is supportive of the week-form PPP, i.e., comovement between the exchange rate and the respective relative prices; but is less in favour of PPP in the strong-form, i.e., comovement *and* proportionality. They argue that given the transportation cost, tariffs, and cross-country differences in the construction of price indices, PPP may be consistent with the above findings.

A few other studies attempt to investigate the validity of PPP under special circumstances such as high inflation and the European Monetary System (EMS). Frenkel (1981) has argued that for countries experiencing high money supply and variable rates of inflation, short-term deviations from PPP will occur, but price movements and nominal exchange rate movements will offset each other over time so that long-run PPP is likely to hold. If, however, the economy suffers real shocks, long-run PPP will not hold. Empirical tests for high inflation can also be found in McNown and Wallace (1989), and Mahdavi and Zhou (1994). These studies generally find some but not clear cut evidence of long-run PPP. They suggest that PPP may hold over a range of inflationary experience, and it is likely to hold more consistently when the inflation rate is very high. The evidence for the EMS, which is a system of managed floating exchange rates, is analysed by Chen (1995), Cheung, et al (1995), Chowdhury and Sdogati (1993) to assess how long-run PPP is affected by the EMS exchange rate arrangement. In general, the results of these studies support the view that currency realignments of the EMS have been effective in maintaining PPP among its member countries.

### *Cross Country Panel Data Approach*

An alternative way to circumvent the low power of many traditional tests has been the use of panel data. A number of competing studies have emerged, arguing that the standard unit root and cointegration tests have low power against stationary alternatives in small samples and suggesting that failure to support the long-run PPP in early studies may result from this shortcoming. Although a few studies have turned to long period time series, these long period samples are available for only a few currencies. More importantly, exchange rate data spanning a very long time period suffer changes in exchange rate regimes. As Mussa (1986) has pointed out, real exchange rates behave very differently under different exchange rate regimes. If there are different parameters governing fixed versus floating exchange rates, test credibility may be heavily reduced by the inclusion of fixed rate period.

In this framework, Frankel and Rose (1996) examine deviations from PPP using a panel of data for 150 countries. The panel shows strong evidence of mean-reversion similar to that observed in long-run time series. The deviations from PPP have a half-life of approximately four years. The panel approach is also adopted by Jorion and Sweeney (1996), Mark (1995), Wu (1996), Oh (1996), Papell and Theodoridis (1998), and Lothian (1997). All have reported similar findings. Recently, O'Connell (1998) raises a potentially important problem with this approach. He points out that the standard practice of calculating all real exchange rates relative to the US dollar leads to cross sectional dependence in time series panel data. Adjusting for this problem appears to make it more difficult to reject the null of non-stationarity. Taylor and Sarno (1998) also point out that there may exist bias, sometimes substantial bias, towards stationarity in such tests.

In summary, the above review and analysis show that, although great efforts have been made over the past decades on empirical tests of PPP, the results and findings are mixed. There are a number of factors causing departures from PPP, each of which is discussed in the following[2].

## Construction of Price Indices

PPP is based on the concept of comparing identical baskets of goods in two economies. An important problem facing researchers in this aspect is that different countries usually attach different weights to different goods and services when constructing their price indices. This means that it is difficult to compare the goods in the two baskets - it is difficult to match the attributes of the goods in the two baskets and it is probably only by chance to allocate the same weights to the same goods in the baskets. This issue is most probably significant in testing for PPP between developed economies and developing economies that have vastly different consumption patterns. People in developing countries usually spend a high proportion of their income on basics such as food and clothing while these sorts of consumption take up a much smaller proportion of people's expenditure in developed economies. But, we should note that it is the difference in the attributes of goods and weightings that primarily give rise to international trade, along with taking advantages in relative prices. Consequently, testing for PPP was, is and will always be difficult.

## Transportation Costs and Trade Impediments

Transportation costs and restrictions on trade may be substantial enough to prevent some goods and services from being traded between countries. Studies, such as Frenkel (1981), note that PPP holds better when the countries concerned are geographically close and trade linkages are high, which can partly be explained by transportation costs and the existence of other trade impediments such as tariffs. Nonetheless, since transportation costs and trade barriers do not change dramatically over time they are not factors explaining sufficiently for the failure of relative PPP.

## Relative Prices of Non-tradable Goods

The existence in all countries of non-traded goods and services whose prices are not linked internationally allows systematic deviations even from relative PPP. Because the price of a non-tradable is determined entirely by its domestic supply and demand, changes in these may cause the domestic price of a broad commodity basket to change relative to the foreign price of the same basket. Other things kept unchanged, a rise in the price of a country's non-tradables will raise its price level

---

[2] For details see, for example, Krugman and Obstfeld (1994).

relative to foreign price levels, or the purchasing power of any given currency will fall in countries where the prices of non-tradables rise.

One well documented striking empirical observation, as in a survey by Rogoff (1996), is that when prices of similar baskets of both traded and non-traded goods are converted into a common currency, the aggregate price indices tend to be higher in rich countries than in poor countries. Further evidence shows that tradable goods prices are nowhere as dissimilar internationally as those of non-traded goods. Consequently the overall higher price index in rich countries is mainly due to the fact that non-tradable goods prices are higher in developed than developing countries.

### Differences Between Capital and Goods Markets

PPP is based on the concept of goods arbitrage and has nothing to say about the role of capital movements. However, as Dornbusch (1976) has put forward, there can be substantial prolonged deviations of the exchange rate from PPP. The basic idea is that goods prices are flexible and adjustable in the long-term but can be considered fixed in the short-term, i.e., prices are sticky. In the short-term, goods prices in both the home and foreign economies are fixed, while the exchange rate adjusts quickly to the arrival of new information and changes in economic policy. Exchange rate movements represent deviations from PPP that can be substantial and prolonged, since it takes substantial longer time for prices to make corresponding adjustments.

### Imperfect Competition

One of the notions underlying PPP is that there is sufficient international competition to prevent the price of a good in one country exceeding notably that in another country. However, it is clear that there is considerable variation in the degree of competition internationally. These differences mean that multinational corporations can often get away with charging different prices in different countries. Monopolistic or oligopolistic practices in goods markets may interact with transport costs and other trade barriers to weaken further the link between the prices of similar goods sold in different countries.

## 3.2  Interest Rate Parities

Interest rate parities are concerned with expected exchange rate changes and the interest rate differential between the two involved countries or currency zones during a certain period. The expected exchange rate change can be *covered* by entering a forward contract for the foreign exchange transaction at a future time. Subsequently, it is called covered interest rate parity (CIRP), which identifies the relationships between the spot exchange rate, the forward exchange rate, and the interest rates in the two countries in a time period. Without a forward contract on future foreign exchange transactions, the expected change in exchange rates is *uncovered*, and then an appropriate relationship between expected exchange rate changes and the interest rate differential between the two countries during a certain period is justified and established by uncovered interest rate parity (UIRP), which is usually associated with the international Fisher effect (IFE) to be discussed in the next section.

### 3.2.1 Covered Interest Rate Parity

CIRP states that the forward premium must be equal to the two countries' interest rate differential, otherwise there exist exploitable profitable arbitrage opportunities. Prior to proving this statement, which is in fact a reasonable approximation, we present an exact relationship between the spot exchange rate, the forward exchange rate, and the interest rates in the two involved countries in a certain period.

Define $F_{0,1}$ the forward exchange rate contracted now and to be delivered in the next period, e.g., in 30 days, $S_0$ the currently prevailing spot exchange rate, $r_h$ the interest rate in the home country, and $r_f$ the interest rate in the foreign country during the period. Then the following relationship (parity) between the spot exchange rate, forward exchange rate, and the interest rates in the two countries must hold to eliminate any arbitrage opportunities:

$$\frac{F_{0,1}}{S_0} = \frac{1+r_h}{1+r_f} \qquad (3.8)$$

The rationale of equation (3.8) can be illustrated by the following example.

Suppose you have €1,000,000 to invest for one year. You can

either invest in the euroland at $r_€$ ($r_h$). The future value of your investment in one year = €1,000,000×(1 + $r_€$);

or convert your € for £ at the spot rate, invest in the UK at $r_£$ ($r_f$) and enter into a forward contract simultaneously to sell £ in one year. The future value of this investment in one year = €1,000,000×($F_{0,1}/S_0$)× (1 + $r_£$).

The two investments must have the same future value; otherwise arbitrage exists, so ($F_{0,1}/S_0$)×(1 + $r_£$) must equal (1 + $r_€$), or equivalently ($F_{0,1}/S_0$) = (1 + $r_€$)/(1 + $r_£$) = (1 +$r_h$)/(1 +$r_f$). This verifies equation (3.8). Deducting 1 from both sides of equation (3.8) leads to another expression of the relationship:

$$\frac{F_{0,1} - S_0}{S_0} = \frac{r_h - r_f}{1 + r_f} \approx r_h - r_f \qquad (3.9)$$

It can be observed that, exactly speaking, the forward premium is equal to the interest rate differential adjusted by a factor of $(1 + r_f)$. Only when $r_f$ is fairly small can the adjustment be comfortably ignored. Now let us progress to the approximate, but commonly used, version of CIRP. Taking logarithms of both sides of equation (3.8) yields:

$$f_{0,1} - s_0 = r_h - r_f \qquad (3.10)$$

where $f_{0,1} = \ln(F_{0,1})$ and $s_0 = \ln(S_0)$. Further define the (approximate) forward premium $p_{0,1} = f_{0,1} - s_0$, equation (3.10) becomes:

$$p_{0,1} = r_h - r_f \qquad (3.10')$$

Notice that it has involved approximation in the process from equation (3.8) to equation (3.10). We should use equation (3.8) if interest rates are not small. However, equations (3.10) and (3.10') present the relationship as a commonly adopted CIRP statement that the forward premium must be equal to the two countries' interest rate differential to eliminate any arbitrage opportunities.

The relationship revealed by CIRP is graphically illustrated in Figure 3.2. Any Points on the 45 degree line indicate that CIRP holds. As a result, no arbitrage opportunities exist and it makes no difference whether one chooses to invest in the home country or the foreign country. A point to the left of the 45 degree line is where the forward premium is smaller than the interest rate differential between the home country and the foreign country. So the benefit of exploiting the forward premium is more than offset by the benefit from the interest rate differential. For example, if the forward premium is 1% and the interest rate differential is 2% during a given period. In this case, the home currency has depreciated but has not depreciated enough to the extent dictated by the interest rate differential. The gain from the foreign exchange transaction (1%) is smaller than the opportunity cost of going abroad (2%). A point to the right of the 45 degree line suggests that the forward premium is greater than the interest rate differential between the home country and the foreign country. Subsequently, it is profitable to exploit the arbitrage opportunity by investing in the foreign country, which involves converting the home currency into the foreign currency at the spot exchange rate prevailing at the beginning of the period, investing in the foreign country and earning interest at the rate of $r_f$ in the period, and converting the foreign return back into the home currency at the end of the period through the use of a forward contracted at the beginning of the period. Notice that the home country and the foreign country are relative terms and one does not necessarily stay in the home country. In the following, we examine some examples to apply the CIRP theory and to exploit the arbitrage opportunities exposed by the violation of CIRP step by step.

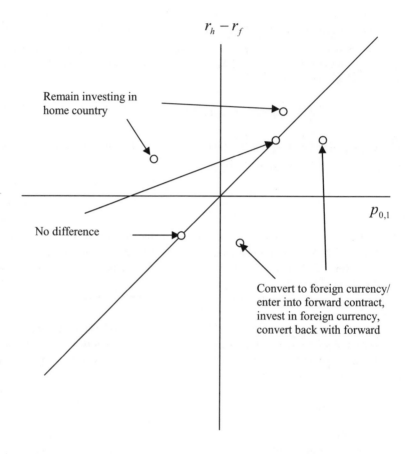

$$r_h - r_f$$

Remain investing in home country

No difference

$$P_{0,1}$$

Convert to foreign currency/ enter into forward contract, invest in foreign currency, convert back with forward

**Figure 3.2.** Graphical illustration of CIRP

Exchange rate and interest rate information in the US and the euroland is given as follows:

| | |
|---|---|
| The $/€ spot rate | $S_0 = 1.1237$ |
| One year $/€ forward rate | $F_{0,360} = 1.1128$ |
| US discount rate | 2.50% pa |
| Euroland discount rate | 3.75% pa |

Let us examine and answer these questions: (a) Do arbitrage opportunities exist? (b) How will you invest to exploit the arbitrage opportunities?

Answers to part (a) are to check whether CIRP holds in this case, or whether the forward premium is equal to the interest rate differential. We adopt the exact version of CIRP and apply equation (3.4) to the above exchange rate and interest rate figures.

The forward premium (exact) $(F_{0,1} - S_0)/S_0$ = (1.1128-1.1237) / 1.1237= -0.0097;

The interest rate differential (exact) $(r_h - r_f)/(1 + r_f)$ = -0.01205.

From the result and referring to Figure 3.2, it can be concluded that:

As forward premium $\neq$ interest rate differential, arbitrage opportunities exist.

As forward premium > interest rate differential, it would be more profitable to invest in €. That is, if you have money in the US dollar to invest, you will convert the dollar to the euro at the beginning of the period, enter into a forward contract simultaneously to sell the euro at the end of the period, invest in the euro, and convert the euro back to the dollar with the forward contract at the end of the period. If you have money in the euro to invest, you simply invest in the euro.

Following the above analysis, we know that there are arbitrage opportunities and it is more profitable to invest in the euroland in this case. We present two procedures for the part (b) question below showing how to exploit the opportunities posed by the infringement of CIRP, one with the investor's own fund, and the other with borrowed fund, to make the investment.

Procedures for (b.1)
Suppose the investor has $1,000,000 and is based in the US, then the procedure to exploit the arbitrage opportunities can be:

Step 1(a): Convert the fund in $ to € at the spot exchange rate $S_0$ = $1.1237/€, which gives $1,000,000/$1.1237/€ = €889917.2;

Step 1(b): Enter into a forward contract simultaneously to sell € at the forward exchange rate $F_{0,360}$ = $1.1128/€, the size of the contract, €923289.1, is decided below;

Step 2: Invest the amount of € 889917.2 for one year in the euroland at the rate of $r_f = r_e$ = 3.75%. At the end of one year, the investment return is €889917.2×(1+0.0375) = €923289.1, all of which is to be converted back into $. So €923289.1 is also the size of the forward contract in step 1(b);

Step 3: Convert €923289.1 to $ with the forward contract in step 1(b), resulting in €923289.1×$1.1128/€ = $1,027,436

If the investor does not engage in the above foreign exchange transaction activities and invest in the US for one year at the rate of $r_h = r_s = 2.50\%$ instead, then the investment return is $1,000,000×(1+0.025) = $1,025,000. Let us call the former the foreign strategy and the latter the home strategy. The arbitrage profit is the difference between the investment returns of the foreign strategy and the home strategy, which is $1027436-$1025000 = $2,436. As discussed earlier, the home country and the foreign country are relative terms. So if the investor has €1,000,000, then she or he adopts the "home strategy" and remains investing in the euroland. It can be concluded that it is the euroland that is a place to make higher returns in this case.

Procedures for (b.2)
Suppose the investor does not use her or his own fund and borrows $1,000,000, then the procedure to exploit the arbitrage opportunities can be:

Step 1: Borrow $1,000,000 at the cost of $r_h = r_s = 2.50\%$;

Step 2(a): Convert the fund in $ to € at the spot exchange rate $S_0 = $1.1237/€$, leading to $1,000,000/$1.1237/€ = €889917.2;

Step 2(b): Enter into a forward contract simultaneously to sell € at the forward exchange rate $F_{0,360} = $1.1128/€$, the size of the contract, €923289.1, is decided below;

Step 3: Invest the amount of € 889917.2 for one year in the euroland at the rate of $r_f = r_\epsilon = 3.75\%$. At the end of one year, the investment return is €889917.2×(1+0.0375) = €923289.1, all of which is to be converted back into $. So €923289.1 is also the size of the forward contract in step 2(b);

Step 4: Convert €923289.1 to $ with the forward contract in step 2(b), resulting in €923289.1×$1.1128/€ = $1,027,436;

Step 5: Repay the lender at the future value of the borrowing (principal plus interest), which is $1,000,000×(1+0.025) = $1,025,000.

After repaying the lender the principal of the borrowing and the interest incurred in one year, there is an amount of $2,436 = $1027436-$1025000 left with the investor or arbitrageur. The result is the same as in part (b1) with the investor's own fund. However, it will make a difference when transaction costs are considered and included, e.g., the borrowing rate is usually higher than the lending rate.

Therefore, there may be situations when there are arbitrage opportunities using one's own funds, but such arbitrage opportunities will not materialise using borrowed funds.

### 3.2.2  CIRP and Arbitrage in the Presence of Transaction Costs

Transaction costs reduce arbitrage opportunities or prevent arbitrage opportunities from materialising. These include bid-ask spreads in foreign exchange rates and in case of using borrowed funds, the difference in lending and borrowing rates.

For example, if in the previous case it is assumed that the lending rate is 3.00% per annum and the borrowing rate is 2.00% per annum in the US, the lending rate is 4.25% per annum and the borrowing rate is 3.25% per annum in the euroland, and a zero bid-ask spread is still assumed for exchange rates, as summarised below, is it possible to make arbitrage profit using borrowed US dollar funds?

| | |
|---|---|
| The $/€ spot rate | $S_0 = 1.1237$ |
| One year $/€ forward rate | $F_{0.360} = 1.1128$ |
| US borrowing rate | 2.00% pa |
| US lending rate | 3.00% pa |
| Euroland borrowing rate | 3.25% pa |
| Euroland lending rate | 4.25% pa |

We repeat the above procedure with the interest rates being replaced their respective borrowing and lending rates.

Step 1: Borrow $1,000,000 at the cost of $r_{\$,lending} = 3.00\%$ (bank's lending rates are borrowers' borrowing rates);

Step 2(a): Convert the fund in $ to € at the spot exchange rate $S_0 = \$1.1237/€$, leading to $\$1,000,000/\$1.1237/€ = €889917.2$;

Step 2(b): Enter into a forward contract simultaneously to sell € at the forward exchange rate $F_{0.360} = \$1.1128/€$, the size of the contract, €918839.5, is decided below;

Step 3: Invest the amount of € 889917.2 for one year in the euroland at the euro borrowing rate of $r_{€,borrowing} = 3.25\%$. At the end of one year, the investment return is €889917.2×(1+0.0325) = €918839.5, all of which is to be converted back into $. So €918839.5 is also the size of the forward contract in step 2(b);

Step 4: Convert €918839.5 to $ with the forward contract in step 2(b), resulting in €918839.5×$1.1128/€ = $1,022,485;

Step 5: Repay the lender at the future value of the borrowing (principal plus interest) at a cost of $r_{\$,lending} = 3.00\%$, which is $\$1,000,000\times(1+0.03)$ $= \$1,030,000$.

It is obvious that the future value of the borrowing, which is $\$1,030,000$, is greater than the investment return from the "arbitrage" process, which is $\$1,022,485$, so there exist no exploitable arbitrage opportunities due to the presence of the transaction cost in the form of differential lending and borrowing interest rates. However, it is still more profitable to adopt the "foreign" strategy if one uses her or his own US dollar funds, illustrated as follows.

Step 1(a): Convert the fund in $ to € at the spot exchange rate $S_0 = \$1.1237/€$, which gives $\$1,000,000/\$1.1237/€ = €889917.2$;

Step 1(b): Enter into a forward contract simultaneously to sell € at the forward exchange rate $F_{0,360} = \$1.1128/€$, the size of the contract, €918839.5, is decided below;

Step 2: Invest the amount of € 889917.2 for one year in the euroland at the euro borrowing rate of $r_{€,borrowing} = 3.25\%$. At the end of one year, the investment return is $€889917.2\times(1+0.0325) = €918839.5$, all of which is to be converted back into $. So €918839.5 is also the size of the forward contract in step 1(b);

Step 3: Convert €918839.5 to $ with the forward contract in step 1(b), resulting in $€918839.5\times\$1.1128/€ = \$1,022,485$;

If the investor does not engage in the above foreign exchange transaction activities and invest in the US for one year at the US rate of $r_{\$,borrowing} = 2.00\%$ instead, then the investment return is $\$1,000,000\times(1+0.02) = \$1,020,000$. Therefore, there is an arbitrage profit of $\$2,480 = \$1,022,485 - \$1,020,000$ from the arbitrage activity. When other kinds of transaction costs are taken into consideration, such as commonly observed bid-ask spreads in exchange rates, arbitrage opportunities will be further reduced.

## 3.2.3 Uncovered Interest Rate Parity

UIRP states that there is a relationship between the expected change in the spot exchange rate and the interest rate differential between the two countries and the expected change in the spot exchange rate is equal to the two countries' interest rate differential. There are no profitable opportunities if:

$$F_{0,1} = E_0\{S_1\} \tag{3.11}$$

while CIRP holds, where $E_0\{S_1\}$ is the expectations, formed at time 0, of the future spot exchange rate at time 1. Therefore, in relation to equation (3.8), the following relationship (parity) must hold:

$$\frac{E_0\{S_1\}}{S_0} = \frac{1+r_h}{1+r_f} \tag{3.12}$$

UIRP implies that the forward exchange rate is an unbiased predictor of the future spot exchange rate. Deducting one from both sides of equation (3.12) yields:

$$\frac{E_0\{S_1\}-S_0}{S_0} = \frac{r_h - r_f}{1+r_f} \approx r_h - r_f \tag{3.13}$$

The above equation states that the expected (percentage) change in the spot exchange rate, exactly speaking, is equal to the two countries' interest differential adjusted by a factor of $(1 + r_f)$. The factor of $(1 + r_f)$ can only be ignored when $r_f$ is fairly small. We can work out an approximate, but commonly used, version of equation (3.12), similar to that for CIRP, by taking logarithms on both sides of equation (3.12):

$$E_0\{\Delta s_1\} = E_0\{s_1\} - s_0 = r_h - r_f \tag{3.14}$$

It has involved approximation in the process from equation (3.12) to equation (3.14), similar to the CIRP case. Although equation (3.14) is an approximation, it presents the relationship as a commonly adopted UIRP statement suggesting that the expected change in the spot exchange rate be equal to the two countries' interest rate differential. There can be profitable opportunities if UIRP does not hold while the expectations about future spot exchange rates are right. But one may make no profits or even make a loss, if UIRP does not hold *and* the expectations about future spot exchange rates are wrong. Unlike CIRP, UIRP is *not* covered by a forward contract and, subsequently, the expected outcome is not guaranteed.

Figure 3.3 illustrates graphically the relationship established by UIRP. Points on the 45 degree line indicate that UIRP holds. As a result, it is not expected to make any difference whether one chooses to invest in the home country or the foreign country. Any points to the right of the 45 degree line mean that the expected depreciation of the home currency is greater than the interest rate differential between the home country and the foreign country. If the expectations are proved correct, then it is profitable to invest in the foreign country, which involves converting the home currency into the foreign currency at the beginning of the period at the prevailing spot exchange rate at the time, investing in the foreign country and earning interest at the rate of $r_f$ in the period, and converting the foreign return back into the home currency at the future spot exchange rate prevailing at the end of the period. The outcome would be the same as that in the CIRP case when the expectations are correct, i.e., $S_1 = E_0\{S_1\} = F_{0,1}$. Any points to the left of the 45 degree line indicate that the expected depreciation of the home currency is smaller than the interest rate differential between the home country and the foreign country. Consequently, the benefit of exploiting the expected changes in the exchange rate is more than offset by the benefit from the interest rate differential if the expectations are proved correct. The cases can be that the expected depreciation of the home currency is smaller than the right extent suggested by the interest rate differential between the home country and the foreign country; or the expected appreciation of the home currency is larger than the interest rate differential between the foreign country and the home country.

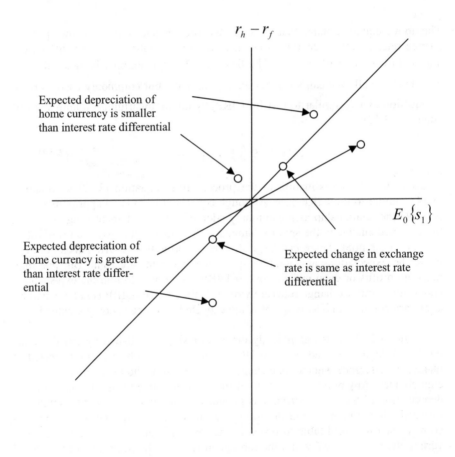

**Figure 3.3.** Graphical illustration of UIRP

We conclude this part with a simple example. Suppose that the UK interest rate is and will remain 3.25% per annum for the next 12 months, the US interest rate is and will remain 2.50% per annum for the next 12 months, and the current spot exchange rate of the US dollar vis-à-vis the British pound is $1.6036/£. (a) What is the expected spot exchange rate in 12 months time? (b) If the UK interest rate is expected to rise in six months by a quarter to two quarter points, what will the expected spot exchange rate be? UIRP is assumed to holds.

The answer to part (a) is an application of UIRP and equation (3.12), which gives:

$$E_0\{S_1\} = S_0 \times \frac{1+r_h}{1+r_f} = \$1.6305/£ \times \frac{1+0.0250}{1+0.0325} = \$1.5587/£ \cdot$$

The answer to part (b) is qualitative. Since the UK interest rate will be higher than 3.25 per annum overall in the next twelve months, the interest rate differential between the US and the UK will be smaller than that used in the above calculation. Therefore, the expected spot exchange rate will be smaller than $1.5587/£ as obtained in part (a).

## 3.3 International Fisher Effect

Prior to studying IFE, we first review the Fisher effect, which is concerned with the relationship between the real interest rate, the nominal interest rate, and inflation, in a domestic economic setting.

Denote $a$ as the real interest rate, $r$ as the nominal interest rate, and $E\{\pi\}$ the expected inflation rate in a certain period ($t-1$, $t$], then:

$$1+r = (1+a) \times [1 + E\{\pi\}]$$
(3.15)

An approximation can be made from the above equation:

$$\begin{aligned} 1+r &= (1+a) \times [1 + E\{\pi\}] \\ &= 1 + a + E\{\pi\} + a \times E\{\pi\} \\ &\approx 1 + a + E\{\pi\} \end{aligned}$$
(3.15')

Deducting one from both sides of equation (3.15') results in:

$$r \approx a + E\{\pi\}$$
(3.16)

Equation (3.16) is a mathematical expression of the Fisher effect, which states that that the nominal interest rate is the sum of the real interest rate and the inflation expectations in the period. The statement is indeed an approximation of the effect of expected inflation on the nominal interest rate, given the real interest rate. The error in the approximation is small when the real interest rate and inflation are low. The Fisher effect suggests that changes in the nominal interest rate reflect the revised inflation expectations; and revised inflation expectations have an impact on the level of the nominal interest rate.

Applying the Fisher effect to two concerned countries leads to the international Fisher effect. This involves combining the two countries' Fisher effects with exchange rate expectations and PPP, assuming real interest rates are equalised across countries.

The Fisher effect for the two countries, one of which is home and the other is foreign, is presented as:

$$r_h \approx a_h + E\{\pi_h\} \tag{3.17a}$$
$$r_f \approx a_f + E\{\pi_f\} \tag{3.17b}$$

A version of PPP, which involves exchange rate expectations, is given as:

$$E\{\Delta s_t\} = E\{\pi_h\} - E\{\pi_f\} \tag{3.18}$$

where $\Delta s_t$ is the (percentage) change in the exchange rate during $(t\text{-}1, t]$, the same period as for the prevailing inflation.

Combining the above equations (3.17) and (3.18) leads to:

$$\begin{aligned} E\{\Delta s_t\} &= E\{\pi_h\} - E\{\pi_f\} \\ &= (r_h - a_h) - (r_f - a_f) \\ &= r_h - r_f \end{aligned} \tag{3.19}$$

assuming real interest rates are equalised across countries, i.e., $a_h = a_f$.

IFE suggests that the expected change in exchange rates be equal to the interest rate differential between the two countries, which is a statement of UIRP derived under different circumstances. IFE pays attention to expected inflation and is derived through analysing the effect of expected inflation and the inflation differential between the two countries on expected changes in exchange rates. Expected inflation is a channel to cause nominal interest rates to change, the differential in the expected inflation of the two countries is a channel to result in the interest rate differential between the two countries, leading to expected relative changes in purchasing power and subsequent adjustment in exchange rate expectations. In contrast, UIRP relies on the forward exchange rate as an unbiased predictor of the future spot exchange rate and the validity of CIRP. A graphical illustration of IFE would be similar to Figure 3.3 for UIRP.

## 3.4    Links Between the Parities: a Summary

The relationships between the spot exchange rate, the forward exchange rate of one currency vis-à-vis the other, and the interest rates and inflation in the two countries give rise to the above examined parities and parity conditions. These relationships are about how changes (expected and *ex ante*) in one or two variables result in changes in other variables. Relevant parities apply when changes or expected changes in relevant variables are examined. That is, the relevance of a specific parity depends on the circumstances, under which the relationships are inspected, and the theme of the issue to be investigated. Figure 3.4 shows the links between different parities and the interactions between various factors.

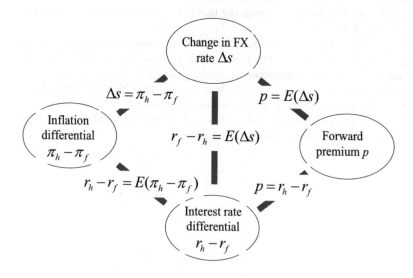

**Figure 3.4.** Links between parities and relationships between factors

The factors involved in these links are expected and realised changes in the spot exchange rate, the forward premium, the expected and realised inflation differential, and the interest rate differential. The upper left branch of the graph is PPP in the relative form, which states that changes in the spot exchange rate between two currencies in a given period is equal to the inflation differential in these two countries in the same period. The lower right branch is CIRP, which states that the forward premium that involves the spot and forward exchange rates for two currencies in a certain period is equal to the interest rate differential in the two countries in the same period. The lower left branch of the graph presents the Fisher effect in two countries, showing that interest rate differentials are equal to inflation differentials in the two countries in concern. This, through the channel of the upper left branch, establishes the IFE as a relationship between expected changes in the exchange rate and the interest rate differential, indicating that the expected changes in the exchange rate is equal to the interest rate differential in the two countries under consideration. The upper right branch illustrates the hypothesis that forward exchange rate be an unbiased predictor of the future spot exchange rate, in the form that the expected change in the spot exchange rate in a given period is equal to the forward premium in the same period for the two currencies involved. Combining the upper right and lower branches of the graph, the link between expected changes in the spot exchange rate and interest rate differentials is derived as UIRP, which states that the expected change in the spot exchange rate in a certain period is equal to the interest rate differential between the two countries in concern in the same period. In the middle of the graph is a direct link between the expected changes in the spot exchange rate and the interest rate differential, which is the IFE through the two left branches and UCIP through the two right branches in the graph.

Figure 3.4 not only presents the links between various parities but also indicates the roles of each of the factors or variable and the way in which they adjust and make corresponding comovements, as suggested by relevant parities. Nevertheless, these parities are in essence theories and hypotheses, and their validity is subject to empirical enquiries under various and relevant circumstances as discussed earlier in this chapter. One should not rely on them in making policy or investment decisions without cautious prior analysis.

# 4 Balance of Payments and International Investment Positions

Similar to book keeping and accounting in business firms, international transactions - international trade activity and the accompanied international financial settlement, must be recorded in a nation's accounts over every certain time period. These are referred to as balance of payments accounts. While the balance of payments records transactions during a certain period, the international investment statement presents a country's financial claims on, and financial liabilities to, the rest of the world at the end of a given period. So they mirror corporate income statements and balance sheets in a sense. Unlike the accounts of individual corporations, the entries to balance of payments accounts are an aggregate of all relevant international transactions carried out by a country's residents - corporations, individuals and government agencies. Therefore, the balance of payments is the *statistical* record of a country's international transactions over a certain period of time. So is the international investment position statement in recording a country's financial assets and liabilities.

The balance of payments and its accounts and the international investment position statement do not only record such international transactions and accumulated stock of assets/liabilities, but also indicate international flows of goods, services and capital, identify a country's international positions in various areas, and demonstrate international economic linkages between nations. Making good use of balance of payments and international investment position information helps government policy formation and formulation, corporate financial management decision-making, as well as inter-governmental cooperation and coordination in international trade and monetary arrangements.

This chapter introduces the balance of payments and the international investment position statement, examining balance of payments accounts and categories, the ways in which entries to balance of payments accounts are recorded, and the relationships between these entries, between balance of payments accounts, and between the balance of payments and the international investment position statement. International economic linkages between nations and, in particular, a country's international linkage with the rest of the world, are examined through analysing flows of goods, services and capital into and out of that country. International positions of individual countries revealed by the balance of payments and the international investment position statement are considered, together with the measures for altering the positions in specific areas.

## 4.1  Balance of Payments

The balance of payments is a statistical statement or record of a country's international economic transactions with the rest of the world over a certain period of time, showing flows of goods, services and capital out and into the country. Transactions represented by flows of goods, services and capital are presented in the form of double-entry bookkeeping, i.e. every transaction is recorded as both a credit and a debit with equal values and opposite signs. A debit entry shows a purchase of foreign goods, services, and assets, which results in a decline in liabilities to foreigners and has a negative sign on a balance of payments account. A credit entry shows a sale of domestic goods, services, and assets, which incurs an increase in liabilities to foreigners and has a positive sign on a balance of payments account. While most entries in the balance of payments refer to transactions in which economic values are provided or received in exchange for other economic values, at times items are given away rather than exchanged. When these happen, recording is one-sided, special types of entries referred to as transfers are made as the required offsets.

Since the publication of the IMF Balance of Payments Manual 5th edition in 1993 and its subsequent implementation, the structure and classification of balance of payments accounts have experienced significant changes. The development of the 5th edition of the Manual took place in conjunction with the development of the System of National Accounts 1993 and the two frameworks are now very closely aligned. According to the Manual, a balance of payments statement is constructed to include a current account and a capital and financial account. There involved major revisions and changes to the 4th edition of the Manual, not only in the names of the accounts, but also in the components of the accounts. Currently, the 5th edition of the Manual is the prevailing guideline for nations to follow in presenting their balance of payments, while proposals to revise and update it towards the 6th edition have been under way since 1999. In October 2000, the 13th meeting of the IMF Committee on Balance of Payments Statistics held in Washington, D.C. identified areas of the 5th edition of the Manual that require updating. This is prompted by the changes that have taken place in the international economy since the publication of the 5th edition of the Manual, the developments that are taking place in international trade negotiations, particularly in the services area, and the increased focus on both transaction and position statistics during and since the financial crises of 1994, 1997, and 1998. The focus of analysis, learned from the financial crises of 1994, 1997 and 1998, will be more on the financial account of the balance of payments and on the financial positions shown in the international investment position statement to be discussed in the following. External debt, reserves, and financial derivatives and other leveraged and complex transactions will be scrutinised in greater details.

The balance of payments provides flow measures for a certain time period, usually in one year. The IMF also compiles international investment position statistics that are stock at a specified time, usually at the year end. There are some relations between flows and stocks. The stock of a country's financial assets at the latest year end is the stock at the previous year end plus net inflows of financial assets between the two year ends, taking into account any valuation changes such as that caused by changes in exchange rates and other adjustments. Knowing a country's last year's international investment position and its balance of payments figures in the current year does not yield this year's international investment position without relevant and appropriate adjustments, which gives rise to the need for a stock measure of a country's international investment position. The international investment position of a country, to be introduced in the next section, is a statistical statement of two sides of a balance sheet: (a) the value and composition of the stock of a country's financial assets, or claims on the rest of the world, and (b) the value and composition of the stock of a country's liabilities to the rest of the world. The difference between the two sides is a measure of the net position that is a country's net worth attributable to, or derived from, its relationship with the rest of the world.

### 4.1.1    Balance of Payments Accounts and Classification

The balance of payments consists of two major categories: the *current account* and the *capital and financial account*. Table 4.1 presents the structure and lists the main components of the balance of payments. The current account covers goods and services, income, and current transfers. The capital and financial account comprises capital transfers, and acquisition or disposal of non-produced, non-financial assets, and financial assets and liabilities. In the following, we discuss the main components and their classification in accordance with the structure and framework presented by Table 4.1.

The largest and most important components in the current account for most economies are balances in goods and services, so important that they are commonly referred to as trade balance. The Goods sub-section covers transactions that usually involve changes of ownership between residents and non-residents. In addition to general merchandise that refers to most movable goods, the scope of this section has been expanded from that in the 4th edition to include the movement of goods for processing when no change of ownership occurs, the value of repairs on goods other than the value of the movement of goods undergoing repair, goods procured in ports by non-resident carriers, non-monetary gold including gold to be held as a store of value or as other gold for, e.g., industrial purposes. The Services sub-section covers traditional items, such as travel and transportation that were included in the 4th edition of the Manual and items that are becoming increasingly important in international transactions – communications services, construction services, computer and information services, financial and insurance services, royalties and license fees, personal, cultural, and recreational services, and many other business services and government services. It is noted that in the 5th edition of the Manual, transactions in services are separated from income transactions, which is consistent with the System of National Accounts and the Central Product Classification.

**Table 4.1.** Balance of payments structure and components

| | | | | |
|---|---|---|---|---|
| CURRENT ACCOUNT | Goods and services | *Goods* | General merchandise | |
| | | | Goods for processing | |
| | | | Repairs on goods | |
| | | | Goods procured in ports by carriers | |
| | | | Non-monetary gold | |
| | | *Services* | Transportation | |
| | | | Travel | |
| | | | Communications services | |
| | | | Construction services | |
| | | | Insurance services | |
| | | | Financial services | |
| | | | Computer and information services | |
| | | | Royalties and license fees | |
| | | | Other business services | |
| | | | Personal, cultural, and recreational services | |
| | | | Government services not included elsewhere | |
| | Income | | Compensation of employees | |
| | | | Investment income | Direct investment |
| | | | | Portfolio investment |
| | | | | Other investment |
| | Current transfers | | General government | |
| | | | Other sectors | Workers' remittances |
| | | | | Other transfers |
| CAPITAL AND FINANCIAL ACCOUNT | Capital account | | Capital transfers | General government |
| | | | | Other sectors |
| | | | Acquisition/disposal of non-produced, non-financial assets | |
| | Financial account | | Direct investment | Abroad |
| | | | | In reporting economy |
| | | | Portfolio investment | Assets |
| | | | | Liabilities |
| | | | Other investment | Assets |
| | | | | Liabilities |
| | | | Reserve assets | Monetary gold |
| | | | | Special drawing rights |
| | | | | Reserve position in the IMF |
| | | | | Foreign exchange |
| | | | | Other claims |

The Income section consists of compensation of employees and investment income from direct investment, portfolio investment and other investment in the form of dividends and interest payments. The purposes of treating income as a separate component of the current account are to make the links between income and financial account flows and between the balance of payments and the international investment position clear and straightforward and to increase the analytical usefulness of these international accounts.

The Current transfers section comprises general government transfers and transfers made by other sectors. One of the most significant revisions in the 5$^{th}$ edition of the Manual is the re-categorisation of unilateral transfers and the distinction between current transfers and capital transfers. Consequently, transfers span two accounts that only current transfers are included in the current account, capital transfers are incorporated into the capital account part of the capital and financial account. The new treatment reflects international efforts to harmonise the Manual with the System of National Accounts and eliminates a major discordance between the two systems. According to the Manual, the following characteristics distinguish current transfers from capital transfers. Firstly, a transfer is a capital transfer when it consists of (a) the transfer of ownership of a fixed asset or (b) the forgiveness of a liability by a creditor when no counterpart is received in return. Secondly, a transfer of cash is a capital transfer when it is linked to, or conditional on, the acquisition or disposal of a fixed asset (for example, an investment grant) by one or both parties to the transaction. A capital transfer should result in a commensurate change in the stocks of assets of one or both parties to the transaction. Capital transfers also may be distinguished by being large and infrequent, but capital transfers cannot be defined in terms of size or frequency. Current transfers are characterised by their direct effect on the level of disposable income and their influence on the consumption of goods or services. Current transfers reduce the income and consumption possibilities of the donor and increase the income and consumption possibilities of the recipient. It should be noted that a cash transfer could be regarded as a capital transfer by one party to a transaction and as a current transfer by the other party. So that when a donor and a recipient do not treat the same transaction differently, it is recommended that a transfer be classified as a capital transfer by both parties – even if the transfer is linked to the acquisition or disposal of a fixed asset by only one of the parties. Whereas if available evidence creates serious doubt that a cash transfer should be classified as a capital transfer, the transfer should be classified as a current transfer.

The capital and financial account of the balance of payments comprises two main categories: a capital account and a financial account. The capital account consists of all transactions that involve the receipt or payment of capital transfers and acquisition or disposal of non-produced, non-financial assets. The financial account covers all transactions associated with changes of ownership in the foreign financial assets and liabilities of a country, including the creation and liquidation of claims on, or by, the rest of the world. Changes that do not involve transactions are excluded from the capital and financial account, such as valuation changes that reflect exchange rate or price changes, in assets for which there are no changes in ownership. All such changes are reflected in the international investment position. When there is a change in ownership and an asset acquired at one price is disposed of at a different price, both assets are recorded at respective market values and the difference in value is included in the balance of payments.

The capital account of the capital and financial account covers capital transfers, which has been discussed in conjunction with current transfers earlier, and acquisition or disposal of non-produced, non-financial assets. Previously prior to the 5$^{th}$ edition of the Manual, capital transfers were included in the current account of the balance of payments as current transfers were. Capital transfers are divided into general government transfers and transfers made by other sectors, due to the significant and distinct part played by governments in such transfers. General government transfers consist of debt forgiveness, when a government creditor entity in one economy formally agrees with a debtor entity in another economy to forgive or extinguish all, or part, of the obligations of the debtor entity to that creditor; and other capital transfers of general government, such as transfers made by a government to non-resident units to finance investment projects or the costs of acquiring fixed assets, or vice versa. Capital transfers by other sectors include migrants' transfers, debt forgiveness, and other transfers, the latter two items being similar to those under the heading of general government transfers but conducted by non-governmental entities.

The financial account of the capital and financial account consists of direct investment, portfolio investment, other investment, and reserve assets. Direct investment involves a significant degree of control and/or management in a corporation or other entities located in a foreign country with a long lasting interest. Three terms of direct investment enterprises, direct investors, and direct investment capital are relevant in the gathering of direct investment information in this context. Direct investment enterprises are defined as incorporated or unincorporated enterprises in which a direct investor who resides in another country owns 10 percent or more of the ordinary shares or voting power for an incorporated enterprise or the equivalent for an unincorporated enterprise. Direct investment enterprises include subsidiaries where a non-resident investor owns more than 50 percent, associates where a non-resident investor owns between 10 to 50 percent, and branches that are unincorporated enterprises wholly or jointly owned by the direct investor directly or indirectly. Direct investors can be individuals, incorporated or unincorporated private or public enterprises, associated groups of individuals or enterprises, governments or government agencies, or other entities that own direct investment enterprises in countries where the direct investors are non-residents. If combined ownership of an associated group of individuals or enterprises equals or exceeds 10 percent of the direct investment enterprise, the group is considered to have a degree of influence on management of the enterprise that is similar to that of an individual with the same degree of ownership. Direct investment capital is capital provided by a direct investor to a direct investment enterprise either directly or through other related enterprises, or capital received from a direct investment enterprise by a direct investor. For the country in which the investment is located, such capital includes funds provided directly by the direct investor and funds provided by other direct investment enterprises associated with the same direct investor. For the country where the direct investor resides, such capital includes only funds provided by the resident investor. In contrast, portfolio investors do not take an interest in the management of the corporation. Portfolio investment includes equity securities, debt securities, money market instruments, and financial derivatives. Each of them, especially the derivatives entry, has sub-categories, as they grow fast and become increasingly sophisticated. Other investment is a residual category that includes all financial transactions not covered in direct investment, portfolio investment, or reserve assets, which covers trade credits, loans, currency and deposits, and other accounts receivables and payables. Financial items are subject to re-classification in accordance with changes in motivation. For example, several independent portfolio investors who hold shares issued by a single foreign enterprise may form an associated group to take a long lasting interest and exert considerable influence on the management of the enterprise. Their holdings will then meet the criteria for direct investment, and the change in the status of the investment could be recorded as a re-classification, to be reflected in the international investment position but not in the balance of payments.

Direct investment is bi-directional, so there are directional distinctions between abroad and in the reporting economy. Equity capital and other capital components in either direction are recorded as assets of the reporting economy that constitute claims on non-residents, which are claims on direct investors in the reporting economy or claims on affiliated enterprises abroad; or liabilities of the reporting economy to non-residents, which are liabilities to direct investors in the reporting economy or liabilities to affiliated enterprises abroad. Portfolio investment and other investment by residents abroad and non-residents in the reporting economy are recorded separately as customary assets or liabilities. The foreign financial assets of an economy comprise holdings of monetary gold, SDRs, and claims on non-residents. The foreign liabilities of an economy consist of indebtedness to non-residents.

Although reserve assets are included in the capital and financial account, they are quite distinctive to other financial assets. Reserve assets are so important to the analysis of a country's external position that this category is often separately listed in parallel with the current account and the capital and financial account (excluding reserve assets). This is particularly evident for balance of payments identities under different exchange rate arrangements to be studied later in this chapter. The Reserve assets category consist of monetary gold, SDRs, reserve position in the IMF, foreign exchange assets with the monetary authorities in other countries and with banks, and other claims that are readily available to, and controlled by, the monetary authorities of a country for such important functions and operations as financing payments imbalances and regulating the extent of payments imbalances through foreign exchange market intervention.

## 4.1.2 Balance of Payments Entries and Recording

Having considered balance of payments accounts and classification, this section first presents examples demonstrating how and where individual transactions are recorded in the balance of payments and how double-entry bookkeeping is applied, and then analyses two recent cases of actual balance of payments to show the entries to the balance of payments and the recording of international transactions.

*Example 1*: Recording export of £10,000 of Sophie Ellis-Bextor CDs from the UK balance of payments perspective.

This is classified as merchandise trade; it is export of goods of the UK, a credit is recorded on the UK balance of payments current account.

|  | Credit |
|---|---|
| Exports of goods |  |
| (general merchandise) | +£10,000 |

*Example 2*: Recording tuition fees of €50 million received by French universities from foreign students from the French balance of payments perspective.

This is classified as services export of France; a credit is recorded on the French balance of payments current account.

|  | Credit |
|---|---|
| Exports of services |  |
| (cultural services) | +€50m |

*Example 3*: Applying double-entry bookkeeping to Citroën's exports of €10 million of cars to the People's Republic who receives payment in the form of a check drawn on a French bank; recording these transactions on French balance of payments accounts.

A credit is recorded on the French balance of payments current account for the increase in French exports and a debit is recorded on the balance of payments capital and financial account to reflect a decrease in liabilities to a foreigner associated with the check drawn on a French bank, which is a private capital outflow.

|  | Credit | Debit |
|---|---|---|
| Exports of goods |  |  |
| (general merchandise) | +€10m |  |
| Other investment |  |  |
| (decrease in liabilities) |  | -€10m |

*Example 4*: Applying double-entry bookkeeping to Sony's investment of ¥3 billion in a video factory in Mexico that is financed by issuing bonds in London; recording these transactions on Japan's balance of payments accounts.

A debit is recorded on Japan's balance of payments capital and financial account to reflect the increase in Japan's direct investment abroad (the acquisition of foreign assets) and a credit is recorded on the balance of payments capital and financial account for the inflow of foreign capital used to finance that investment, which is an increase in liabilities to foreigners.

|  | Credit | Debit |
|---|---|---|
| Direct investment abroad (claims on affiliated enterprises) |  | -¥3 b |
| Portfolio investment: bonds (increase in liabilities) | +¥3 b |  |

*Example 5*: John Morrison, a UK resident, buys 1,000 shares of IMB stock on March 31, 2003 at the price of $80 per share, financed by his bank deposit with Lloyds TSB in England; He receives dividends of 45 cents per share in quarters 1-3 in 2003 and deposits the dividend payment into his bank account at Lloyds TSB back in England; On February 13, 2004 he sells all the shares at the price of $100 and deposit the net proceeds of $90,000 in his bank account in the US. Record these transactions from the US balance of payments perspective.

A credit of $80,000 is recorded on the US balance of payments capital and financial account in year 2003 to reflect the increase of foreign portfolio investment in the US; a debit of $450 is recorded on the US balance of payments current account in year 2003 to reflect income on equity (dividends) paid to foreigners. A debit of $90,000 is recorded on the US balance of payments capital and financial account in year 2004 to reflect the decrease of foreign portfolio investment in the US; a credit of $90,000 is recorded on the US balance of payments capital and financial account in year 2004 to reflect John Morrison's deposit of the proceeds in the US bank, an increase in liabilities to foreigners.

Transactions 2003

|  | Credit | Debit |
|---|---|---|
| Portfolio investment (increase in liabilities) | +$80,000 |  |
| Income payments (portfolio investment: income on equity) |  | -$450 |

Transactions 2004

|  | Credit | Debit |
| --- | --- | --- |
| Portfolio investment (decrease in liabilities) |  | -$90,000 |
| Other investment (increase in liabilities) | $90,000 |  |

In the following, we make use of a few recent sets of actual balance of payments to show the entries to the balance of payments and the recording of international transactions. Table 4.2, US international transactions 2002 shows US balance of payments accounts in 2002 that follows exactly the framework of the 5th edition of the Manual. A credit entry has a + sign and debit entry has a – sign in the table. It is entitled international transactions, a reference to its flow nature, to contrast the other international statistical statement, the international investment position that is a stock measure. Nevertheless, we should note that, strictly speaking, while most entries in the balance of payments refer to transactions, some items, such as transfers, are not.

Exports and imports of goods and services are the largest components of the current account. Exports of goods and services are credits, while imports of goods and services are debits. Comparing line 2 and line 19, we can observe a deficit of $418,038 million in the balance on goods and services in 2002, which is also recorded on line 73 under Memoranda. Considering trade in goods and services separately, the US run a deficit of $482,872 million in the balance on goods, indicated by line 71, but a smaller surplus of $64,834 million in the balance on services, indicated by line, in 2002. Income balance is fairly small relative to balance on goods and services. The US income receipts in 2002 are dominated by income from direct investment abroad (line 14), while income payments for direct investment (line 31) are less than half of income payments for other private investments (line 32) including portfolio investment. This feature is also reflected on the financial account that US direct investment abroad (line 51) is much greater than direct investment in the US by foreign residents (line 64); and foreign residents' investment in US treasury and corporate securities (lines 65 and 66) is much greater than US residents' investment in foreign securities (line 52). The capital and financial account consists of a capital account (line 39) and a financial account (lines 40-69). The financial account is arranged in two parts. US owned assets abroad are recorded as debits with a – sign, indicating capital outflow from the US to the rest of the world and showing US purchases of foreign assets, which results in a decline in liabilities to foreigners. Foreign owned assets in the US that are credits with a + sign, indicating capital inflow into the US from the rest of the world and showing sales of US domestic assets to foreigners, which incurs an increase in liabilities to foreigners. US owned assets have three major components, US official reserve assets, US government assets other than official reserves, and private assets in the form of direct investment, portfolio investment and other investment.

**Table 4.2.** US international transactions 2002

(US$ million)

| (Credits +, debits -) | 2002 |
|---|---|
| **Current account** | |
| **1 Exports of goods and services and income receipts**............... | **1,229,649** |
| 2    Exports of goods and services.................... | 974,107 |
| 3        Goods, balance of payments basis................ | 681,874 |
| 4        Services................................. | 292,233 |
| 5            Transfers under U.S. military agency sales contracts........ | 11,943 |
| 6            Travel................................ | 66,547 |
| 7            Passenger fares........................ | 17,046 |
| 8            Other transportation..................... | 29,166 |
| 9            Royalties and license fees................ | 44,142 |
| 10           Other private services................... | 122,594 |
| 11           U.S. Government miscellaneous services....... | 795 |
| 12   Income receipts............................ | 255,542 |
| 13       Income receipts on U.S.-owned assets abroad........ | 252,379 |
| 14           Direct investment receipts............... | 142,933 |
| 15           Other private receipts.................. | 106,143 |
| 16           U.S. Government receipts................ | 3,303 |
| 17       Compensation of employees................. | 3,163 |
| **18 Imports of goods and services and income payments**....... | **-1,651,657** |
| 19   Imports of goods and services................. | -1,392,145 |
| 20       Goods, balance of payments basis............. | -1,164,746 |
| 21       Services............................... | -227,399 |
| 22           Direct defense expenditures.............. | -19,245 |
| 23           Travel.............................. | -58,044 |
| 24           Passenger fares........................ | -19,969 |
| 25           Other transportation..................... | -38,527 |
| 26           Royalties and license fees................ | -19,258 |
| 27           Other private services................... | -69,436 |
| 28           U.S. Government miscellaneous services....... | -2,920 |
| 29   Income payments............................ | -259,512 |
| 30       Income payments on foreign-owned assets in the United States....... | -251,108 |
| 31           Direct investment payments............... | -49,458 |
| 32           Other private payments.................. | -127,735 |
| 33           U.S. Government payments................ | -73,915 |
| 34       Compensation of employees................. | -8,404 |
| **35 Unilateral current transfers, net**................. | **-58,853** |
| 36   U.S. Government grants...................... | -17,097 |
| 37   U.S. Government pensions and other transfers........ | -5,125 |
| 38   Private remittances and other transfers........... | -36,631 |

**Table 4.2.** (cont.)

| | |
|---|---:|
| **Capital and financial account** | |
| **Capital account** | |
| 39  Capital account transactions, net............................................................................................ | **-1,285** |
| **Financial account** | |
| **40  U.S.-owned assets abroad, net (increase/financial outflow (-))............................................** | **-178,985** |
| 41    U.S. official reserve assets, net............................................................................................. | -3,681 |
| 42      Gold................................................................................................................................... | ..... |
| 43      Special drawing rights...................................................................................................... | -475 |
| 44      Reserve position in the International Monetary Fund........................................................ | -2,632 |
| 45      Foreign currencies............................................................................................................ | -574 |
| 46    U.S. Government assets, other than official reserve assets, net............................................ | -32 |
| 47      U.S. credits and other long-term assets........................................................................... | -5,611 |
| 48      Repayments on U.S. credits and other long-term assets................................................... | 5,684 |
| 49      U.S. foreign currency holdings and U.S. short-term assets, net......................................... | -105 |
| 50    U.S. private assets, net....................................................................................................... | -175,272 |
| 51      Direct investment............................................................................................................. | -137,836 |
| 52      Foreign securities............................................................................................................. | 15,801 |
| 53      U.S. claims on unaffiliated foreigners reported by U.S. nonbanking concerns | -31,880 |
| 54      U.S. claims reported by U.S. banks, not included elsewhere............................................. | -21,357 |
| **55  Foreign-owned assets in the United States, net (increase/financial inflow (+))......................** | **706,983** |
| 56    Foreign official assets in the United States, net.................................................................. | 94,860 |
| 57      U.S. Government securities............................................................................................... | 73,521 |
| 58        U.S. Treasury securities................................................................................................ | 43,144 |
| 59        Other............................................................................................................................. | 30,377 |
| 60      Other U.S. Government liabilities....................................................................................... | 137 |
| 61      U.S. liabilities reported by U.S. banks, not included elsewhere........................................ | 17,594 |
| 62      Other foreign official assets.............................................................................................. | 3,608 |
| 63    Other foreign assets in the United States, net.................................................................... | 612,123 |
| 64      Direct investment............................................................................................................. | 39,633 |
| 65      U.S. Treasury securities.................................................................................................... | 96,217 |
| 66      U.S. securities other than U.S. Treasury securities.......................................................... | 291,492 |
| 67      U.S. currency................................................................................................................... | 21,513 |
| 68      U.S. liabilities to unaffiliated foreigners reported by | |
| | U.S. nonbanking concerns............................................................................................ | 72,142 |
| 69      U.S. liabilities reported by U.S. banks, not included elsewhere......................................... | 91,126 |
| **70  Statistical discrepancy (sum of above items with sign reversed)............................................** | **-45,852** |
| **Memoranda:** | |
| 71  Balance on goods (lines 3 and 20)............................................................................................ | -482,872 |
| 72  Balance on services (lines 4 and 21)......................................................................................... | 64,834 |
| 73  Balance on goods and services (lines 2 and 19)........................................................................ | -418,038 |
| 74  Balance on income (lines 12 and 29).......................................................................................... | -3,970 |
| 75  Unilateral current transfers, net (line 35).................................................................................. | -58,853 |
| 76  Balance on current account (lines 1, 18, and 35 or lines 73, 74, and 75)................................... | -480,861 |

<sup>r</sup> Revised.  <sup>p</sup> Preliminary.

Source: US Bureau of Economic Analysis

**Table 4.3.** Balance of payments of Japan 2002

### 平成14年中国際収支状況
**Balance of Payments C.Y. 2002**

(単位：億円、%) (100 million yen, %)

| 項目<br>Item | 2002年<br>2002 | 前年<br>2001 | 前年比増減<br>Changes from previous year |
|---|---|---|---|
| 経常収支 current Account | 142,484 | 106,523 | 35,961 |
| (対前年比) (Changes from previous year) | (33.8%) | (-17.3%) | |
| 貿易・サービス収支 Goods and services | 65,653 | 32,120 | 33,533 |
| (対前年比) (Changes from previous year) | (104.4%) | (-56.8%) | |
| 貿易収支 Trade balance | 117,280 | 85,270 | 32,009 |
| (対前年比) (Changes from previous year) | (37.5%) | (-32.1%) | |
| 輸出 Exports | 494,710 | 465,835 | 28,876 |
| (対前年比) (Changes from previous year) | (6.2%) | (-5.9%) | |
| 輸入 Imports | 377,431 | 380,564 | -3,133 |
| (対前年比) (Changes from previous year) | (-0.8%) | (3.0%) | |
| サービス収支 Services | -51,627 | -53,150 | 1,523 |
| 所得収支 Income | 82,784 | 84,007 | -1,223 |
| 経常移転収支 Current transfers | -5,952 | -9,604 | 3,652 |
| 資本収支 Capital and Financial Account | -79,784 | -61,726 | -18,058 |
| 投資収支 Financial Account | -75,567 | -58,264 | -17,303 |
| 直接投資 Direct investment | -27,780 | -39,000 | 11,220 |
| 証券投資 Portfolio investment | -126,815 | -56,291 | -70,524 |
| (証券貸借取引を除く) Excl. securities lending | (-181,289) | (-76,133) | (-105,156) |
| 金融派生商品 Financial derivatives | 2,629 | 1,853 | 777 |
| その他投資 Other investment | 76,398 | 35,175 | 41,224 |
| (証券貸借取引を除く) Excl. securities lending | (126,672) | (54,922) | (71,750) |
| その他資本収支 Capital Account | -4,217 | -3,462 | -755 |
| 外貨準備増減 Changes in Reserve Assets | -57,969 | -49,364 | -8,605 |
| 誤差脱漏 Errors & Omissions | -4,731 | 4,567 | -9,298 |

Source: Ministry of Finance of Japan

Foreign owned assets in the US have the similar components except for official reserve assets and are mainly foreign investment in US government securities and in the private sector. It is worthwhile to single out official reserve assets as they play an important role. Overall, the US runs a current account deficit of $480,861 million in 2002, as summarised on line 76. This balance on the current account, in theory, must be offset by the balance on the capital and financial account – a balance of payments identity to be studied in the next section. However, the balance on the capital and financial account is $526,713 million in surplus. So the two balances do not offset each other, which is rather common, and the difference is attributed to statistical discrepancy or called errors and omissions that is $45,852 million, the sum of the current account balance and the capital and financial account balance with the sign being reversed. As the US runs a current account deficit in 2002 that US residents have consumed more than it has produced, it has experienced a capital and financial account surplus in the same year that its liabilities to the rest of world has increased as a consequence.

Table 4.3 presents the balance of payments of Japan in the 2002 calendar year, both in Japanese and English. Japan is one of leading industrialise economies, playing an important role in international trade. The Japanese language is spoken by over 100 million people and its writing can be easily understood by 1.2 billion Mandarin speakers. For these reasons, the presentation of Japan's balance of payments in both Japanese and English conveys helpful information and messages. It can be observed that it follows the structure and guideline of the 5$^{th}$ edition of the Manual to have a current account and a capital and financial account. However, its reserve assets are separate from the capital and financial account and listed as a category at the same level as the capital and financial account, so is the errors and omissions entry. That is, the balance of payments shown by Table 4.2 has four categories that were prevailing before the 5$^{th}$ edition; nevertheless, with its treatment of current transfers and inclusion of capital transfers in the capital and financial account, the structure and classification is largely in the framework of the 5$^{th}$ edition of the Manual.

In contrast to the US, Japan runs a current account surplus in 2002, largely accounted for by a positive balance on goods. Japan has a sizable net income in 2002, indicating its residents own more assets abroad, which generate income receipts for Japan's residents, than foreigners own assets in Japan, which generate income payments to foreigners. With a current account surplus, Japan must run a capital and financial account deficit, with increase in net assets abroad mainly in the form of direct investment and portfolio investment, as well as official reserves. In the above, we have inspected the balance of payments of two large industrialised countries. In these two cases, one country runs a current account deficit and a capital and financial account surplus, and the other country experiences the opposite with a current account surplus and a capital and financial account deficit. Indeed, one country's net imports of goods must be some other countries' net exports of goods and one country's net capital inflow must be some other countries' net capital outflows - the sum of the net imports or net exports of goods of all the countries in the world must be zero and the sum of net capital inflows of all the countries must be zero. This is true for trade in services, for the current account, as

**Table 4.4.** Regional balance of payments current accounts

平成14年中地域別国際収支状況 (Regional Balance of Payments for C.Y. 2002)

経常収支 (Current account)

(単位：億円) (100 million yen)

| 項目 Item<br>地域 Region | 経常収支 Current account | | 貿易・サービス収支 Goods and services | | 貿易収支 Trade balance | | 輸出 Exports | | 輸入 Imports | | サービス収支 Services | |
|---|---|---|---|---|---|---|---|---|---|---|---|---|
| | 2001 | 2002 | 2001 | 2002 | 2001 | 2002 | 2001 | 2002 | 2001 | 2002 | 2001 | 2002 |
| 合計 Total | 106,523 | 141,397 | 32,120 | 64,690 | 85,270 | 117,333 | 465,835 | 494,797 | 380,564 | 377,464 | -53,150 | -52,643 |
| アジア Asia 1/ | 18,894 | 43,899 | 15,392 | 39,108 | 25,294 | 49,157 | 185,968 | 211,027 | 160,674 | 161,870 | -9,902 | -10,048 |
| 中国 P.R.China | -30,010 | -24,637 | -30,589 | -25,117 | -28,634 | -23,157 | 36,088 | 47,551 | 64,722 | 70,708 | -1,954 | -1,960 |
| 香港 Hong Kong | 23,990 | 28,661 | 24,263 | 28,007 | 25,981 | 29,542 | 26,717 | 29,954 | 735 | 411 | -1,719 | -1,535 |
| 台湾 Taiwan | 13,208 | 17,442 | 13,036 | 16,998 | 13,180 | 16,785 | 27,579 | 30,778 | 14,399 | 13,992 | -144 | 213 |
| 韓国 R.Korea | 8,499 | 14,479 | 8,197 | 14,520 | 10,824 | 17,335 | 29,185 | 34,101 | 18,361 | 16,766 | -2,627 | -2,815 |
| シンガポール Singapore | 6,687 | 7,896 | 8,975 | 9,010 | 10,202 | 10,492 | 15,933 | 15,380 | 5,731 | 4,888 | -1,227 | -1,482 |
| タイ Thailand | 3,547 | 4,784 | 2,370 | 3,650 | 2,569 | 4,115 | 13,435 | 15,431 | 10,866 | 11,316 | -199 | -465 |
| インドネシア Indonesia | -7,879 | -8,329 | -9,714 | -9,531 | -9,289 | -8,972 | 7,556 | 7,500 | 16,846 | 16,472 | -425 | -559 |
| マレイシア Malaysia | -1,173 | 648 | -2,120 | -263 | -1,307 | 478 | 12,664 | 12,941 | 13,971 | 12,463 | -812 | -741 |
| フィリピン Philippines | 2,763 | 3,050 | 2,171 | 2,405 | 2,628 | 2,938 | 9,256 | 9,651 | 6,628 | 6,713 | -458 | -532 |
| インド India | 95 | 115 | -229 | -118 | -177 | -123 | 2,272 | 2,290 | 2,449 | 2,413 | -52 | 5 |
| 北米 North America 2/ | 101,496 | 105,970 | 54,818 | 64,590 | 72,937 | 79,768 | 147,402 | 149,996 | 74,465 | 70,228 | -18,118 | -15,178 |

**Table 4.4.** (cont.)

| | | | | | | | | | | | | |
|---|---|---|---|---|---|---|---|---|---|---|---|---|
| 中南米 Central and South America 3/ | 12,686 | 11,993 | 5,616 | 4,313 | 10,285 | 9,042 | 21,429 | 20,304 | 11,145 | 11,262 | -4,668 | -4,729 |
| 大洋州 Oceania 4/ | -11,133 | -9,432 | -12,900 | -11,561 | -8,222 | -6,528 | 11,057 | 12,465 | 19,279 | 18,993 | -4,678 | -5,033 |
| オーストラリア Australia | -7,140 | -6,023 | -8,927 | -8,067 | -7,133 | -5,930 | 9,158 | 10,191 | 16,291 | 16,121 | -1,794 | -2,137 |
| ニュージーランド New Zealand | -1,201 | -873 | -1,269 | -964 | -910 | -437 | 1,377 | 1,712 | 2,287 | 2,149 | -359 | -527 |
| 西欧 Western Europe 5/ | 28,291 | 24,496 | 15,091 | 8,802 | 25,832 | 22,120 | 79,446 | 77,609 | 53,614 | 55,489 | -10,741 | -13,318 |
| 中東 Middle East 7/ | -39,360 | -34,878 | -39,494 | -34,938 | -37,500 | -33,068 | 13,051 | 14,855 | 50,551 | 47,923 | -1,995 | -1,870 |
| アフリカ Africa 8/ | -2,494 | -2,949 | -2,913 | -3,372 | -492 | -1,545 | 4,553 | 4,982 | 5,045 | 6,527 | -2,420 | -1,827 |
| 国際機関 International Organization | 1,027 | 4,081 | 14 | 16 | 0 | 0 | 0 | 0 | 0 | 0 | 14 | 16 |
| 参 OECD諸国 OECD Countries 9/ | 133,326 | 141,928 | 70,662 | 82,015 | 104,214 | 115,725 | 271,928 | 278,930 | 167,714 | 163,205 | -33,553 | -33,709 |
| □ EU 11/ | 29,907 | 26,975 | 16,617 | 11,440 | 26,085 | 22,834 | 74,650 | 72,862 | 48,565 | 50,028 | -9,468 | -11,394 |

Source: Ministry of Finance of Japan

well as the capital and financial account as a whole. That is, the sum of the current account deficits or surpluses of all the countries must be zero and the sum of the capital and financial account deficits or surpluses of all the countries must be zero.

Balance of payments information can also be compiled with reference to a country's trading partners in terms of geographical distributions and trading blocs. While a country experiences, for example, an overall surplus in trade in goods, it may have a trade deficit with one or more countries. While its capital flows out to some countries, some other countries' capital may flow in at the same time. Table 4.4, Japan's regional balance of payments current accounts for 2002 calendar year, provides such an example for analysis. To save the space, only economies in Asia and Oceania are individually listed. It is observed that while Japan has an overall current account surplus of ¥10,652 billion, this surplus is largely from North America and Western Europe in geographical terms, or from OECD countries and the EU. Japan runs considerable current account deficits with the People's Republic and the Middle East, mainly in trade in goods. Nevertheless, Japan runs an overall current account surplus in Asia, due largely to its surpluses with Hong Kong, Taiwan, Korea, and Singapore. In a sense, a country tends to have trade surpluses with countries where consumption is higher, labour costs are more expensive or the manufacturing industry is less competitive, and is likely to incur trade deficits with countries where consumption is lower, labour costs are cheaper, or the manufacturing industry is more competitive.

### 4.1.3 The Balance of Payment Identity

The double-entry bookkeeping principle and practice applied to the balance of payments recording means that the sum of all international transactions must be zero in theory. As noted earlier, although reserve assets are included in the capital and financial account, they are crucial to the analysis of a country's external position and are separately listed in parallel with the current account and the capital and financial account (excluding reserve assets). Therefore, the balance of payments identity is stated as follows:

$$CAB + KAB + ORT = 0 \qquad (4.1)$$

where $CAB$ stands for the current account balance, covering balance on goods and services, net income from abroad and net current transfers; $KAB$ stands for balance on the capital and financial account exclusive of transactions in official reserve assets, which, for convenience, is simply referred to as capital and financial account balance; and $ORT$ stands for transactions in official reserve assets.

Equation (4.1) indicates that the current account balance must equal the balance on capital and financial account balance and official reserve asset transactions. This relationship shows that the net provision of resources to or from the rest of the world, measured by the current account balance, must by definition be matched by changes in net claims on, or net liabilities to, the rest of the world. Under a pure floating exchange rate regime involving no foreign exchange market intervention, *ORT* is zero and equation (4.1) becomes:

$$CAB + KAB = 0 \tag{4.2}$$

Equation (4.1) and equation (4.2) suggest that, under a pure floating exchange rate regime, a current account deficit is offset through the market force and mechanism by a capital and financial account surplus of equal size and opposite sign and vice versa; and with pegged exchange rate arrangements, transactions in official reserve assets take place to settle the difference between the current account balance and the capital and financial account balance. It is because that, under pegged exchange rate arrangements, exchange rates are not allowed to adjust freely so that the current account balance and the capital and financial account balance adjust accordingly to offset each other. Under a pure floating exchange rate arrangement, exchange rate movements are not restricted; they are only influenced by the market force and mechanism and can adjust freely, which allows the current account balance and the capital and financial account balance to offset each other.

Since the balance of payments is a statistical statement or record of a country's international economic transactions with the rest of the world over a certain period, with data for balance of payments entries being usually derived from different sources, it inevitably involves errors in the compilation so that the above identities may not hold. When these happen, a net credit or net debit is attributed to errors and omissions of opposite sign, so the identity is the sum of the current account balance, the capital and financial account balance, official reserve asset transactions and errors and omissions under pegged exchange rate regimes, and is the sum of the current account balance, the capital and financial account balance and errors and omissions under a pure floating exchange rate regime.

## 4.2  International Investment Position Statements and Analysis

The international investment position provides the stock information of an economy's international accounts that deal specifically with its external assets and liabilities, while the balance of payments presents the flow information of an economy's international accounts that record its external transactions. The international investment position is the balance sheet of the stock of external financial assets and liabilities, and the balance of payments is the income statement of the inflow and outflow of goods, services and capital. The entries to the international investment position are the same and consistent with the balance of payments financial account. However, changes in the international position statement in two consecutive year ends do not straightforwardly produce corresponding figures in the

**Table 4.5.** International investment position structure and main components

| | | Position at beginning of year | Changes in position reflecting | | | | Position at end of year |
|---|---|---|---|---|---|---|---|
| | | | Trans-actions | Price changes | Exchange rate changes | Other adjust-ments | |
| **Assets** | | | | | | | |
| *Direct investment abroad* | | | | | | | |
| | Equity capital and re-invested earnings | | | | | | |
| | Other capital | | | | | | |
| *Portfolio investment* | | | | | | | |
| | Equity securities | | | | | | |
| | Debt securities | | | | | | |
| *Other investment* | | | | | | | |
| | Trade credits | | | | | | |
| | Loans | | | | | | |
| | Currency and deposits | | | | | | |
| | Other assets | | | | | | |
| *Reserve assets* | | | | | | | |
| | Monetary gold | | | | | | |
| | Special drawing rights | | | | | | |
| | Reserve position in the IMF | | | | | | |
| | Foreign exchange | | | | | | |
| | Other claims | | | | | | |
| **Liabilities** | | | | | | | |
| *Direct investment in reporting economy* | | | | | | | |
| | Equity capital and re-invested earnings | | | | | | |
| | Other capital | | | | | | |
| *Portfolio investment* | | | | | | | |
| | Equity securities | | | | | | |
| | Debt securities | | | | | | |
| *Other investment* | | | | | | | |
| | Trade credits | | | | | | |
| | Loans | | | | | | |
| | Currency and deposits | | | | | | |
| | Other liabilities | | | | | | |

balance of payments financial account, since it involves valuation changes and adjustments in compiling the international financial position statement, in addition to the financial transactions taking place between these two consecutive year ends. Because one set of the international accounts cannot be derived from the other set, it is necessary to prepare and present both sets of the international accounts of the international investment position and the balance of payments for an economy.

Table 4.5 presents the structure and main components of the international investment position. Consistent with the balance of payments financial accounts, the assets part has four sections, direct investment, portfolio investment, other investment, and official reserve assets; and the liabilities part does not cover official reserve assets and is made up of direct investment, portfolio investment and other investment. A country's net international investment position is its assets minus its liabilities, which measures its net claims on the rest of the world.

Direct investment covers equity capital and reinvested earnings and other capital (inter-company debt). Since direct investment is bi-directional, they are differentiated between direct investment abroad in the assets part and direct investment in the reporting economy in the liabilities part. For the former, these types of direct investment are claims on affiliated enterprises and liabilities to affiliated enterprises; and for the latter, they are claims on direct investors and liabilities to direct investors. Because direct investment is classified on such bi-directional basis, these entries do not strictly conform to the overall headings of assets and liabilities. Portfolio investment consists of equity securities and debt securities. Financial derivatives, together with traditional bonds, notes and money market instruments, are covered by debt securities. Other investment includes trade credits, loans, currency and deposits, and other assets (under the assets heading) and liabilities (under the liabilities heading) not included elsewhere. Official reserve assets cover monetary gold, special drawing rights, position in the IMF, foreign currency, deposits and securities.

The international investment position at the end of a period is the accumulation of financial transactions, valuation adjustments attributed to price changes, valuation adjustments attributed to foreign exchange rate changes, and other adjustments that occurred during the period the affected the level or stock of assets and liabilities. Factors that result in valuation changes and other adjustments are important considerations in the international investment position. Transactions in the balance of payments reflect only part of the changes in the international investment position. This is evident in Table 4.6 for US international investment position in 2001 and 2002. Consequently, the balance of payments alone cannot determine the financial relationship of an economy with the rest of the world and one has to resort to both the balance of payments and the international investment position. Let us examine Table 4.2 for US balance of payments 2002 and Table 4.6 for US international investment position at year ends of 2001 and 2002 together. In the first column under the heading of changes in positions in 2002 are financial flow items, with the figures coming from US balance of payments statement 2002. For instance, US owned assets abroad is $178,985 million (line 3 or line 4), which is line 40 on the US balance of payments financial account 2002 in Table 4.2; and foreign owned assets in the US is $706,983 million (line 16 or line 17), which is line 55 in Table 4.2. US owned assets abroad can be broken down as US official reserve assets at $2,681 million (line 5), which corresponds to line 41 on US balance of payments financial account 2002 in Table 4.2; US Government assets

**Table 4.6.** International Investment Position of the US (Year Ends of 2001 and 2002)

International Investment Position of the United States at Yearend, 2001 and 2002
[Millions of dollars]

| Line | Type of investment | Position, 2001 /r/ | Changes in position in 2002 (decrease (-); increase (+)) Attributable to: | | | | | Position, 2002 /p/ |
|---|---|---|---|---|---|---|---|---|
| | | | Financial flows (a) | Valuation adjustments | | | Total (a+b+c+d) | |
| | | | | Price changes (b) | Exchange rate changes /1/ (c) | Other changes /2/ (d) | | |
| | **Net international investment position of the United States:** | | | | | | | |
| 1 | With direct investment positions at current cost (line 3 less line 16) | -1,979,906 | -527,998 | -83,284 | 147,129 | 56,848 | -407,305 | -2,387,211 |
| 2 | With direct investment positions at market value (line 4 less line 17) | -2,314,271 | -527,998 | -42,105 | 230,053 | 49,166 | -290,884 | -2,605,155 |
| | **U.S.-owned assets abroad:** | | | | | | | |
| 3 | With direct investment positions at current cost (lines 5+6+7) | 6,187,410 | 178,985 | -365,107 | 182,335 | 5,568 | 1,781 | 6,189,191 |
| 4 | With direct investment positions at market value (lines 5+6+8) | 6,891,251 | 178,985 | -847,812 | 264,680 | -13,542 | -417,689 | 6,473,562 |
| 5 | U.S. official reserve assets | 129,961 | 3,681 | 18,492 | 6,482 | -14 | 28,641 | 158,602 |
| 6 | U.S. Government assets, other than official reserve assets | 85,654 | 32 | ... | ... | ... | 32 | 85,686 |
| | **U.S. private assets:** | | | | | | | |
| 7 | With direct investment at current cost (lines 9+11+14+15) | 5,971,795 | 175,272 | -383,599 | 175,853 | 5,582 | -26,892 | 5,944,903 |
| 8 | With direct investment at market value (lines 10+11+14+15) | 6,675,636 | 175,272 | -866,304 | 258,198 | -13,528 | -446,362 | 6,229,274 |
| | Direct investment abroad: | | | | | | | |
| 9 | At current cost | 1,598,072 | 137,836 | -5,215 | 25,577 | -4,418 | 153,780 | 1,751,852 |
| 10 | At market value | 2,301,913 | 137,836 | -487,920 | 107,922 | -23,528 | -265,690 | 2,036,223 |
| 11 | Foreign securities | 2,114,734 | -15,801 | -378,384 | 126,427 | ... | -267,758 | 1,846,976 |
| 12 | Bonds | 502,061 | -33,478 | 21,274 | 11,927 | ... | -277 | 501,784 |
| 13 | Corporate stocks | 1,612,673 | 17,677 | -399,658 | 114,500 | ... | -267,481 | 1,345,192 |
| 14 | U.S. claims on unaffiliated foreigners reported by U.S. nonbanking concerns | 835,780 | 31,880 | ... | 13,301 | 10,000 | 55,181 | 890,961 |
| 15 | U.S. claims reported by U.S. banks, not included elsewhere | 1,423,209 | 21,357 | ... | 10,548 | ... | 31,905 | 1,455,114 |

**Table 4.6. (cont.)**

| | | | | | | | |
|---|---|---|---|---|---|---|---|
| | **Foreign-owned assets in the United States:** | | | | | | |
| 16 | With direct investment at current cost (lines 18+19).......... | 8,167,316 | 706,983 | -281,823 | 35,206 | -51,280 | 8,576,402 |
| 17 | With direct investment at market value (lines 18+20).......... | 9,205,522 | 706,983 | -805,707 | 34,627 | -62,708 | 9,078,717 |
| 18 | Foreign official assets in the United States.......... | 1,027,194 | 94,860 | 10,476 | ... | ... | 1,132,530 |
| | Other foreign assets: | | | | | | |
| 19 | With direct investment at current cost (lines 21+23+24+27+28+29).......... | 7,140,122 | 612,123 | -292,299 | 35,206 | -51,280 | 7,443,872 |
| 20 | With direct investment at market value (lines 22+23+24+27+28+29).......... | 8,178,328 | 612,123 | -816,183 | 34,627 | -62,708 | 7,946,187 |
| | Direct investment in the United States: | | | | | | |
| 21 | At current cost.......... | 1,514,374 | 39,633 | -6,060 | 579 | -44,098 | 1,504,428 |
| 22 | At market value.......... | 2,552,580 | 39,633 | -529,944 | ... | -55,526 | 2,006,743 |
| 23 | U.S. Treasury securities.......... | 389,000 | 96,217 | 18,413 | ... | 114,630 | 503,630 |
| 24 | U.S. securities other than U.S. Treasury securities.......... | 2,855,705 | 291,492 | -304,652 | 18,570 | 5,410 | 2,861,115 |
| 25 | Corporate and other bonds.......... | 1,391,616 | 236,309 | 43,801 | 18,570 | 298,680 | 1,690,296 |
| 26 | Corporate stocks.......... | 1,464,089 | 55,183 | -348,453 | ... | -293,270 | 1,170,819 |
| 27 | U.S. currency.......... | 275,569 | 21,513 | ... | ... | 21,513 | 297,082 |
| 28 | U.S. liabilities to unaffiliated foreigners reported by U.S. nonbanking concerns.......... | 799,120 | 72,142 | ... | 6,179 | 71,139 | 870,259 |
| 29 | U.S. liabilities reported by U.S. banks, not included elsewhere.......... | 1,306,354 | 91,126 | ... | 9,878 | 101,004 | 1,407,358 |

p Preliminary.

r Revised.

1. Represents gains or losses on foreign-currency-denominated assets due to their revaluation at current exchange rates.

2. Includes changes in coverage, capital gains and losses of direct investment affiliates, and other statistical adjustments to the value of assets.

Source: US Bureau of Economic Analysis

other than official reserve assets at $32 million (line 6), which corresponds to line 56 in Table 4.2; and US private assets abroad at $175,272 million (line 7), which corresponds to line 50 in Table 4.2. Foreign owned assets in the US are comprised of foreign official assets in the US valued at $94,860 million (line 18), which matches up with line 56 in Table 4.2; and other foreign assets at $612,123 million, which is indicated by line 63 in Table 4.2. The net international investment position of the US is the sum of US owned assets abroad and foreign owned in the US with the signs reversed, which is -$527,998 million = -(-$178,985 million +$706,983 million). A + sign for changes in the net international investment position due to financial transactions indicates an increase in net assets or a net capital outflow during the period between the two year ends; and a – sign for changes in the net international investment position due to financial transactions indicates a decrease in net assets or a net capital inflow during the period between the two year ends, which is in contrast to the signs in the balance of payments statement, since the treatment in the former reflects a country's claims on, and liabilities to, the rest of the world.

Changes in US international investment positions at year ends 2001 and 2002 attributed to valuation changes are recorded under the sub-heading of valuation adjustments in Table 4.6, for those due to price changes, foreign exchange rate changes and other changes including changes in coverage, capital gains and losses of direct investment affiliates, and other statistical adjustments to the value of assets, respectively. Valuation adjustments due to price changes result in a substantial decrease in US asset values abroad, as well as a similar decrease in foreign asset values in the US, leading to a decrease of $83,284 million (valued at the current cost) or $42,105 million (market value) in US net position. In contrast, exchange rate changes cause upward adjustments for both US assets abroad and foreign assets in the US, with a net effect of $147,129 million (current cost) or $230,053 million (market value). Total valuation changes amount to an increase of $120,693 million (current cost) or $237,114 million (market value) in the US net international investment position, which offsets the $527,998 million decline in the US net international position due to financial transactions to a large extent. The overall changes in position in 2002, attributed to transactions and to valuation adjustments, are -$407,305 million (current cost) or -$290,884 million (market value). Measured in market values, valuation adjustments have reduced the US liabilities that arise from transactions by 45%. The US international investment position at the 2002 year end, -$2,387,211 million (current cost) or -$2,605,155 million (market value), is its position at the 2001 year end, -$1,979,906 million (current cost) or -$2,314,271 million (market value), plus total changes in position in 2002, -$407,305 million (current cost) or -$290,884 million (market value).

Table 4.7 presents the international investment position of Japan at year ends 2001 and 2002. The statement is arranged that there is one to one match between assets entries and liabilities entries, except for official reserve assets. Financial derivatives are separate from portfolio investment and are at the same level as portfolio investment. So, there are five sections for assets and four sections for liabilities. In contrast to the US, Japan has maintained a positive net international investment position over a few decades, so Japan has net claims on the rest of the

**Table 4.7.** International Investment Position of Japan (Year Ends of 2001 and 2002)

(¥ billion)

| Assets | End of 2001 | End of 2002 | Changes from previous year-end | Liabilities | End of 2001 | End of 2002 | Changes from previous year-end |
|---|---|---|---|---|---|---|---|
| 1. Direct Investment | 39,555 | 36,478 | - 3,077 | 1. Direct Investment | 6,632 | 9,369 | 2,737 |
| 2. Portfolio Investment | 169,990 | 167,203 | - 2,786 | 2. Portfolio Investment | 87,752 | 73,189 | - 14,563 |
| Equity Securities | 29,965 | 25,277 | - 4,688 | Equity Securities | 49,563 | 40,757 | - 8,806 |
| Public Sector | 0 | 0 | 0 | | | | |
| Banks | 636 | 541 | - 95 | Banks | 1,492 | 1,061 | - 432 |
| Other Sectors | 29,329 | 24,736 | - 4,593 | Other Sectors | 48,071 | 39,697 | - 8,374 |
| Debt Securities | 140,025 | 141,926 | 1,901 | Debt Securities | 38,189 | 32,432 | - 5,757 |
| Bonds and Notes | 132,443 | 136,149 | 3,706 | Bonds and Notes | 33,546 | 27,799 | - 5,747 |
| Public Sector | 6,948 | 5,626 | - 1,322 | Public Sector | 23,651 | 19,135 | - 4,516 |
| Banks | 40,098 | 40,989 | 891 | Banks | 1,520 | 1,138 | - 382 |
| Other Sectors | 85,396 | 89,533 | 4,137 | Other Sectors | 8,375 | 7,527 | - 848 |
| Money Market Instruments | 7,582 | 5,777 | - 1,805 | Money Market Instruments | 4,643 | 4,633 | - 10 |
| Public Sector | 8 | 13 | 5 | Public Sector | 4,643 | 4,582 | - 60 |
| Banks | 1,094 | 1,800 | 707 | Banks | 0 | 0 | 0 |
| Other Sectors | 6,480 | 3,964 | - 2,516 | Other Sectors | 0 | 50 | 50 |
| 3. Financial Derivatives | 395 | 404 | 8 | 3. Financial Derivatives | 467 | 445 | - 23 |
| Public Sector | 0 | 0 | 0 | Public Sector | 0 | 0 | 0 |
| Banks | 249 | 230 | - 19 | Banks | 325 | 330 | 5 |
| Other Sectors | 146 | 174 | 28 | Other Sectors | 143 | 115 | - 28 |
| 4. Other Investment | 117,069 | 105,792 | - 11,276 | 4. Other Investment | 105,673 | 107,628 | 1,955 |
| Loan | 81,448 | 81,353 | - 96 | Loan | 79,538 | 83,757 | 4,219 |
| Public Sector | 19,615 | 19,105 | - 511 | Public Sector | 0 | 0 | 0 |
| Banks | 49,528 | 48,819 | - 708 | Banks | 54,299 | 57,500 | 3,201 |
| Other Sectors | 12,305 | 13,429 | 1,123 | Other Sectors | 25,239 | 26,257 | 1,018 |
| [Long-Term] | 41,109 | 37,042 | - 4,067 | [Long-Term] | 18,408 | 15,934 | - 2,474 |
| [Short-Term] | 40,340 | 44,310 | 3,971 | [Short-Term] | 61,130 | 67,823 | 6,693 |
| Trade Credit | 4,317 | 4,332 | 15 | Trade Credit | 1,149 | 1,334 | 186 |
| Public Sector | 918 | 907 | - 11 | Public Sector | 0 | 0 | 0 |
| Other Sectors | 3,399 | 3,426 | 26 | Other Sectors | 1,149 | 1,334 | 186 |
| [Long-Term] | 1,995 | 1,651 | - 344 | [Long-Term] | 123 | 123 | 0 |
| [Short-Term] | 2,322 | 2,682 | 360 | [Short-Term] | 1,026 | 1,211 | 185 |

**Table 4.7.** (cont.)

| | | | | | | | | |
|---|---|---|---|---|---|---|---|---|
| Currency and Deposit | 15,005 | 7,859 | - 7,146 | Currency and Deposit | 12,647 | 9,291 | - 3,356 |
| Public Sector | 0 | 0 | 0 | Public Sector | 924 | 1,370 | 446 |
| Banks | 8,854 | 3,905 | - 4,948 | Banks | 11,723 | 7,921 | - 3,802 |
| Other Sectors | 6,151 | 3,953 | - 2,198 | | | | |
| Other Assets | 16,298 | 12,248 | - 4,050 | Other Liabilities | 12,339 | 13,246 | 906 |
| Public Sector | 4,763 | 4,804 | 41 | Public Sector | 1,075 | 630 | - 444 |
| Banks | 3,230 | 5,626 | 2,396 | Banks | 7,970 | 8,881 | 911 |
| Other Sectors | 8,305 | 1,818 | - 6,487 | Other Sectors | 3,295 | 3,735 | 440 |
| [Long-Term] | 12,255 | 8,638 | - 3,617 | [Long-Term] | 388 | 435 | 47 |
| [Short-Term] | 4,043 | 3,610 | - 433 | [Short-Term] | 11,951 | 12,810 | 859 |
| 5. Reserve Assets | 52,772 | 56,063 | 3,291 | | | | |
| **Assets Total** | 379,781 | 365,940 | - 13,841 | **Liabilities Total** | 200,524 | 190,631 | - 9,893 |
| | | | | Net Assets Total | 179,257 | 175,308 | - 3,948 |
| | | | | Public Sector | 54,732 | 60,800 | 6,068 |
| | | | | Private Sector | 124,525 | 114,508 | - 10,017 |
| | | | | (Banks) | 26,360 | 25,082 | - 1,279 |

Source: Ministry of Finance of Japan

world, whereas the US owes net liabilities to the rest of the world. In 2002, Japan's total assets have declined by ¥14,381 billion, while its total liabilities also fall by ¥9,893 billion, resulting in a decrease of ¥3,948 billion in its net international investment position. Japan's net international investment position is ¥175,308 billion by the end of 2002, which is about half of the size of the US liabilities at the time.

# 5  Open Economy Macroeconomics

The balance of payments examined in the previous chapter is an extension of national accounts in a closed economy to national accounts with an external sector, and deals specifically with the external sector. Therefore, this chapter extends the basic IS-LM analytical framework for a closed economy through incorporating the balance of payments into IS-LM analysis in an open economy, which is particularly helpful and relevant to the Mundell-Fleming model of foreign exchange rate determination, to be introduced in the following chapter. Various assumptions on the attributes of prices adopted by different models for exchange rate determination are presented, providing a background for the study of these models in the later chapters.

## 5.1  The Balance of Payments, National Accounts and International Economic Linkages

The balance of payments and the international investment position are designed to measure and present an economy's external activity engaged with the rest of the world, such as flows of goods, services and capital during certain periods and the accumulated stocks of assets or liabilities at certain times. Analysis of the balance of payments, which extends national accounts for a closed economy to national accounts for an open economy, demonstrates a country's international economic linkages with the rest of the world.

### 5.1.1  National Accounts with an External Sector

In a closed economy involving no government activity, the following accounting identities hold:

$$GDP = C + I \qquad (5.1a)$$
$$GDP = C + S \qquad (5.1b)$$

where *GDP* is gross domestic product, *C* is consumption expenditure, *I* is investment and *S* is savings. The first equation the compositions of spending, the second equation is the compositions of income, and total spending is equal to total income. The above equations imply:

$$S = I \tag{5.1c}$$

which states that investment is equal to savings in a closed economy without a government.

Incorporating government activities, the equations become:

$$GDP = C + I + G \tag{5.2a}$$
$$GDP = C + S + T \tag{5.2b}$$

where *G* is government spending, *C* is consequently confined to private consumption, *I* is consequently confined to private investment, *T* is taxation or government income, and *S* is consequently confined to private savings. Still, total spending must equal total income. A relationship

$$S - I = G - T \tag{5.2c}$$

is derived, which states that government budget deficit must be offset by surplus in private savings.

In an open economy, national spending does not necessarily always equal national income. National spending can be in excess of national income at times or over a not too long period. Further incorporating an external sector, the equations become:

$$GDP = C + I + G + X - M \tag{5.3a}$$
$$GDP = C + S + T - NYF - NCT \tag{5.3b}$$

where *X* stands for exports of goods and services, *M* stands for imports of goods and services, and *X* − *M* is balance on goods and services; *NYF* stands for net income from abroad, and *NCT* stands for net current transfers. When *X* − *M* > 0, the economy is a net exporter and has produced more than it has spent, and when *X* − *M* < 0, the economy is a net importer and has spent more than it has produced. Moreover, a nation's total income in an open economy, due to income receipts from abroad, income payments to foreigners, and current transfers, can be different from its *GDP* and is the sum of *GDP*, *NYF* and *NCT*. Equation (5.3a) and equation (5.3b) entail a relationship:

$$(S - I) - (G - T) = (X - M) + NYF + NCT = CAB \tag{5.3c}$$

where *CAB* stands for current account balance. Equation (5.3c) indicates that if government budget deficit is not offset by private savings surplus, the country must run a current account deficit, or must be a net importer of goods and services when net income from abroad and net current transfers are negligible.

From the balance of payments identity, equation (4.1), and equation (5.3c), it can be worked out that:

$$(S - I) - (G - T) = NFI - NKT + NAN \qquad (5.4)$$

where *NFI* is net foreign investment including official and private investment, *NKT* is net capital transfers and *NAN* is net acquisition of non-produced, non-financial assets. ($NKT - NAN$) together is balance on the capital account. The sign of *NFI* is reversed from that for the financial account, with + indicating net foreign investment abroad of the reporting country or capital outflow, and − indicating net foreign investment in the reporting country or capital inflow. Equation (5.4) shows that if a country saves more than it invests domestically by the private sector and the government, the country will have surplus capital to invest abroad; and if a country invests more domestically by the private sector and the government than it saves, the extra capital has to be flowed in from the rest of the world. When balance on the capital account ($NKT - NAN$) is ignored, such capital surplus or shortage will be in the form of net foreign investment.

### 5.1.2 International Economic Linkages

Equations (5.3) and (5.4) illustrate and explain a country's economic linkages with the rest of the world in terms of savings, spending, and foreign investment. To concentrate our analysis on international trade and foreign investment, usually the largest and the most important components on the current account and the capital and financial account, we remove net foreign income, net transfers and net acquisition of non-produced, non-financial assets from equations (5.3) and (5.4), designate $TB = (X\text{-}M)$ for trade balance, and re-write the equations as follows:

$$GDP = C + I + G + X - M \qquad (5.3a)$$
$$GDP = C + S + T \qquad (5.3b')$$
$$(S - I) - (G - T) = (X - M) = TB \qquad (5.3c')$$
$$(S - I) - (G - T) = NFI \qquad (5.4')$$

If a country has spent more than it has produced, the country must acquire the excess through international trade as a net importer of goods and services (equation (5.3a)), and becomes a net importer of capital in the meantime with more foreign investment inflow, as suggested by the balance of payments identity (equation (5.3c') and equation (5.4')). The larger the excess, the more indebted the country is to the rest of the world. Accompanied by capital inflows, more domestic assets, financial and real, fall in the hands of foreigners. If a country has produced more than it has spent, the country is a net exporter of goods and services and exports the excess through international trade to the rest of the world (equation (5.3a)), and increases its net foreign investment abroad in the meantime (equation (5.3c') and equation (5.4')). The larger the excess, the more claims the country is to make on the rest of the world. Accompanied by capital outflows, the country acquires more real and/or financial assets abroad.

From the budget perspective, spending is related and constrained by savings. When savings are less than the sum of domestic private investment and government budge deficit, the country has to import capital from the rest of the world in the form of foreign investment to fill the overall domestic private and government budgetary shortfall financially (equation (5.4'), and then to implement foreign investment physically through imports (equation (5.3c')). When a country saves more than the sum of domestic private investment and government budge deficit, the country exports capital to the rest of the world in the form of foreign investment abroad financially (equation (5.4'), and then to implement foreign investment physically through exports (equation (5.3c')). It can be observed that capital flows always and eventually go with goods and services flows.

$(S - I) - (G - T)$ is the overall budgetary surplus or deficit of a country. It consists of two components, $(S - I)$ and $(G - T)$. $(S - I)$ is private savings surplus when private savings are greater than private investment or private savings deficit when its sign is negative. $(G - T)$ is government budget deficit when $G > T$, i.e., the government spends more than its tax revenue, or government budget surplus when $G < T$, i.e., the government's revenue is greater than its spending. In a closed economy, these two parts must offset each other. That is, private savings surplus must have the same sign as government budget deficit with an equal amount. In an open economy, they do not necessarily offset each other completely, since the balance can be made up through international trade and foreign investment. So, it is possible that a country runs both a private savings deficit and a government budgetary deficit. When this happens, it is said that the country experiences twin deficits. Obviously, when a country experiences twin deficits, it runs an overall budgetary deficit. While an overall budgetary deficit may or may not be associated with twin deficits, e.g., when private savings are in surplus but the surplus is not large enough to offset government budget deficit completely.

The international economic linkages of a country with the rest of the world revealed by the above equations and relationships show the potential measures and means to solve for a country's trade balance problems. These measures and means include increasing private savings, reducing private investment, boosting government revenue and cutting government spending, which is typically domestic budgetary issues; lessening trade balance deficit through increasing exports and reducing imports, which is affected by the foreign exchange policy and international competitive advantages of a country; and increasing output through raising productivity, R&D, innovation, and other aspects of the real economy, which is probably the most important and effective amongst all.

## 5.2   IS–LM in Open Economy Macroeconomics

IS–LM analysis is one of the most fundamental and widely adopted means in macroeconomics. This section first introduces the standard IS–LM analytical framework, and then extends it to IS–LM–BP analysis through including an external sector represented by the balance of payments for the analysis of an open economy. The importance and relevance of IS–LM analysis for an open economy are evident by the fact that one of the most influential models for foreign exchange rate determination and policy analysis, the Mundell–Fleming model, is explicitly based on this analytical framework; the flexible price monetary model of exchange rate determination is associated with part of IS–LM; and so is the Dornbusch model, the sticky price model of exchange rate determination, with pertinent adaptations.

### 5.2.1   IS–LM Analysis

There are two parts in IS–LM analysis, one is the IS plane for investment and savings, and the other is the LM plane referring to liquidity of money. The former the equilibrium on the goods market and the latter is the equilibrium on the money market.

The goods market equilibrium and the corresponding IS curve are derived from analysing the following equation that are resulted from subtracting equation (5.3a) from equation (5.3b'):

$$S + T - I = G + TB \tag{5.5}$$

Taking derivatives of the variables in equation (5.5) with respect to the interest rate, income and the real exchange rate, following partial derivatives

$$S'_r > 0, \ I'_r < 0, \ S'_Y > I'_Y > 0, \ T'_Y > 0, \ TB'_Q > 0, \text{ and } TB'_Y < 0$$

are obtained, which indicate that:

Savings are an increasing function of the interest rate $r$;

Investment is a decreasing function of the interest rate $r$;

Both savings and investment increase with the level of income $Y$ ($GDP$), but savings increase more than investment for a same size of increase in $Y$;

Government tax revenue is an increasing function of income $Y$;

Trade balance is an increasing function of the real exchange rate $Q$ (An increase in $Q$ means the depreciation of the domestic currency in real terms. It can be the nominal exchange rate and the analysis is the same) – depreciation in the real exchange rate boosts exports and deters imports by making domestic goods cheaper and more competitive abroad and imported foreign goods more expensive and less competitive on the domestic market; and

Trade balance is a decreasing function of income $Y$ – domestic residents will spend more on imported goods with income increases.

Expressing $S$, $T$, $I$, $G$ and $TB$ as linear functions of $r$, $Y$, and $Q$ yields:

$$S(Y,r) = \beta_1 Y + \lambda_1 r$$

$$T(Y) = \beta_2 Y$$

$$I(Y,r) = \beta_3 Y - \lambda_2 r$$

$$TB(Y,Q) = hQ - \beta_4 Y$$

where all the parameters are positive and $\beta_2 > \beta_3$.

Bringing the above variables expressed as functions of $r$, $Y$, and $Q$ into equation (5.5) results in:

$$\beta_1 Y + \beta_2 Y - \beta_3 Y + \lambda_1 r + \lambda_2 r = G + hQ - \beta_4 Y$$

Moving $\beta_4 Y$ to the left hand side of the equation, it becomes:

$$(\beta_1 + \beta_2 - \beta_3 + \beta_4)Y + (\lambda_1 + \lambda_2)r = G + hQ$$

or:

$$\beta Y + \lambda r = hQ + G \qquad\qquad (5.6)$$

after re-arrangements, where $\beta = (\beta_1 + \beta_2 - \beta_3 + \beta_4) > 0$, $\lambda = (\lambda_1 + \lambda_2) > 0$ and $h > 0$. Equation (5.6) is the IS curve when plotted on the $Y$-$r$ plane showing the relationship between the level of the interest rate and the level of income when the goods market clears or is in equilibrium. Government spending and the real exchange rate are exogenous on the $Y$-$r$ plane. The lower the level of the interest rate, the higher is the level of income, when the goods market equilibrium is considered alone.

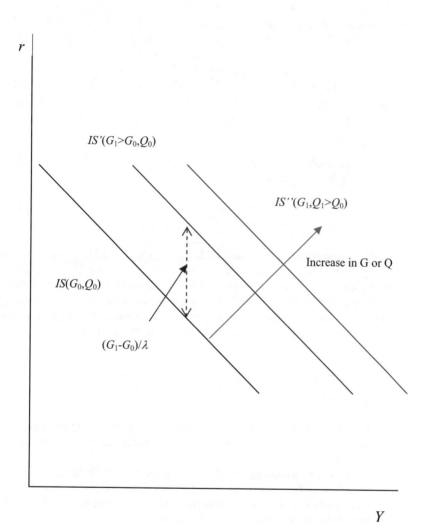

**Figure 5.1.** IS curve

Figure 5.1 shows the IS curves and the goods market equilibria at various levels of the exogenous variables, government spending, $G$, and the real exchange rate, $Q$. Let us re-arrange equation (5.6) as follows:

$$r = -\frac{\beta}{\lambda}Y + \frac{h}{\lambda}Q + \frac{1}{\lambda}G \qquad (5.6')$$

It is clear that the slope the curve is $-\beta/\lambda$, which is down sloping. Both increases in government spending and the real exchange rate shift the entire IS curve in the up right direction. When $Q$ is kept unchanged, a unit increase in $G$ will cause the curve to move upwards by $1/\lambda$. Therefore, an increase in government spending from $G_0$ to $G_1$ will move the position of the curve at $IS(G_0,Q_0)$ upwards by $(G_1 - G_0)/\lambda$ to the position at $IS'(G_1,Q_0)$, as shown by the graph. Likewise, when $G$ is fixed at $G_1$, an increase in the real exchange rate from $Q_0$ to $Q_1$ will move the position of the curve at $IS'(G_1,Q_0)$ upwards by $\frac{h}{\lambda}(Q_1 - Q_0)$ to the position at $IS''(G_1,Q_1)$.

The money market equilibrium and the corresponding LM curve are derived from analysing the following equation:

$$\frac{M^D}{P} = \frac{M^S}{P} = L(r,Y) \tag{5.7}$$

where $M^D$ is demand for money and $M^S$ is money supply and they are equal when the money market is in equilibrium; $P$ is price; and $L$ stands for liquidity of money, which is a function of the interest rate $r$ and income $Y$. $L(r,Y)$ is a measure of the velocity of money in circulation. With a fixed amount of money supply, the lower the price level, the more liquid is the money market. Taking derivatives of $L(r,Y)$ with respect to $r$ and $Y$ yields the following partial derivatives:

$L'_r < 0$ and $L'_Y > 0$,

which indicate that:

> $L(r,Y)$ is a decreasing function of the interest rate $r$ – a higher level of the interest rate will induce more savings and reduce demand for money; and

> $L(r,Y)$ is an increasing function of income $Y$ – with the price level and money supply unchanged, a higher level of income means the same money has to circulate for more times in a given period, or the velocity of money has to increase.

Let us express $L(r,Y)$ as a linear function of $r$ and $Y$:

$$L(r,Y) = kY - \gamma r$$

where $k > 0$ and $\gamma > 0$. Bringing the above expression into equation (5.7), with $M^D = M^S = M$, yields:

$$kY - \gamma r = \frac{M}{P} \tag{5.8}$$

Equation (5.8) represents the LM curve plotted on the *Y-r* plane demonstrating the relationship between the level of the interest rate and the level of income when the money market clears or is in equilibrium. Money supply or demand for money and the price level are exogenous on the *Y-r* plane. Government spending and the real exchange rate do not exist on the *Y-r* plane. The higher the level of the interest rate, the higher is the level of income, when the money market equilibrium is considered alone.

Figure 5.2 exhibits the LM curves and the money market equilibria at various levels of the exogenous variables, money supply or demand for money, *M*, and the price level, *P*. Re-arrangement of equation (5.8) leads to:

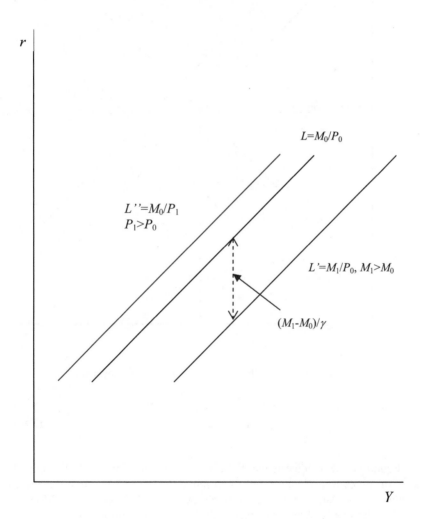

**Figure 5.2.** LM curve

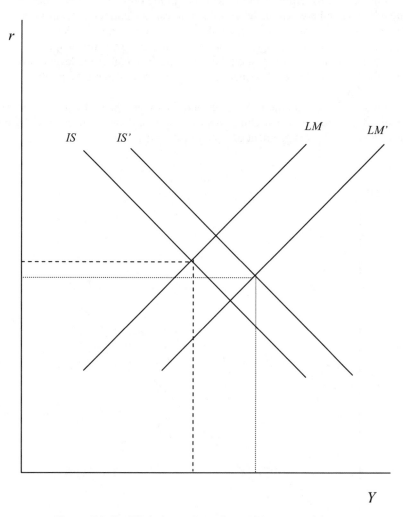

**Figure 5.3.** Equilibria in goods market and money market

$$r = \frac{k}{\gamma} Y - \frac{1}{\gamma} \frac{M}{P} \qquad (5.8')$$

Equation (5.8') suggests that the LM curve is up sloping with the slope being $k/\gamma$. An increase in money supply will move the entire LM curve downwards or rightwards; and an increase in the price level will shift the entire LM curve upwards or leftwards. When $P$ is fixed at $P_0$, an increase in money supply from $M_0$ to $M_1$ will move the position of the LM curve at $L=M_0/P_0$ downwards by $(M_1-M_0)/\gamma$

to the position at $L'=M_1/P_0$, as shown in Figure 5.2. When $M$ is fixed at $M_0$, an increase in the price level from $P_0$ to $P_1$ will move the position of the LM curve at $L=M_0/P_0$ upwards by $(1/P_0-1/P_1)/\gamma$ to the position at $L''=M_0/P_1$.

General equilibrium attains when both the goods market and the money market clear or are in equilibrium. This happens when the IS curve and the LM curve cross on the $Y$-$r$ plane. The level of income and the level of the interest rate can therefore be determined, as shown in Figure 5.3. When the IS curve and/or the LM curve shift due to changes in the value of the exogenous variables, the level of income and the corresponding interest rate will also change accordingly to settle down at a new equilibrium point.

## 5.2.2 IS–LM–BP Analysis

In the above IS–LM analysis, the foreign exchange rate is treated as an exogenous variable, so is trade balance. While this treatment works for domestic policy analysis, it is not appropriate for the analysis of issues in international finance and trade where foreign exchange, international trade and capital flows are amongst major considerations. Moreover, the effect of various monetary and fiscal policies in an open economy may substantially differ from that in a closed economy. Measures that are confined to domestic issues exclusively will have to be reconsidered and extended to cover the external sector endogenously. It is of critical importance to integrate domestic analysis and international analysis methodically, since domestic issues and international issues are complicatedly interwoven; or in other words, there are no pure domestic issues in an open economy.

Therefore, this section adds another dimension to the IS–LM framework by incorporating the balance of payments (BP) into the analysis, in which the foreign exchange rate and trade balance are endogenous. Under this extended framework of IS–LM–BP analysis, income, the interest rate, the exchange rate, and the balance of payments accounts are jointly determined, e.g., the implementation of a specific policy may firstly have effect on the level of the interest rate and income, which passes onto the exchange rate, which in turn impacts trade balance, income and the interest rate.

In the same spirit as for IS–LM analysis, the balance of payments accounts are expressed as functions of income, $Y$, the real foreign exchange rate, $Q$, and the interest rate, $r$:

$$BP = CAB(Q,Y) + KAB(r) \qquad (5.9)$$

where $BP$ stands for the balance of payments, $CAB$ stands for the current account balance, and $KAB$ stands for the capital and financial account balance. As suggested earlier, our analysis concentrates on trade balance, $TB = (X-M)$, so we rewrite equation (5.9) as follows:

$$BP = TB(Q,Y) + KAB(r) \qquad (5.9')$$

Equation (5.9') indicates that trade balance is a function of income and the foreign exchange rate, and the capital and financial account balance is only influenced by the level of the interest rate. Taking derivatives of $TB$ and $KAB$ with respect to the foreign exchange rate, income and the interest rate respectively yields:

$$TB'_Q > 0, \ TB'_Y < 0, \text{ and } KAB'_r > 0,$$

which indicate that:

Trade balance is an increasing function of the real foreign exchange rate $Q$ (it can be the nominal exchange rate and the analysis is the same) – depreciation in the real exchange rate boosts exports and deters imports by making domestic goods cheaper and more competitive abroad and imported foreign goods more expensive and less competitive on the domestic market;

Trade balance is a decreasing function of income $Y$ – domestic residents will spend more on imported goods with income increases; and

Capital and financial account balance is an increasing function of the level of interest rate $r$ – a higher level of the interest rate will induce more capital inflows and reduce capital outflows. Capital is perfectly mobile when $KAB'_r = \infty$, which is usually applicable to a small open economy, and capital is completely immobile when $KAB'_r = 0$.

Same as with IS–LM analysis, we express $TB$ and $KAB$ as linear functions of and $Y$, $Q$ and $r$:

$$TB(Y,Q) = hQ - \theta Y$$
$$KAB(r) = \kappa(r - r^*)$$

where $\theta = \beta_4$ and $\theta < \beta$ in equation (5.6), $0 \leq \kappa < \infty$, and $r^*$ is the equilibrium interest rate. Bringing the above expressions into equation (5.9'), noting that the two balances sum to zero, yields:

$$hQ - \theta Y + \kappa(r - r^*) = 0 \qquad (5.10)$$

Now we extend the IS–LM framework by introducing a new dimension of the foreign exchange rate on a new $Y$–$Q$ plane in association with the $Y$–$r$ plane, as shown in Figure 5.4. Equation (5.10) represents two BP curves, one on the $Y$–$r$ plane while the exchange rate is treated as exogenous, and one on the $Y$–$Q$ plane where the interest rate is exogenous. In the meantime, equations (5.6) and (5.8)

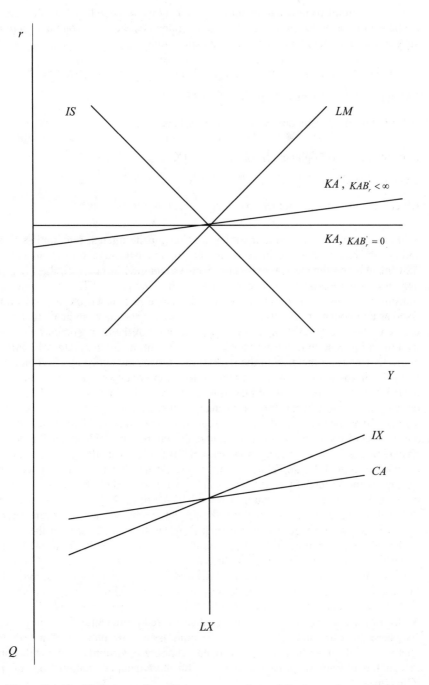

**Figure 5.4.** Equilibria in goods market, money market and foreign exchange market

bring into being two new curves on the new $Y–Q$ plane as well, where the foreign exchange rate is endogenous but the interest rate is exogenous. Together there are six curves, represented by the following expressions:

IS curve on the $Y–r$ plane: $\beta Y + \lambda r = hQ + G$, IS

LM curve on the $Y–r$ plane: $kY - \gamma r = \dfrac{M}{P}$, LM

BP curve on the $Y–r$ plane: $\theta Y - \kappa(r - r^*) = hQ$, KA

IS curve on the $Y–Q$ plane: $\beta Y - hQ = G - \lambda r$, IX

LM curve on the $Y–r$ plane: $kY = \dfrac{M}{P} + \gamma r$, LX

BP curve on the $Y–r$ plane: $\theta Y - hQ = \kappa(r - r^*)$, CA

For consistency, the same treatment as that for the interest rate applies to the foreign exchange rate: an increase in the foreign exchange rate is an upward movement along the vertical axis. The IS curve and the LM curve on the $Y–r$ plane need no further explanation. The IS curve on the $Y–Q$ plane, IX, exhibits the relationship between income and the foreign exchange rate, when the interest rate is fixed as an exogenous variable. The relationship and the curve indicate that an increase in the foreign exchange rate, or depreciation of the domestic currency, will lead to an increase in domestic income. A change in the interest rate will shift the entire IX curve: an increase in the interest rate moves the entire IX curve upwards and a fall in the interest rate moves the entire IX curve downwards. The LM curve on the $Y–r$ plane, LX, is a vertical line, since only the income variable $Y$ is endogenous. Changes in the foreign exchange rate have no effect on the LX curve. The BP curve on the $Y–r$ plane, KA, represents the capital and financial account and the relationship between income and the interest rate when the foreign exchange rate is fixed as an exogenous variable. It is a horizontal line when capital is completely immobile, i.e., changes in the interest rate have no whatsoever effect on capital movement. In general, it is an upward line. The BP curve on the $Y–r$ plane, CA, is the current account or trade balance in the balance of payments for the relationship between income and the foreign exchange rate when the interest rate is fixed as an exogenous variable. It suggests that an increase in the foreign exchange rate, or depreciation of the domestic currency, results in an increase in domestic income. An increase in the interest rate moves the entire CA curve downwards with the effect of an rising capital and financial account surplus (falling capital and financial account deficit), offset by an rising current account deficit (falling current account surplus).

IS–LM–BP analysis is one of the most structured frameworks for policy analysis where domestic and international economic issues are interwoven and, consequently, are dealt with jointly in an open economy environment. We will apply this analytical framework later in the book for more detailed examinations of specific issues.

## 5.3   Aggregate Supply and Assumptions on Price Attributes

Economists make different assumptions on the properties of prices. Analysis based on different assumptions may proceed with different approaches and reach different conclusions. Depending on the circumstances, one assumption or one set of assumptions can be more appropriate and relevant than others. This section briefly introduce three assumptions on the attributes of prices, based on which three major models of foreign exchange rate determinations were developed, and presents their implications respectively.

With the flexible prices assumption, aggregate supply curve is vertical. This means that a shift in aggregate demand has no whatsoever effect on output. The level of output cannot be easily changed as it is mainly determined by supply side factors. Since a shift in demand will not cause shifts in aggregate supply or output, the shift in aggregate demand will only cause prices to change. e.g., since a shift to a higher aggregate demand level will not lead to a higher aggregate output level, the price level has to and will rise.

Figure 5.5 demonstrates what may happen under the flexible prices assumption. For example, if initially the aggregate supply curve is at the position $AS_1$ and the aggregate demand curve is the position $AD_1$. Output is at the level of $Y_1$, the price level is at $P_1$, and the aggregate demand curve and the aggregate supply curve cross at point $A$ in equilibrium. If for some reason the aggregate demand curve shifts to a new position $AD_2$, then $A$ is no longer the equilibrium point. The aggregate supply curve and the new aggregate demand curve cross at point $B$ in a new equilibrium where output remains $Y_1$ but the price level increases from $P_1$ to $P_2$. Only a shift in aggregate supply will change the level of output, e.g., from $Y_1$ to $Y_2$. The price level can be lowered in a new equilibrium at point $C$ or higher at point $D$, depending on whether aggregate demand shifts as well and how it shifts.

The flexible price monetary model of foreign exchange rate determination adopts this assumption on price attributes. Since there is not much role for the goods market equilibrium, the monetary model, unlike the Mundell-Fleming model, does not follow the IS–LM framework. If it dose in some sense, it works with the LM part only.

When fixed prices are assumed, the aggregate supply curve is fairly flat or horizontal in the extreme. This suggests that a shift in aggregate demand is almost everything to concern. Changes in aggregate supply or output are almost entirely induced by shifts in aggregate demand. In contrast to the flexible price case, the level of output can be easily adjusted in response to shifts in aggregate demand so the price level need not change.

Figure 5.6 shows the fixed prices case. Since the aggregate supply is flat, the amount of supply changes, increase or decrease, induced by a shift in demand can be enormous, indicating supply side factors can be easily mobilised. Assuming the initial equilibrium has been reached at point $A$, a shift of the aggregate demand curve from $AD_1$ to $AD_2$ induces aggregate supply to increase so the level of output increases from $Y_1$ to $Y_2$, with little effect on the price level, since the consequences of the shift in demand are almost absorbed by adjustments in output.

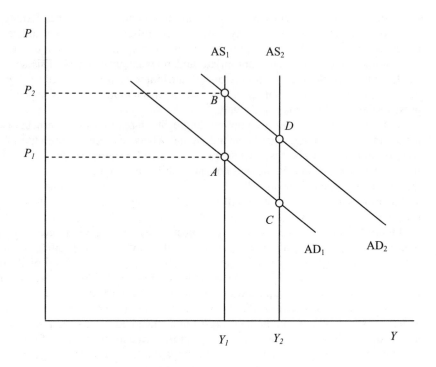

**Figure 5.5.** Flexible prices

With the fixed prices assumption, demand analysis is important and, consequently, the IS–LM framework or its international extension, IS–LM–BP analysis, is usually adopted. The Mundell-Fleming model adopts this assumption on price attributes.

Flexible prices and fixed prices are two extreme assumptions on price attributes. A more appropriate assumption may be that prices are neither totally flexible nor totally fixed, which leads to the sticky price assumption. The aggregate supply curve is flat in the short term, the slope of the aggregate supply curve gradually becomes steeper and steeper with increases in time horizon, and the curve is vertical in the long run. In the short term, increases in output are induced by shifts in aggregate demand; in the medium term, increases in output are caused by shifts in aggregate demand or shifts in aggregate supply or both; and in the long run, only a shift in aggregate supply changes output. The stick price is the assumption adopted by the Dornbusch model of foreign exchange rate determination.

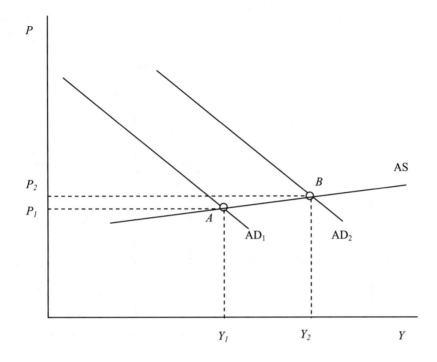

**Figure 5.6.** Fixed prices

Figure 5.7 exhibits the short term, medium term and long run features of aggregate supply with the sticky prices assumption. In the short term, the aggregate supply curve $AS_S$ is flat or horizontal, so a shift of the aggregate demand curve from $AD_1$ to $AD_2$ induces aggregate supply to increase so the level of output increases from $Y_1$ to $Y_2$, while the price is unchanged or fixed at $P_1$. Assuming the initial equilibrium has been reached at point $A$, the shift of the aggregate demand curve from $AD_1$ to $AD_2$ will lead to the temporary equilibrium point $B$, as indicated in Figure 5.7. In the medium term, the aggregate supply curve $AS_M$ is neither horizontal nor vertical and output is determined by both aggregate demand and aggregate supply. At point $C$, the price level is between $P_1$, the fixed price, and $P_2$, the flexible price with the aggregate demand shift; and the increase in output is lower than that in the fixed price case. In the long run, the aggregate supply curve $AS_{L1}$ is vertical, so at point $D$ there is only increase in the price level but no change in output. Only a shift in aggregate supply from $AS_{L1}$ to $AS_{L2}$ increases output from $Y_1$ to $Y_2$.

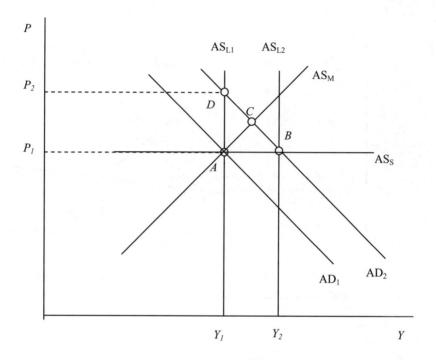

**Figure 5.7.** Sticky prices

# 6 The Mundell-Fleming Model

The Mundell-Fleming model works with the assumption that prices are fixed. This means that the aggregate supply curve is flat (horizontal in the extreme) and income is determined by the aggregate demand only. Therefore, analysis in this chapter is in the IS-LM framework, extended to incorporate the external sector – the balance of payments, to become IS–LM–BP analysis, as studied in Section 5.2 of the previous chapter. The model has been originated in a series of papers and collections by Mundell (1960, 1961, 1962, 1963 and 1964) and Fleming (1962 and 1971). The background, history and development of the Mundell-Fleming model can be found in Mundell (2001) and Obstfeld (2001), which the interested reader may refer to.

This chapter examines the effects of monetary policy and fiscal policy under various assumptions on exchange rate regimes and capital mobility in the IS-LM-BP framework. Specifically, we analyse and discuss the effects and effectiveness of monetary policy and fiscal policy under the following scenarios: perfect capital mobility or small open economy (SOE) with flexible exchange rates and fixed exchange rates respectively; and imperfect capital mobility or non-SOE with flexible exchange rates and fixed exchange rates respectively. Under each of the scenarios the effects of monetary policy changes and fiscal policy changes are considered respectively, so there are eight sets of individual cases. Finally we compare the outcomes and comment on the use of one policy against the other under certain circumstances.

## 6.1 Effects and Effectiveness of Monetary Policy and Fiscal Policy - *Perfect Capital Mobility*

Under perfect capital mobility (PCM), the domestic interest rate, after enduring a shock such as a monetary/fiscal expansion/contraction, returns to its original level eventually. In the SOE case, the original level of the interest rate is the world rate of interest. We know from the standard closed economy IS-LM analysis that a change in monetary policy shifts the LM curve while a change in fiscal policy shifts the IS curve. In an open economy, one policy change may shift both LM and IS curves. For example and under a flexible exchange rate regime, a monetary expansion has direct effect on the LM curve and shifts the LM curve towards the right initially; then the resulted increase in the exchange rate (depreciation) has the consequence of moving the IS curve to the right as well, a phenomenon similar to the effect of a fiscal expansion. Likewise and under a fixed exchange rate regime, a fiscal expansion has direct effect on the IS curve and shifts the curve towards the right initially. However, since the exchange rate is fixed, the deterioration in the current account may not be exactly offset by the amount of capital inflows, leading to an adjustment or change in official reserves and money supply. This consequently changes the LM curve position. From such preliminary reasoning, we become aware that, in an open economy, the economy may benefit from the implementation of a policy in more areas and to a larger extent than in a closed economy. The opposite is also true and the economy can be put in a state of complete mess.

### 6.1.1  Monetary Expansion - Perfect Capital Mobility, Flexible Exchange Rates

The first case we analyse is the effects and effectiveness of an expansionary monetary policy. Suppose the goods market, the money market and the balance of payments were in equilibrium at point A before the monetary expansion. As Figure 6.1 indicates, a monetary expansion shifts the LM curve to the right but has no immediate effect on the IS curve, so the latter maintains its original position, leading to a temporary equilibrium at point B. As the domestic interest rate is lower than the interest rate in the rest of the world, capital flows out of the country, net deficit in the capital account accumulating (net surplus decreasing). This takes effect on the current account of the balance of payments, resulting in an increase in net current account surplus (decrease in net deficit) and shifting the CA curve to a more favourable position CA', accompanied by the depreciation of the domestic currency. The wealth effect can be seen as the IS curve shifts to the right due to a net increase in trade balance. A new equilibrium attains at point C. The IX curve shifts to $IX^T$ temporarily when the domestic interest rate is lower than that in the rest of the world and returns to its original position after the two interest rates become equal again. The process can be more precisely described by changes in the values of the variables in relevant equations as follows:

(1).    Monetary expansion: the LM curve in the i-Y plane shifts from $\gamma Y - \varphi i = \dfrac{M}{P}$ to $\gamma Y - \varphi i = \dfrac{M + \Delta M}{P}$.

(2).    Capital outflow: $\Delta K = -k, k > 0$ ($\kappa = \infty$, $\Delta i = -0.$).
        The LX curve in the S-Y plane[1] shifts to $LX^T$.

---

[1] Slightly different from the analysis in Chapter 5, we use the nominal exchange rate S in this chapter in place of the real exchange rate Q, so the Q-Y plane become the S-Y plane.

The IX curve in the S-Y plane shifts from IX ( $\beta Y - \delta S = G - \lambda i^*$ ) to IX$^T$ ( $\beta Y - \delta S = G - \lambda i$ ).

(3).    Current account improvement: the CA curve shifts from CA ( $\theta Y - \eta S = K$ ) to CA' ( $\theta Y - \eta S = K - k$ ).
The LX curve in the S-Y plane shifts from LX$^T$ to LX'.
The IX curve in the S-Y plane shifts from IX$^T$ ( $\beta Y - \delta S = G - \lambda i$ ) back to IX ( $\beta Y - \delta S = G - \lambda i^*$ ).
New equilibrium in the S-Y plane attains.

(4).    Wealth effect: the IS curve in the i-Y plane shifts from IS ( $\beta Y + \lambda i = G + \delta S$ ) to IS' ( $\beta Y + \lambda i = G + \delta S'$ ). New equilibrium in the i-Y plane attains.

We can work out the values of these variables in the new equilibrium. Since in the new equilibrium the interest rate is equal to that in the old equilibrium, we have $\gamma \Delta Y = \dfrac{\Delta M}{P}$ calculated from the LM curve equations, i.e., increase in wealth is:

$$\Delta Y = \frac{\Delta M}{\gamma P} \cdot$$

From the IS curve equations we know that $\delta \Delta S = \beta \Delta Y = \dfrac{\beta \Delta M}{\gamma P}$ , i.e., the currency depreciates to the extent of:

$$\Delta S = \frac{\beta}{\delta \gamma P} \Delta M \cdot$$

Comparing the CA curve and CA' curve, we know that the current account position has improved by

$$\eta \Delta S - \theta \Delta Y = \frac{1}{\gamma P} \left( \frac{\eta \beta}{\delta} - \theta \right) \Delta M \cdot$$

We know from the parameter condition $\dfrac{\beta}{\delta} > \dfrac{\theta}{\eta}$ that the above figure is greater than zero. This figure offsets the increase in the net deficit in the capital account or net capital outflow, so:

$$-k = \frac{1}{\gamma P} \left( \frac{\eta \beta}{\delta} - \theta \right) \Delta M$$

The above figure is also the extent to which the current account has improved, i.e., increase in the net current account surplus.

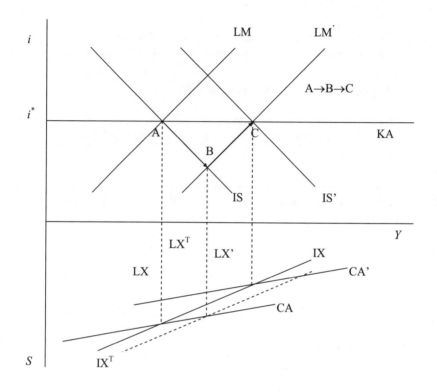

**Figure 6.1.** Monetary expansion – PCM and flexible exchange rates

It can be concluded that a monetary expansion of the amount $\Delta M$ in the case of a small open economy or perfect capital mobility with a flexible exchange rate has the effects leading to:

- Increase in income by $\Delta Y = \dfrac{\Delta M}{\gamma P}$.

- A once for all capital outflow of $-k = \dfrac{1}{\gamma P}\left(\dfrac{\eta\beta}{\delta} - \theta\right)\Delta M$.

- Improvement in the current account to the extent of $\dfrac{1}{\gamma P}\left(\dfrac{\eta\beta}{\delta} - \theta\right)\Delta M$.

- Depreciation of the domestic currency by $\Delta S = \dfrac{\beta}{\delta\gamma P}\Delta M$.

### 6.1.2 Fiscal Expansion - Perfect Capital Mobility, Flexible Exchange Rates

In contrast to monetary policy changes, a fiscal expansion shifts the IS curve to the right but has no effect on the LM curve. Figure 6.2 demonstrates the case of fiscal expansion under PCM with flexible exchange rates. The equilibrium at point B is temporary, because the domestic interest rate is higher than that in the rest of the world at this point which will be reduced to the world level gradually and eventually due to the assumption of perfect capital mobility. The IX curve also shifts to the right caused by increased government spending G, though an increasing interest rate offsets the shift to a certain degree. When the domestic interest rate returns to the level of the world interest rate, the IX curve shifts through a transitional position $LX^T$ then settles down at the position LX' and the effect is purely from the increase in G. The decrease in S (appreciation of the domestic currency) or the worsening in trade balance eventually offsets the increase in G, pulling the IS curve back to its original position. Equilibrium is only restored in the i-Y plane at point A, with a deteriorated external balance situation. Describing the process by changes in the values of the variables in the relevant equations, we obtain:

(1).   Fiscal expansion: the IS curve in the i-Y plane shifts from $\beta Y + \lambda i = G + \delta S$ to $\beta Y + \lambda i = G + \Delta G + \delta S$ with temporary increase in income. Comparing the cross points of LM and IS and LM and $IS^T$ yields

$$\Delta Y^T = \frac{\varphi \Delta G}{\beta \varphi + \lambda \gamma} \quad .$$

(2).   Capital inflow: $\Delta K = k, k > 0$ ($\kappa = \infty$, $\Delta i = +0.$).
The IX curve in the S-Y plane shifts from IX ($\beta Y - \delta S = G - \lambda i^*$) to $IX^T$ ($\beta Y - \delta S = G + \Delta G - \lambda i$).
The LX curve in the S-Y plane shifts to $LX^T$.

(3).   Current account deterioration: the CA curve shifts from CA ($\theta Y - \eta S = K$) to CA' ($\theta Y - \eta S = K + k$).
The IX curve in the S-Y plane shifts from $IX^T$ ($\beta Y - \delta S = G + \Delta G - \lambda i$) to settle down at IX' ($\beta Y - \delta S = G + \Delta G - \lambda i^*$).
The LX curve in the S-Y plane shifts from $LX^T$ back to LX.
New equilibrium in the S-Y plane attains, with deteriorated external balance conditions.

(4).   Wealth effect: the IS curve in the i-Y plane shifts from $IS^T$ ($\beta Y + \lambda i = G + \Delta G + \delta S$) back to IS ($\beta Y + \lambda i = G + \Delta G + \delta S' = G + \Delta G + \delta \Delta S$, with $G + \Delta G + \delta S' = G + \delta S$, or $\Delta G + \delta \Delta S = 0$). Equilibrium in the i-Y plane is restored.

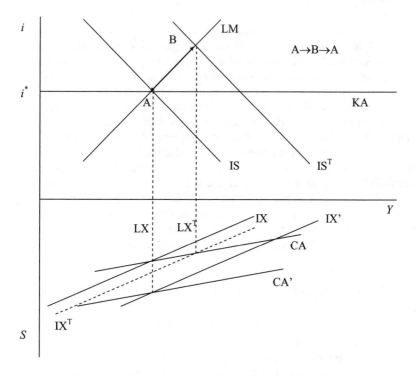

**Figure 6.2.** Fiscal expansion – PCM and flexible exchange rates

Comparing the IX' curve and the IX curve, we can infer how much the currency has appreciated. With Y and i having returned to their original levels in equation $\beta Y - \delta S = G + \Delta G - \lambda i^*$, the only variable which has changed is S. So, $-\delta \Delta S = \Delta G$, i.e. the currency has appreciated by:

$$\Delta S = -\frac{\Delta G}{\delta}$$

At the new exchange rate level, we know from the current account balance equations, that $k = -\eta \Delta S$, i.e., increase in net capital account surplus (decrease in net deficit) is:

$$k = \frac{\eta \Delta G}{\delta}$$

This is also the decrease in net trade balance surplus (increase in net trade balance deficit).

We can reach conclusions that a fiscal expansion of the amount $\Delta G$ in the case of a small open economy or perfect capital mobility under a flexible exchange rate regime results in:

- Temporary increase in income $\Delta Y^T = \dfrac{\varphi \Delta G}{\beta \varphi + \lambda \gamma}$, income is later restored to its original level.

- Appreciation of the domestic currency to the extent of $\Delta S = -\dfrac{\Delta G}{\delta}$.

- A once for all capital inflow of $k = \dfrac{\eta \Delta G}{\delta}$.

- Deterioration in the current account by $-\dfrac{\eta \Delta G}{\delta}$.

### 6.1.3 Monetary Expansion - Perfect Capital Mobility, Fixed Exchange Rates

A monetary expansion shifts the LM curve to the right, reduces the domestic interest rate and causes capital outflow from the country. However, with a fixed exchange rate regime, a more favourable current account position will not emerge as a result of the depreciation of the domestic currency – the CA curve does not move up to cross the IX curve as the exchange rate cannot be changed to that level, instead the CA curve moves down across the line of $S = S^*$ at the level of the fixed exchange rate. Consequently, a rightwards shift of the IS curve does not materialise either. Figure 6.3 shows the case of monetary expansion under PCM with fixed exchange rates.

Previously, we have ignored changes in official reserves in flexible exchange rate cases and all we considered are private capital account transactions, because, by definition, changes in official reserves are zero under the flexible exchange rate regime. Now that the exchange rate is fixed, an increase in official reserves is inevitable to offset both current and capital account deficits. A direct consequence of this change in official reserves is a reduction of money in circulation, and quantitatively the volume of reduction is exactly the amount expanded at the monetary expansion stage. All have happened are a temporary increase in income, once for all capital outflow and temporary worsening of the current account balance, which are all restored to the pre-expansion levels, accompanied by an increase in official reserves. In description, the LM curve in the i-Y plane shifts to $LM^T$ then back to LM; similarly move the LX curve and the CA curve in the S-Y plane; and the positions of the IS curve in the i-Y plane and IX curve in the S-Y plane remain unchanged. The process is shown in the following steps:

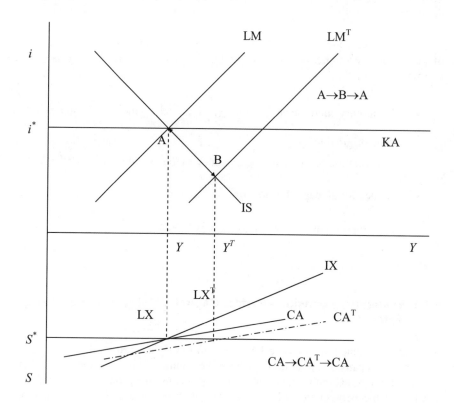

**Figure 6.3.** Monetary expansion – PCM and fixed exchange rates

(1).    Monetary expansion: the LM curve in the i-Y plane shifts from $\gamma Y - \varphi i = \dfrac{M}{P}$ to $\gamma Y - \varphi i = \dfrac{M + \Delta M}{P}$, temporary increase in income of $\Delta Y^T$ from Y to $Y^T$.

(2).    Capital outflow: $\Delta K = -k, k > 0$ ($\kappa = \infty$, $\Delta i = -0.$).
        The LX curve in the S-Y plane shifts to $LX^T$.

(3).    Current account deterioration: the CA curve shifts from CA ($\theta Y - \eta S = K$) to $CA^T$ [$\theta(Y - \Delta Y^T) - \eta S = K$, or $\theta Y - \eta S = K + \theta \Delta Y^T$], as the curve shifts rightwards by $\Delta Y^T$. This is not determined by private capital account changes but the fixed exchange rate.

(4).    Increase in official reserves and reduction of money in circulation to the original amount before the expansion. The LM curve in the i-Y plane shifts from $LM^T$ back to LM. Equilibrium in the i-Y plane is restored.

The temporary increase in income can be derived by comparing the value of Y at the cross point of LM and IS and that of $LM^T$ and IS. It is solved as:

$$\Delta Y^T = \frac{\lambda \Delta M}{P(\beta \varphi + \lambda \gamma)}$$

The extent to which the current temporally deteriorated is $\theta \Delta Y^T$, i.e.:

$$\Delta CA = \frac{-\lambda \theta \Delta M}{P(\beta \varphi + \lambda \gamma)}$$

From the balance of payments identity we know that changes in the current account ($-\frac{\lambda \theta \Delta M}{P(\beta \varphi + \lambda \gamma)}$), the private capital account (-k) and official reserves ($\Delta M$) sum to zero. So, change in the private capital account or net capital outflow is:

$$-k = \left(1 - \frac{\lambda \theta}{P(\beta \varphi + \lambda \gamma)}\right)\Delta M$$

We conclude that a monetary expansion of the amount $\Delta M$ in the case of a small open economy or perfect capital mobility under a fixed exchange rate regime has the following effects:

- Temporary increase in income by $\Delta Y^T = \frac{\lambda \Delta M}{P(\beta \varphi + \lambda \gamma)}$, income is later restored to its original level.
- Increase in official reserves by the amount of the monetary expansion $\Delta M$.
- A once for all capital outflow of $\left(1 - \frac{\lambda \theta}{P(\beta \varphi + \lambda \gamma)}\right)\Delta M$.
- Temporary deterioration in the current account to the extent of $\Delta CA = -\frac{\lambda \theta \Delta M}{P(\beta \varphi + \lambda \gamma)}$.

### 6.1.4 Fiscal Expansion - Perfect Capital Mobility, Fixed Exchange Rates

A fiscal expansion under the fixed exchange rate regime differs from that under the flexible exchange rate regime in that its wealth effect is permanent. The shift of the IS curve to IS' is permanent due to the fact that the exchange rate is fixed, in contrast to the case of flexible exchange rates where appreciation of the domestic currency (decrease) eventually offsets the increase in government spending G. A second point to differ from the flexible exchange rate regime is that changes in the current account may not be exactly offset by changes in the private capital account, because they are determined by different factors respectively. This implies that official reserves may change as well in response to any balance unsettled by the private capital account and the current account in the balance of payments.

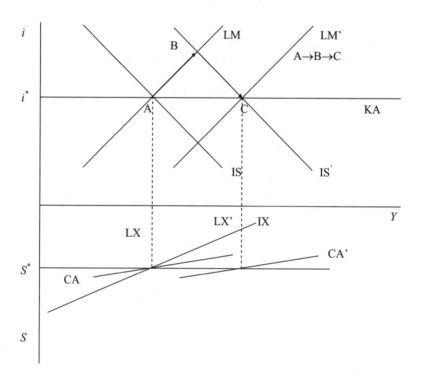

**Figure 6.4.** Fiscal expansion – PCM and fixed exchange rates

Figure 6.4 presents the case of fiscal expansion under PCM with fixed exchange rates. A fiscal expansion shifts the IS curve to the right, from IS to IS' in the i-Y plane. Correspondingly, the IX curve in the S-Y plane moves from IX to IX' (not shown as it has no role in determining the exchange rate). The domestic interest rate is higher that that in the rest of the world at point B, inducing capital inflow into the country. As the CA curve has to cross the line S=S*, the degree of deterioration in the current is less than that with the flexible exchange rate, suggesting that private capital inflow is greater than the increase in net deficit in the current account (decrease in surplus). Consequently, money in circulation increases, shifting the LM curve to LM'. A new equilibrium attains at point C at a higher income level when the domestic interest rate equals that in the rest of the world.

The process of adjustment is described by changes in the values of the variables as follows:

(1).    Fiscal expansion: the IS curve in the i-Y plane shifts from $\beta Y + \lambda i = G + \delta S$ to $\beta Y + \lambda i = G + \Delta G + \delta S$.

(2).    Capital inflow: $\Delta K = k, k > 0$ ($\kappa = \infty$, $\Delta i = +0.$).
The IX curve in the S-Y plane shifts from IX ($\beta Y - \delta S = G - \lambda i^*$) through $IX^T$ ($\beta Y - \delta S = G + \Delta G - \lambda i$, not depicted) to IX' ($\beta Y - \delta S = G + \Delta G - \lambda i^*$).
The LX curve in the S-Y plane shifts through $LX^T$ (not depicted) to LX'.

(3).    Current account deterioration: the CA curve shifts from CA ($\theta Y - \eta S = K$) to CA' [$\theta(Y - \Delta Y) - \eta S = K$, or $\theta Y - \eta S = K + \theta \Delta Y$, as the curve shifts rightwards by $\Delta Y$).
New equilibrium in the S-Y plane attains, with deteriorated external balance conditions which are less serious than the flexible exchange rate arrangement.

(4).    Wealth effect: Decrease in official reserves and increase in money in circulation. The LM curve in the i-Y plane shifts from LM ($\gamma Y - \varphi i = \dfrac{M}{P}$) to LM' ($\gamma Y - \varphi i = \dfrac{M - \Delta OR}{P}$, OR-official reserves). New equilibrium in the i-Y plane attains, with a higher level of income.

We can work out the change of value in these relevant variables. At the new equilibrium point C the interest rate is the same as before and the exchange rate is fixed, so $\beta \Delta Y = \Delta G$, i.e., changes in income are:

$$\Delta Y = \frac{\Delta G}{\beta}.$$

The current account has deteriorated by the amount of $\theta \Delta Y$, i.e.:

$$\Delta CA = -\frac{\theta \Delta G}{\beta}.$$

Comparing the LM and LM' curves, we get $\gamma \Delta Y = \frac{-\Delta OR}{P}$, i.e., changes in official reserves are:

$$\Delta OR = \frac{-\gamma P \Delta G}{\beta}$$

The balance of payments identity dictates that changes in the private capital account (k), in the current account $(\Delta CA = -\frac{\theta \Delta G}{\beta})$ and official reserves $(\Delta OR = \frac{-\gamma P \Delta G}{\beta})$ sum to zero. So net increase in the private capital account surplus is:

$$k = \frac{1}{\beta}(\theta + \gamma P)\Delta G$$

It is concluded that that a fiscal expansion of the amount $\Delta G$ in the case of a small open economy or perfect capital mobility under a fixed exchange rate regime has the effects of:

- Increase in income by $\Delta Y = \frac{\Delta G}{\beta}$.

- Deterioration in the current account to the extent of $\frac{\theta \Delta G}{\beta}$.

- Decrease of official reserves by $\Delta OR = \frac{-\gamma P \Delta G}{\beta}$.

- Capital inflow of amount $k = \frac{1}{\beta}(\theta + \gamma P)\Delta G$.

## 6.2    Effects and Effectiveness of Monetary Policy and Fiscal Policy - *Imperfect Capital Mobility*

Under imperfect capital mobility (ICM), the domestic interest rate, after enduring a shock such as a monetary/fiscal expansion/contraction, may not return to its original level eventually. Also, the original level of the interest rate may or may not be the interest rate in the rest of the world. Nevertheless, while working with the general setting of imperfect capital mobility in this section, we also present the extreme cases of complete immobility of capital, as well as those of perfect mobility of capital - as special instances.

### 6.2.1 Monetary Expansion - Imperfect Capital Mobility, Flexible Exchange Rates

Having discussed monetary expansions under perfect capital mobility, it is straightforward to modify the model to accommodate matters arising from imperfect capital mobility – a more realistic assumption about capital movement across borders, sometimes referred to as non-small open economies (Non-SOE). ICM is reflected by an up-sloping KA curve in the i-Y plane. So to counterbalance deterioration (improvement) in the current account position due to an increase (decrease) in income, the domestic interest rate must increase (decrease) to improve (reduce) the capital account balance. The equation for the KA curve $\theta Y - \kappa(i - i^o) = \eta S$ means the relationship between income and the interest rate or the capital account balance at a given level of the exchange rate, as the exchange rate is exogenous in the i-Y plane. Likewise, the interest rate or the capital account balance is exogenous to the CA equation $\theta Y - \eta S = \kappa(i - i^o)$ which explains the relationship between income and the exchange rate at a given amount of the capital account balance in the S-Y space. Moreover, whenever a policy change brings about an increase in the domestic interest rate, the interest rate may or may not eventually return to its original level in the pre-policy change equilibrium – it will stop at the point where the new LM or IS curve crosses the new KA curve, depending on the degree of imperfect mobility of capital. Vice versa is a fall in the interest rate caused by a policy change. Figure 6.5(a) shows a case of less immobile capital, so that the change in the (private) capital account position is modest and is mostly offset by an opposite change in the current account. While in Figure 6.5(b), the degree of capital immobility is higher and the change in the private capital account is not offset by the change in the current account to a large extent. Consequently, changes in official reserves to varied degrees are inevitable, bearing some similarity with fixed exchange rate regimes even if the policy works in a framework of flexible exchange rates. The initial domestic interest rate is $i^o$ which may or may not be equal to the interest rate in the rest of the world.

We analyse Figure 6.5(a) to see the similarities with the case in 6.1.1, except $\kappa \neq \infty$ in the KA equation $\theta Y - \kappa(i - i^*) = \eta S$ and the world rate of interest $i^*$ is replaced by $i^o$. As the slope of the KA curve is not zero, we are able to quantify the shift of the curve as well the change in capital account positions. Comparing the KA curve and the KA' curve, we recognise the curve has shifted rightwards by $\Delta Y$ and that the capital account has deteriorated by $\theta \Delta Y - \eta \Delta S$. From the analysis in 6.1.1 the current account is known to have improved by $\eta \Delta S - \theta \Delta Y = \left( \dfrac{\eta \beta}{\delta} - \theta \right) \Delta Y$. These are the same as in 6.1.1. The difference is that a shift of a horizontal KA curve in 6.1.1. cannot be observed while in this section we clearly view the shift from KA to KA'.

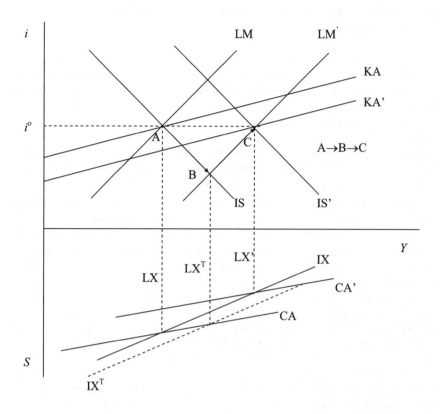

**Figure 6.5(a).** Monetary expansion – ICM and flexible exchange rates

Then in Figure 6.5(b) the domestic interest rate does not return to its original value fully. So the increase in income and the improvement in the current (deterioration in the capital account) are all smaller that those in Figure 6.5(a) or in the perfect capital mobility case. To an extreme extent, if capital is completely immobile the KA curves would be vertical, one (KA) across point A and the other (KA') across point B. The IX curve in the S-Y plane moves $IX^T$ permanently and the CA curve nerve moves its position. Point B would be the new equilibrium, just as in a closed economy. There is no deterioration in the capital account as capital cannot flows out from the country nor flows into the country. There is no improvement in the current account position either, though the currency depreciates which exactly offset the effect of increased income on the current account position, leading to a decrease of amount $\left( \dfrac{\eta\beta}{\delta} - \theta \right)\Delta Y$ in official reserves. Compared with the case in 6.1.1, other things being equal, ICM means there is deterrent to capital outflow and the amount of capital outflow caused by a reduced domestic interest rate is smaller.

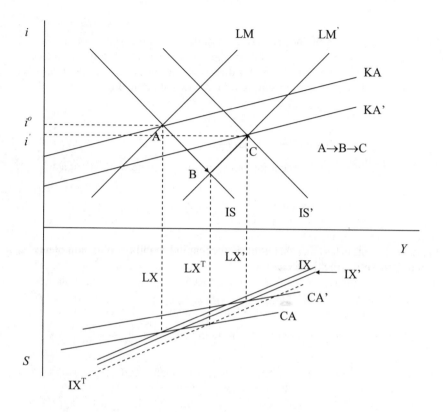

**Figure 6.5(b).** Monetary expansion – ICM and flexible exchange rates
(higher degree of capital immobility)

Inspecting Figure 6.5(b), the capital account position has deteriorated by $\theta \Delta Y - \kappa \Delta i$ where $\Delta i = i' - i^\circ < 0$; changes in the IX curves suggests the depreciation of the currency is $\Delta S = \frac{\beta}{\delta} \Delta Y + \lambda \Delta i$, less than that in perfect capital mobility. A reduced domestic interest rate does not mean that the rate is lower in the country than the rest of the world. In a large country case, a reduced domestic rate can lower the rates elsewhere in the world. In the following, we present changes in the relevant variables in terms of the monetary expansion $\Delta M$ and the imperfect capital mobility $\Delta i \neq 0$. The increase in income can be inferred from the new LM' curve:

$$\Delta Y = \frac{\Delta M}{\gamma P} + \frac{\varphi}{\gamma} \Delta i \,.$$

It is lower than that in the perfect capital mobility case. But if the country is large enough, as the interest rate may fall in the rest of the world, there could be increase in income in the rest of the world as well. In the extreme case of complete capital immobility, new equilibrium is settled down at point B with:

$$\Delta Y = \frac{\lambda \Delta M}{P(\varphi \beta + \lambda \gamma)}$$

From the IX curves, the depreciation in the currency can be worked out as:

$$\Delta S = \frac{\beta \Delta M}{\delta \gamma P} + \left( \frac{\beta \varphi}{\delta \gamma} + \frac{\lambda}{\delta} \right) \Delta i \,.$$

The depreciation is less that that with perfect capital mobility. With complete capital immobility, the depreciation is:

$$\Delta S = \frac{\theta}{\eta} \Delta Y = \frac{\theta \lambda \Delta M}{\eta P(\varphi \beta + \lambda \gamma)}$$

From the CA equations, the improvement in the current account is:

$$\eta \Delta S - \theta \Delta Y = \frac{(\eta \beta - \delta \theta) \Delta M}{\delta \gamma P} + \left( \frac{\eta \beta \varphi}{\delta \gamma} + \frac{\eta \lambda}{\delta} - \frac{\theta \varphi}{\lambda} \right) \Delta i$$

It is also less than that in the perfect capital mobility case, and becomes zero with complete capital immobility. This figure is also the extent to which the capital account has deteriorated.

From the above analysis, it can be concluded that a monetary expansion of the amount $\Delta M$ in the case of imperfect capital mobility with a flexible exchange rate has the effects on the domestic economy:

- Increase in income by $\Delta Y = \frac{\Delta M}{\gamma P} + \frac{\varphi}{\gamma} \Delta i$ (complete mobility: $\Delta Y = \frac{\Delta M}{\gamma P}$, complete immobility: $\Delta Y = \frac{\lambda \Delta M}{P(\varphi \beta + \lambda \gamma)}$ ).

- Depreciation of the domestic currency by $\Delta S = \dfrac{\beta \Delta M}{\delta \gamma P} + \left( \dfrac{\beta \varphi}{\delta \gamma} + \dfrac{\lambda}{\delta} \right) \Delta i$ (com-

  plete     mobility:     $\Delta S = \dfrac{\beta}{\delta \gamma P} \Delta M$ ,     complete     immobility:

  $\Delta S = \dfrac{\theta}{\eta} \Delta Y = \dfrac{\theta \lambda \Delta M}{\eta P (\varphi \beta + \lambda \gamma)}$ ).

- Improvement   in   the   current   account   to   the   extent   of

  $\eta \Delta S - \theta \Delta Y = \dfrac{(\eta \beta - \delta \theta) \Delta M}{\delta \gamma P} + \left( \dfrac{\eta \beta \varphi}{\delta \gamma} + \dfrac{\eta \lambda}{\delta} - \dfrac{\theta \varphi}{\lambda} \right) \Delta i$   (complete   mobility:

  $\dfrac{1}{\gamma P} \left( \dfrac{\eta \beta}{\delta} - \theta \right) \Delta M$ , complete immobility: 0).

- Deterioration in the capital account by $\dfrac{(\eta \beta - \delta \theta) \Delta M}{\delta \gamma P} + \left( \dfrac{\eta \beta \varphi}{\delta \gamma} + \dfrac{\eta \lambda}{\delta} - \dfrac{\theta \varphi}{\lambda} \right) \Delta i$

  (complete mobility: $\dfrac{1}{\gamma P} \left( \dfrac{\eta \beta}{\delta} - \theta \right) \Delta M$ , complete immobility: 0).

## 6.2.2 Fiscal Expansion - Imperfect Capital Mobility, Flexible Exchange Rates

Under ICM, a fiscal expansion causes deterioration in the current to a lesser degree than that under perfect capital mobility. As a result, it has some effect on income, to compare with that under perfect capital mobility where the wealth effect is completely annulled by the deterioration in the current account. We can observe from Figure 6.6 that the IS curve in the i-Y plane shifts to $\mathrm{IS}^T$ to the scale of the fiscal expansion, then it is pulled back to settle down at IS'. In the S-Y plane, the joint effect of increased government spending and the changing domestic interest rate shifts the IX curve through $\mathrm{IX}^T$ to IX'. Correspondingly, the LX curve moves to LX' through $\mathrm{LX}^T$. The decrease in S (appreciation of the domestic currency) or the worsening in trade balance offsets the effect of increased government spending G to a certain degree, pulling the IS curve back which settles eventually down at IS'. Equilibrium is reached in the i-Y plane at point C, with an improved capital account. In the S-Y plane, the current account has deteriorated but the degree of deterioration is lesser than that in the perfect capital mobility case. Changes in the values of the variables in the relevant equations are as follows. The amount of temporary increase in income can be obtained from comparing the cross points of LM with IS and LM with $\mathrm{IS}^T$, yielding:

$$\Delta Y^T = \dfrac{\varphi \Delta G}{\beta \varphi + \lambda \gamma} \ .$$

Clearly it is the amount of permanent increase in income when capital is completely immobile. The general solution of permanent increase in income is indeed a function of the degree of capital immobility $\Delta i = i - i^o$. Comparing points A and C on the LM curve, we get:

$$\Delta Y = \frac{\varphi}{\gamma}\Delta i \cdot$$

When capital is perfect mobile, the change in income is zero as in 6.1.2.

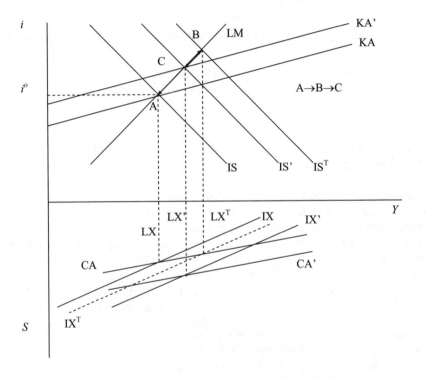

**Figure 6.6.** Fiscal expansion – ICM and flexible exchange rates

From the IX equations, appreciation in the currency is:

$$\Delta S = \frac{\beta \Delta Y - \Delta G + \lambda \Delta i}{\delta} \cdot$$
$$= \frac{(\beta \varphi + \lambda \gamma)\Delta i}{\delta \gamma} - \frac{\Delta G}{\delta}$$

It is less than that with perfect capital mobility. Under complete capital immobility, appreciation is zero. The deterioration in the current account is:

$$\eta \Delta S - \theta \Delta Y = \frac{[\eta(\beta\varphi + \lambda\gamma) - \theta\varphi\delta]\Delta i}{\delta\gamma} - \frac{\eta \Delta G}{\delta}.$$

The capital account position improves by this amount as well. With complete capital immobility, the deterioration in the current account is:

$$-\theta \Delta Y = -\frac{\theta\varphi\Delta G}{\beta\varphi + \lambda\gamma}$$

To conclude, a fiscal expansion of the amount $\Delta G$ in the case of imperfect capital mobility under a flexible exchange rate regime results in:

- Temporary increase in income $\Delta Y^{T} = \dfrac{\varphi\Delta G}{\beta\varphi + \lambda\gamma}$ ; permanent increase in income $\Delta Y = \dfrac{\varphi}{\gamma}\Delta i$ (complete mobility: $\Delta Y = 0$, complete immobility: $\Delta Y = \dfrac{\varphi\Delta G}{\beta\varphi + \lambda\gamma}$ ).

- Appreciation of the domestic currency to the extent of $\Delta S = \dfrac{(\beta\varphi + \lambda\gamma)\Delta i}{\delta\gamma} - \dfrac{\Delta G}{\delta}$ (complete mobility: $\Delta S = -\dfrac{\Delta G}{\delta}$, complete immobility: $\Delta S = 0$ ).

- Deterioration in the current account by $\eta \Delta S - \theta \Delta Y = \dfrac{[\eta(\beta\varphi + \lambda\gamma) - \theta\varphi\delta]\Delta i}{\delta\gamma} - \dfrac{\eta \Delta G}{\delta}$ (complete mobility: $-\dfrac{\eta \Delta G}{\delta}$, complete immobility: $-\dfrac{\theta\varphi\Delta G}{\beta\varphi + \lambda\gamma}$ ).

- Improvement in the capital account by $\dfrac{[\eta(\beta\varphi + \lambda\gamma) - \theta\varphi\delta]\Delta i}{\delta\gamma} - \dfrac{\eta \Delta G}{\delta}$ (complete mobility: $-\dfrac{\eta \Delta G}{\delta}$, complete immobility: $-\dfrac{\theta\varphi\Delta G}{\beta\varphi + \lambda\gamma}$ ).

### 6.2.3 Monetary Expansion - Imperfect Capital Mobility, Fixed Exchange Rates

A monetary expansion under perfect capital mobility and fixed exchange rates has no long run effects on income and trade balance. However, the expansion does cause capital outflow and changes in official reserves. When capital is not perfectly mobile, a monetary expansion brings about an increase in income and, consequently, deterioration in the current account since the exchange rate is fixed, as illustrated in Figure 6.7. The temporary increase in income and temporary deterioration in the current account has been derived in 6.1.3, so we look at the permanent effects left by a monetary expansion. We know from 6.1.3 that there are changes in official reserves, so change in income is:

$$\Delta Y = \frac{\lambda(\Delta M - \Delta OR)}{P(\beta\varphi + \lambda\gamma)}.$$

As the exchange rate is fixed, deterioration in the current account is due to the increase in income only:

$$-\theta\Delta Y = -\frac{\theta\lambda(\Delta M - \Delta OR)}{P(\beta\varphi + \lambda\gamma)}.$$

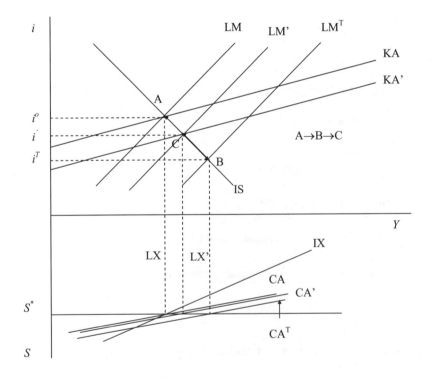

**Figure 6.7.** Monetary expansion – ICM and fixed exchange rates

The position of the KA' curve is derived as if the exchange rate were flexible, and there were improvement in the current to offset the deterioration in the capital account. The deterioration in the capital account is a function of capital mobility. If capital is perfectly mobile, the $LM^T$ curve will return to its original position, incurring the largest capital outflow measured by $\kappa(i^T - i^\circ)$. When capital is not perfectly mobile, the $LM^T$ curve will stay in the between at LM', the less mobile, the closer to $LM^T$ is the LM'. So, capital outflow is $\kappa(i^T - i')$ in general.

From the balance of payments identity we know that changes in the current account ($-\theta\Delta Y = -\dfrac{\theta\lambda(\Delta M - \Delta OR)}{P(\beta\varphi + \lambda\gamma)}$), the private capital account $[\kappa(i^T - i')]$ and official reserves ($\Delta OR$) sum to zero. So, change in official reserves is solved as:

$$\Delta OR = \frac{\theta\lambda\Delta M}{P(\beta\varphi + \lambda\gamma) + \theta\lambda} - \frac{P(\beta\varphi + \lambda\gamma)\kappa(i^T - i')}{P(\beta\varphi + \lambda\gamma) + \theta\lambda}.$$

When capital is perfectly mobile, $\Delta OR = -\Delta M$, so $\kappa(i^T - i') = \kappa(i^T - i^\circ) = -\Delta M$. That is, monetary expansion is completely offset by the change in official reserves, which in turn offsets the capital outflow (no change in the current account). When capital is completely immobile, the LM curve will stay at position $LM^T$, change in official reserves is to offset the deterioration in the current account (no change in the private capital account).

It can be concluded that a monetary expansion of the amount $\Delta M$ with ICM under a fixed exchange rate regime has the following effects:

- Temporary increase in income by $\Delta Y^T = \dfrac{\lambda\Delta M}{P(\beta\varphi + \lambda\gamma)}$, which gradually transits to $\Delta Y = \dfrac{\lambda(\Delta M - \Delta OR)}{P(\beta\varphi + \lambda\gamma)}$ upon changes in official reserves set off (complete mobility: 0, complete immobility: $\Delta Y = \dfrac{\lambda\Delta M}{P(\beta\varphi + \lambda\gamma) + \theta\lambda}$).

- Increase in official reserves by the amount of $\Delta OR = \dfrac{\theta\lambda\Delta M}{P(\beta\varphi + \lambda\gamma) + \theta\lambda} - \dfrac{P(\beta\varphi + \lambda\gamma)\kappa(i^T - i')}{P(\beta\varphi + \lambda\gamma) + \theta\lambda}$ (complete mobility: $\Delta M$, complete immobility: $\dfrac{\theta\lambda\Delta M}{P(\beta\varphi + \lambda\gamma) + \theta\lambda}$).

- Capital outflow of $\kappa(i^T - i')$ (complete mobile: $\kappa(i^T - i^\circ)$, complete immobility: 0).

- Temporary deterioration in the current account to the extent of $-\dfrac{\lambda\theta\Delta M}{P(\beta\varphi+\lambda\gamma)}$ which gradually transits to $-\dfrac{\theta\lambda(\Delta M-\Delta OR)}{P(\beta\varphi+\lambda\gamma)}$ upon changes in official reserves set off (complete mobility: 0, complete immobility: $-\dfrac{\theta\lambda\Delta M}{P(\beta\varphi+\lambda\gamma)+\theta\lambda}$ ).

## 6.2.4 Fiscal Expansion - Imperfect Capital Mobility, Fixed Exchange Rates

We draw two pictures for this case of a fiscal expansion under a fixed exchange rate regime with ICM. In one the new KA' curve moves upwards (Figure 6.8(a)) and the other the new KA' curve moves downwards (Figure 6.8(b)). Depending on the degree of capital immobility, the KA' curve can cross point B (C overlaps B, complete immobility), overlap with the KA curve, or further down until the interest rate returns to its original level (complete mobility).

A fiscal expansion shifts the IS curve to the right, from IS to IS' in the i-Y plane. As with 6.1.4, the shift of the LM curve is due to changes in official reserves, not a direct monetary expansion. From the IS' curve, it can be worked out that:

$$\Delta Y = \frac{\Delta G - \lambda\Delta i}{\beta}.$$

At this level of income and through the LM' curve, changes in official reserves are obtained as $\Delta OR = -P(\gamma\Delta Y - \varphi\Delta i)$, or:

$$\Delta OR = -P\left(\frac{\gamma}{\beta}\Delta G - \frac{\lambda\gamma + \beta\varphi}{\beta}\Delta i\right)$$

The current account has deteriorated by the amount of $\theta\Delta Y$, i.e.:

$$\Delta CA = -\theta\frac{\Delta G - \lambda\Delta i}{\beta}.$$

When capital is completely immobile, increase in income can be solved from the cross-point of the IS' curve and the LM curve.

$$\Delta Y = \frac{\varphi\Delta G}{\beta\varphi + \lambda\gamma}.$$

The corresponding deterioration in the current account is:

$$\Delta CA = -\frac{\theta \varphi \Delta G}{\beta \varphi + \lambda \gamma},$$

and changes in official reserves are zero since the LM curve does not move.

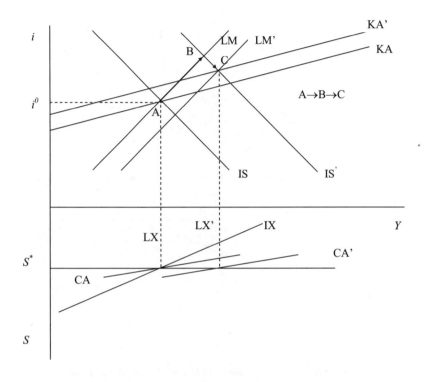

**Figure 6.8(a).** Fiscal expansion – ICM and fixed exchange rates
(Upwards movement of KA curve)

When capital is perfectly mobile, change in income is:

$$\Delta Y = \frac{\Delta G}{\beta}.$$

Working through the KA' curve, changes in official reserves are $\Delta OR = -P\gamma \Delta Y$, or:

$$\Delta OR = -\frac{P\gamma \Delta G}{\beta}.$$

The corresponding deterioration in the current account is:

$$\Delta CA = -\frac{\theta \Delta G}{\beta}.$$

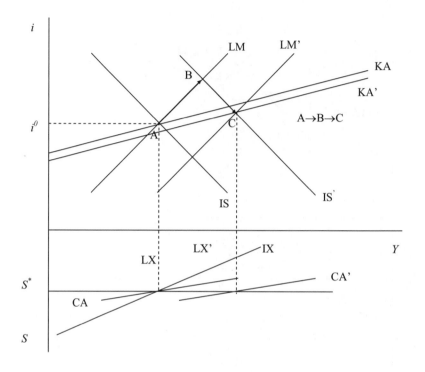

**Figure 6.8(b).** Fiscal expansion – ICM and fixed exchange rates
(Downwards movement of KA curve)

The balance of payments identity dictates that changes in the private capital account (k), in the current account ($\Delta CA = -\theta \dfrac{\Delta G - \lambda \Delta i}{\beta}$) and official reserves ($\Delta OR = -P\left(\dfrac{\gamma}{\beta} \Delta G - \dfrac{\lambda \gamma + \beta \varphi}{\beta} \Delta i\right)$) sum to zero. So net increase in the private capital account surplus is:

$$k = \frac{(\gamma P + \theta)}{\beta} \Delta G - \frac{\lambda(\gamma + \theta) + \beta \varphi}{\beta} \Delta i$$

It is zero with complete capital immobility, and:

$$k = \frac{(\gamma P + \theta)}{\beta} \Delta G$$

when capital is perfectly mobile.

It is concluded that that a fiscal expansion of the amount $\Delta G$ in the case of imperfect capital mobility under a fixed exchange rate regime has the effects of:

- Increase in income by $\Delta Y = \frac{\Delta G - \lambda \Delta i}{\beta}$ (complete mobility: $\Delta Y = \frac{\Delta G}{\beta}$,

  complete immobility: $\Delta Y = \frac{\varphi \Delta G}{\beta \varphi + \lambda \gamma}$ ).

- Deterioration in the current account to the extent of $-\theta \frac{\Delta G - \lambda \Delta i}{\beta}$ (com-

  plete mobility: $-\frac{\theta \Delta G}{\beta}$ , complete immobility: $-\frac{\theta \varphi \Delta G}{\beta \varphi + \lambda \gamma}$ ).

- Decrease of official reserves by $\Delta OR = -P\left( \frac{\gamma}{\beta} \Delta G - \frac{\lambda \gamma + \beta \varphi}{\beta} \Delta i \right)$ (com-

  plete mobility: $\Delta OR = \frac{-\gamma P \Delta G}{\beta}$ , complete immobility: 0).

- Capital inflow of amount $k = \frac{(\gamma P + \theta)}{\beta} \Delta G - \frac{\lambda (\gamma + \theta) + \beta \varphi}{\beta} \Delta i$ (complete

  mobility: $k = \frac{1}{\beta}(\theta + \gamma P) \Delta G$, complete immobility: 0).

## 6.3 Monetary Policy Versus Fiscal Policy

It has been observed in the previous sections that monetary policy and fiscal policy have varied degrees of effect on national income, the current account balance, cross border capital flows and official reserves, depending on the exchange rate regime the countries adopt and capital mobility between them. This section summarises the conclusions reached at earlier with commentary remarks.

### 6.3.1 Effect on Income

#### *Flexible Exchange Rates*

With a flexible exchange rate regime, a monetary expansion has the effect on income to a substantial extent – greater than that in a closed economy. It is because the monetary expansion not only has the effect on income due to a shift of the LM curve which happens to a closed economy, but also through the consequent shift of the IS curve to the right induced by the depreciated currency. On the contrary, a fiscal expansion has none or little effect on income because the initial effect due to the fiscal expansion is completely offset by the appreciated currency if capital is perfectly mobile, or is offset to a certain extent depending on the degree of capital mobility. Fiscal policy achieves the greatest effect on income when capital is completely immobile, that is equivalent to a closed economy, implying that its effect is always lesser than that in a closed economy. Whereas a monetary expansion achieves the least effect when capital is completely immobile, implying that its effect is always greater than that in a closed economy. Figure 6.9 illustrates the effect of monetary policy and fiscal policy as a function of capital mobility under flexible exchange rate regimes.

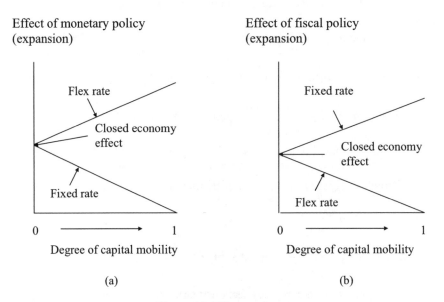

**Figure 6.9.** Effects on income

### Fixed Exchange Rates

When exchange rates are fixed, the results of monetary policy and fiscal policy are opposite to those in a flexible exchange rate regime. That is, the effect on income due to a monetary expansion is offset by changes in official reserves caused by changes in the external sector - the balance of payments, to varied degrees. Whereas the effect of a fiscal expansion is reinforced by changes in official reserves and the effect is greater than that in a closed economy, i.e., the rightwards shift of the IS curve is followed by a consequential rightwards shift of the LM curve. A monetary expansion achieves the greatest effect on income when capital is completely immobile and no effect when capital is perfectly mobile. On the contrary, the effect of fiscal policy is the least when capital is completely immobile, which increases with the degree of capital mobility. Figure 6.9 also demonstrates the effect of monetary policy and fiscal policy as a function of capital mobility under fixed exchange rate regimes.

### 6.3.2 Effects on the Exchange Rate and Official Reserves

#### Exchange Rates

A monetary expansion leads to depreciation of the currency while a fiscal expansion results in appreciation of the currency. This explains the opposite effects on the balance of payments current account of monetary policy and fiscal policy, though their effects on income are in the same direction but to varied degrees. Monetary policy is preferred in expansion as it raises income and promotes the trade balance at the same time. Fiscal policy is preferred in contraction since it improves the trade balance.

#### Official Reserves

Under flexible exchange rate regime, current account balance changes are completely offset by the same amount but opposite sign changes in the capital account. Under the fixed exchange rate regime official reserves have to respond to unsettled balance in the current account and private capital account, which results in changes in money supply and the shift of the LM curve. This has wealth implications absent in a closed economy and balance of payments implications unobserved under the flexible exchange rate regime.

### 6.3.3 Effect on the Balance of Payments Current Account

Monetary policy works effectively with the flexible exchange rate regime to improve the current account position at the same time of raising income, but it has very little and unfavourable impact on the balance of payments current account under the fixed exchange rate regime. Whereas a fiscal expansion always deteriorates the current account position whether under a flexible or fixed exchange rate regime, implying that an improvement in the current account balance can only be achieved by a sacrifice in income. The effects are illustrated in Figure 6.10(a) and Figure 6.10(b). From the parameter condition $\frac{\eta}{\delta} > \frac{\theta}{\beta}$ we know that the deterioration is greater under the flexible exchange rate arrangement than that under the fixed exchange rate regime, so the curve for the flexible rate in below the curve for the fixed rate in Figure 6.10(a).

Effect of monetary policy
(expansion)

Effect of fiscal policy
(expansion)

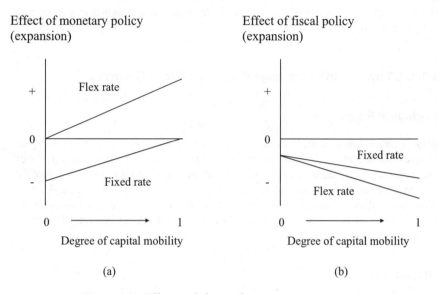

(a)

(b)

**Figure 6.10.** Effects on balance of payments current account

# 7 The Flexible Price Monetary Model

In contrast to the Mundell-Fleming model, the flexible price monetary model proposed by Frenkel (1976), as suggested by the name, works with the assumption that all prices are flexible. This means that the aggregate supply curve is vertical, and a shift in aggregate demand has no whatsoever effect on output. The level of output cannot be easily adjusted either up or down as it is mainly determined by supply side factors. Only a shift in aggregate supply can result in changes in output. Therefore, the IS part of IS–LM analysis is irrelevant here. The model assumes that PPP holds continuously, so does the IFE or UIRP. It further assumes that money supply and real income are exogenously determined. In the following, we simply call the model the monetary model in short when there is no confusion. The other version of the monetary models, the sticky price monetary model by Dornbusch to be introduced in the next chapter, will be simply termed as the Dornbusch model.

This chapter begins with workings on demand for money in a framework similar to the LM part of IS–LM analysis. Then demand for money functions in two relevant countries are jointly analysed and linked through PPP, leading to the derivation of the monetary model for the determination the foreign exchange rate between the two currencies, involving relative real income, demand for money, and interest rate levels in the two countries. Incorporating the IFE, the model takes another form with an inflation dimension in the model. Effects of various shocks on the foreign exchange rate are evaluated through applying the monetary model.

Next the chapter examines the roles of the fundamentals and expectations in foreign exchange rate determination. The relationship between the fundamentals and the foreign exchange rate is illustrated and rational bubbles and testing for rational bubbles are discussed, within the framework of the monetary model, revealing important implications for foreign exchange market activity and operations.

## 7.1 Demand for Money in Two Countries and Foreign Exchange Rate Determination

As learned in Chapter 5, demand for money is a function of real income, the interest rate and the price level. More precisely, the velocity of money, defined as the ratio of demand for money and the price level, is an increasing function of the level of real income and a decreasing function of the level of the interest rate. Reserving these qualitative features, the relationship between these variables in the domestic country can be expressed as follows:

$$\frac{M_t^D}{P_t} = \frac{Y_t^\alpha}{(1+r_t)^\beta}$$    (7.1)

where $M_t^D$ is demand for money, $P_t$ is the price level, $Y_t$ is real income and $r_t$ is the interest rate, all at time $t$, for the domestic country; $\alpha > 0$ and $\beta > 0$ are coefficients representing the income elasticity of money demand, and the interest rate semi-elasticity of money demand. Taking logarithms of equation (7.1) yields:

$$m_t^d - p_t = \alpha y_t - \beta r_t$$    (7.2)

where $m_t^d = Ln(M_t^D)$, $p_t = Ln(P_t)$, and $y_t = Ln(Y_t)$. The only differences between equation (5.8) and equation (7.2) are that demand for money, real income and the price level are in their original forms in the former, while they are in logarithms in the latter. Nevertheless, both equation (5.8) and equation (7.2) point out that the velocity of money increases with real income and decreases with the interest rate.

Similarly, demand for money in the foreign country is:

$$\frac{M_t^{D*}}{P_t^*} = \frac{Y_t^{*\alpha}}{(1+r_t^*)^\beta}$$    (7.3)

and in logarithms:

$$m_t^{d*} - p_t^* = \alpha y_t^* - \beta r_t^*$$    (7.4)

where * denotes the foreign country, $M_t^{D*}$ is demand for money, $P_t^*$ is the price level, $Y_t^*$ is real income and $r_t^*$ is the interest rate, all at time $t$, for the foreign country; $m_t^{d*} = Ln(M_t^{D*})$, $p_t^* = Ln(P_t^*)$, and $y_t^* = Ln(Y_t^*)$. $\alpha$ and $\beta$ are assumed to be equalised across countries, i.e., the effect of a unit increase or decrease in real income and/or the interest rate on the velocity of money is the same in the domestic country and in the foreign country.

Money demand equals money supply in the domestic country and the foreign country respectively, when the money market is in equilibrium in the two countries:

$$m_t^d = m_t^s = m_t$$    (7.5)
$$m_t^{d*} = m_t^{s*} = m_t^*$$    (7.6)

So, we may use either money demand or money supply or simply money in the above equations. It is further assumed that money supply and real income in each country are exogenously determined. Equation (7.2) and equation (7.4) suggest that the price level is a function of demand for money, real income and the interest rate with the following relationships:

$$p_t = m_t - \alpha y_t + \beta r_t \qquad (7.7)$$
$$p_t^* = m_t^* - \alpha y_t^* + \beta r_t^* \qquad (7.8)$$

Combining equation (7.7) and equation (7.8) yields the relative price of the domestic country and the foreign country:

$$p_t - p_t^* = \left(m_t - m_t^*\right) - \alpha\left(y_t - y_t^*\right) + \beta\left(r_t - r_t^*\right) \qquad (7.9)$$

According to relative PPP, equation (7.9) is the logarithm of the foreign exchange rate:

$$s_t = \left(m_t - m_t^*\right) - \alpha\left(y_t - y_t^*\right) + \beta\left(r_t - r_t^*\right) \qquad (7.10)$$

From the IFE we know that:

$$r_t - r_t^* = E_t(\pi_{t+1}) - E_t(\pi_{t+1}^*) \qquad (7.11)$$

where $\pi_t = \Delta p_t$ and $\pi_t^* = \Delta p_t^*$ are the domestic inflation rate and the foreign inflation rate respectively. Substituting equation (7.11) into equation (7.10), another version of the monetary model is derived:

$$s_t = \left(m_t - m_t^*\right) - \alpha\left(y_t - y_t^*\right) + \beta\left[E_t(\Delta p_{t+1}) - E_t(\Delta p_{t+1}^*)\right] \qquad (7.12)$$

$s_t$, $r_t$, and $\Delta p_t$ or $p_t$ are endogenous variables and $m_t$, $m_t^*$, $y_t$, $y_t^*$, $r_t^*$, and $\Delta p_t^*$ or $p_t^*$ are exogenous variables from the domestic country's perspective. Alternatively, the interest rate differential in equation (7.10) can be substituted by the forward premium (originally used by Frenkel (1976)) through applying CIRP:

$$r_t - r_t^* = f_{t,t+1} - s_t \qquad (7.13)$$

and another expression of the monetary model is derived as follows:

$$s_t = \left(m_t - m_t^*\right) - \alpha\left(y_t - y_t^*\right) + \beta\left(f_{t,t+1} - s_t\right) \qquad (7.14)$$

Equation (7.10) and equation (7.12) state that the foreign exchange rate for the two currencies is a function of money supply differentials, real income differentials and interest rate differentials or inflation expectations differentials in the two countries. The foreign exchange rate will adjust to the movements in relative money supplies, relative real income levels, relative interest rate levels or relative inflation expectations in the two countries. Holding other variables constant, if domestic money supply increases faster than foreign money supply in a time period, the foreign exchange rate will increase or the domestic currency will depreciate in that period; if domestic real income increases faster than foreign real income, the foreign exchange rate will fall or the domestic currency will appreciate; if domestic interest rates increase more than foreign interest rates or if domestic interest rates fall less than foreign interest rates, the foreign exchange rate will increase or the domestic currency will depreciate; if inflation expectations are higher in the domestic country than in the foreign country, the foreign exchange rate will increase or the domestic currency will depreciate. The effects of various shocks are analysed as follows.

Domestic money supply shocks. A positive shock to domestic money supply or domestic monetary expansion will cause the price level to rise accordingly since output is fixed in the short term, which increases the foreign exchange rate or depreciate the domestic currency to maintain PPP. Domestic monetary expansions can be a response to an upward shift of the aggregate demand curve, which has only the proportional effect on the price level and no effect on income. The foreign exchange rate, as the ratio of the domestic price level relative to the foreign price level, adjusts accordingly.

Domestic real income shocks. A positive real income shock in the domestic country will lower the domestic price level, the foreign exchange rate will decrease or the domestic currency will appreciate for PPP to uphold. This is valid in the short term as well as in the long run and works for the flexible price as well as fixed price assumptions.

Domestic interest rate shocks. A positive interest rate shock in the domestic country will raise the domestic price level, decrease the foreign exchange rate or depreciate the domestic currency through the mechanism of PPP. Nevertheless, the domestic interest rate is an endogenous variable in the monetary model. So, while changes or expected changes in domestic interest rates can have an effect on the foreign exchange rate, they can be a response to changes or expected changes in the foreign exchange rate as well, though like money supply, they are set by monetary authorities.

Domestic inflation shocks. The foreign exchange rate will increase or the domestic currency will depreciate in response to a positive inflation shock in the domestic country, reflecting the expected purchasing power loss of the domestic currency. A positive inflation shock raises the prospect of an interest rate increase via the IFE. Since the domestic price level or inflation is an endogenous variable, it can cause the foreign exchange rate to change and vice versa, e.g. the depreciation of the domestic currency may bring about a rise in the domestic price level or higher domestic inflation.

Foreign inflation shocks. A foreign inflation shock or change in the foreign price level has the most straightforward effect on the foreign exchange rate through the functioning of PPP, and has no effect whatsoever on all the domestic variables, since this is the one of the most fundamental assumptions of the monetary model and the way in which the model is derived, referring to equation (7.9) and equation (7.10). In particular, inflation will not transmit from the foreign country to the domestic country and vice versa with a pure floating foreign exchange rate arrangement.

In the above, various shocks and effects are discussed separately based on the monetary model. However, upholding the monetary model's assumptions, more than one event may take place at one time, though none is assumed to be the cause of, or the effect on, the other. Under such circumstances, there can be shocks to, or changes in, more than one exogenous variable, e.g., a domestic real income shock and a domestic monetary expansion. If in response to a positive real income shock or a real income increase in the domestic country, the monetary authority decides to increase money supply, the foreign exchange rate may remain unchanged or the domestic currency may depreciate to an extent smaller than what is expected from an isolated monetary expansion with no real income implications. It is not assumed in the case that the increase in real income necessarily leads to an increase in money supply that remains exogenous. Similarly, the real income shock or increase in real income is neither assumed to be caused by the monetary expansion nor assumed to be induced by the aggregate demand shift in the flexible price monetary model, but they do happen independently as exogenous variables.

Originally, money supply and real income are assumed to be exogenously determined in the monetary model. So the model is mainly used to evaluate or assess the impact of changes or movements in various endogenous and exogenous variables, individually or jointly, on the endogenous variables only, i.e., the foreign exchange rate and the domestic interest rate and inflation from the domestic country's point of view, or the foreign exchange rate and the foreign interest rate and inflation from the foreign country's point of view. Nevertheless, some of the assumptions may be relaxed and the model may be modified to deal with various issues under certain circumstances. Bearing these in mind, let us examine several examples in the following through applying the monetary model.

*Example 1*: Suppose real income increases by 1.5% in the domestic country and 2.0% in the foreign country in 2003; the interest rate remain unchanged at 3.25% per annum in the domestic country and is increased from 3.75% to 4.00% in the foreign country; and money supply increases by 2% in the home country and increases by 1% in the foreign country.

a)    Demonstrate the effects of these changes in the relevant variables on the exchange rate in the framework of the monetary model.

b)    Explain the overall effect on the exchange rate due to these changes. Would the domestic currency appreciate or depreciate according to the monetary model, assuming $\alpha=0.5$ and $\beta=0.8$ in the model?

c)    What should be the exchange rate at the end of 2003, assuming the exchange rate was 1.4185 at the end of 2002?

*Solutions:*

a)    With the help of equation (7.10), it is expected that the real income differential alone would cause the foreign exchange rate to increase or the domestic currency to depreciate since real income in the domestic country grows slower than that in the foreign country; the interest rate differential alone would cause the foreign exchange rate to decrease or the domestic currency to appreciate since the interest rate level in the domestic country increases less than the interest rate in the foreign country; in other words, inflation expectations are lower in the domestic country than in the foreign country, applying equation (7.12); the money supply differential alone would cause the foreign exchange rate to increase or the domestic currency to depreciate since money supply grows faster in the domestic country than in the foreign country

b)    Again applying equation (7.10) with modifications and filling in the figures yields:

$$\Delta s_t = \left(\Delta m_t - \Delta m_t^*\right) - \alpha\left(\Delta y_t - \Delta y_t^*\right) + \beta\left(\Delta r_t - \Delta r_t^*\right)$$
$$= (2.00 - 1.00) - 0.5 \times (1.50 - 2.00) + 0.8 \times (0.00 - 0.25)$$
$$= 1.00 + 0.25 - 0.20 = 1.05\% > 0$$

The overall effect would be that the foreign exchange rate increases or the domestic currency depreciates.

c)    Since $\Delta s_t = Ln\left(\dfrac{S_t}{S_{t-1}}\right)$, so $\left(\dfrac{S_t}{S_{t-1}}\right) = Exp(\Delta s_t)$ or $S_t = S_{t-1} Exp(\Delta s_t)$.

Bringing the figures into the formula yields:

$$S_{2003\,end} = S_{2002\,end} Exp(\Delta s_{2003\,end})$$
$$= 1.4185 \times Exp(0.0105) = 1.4335$$

Or, since $\Delta s_t = \dfrac{S_t - S_{t-1}}{S_{t-1}}$, then $S_t = S_{t-1}(1 + \Delta s_t)$. Bringing the figures into the formula yields:

$$S_{2003\,end} = S_{2002\,end}(1 + \Delta s_{2003\,end})$$
$$= 1.4185 \times (1 + 0.0105) = 1.4334$$

(The difference between the results is due to the logarithm approximation.)

So, according to the monetary model, the foreign exchange rate would be 1.4334.

*Example 2*: Since the domestic price level or expected inflation is endogenous, a shock to real income or money demand may have effect on the foreign exchange rate, as well as on the domestic price level or expected inflation, according to the monetary model. Suppose there is a money demand shock in the home country and money supply increases by 1% in the third quarter of 2003, there is no change in foreign money supply, the foreign interest rate remains 2.25%, and the real income differential between the two countries is zero during the period. If the domestic currency depreciates by 1.2% from 4.2397 to 4.3108, what are the market expectations about the domestic inflation relative to that in the foreign country, assuming $\alpha=0.5$ and $\beta=0.8$ in the model?

*Solutions*:

From $\Delta s_t = (\Delta m_t - \Delta m_t^*) - \alpha(\Delta y_t - \Delta y_t^*) + \beta(\Delta r_t - \Delta r_t^*)$ we have:

$$(\Delta r_t - \Delta r_t^*) = \frac{1}{\beta}\left[\Delta s_t - (\Delta m_t - \Delta m_t^*) + \alpha(\Delta y_t - \Delta y_t^*)\right]$$

$$= \frac{1}{0.8}[1.2 - 1.0] = 0.25\%$$

The result suggests that the market expects a domestic interest rate increase of quarter percent point in the period and, working through the IFE, the domestic inflation is expected to be 0.25% higher than the foreign inflation in the period. Since the market has expected an increase in the foreign exchange rate that is larger than that caused by the domestic money supply shock, the domestic interest rate is expected to rise by the extent unexplained by the money supply shock and the domestic inflation is expected to be higher than that in the foreign country by the same extent.

# 7.2 Expectations, Fundamentals, and the Exchange Rate[1]

The last term in equation (7.10) and equation (7.12), $r_t - r_t^*$ or $E_t(\Delta p_{t+1}) - E_t(\Delta p_{t+1}^*)$, is indeed:

---

[1] This section requires knowledge in co-integration. However, the ideas and relationships are explained intuitively, avoiding technical terms.

$$E_t(\Delta s_{t+1}) = E_t(s_{t+1}) - s_t \qquad (7.15)$$

according to UIRP and the IFE, i.e., the expected change in the spot exchange rate during a certain time period is equal to the effective interest rate differential in the same time period between the two countries (UIRP), or is equal to the expected inflation differential in the same time period between the two countries (IFE). Replacing the last term in equation (7.10) or equation (7.12), the exchange rate can be expressed as a forward-looking function with expectations:

$$s_t = (m_t - m_t^*) - \alpha(y_t - y_t^*) + \beta[E_t(s_{t+1}) - s_t] \qquad (7.16)$$

Re-arrangement through bringing all $s_t$ terms to the left hand side of the equation gives rise to:

$$s_t = \frac{(m_t - m_t^*) - \alpha(y_t - y_t^*)}{1 + \beta} + \frac{\beta}{1 + \beta} E_t(s_{t+1}) \qquad (7.17)$$

Define the following term:

$$x_t = (m_t^d - m_t^{d*}) - \alpha(y_t - y_t^*) \qquad (7.18)$$

as the fundamentals, then the foreign exchange rate is determined by two terms: the fundamentals and future exchange rate expectations:

$$s_t = \frac{1}{1 + \beta} x_t + \frac{\beta}{1 + \beta} E_t(s_{t+1}) \qquad (7.19)$$

Solving equation (7.19) forward yields:

$$
\begin{aligned}
s_t &= \frac{1}{1+\beta} x_t + \frac{1}{1+\beta} \times \frac{\beta}{1+\beta} E_t(x_{t+1}) + \left(\frac{\beta}{1+\beta}\right)^2 E_{t+1}(s_{t+2}) \\
&= \frac{1}{1+\beta} x_t + \frac{1}{1+\beta} \times \frac{\beta}{1+\beta} E_t(x_{t+1}) + \frac{1}{1+\beta} \times \left(\frac{\beta}{1+\beta}\right)^2 E_t(x_{t+1}) \\
&\quad + \left(\frac{\beta}{1+\beta}\right)^3 E_{t+2}(s_{t+3}) \\
&= \dots \\
&= \sum_{\tau=0}^{T} \frac{\beta^\tau}{(1+\beta)^{\tau+1}} E_{t+\tau}(x_{t+\tau+1}) + \left(\frac{\beta}{1+\beta}\right)^{T+1} E_T(s_{T+1})
\end{aligned}
\qquad (7.20)
$$

Notice that the last term in equation (7.20) approaches zero when $T \to \infty$, since $\frac{\beta}{1+\beta} < 1$, then the foreign exchange rate is a function of all expected future fundamentals:

$$s_t = \sum_{\tau=0}^{T} \frac{\beta^{\tau}}{(1+\beta)^{\tau+1}} E_{t+\tau}(x_{t+\tau+1}) \qquad (7.21)$$

Further defining $\lambda = \frac{\beta}{1+\beta}$, $1-\lambda = \frac{1}{1+\beta}$, equation (7.21) becomes:

$$s_t = (1-\lambda)\sum_{\tau=0}^{\infty} \lambda^{\tau} E_{t+\tau}(x_{t+\tau+1}) \qquad (7.22)$$

If we treat $\lambda = \frac{\beta}{1+\beta}$ as the effective discount factor, then equation (7.22) suggests that the foreign exchange rate is the sum of all future fundamentals expectations discounted, or the present value of all expected future values of the fundamentals.

Although equation (7.22) reveals what determine the foreign exchange rate clearly in a common economic analytical framework of income–value relations, the future fundamentals, like future income, are not readily observable. Moreover, what matter are not the fundamentals themselves, but people's current and future expectations about all future fundamentals in this forward-looking model. As expectations about future fundamentals, such as growth in money supply or inflation evolution in the two countries, differ among people even in a few quarters time horizon, let alone in the remote future, this forward-looking model has little practical use in determining or predicting foreign exchange rate. Therefore, it is of great practical interest to establish and scrutinise the relationship between the foreign exchange rate in the present period and the fundamentals in the same. Subtracting the present period fundamentals, $x_t$, from both sides of equation (7.22) and making necessary re-arrangement, we obtain:

$$s_t - x_t = (1-\lambda)\sum_{\tau=0}^{\infty} \lambda^{\tau} E_{t+\tau}(x_{t+\tau+1}) - x_t$$

$$= \sum_{\tau=0}^{\infty} \lambda^{\tau} E_{t+\tau}(\Delta x_{t+\tau+1}) \qquad (7.23)$$

Using a similar term by Campbell and Shiller (1987), $s_t - x_t$ is the spread between the foreign exchange rate and the fundamentals. Equation (7.23) indicates that the spread is the sum of expected changes in all future fundamentals discounted, or is the change in the present value of all expected future values of the fundamentals.

Since the right hand side of equation (7.23) is expected changes in the funda-mentals, equation (7.23) implies a long-run relationship or a co-integration rela-tionship in a time series econometrics term, between the foreign exchange rate and the fundamentals, as changes in the fundamentals usually possess the time series characteristics of stationarity. This means that the foreign exchange rate and the fundamentals would move together in the long-run and any departure away from each other in the evolution path would be temporary and be reverted. If, however, the spread is subject to the influence of factors other than expected changes in the fundamentals, the spread may be non-stationary and there may be no long-run co-integration relationship between the foreign exchange rate and the fundamentals. Tests for the forward-looking monetary model as represented by equation (7.22) then amount to testing for co-integration between the foreign exchange rate and the fundamentals or the stationarity of the spread. The next section will introduce the concept of rational bubbles and progress to the test for the forward-looking monetary model.

## 7.3   Rational Bubbles and Tests for the Forward-Looking Monetary Model[2]

A rational bubble is defined as a seemingly existent object that grows at the same discount rate as that for future income or cash flows generated by an asset. The value or the market price of an asset is derived from all the future income or cash flows generated by the asset discounted, i.e., it is the present value of the sum of all future income or cash flows. This relationship is a fundamental relationship be-tween economic income and economic value and must be upheld for the asset value or price to be the true economic value or market value. However, when a bubble grows at the same discount rate as that for income, it will not be easy to discern whether the price of an asset has correctly reflected its true economic value or contains a rational bubble, since the price continues to grow at the right discount rate with or without a rational bubble.

In the case of foreign exchange rate determination, the fundamentals as de-fined by equation (7.16) in a forward looking monetary model are equivalent to "income" or "cash flows" and the foreign exchange rate is equivalent to "value" in an income-value relationship. Let us define a rational bubble $b_t$, satisfying $b_t = \lambda E_t(b_{t+1})$, i.e.:

$$b_{t+1} = \frac{1}{\lambda} b_t + \varepsilon_{t+1}$$

$$\varepsilon_t \sim iid(0, \sigma_\varepsilon^2)$$

(7.24)

---

[2] This section requires knowledge in co-integration and related subjects in econometrics and algebra. The reader who does not have such knowledge can skip this section and go to the next directly without losing much continuity.

When a rational bubble, as defined by equation (7.24), is added to equation (7.22), the foreign exchange rate containing a rational bubble is then the sum of the fundamentals and a rational bubble, which appears to be rational:

$$s_t + b_t = (1-\lambda)\sum_{\tau=0}^{\infty} \lambda^{\tau} E_{t+\tau}(x_{t+\tau+1}) + b_t$$

$$= (1-\lambda)\sum_{\tau=0}^{\infty} \lambda^{\tau} E_{t+\tau}(x_{t+\tau+1}) + \lambda E_t(b_{t+1})$$

(7.25)

since the bubble is discounted in the same way as the fundamentals are. Therefore, it is difficult to detect the existence of a rational bubble. In other words, it is difficult to distinguish the right foreign exchange rate determined by the fundamentals and reflecting the true worth of the currency, $s_t$, from the untrue exchange rate containing a rational bubble, $s_t + b_t$, since they behave almost the same.

Helpfully, however, a rational bubble added to equation (7.22) also appears in equation (7.23):

$$s_t - x_t + b_t = (1-\lambda)\sum_{\tau=0}^{\infty} \lambda^{\tau} E_{t+\tau}(x_{t+\tau+1}) - x_t$$

$$= \sum_{\tau=0}^{\infty} \lambda^{\tau} E_{t+\tau}(\Delta x_{t+\tau+1}) + b_t$$

(7.26)

It is obvious that there is detectable difference between equation (7.23) and equation (7.26): the right hand side of equation (7.23) possesses current and future expected changes in the fundamentals only and is stationary, while the right hand side of equation (7.26) contains, in addition to current and future expected changes in the fundamentals, a rational bubble, $b_t$. The rational bubble is by definition explosive, so the right hand side of equation (7.26) is non-stationary. Therefore, to detect the existence of a rational bubble in the foreign exchange rate amounts to testing for stationarity of the spread of the foreign exchange rate and the fundamentals. If the foreign exchange rate observed is the right one determined by the fundamentals and reflecting the true worth of the currency, $s_t$, then the spread is $s_t - x_t$ and must be stationary. If however the foreign exchange rate observed is untrue and contains a rational bubble, $s_t + b_t$, then the spread is $s_t + b_t - x_t$ and is non-stationary.

Having examined rational bubbles and associated behaviour and tests, let us turn to the test of the forward-looking monetary model. It happens that, while a rational bubble is ruled out in the foreign exchange rate, the forward-looking monetary model is rejected by using a certain set of data. So testing for validity of the forward-looking monetary model is a weaker hypothesis than testing for rational bubbles. That is, when the spread is non-stationary and a rational bubble is found in the foreign exchange rate, the forward-looking monetary model is rejected;

when the spread is stationary and there is no rational bubble in the foreign exchange rate, the forward-looking monetary model may or may not be valid, subject to further scrutiny. The validity of the forward-looking monetary model can be tested in a Vector Auto Regression (VAR) system. Let $d_t$ be a vector of the present and past spread of the foreign exchange rate and the fundamentals and $\Delta x_t$ be a vector of changes in the present and past fundamentals, i.e.:

$$\mathbf{d}_t = \begin{bmatrix} d_t & \cdots & d_{t-p+1} \end{bmatrix}'$$
$$\Delta \mathbf{x}_t = \begin{bmatrix} \Delta x_t & \cdots & \Delta x_{t-p+1} \end{bmatrix}'.$$

The VAR for the foreign exchange rate and the fundamentals can be written in the companion form:

$$\begin{bmatrix} \mathbf{d}_t \\ \Delta \mathbf{x}_t \end{bmatrix} = \begin{bmatrix} \mathbf{a}_{11}(L) & \mathbf{a}_{12}(L) \\ \mathbf{a}_{21}(L) & \mathbf{a}_{22}(L) \end{bmatrix} \begin{bmatrix} \mathbf{d}_{t-1} \\ \Delta \mathbf{x}_{t-1} \end{bmatrix} + \begin{bmatrix} \mu_{1t} \\ \mu_{2t} \end{bmatrix} \qquad (7.27)$$

where

$$\mathbf{a}_{11}(L) = \begin{bmatrix} a_{11,1} & \cdots & \cdots & a_{11,p} \\ 1 & \cdots & & \\ & & \cdots & \\ & & & 1 \end{bmatrix}, \quad \mathbf{a}_{12}(L) = \begin{bmatrix} a_{12,1} & \cdots & \cdots & a_{12,p} \\ 0 & \cdots & & \\ & & \cdots & \\ & & & 0 \end{bmatrix},$$

$$\mathbf{a}_{21}(L) = \begin{bmatrix} a_{21,1} & \cdots & \cdots & a_{21,p} \\ 0 & \cdots & & \\ & & \cdots & \\ & & & 0 \end{bmatrix}, \quad \mathbf{a}_{22}(L) = \begin{bmatrix} a_{22,1} & \cdots & \cdots & a_{22,p} \\ 1 & \cdots & & \\ & & \cdots & \\ & & & 1 \end{bmatrix}$$

are coefficient matrices, and

$$\mu_{1t} = \begin{bmatrix} v_{1t} & 0 & \cdots \end{bmatrix}', \quad \mu_{2t} = \begin{bmatrix} v_{2t} & 0 & \cdots \end{bmatrix}'$$

are residual vectors for the spread and the fundamentals respectively. Equation (7.27) can be written in a compact form:

$$\mathbf{z}_t = \mathbf{A}\mathbf{z}_{t-1} + \mu_t \qquad (7.28)$$

where $\mathbf{z}_t$ is a vector of $\mathbf{d}_t$ and $\Delta \mathbf{x}_t$ :

$$\mathbf{z}_t = \begin{bmatrix} d_t & \cdots & d_{t-p+1} & \Delta x_t & \cdots & \Delta x_{t-p+1} \end{bmatrix}'$$

$$A = \begin{bmatrix} a_{11} & a_{12} \\ a_{21} & a_{22} \end{bmatrix}$$

and

$$\mu_t = \begin{bmatrix} \mu_{1t} & \mu_{2t} \end{bmatrix}'$$

Further, let **e1'** and **e2'** be (1×2p) row vectors with zero in all cells except unity in the first element for the former and in the (p+1) element for the latter respectively, i.e.:

$$d_t = e1' z_t \tag{7.29}$$

$$\Delta x_t = e2' z_t \tag{7.30}$$

Notice:

$$E\{z_{t+k}|H_t\} = A^k z_t \tag{7.31}$$

where $H_t$ is the information set with all available information about $s_t$ and $\Delta x_t$ at time $t$. Applying equations (7.29), (7.30) and (7.31) to equation (7.23) yields:

$$e1' z_t = \sum_{\tau=1}^{\infty} \lambda^{\tau-1} e2' A^\tau z_t = e2' \frac{1}{\lambda} A[I - \lambda A]^{-1} z_t \tag{7.32}$$

Equation (7.32) imposes restrictions on the VAR parameters if rationality is to uphold, i.e.:

$$e1'[I - \lambda A] = e2' \frac{1}{\lambda} A \tag{7.33}$$

Subsequently, the "theoretical" spread can be introduced as:

$$d_t^* = e2' \frac{1}{\lambda} A[I - \lambda A]^{-1} z_t \tag{7.34}$$

Tests for the validity of the forward-looking monetary model can be carried out in two ways. One is to impose restrictions on the VAR. The other is the variance ratio test, $Var(d_t)/Var(d_t^*)$, a ratio of the variance of the observed spread over the variance of the theoretical spread given by equation (7.34). Intuitively, if the variance of the observed spread is not much larger than that of the theoretical spread, then the reality is close to what suggested by the forward-looking monetary model, and the validity of the model is accepted. Otherwise, if the variance of the observed spread is significantly greater than that of the theoretical spread, then the forward-looking monetary model does not fit the real story implied by the used data and is consequently rejected in that case. Similar analysis applies to the restrictions on the VAR as well.

The implications of above analysis can be summarised in the following. If the foreign exchange market is rational for a currency, e.g., the domestic currency, then its value, the foreign exchange rate or the relative price of the currency in terms of the foreign currency, and the fundamentals determining its value, should be cointegrated and the spread of the foreign exchange rate and the fundamentals should be stationary. The spread is non-stationary without a cointegration relationship between the foreign exchange rate and the fundamentals, and a rational bubble, which by definition is explosive, may exist in the foreign exchange market. If the foreign exchange market is efficient and the forward-looking monetary model holds, then the actual observed spread should not substantially differ from the "theoretical" spread, and the variance ratio should not be significantly larger then unity.

## 7.4    Empirical Evidence on the Validity of the Monetary Model

Earlier empirical studies of the monetary model are mainly based on the regression of the logarithm of the foreign exchange rate on the variables of money supply differentials, interest rate differentials, inflation differentials and/or income differentials. The validity of the model is judged by whether the coefficient for the money differential variable is not significantly different from unity, the coefficient for the interest rate differential variable, $\beta$ in equation (10) or equation (12), is positive, and the coefficient for the income differential variable, $-\alpha$ in equation (10) or equation (12), is negative. For example, the original paper by Frenkel (1976) examining the DM/$ exchange rate data between February 1920 and November 2003 during the German hyperinflation period, regresses the logarithm of the foreign exchange rate on money stock and the forward premium that is a substitute for the interest rate differential. He confirms the monetary model with the following findings: the coefficient for the money stock variable is 0.975 that does not differ significantly from unity and the coefficient for the forward premium is positive at 0.591 that differs significantly from zero. The model enjoyed some success, mostly applying pre Bretton Woods data since it was only several years into the recent floating.

However, with the progress in time series econometrics, researchers have gradually become aware of the non-stationarity characteristics of the foreign exchange rate and the fundamentals. On the other hand, the availability of longer period recent data makes advanced econometric tests possible and feasible. These have shoved research on foreign exchange and the test on the monetary model to a large extent. Consequently, doubts are cast on the empirical results that support the monetary model. As Boothe and Glassman (1987) point out that the initial empirical support of the monetary model was an illusion created by the failure to account for exchange rate non-stationarity and the arbitrary imposition of dynamic restrictions. It follows that more recent empirical studies predominantly adopt the econometric analytical framework of cointegration and test for the restrictions on, and the dynamics of, the forward-looking monetary model.

Using a multivariate cointegration technique, MacDonald and Taylor (1991) re-examine the monetary model for three major currencies, using data for the recent floating exchange rates. They demonstrate that an unrestricted monetary model is a valid framework for analysing the long-run exchange rate. That is, there exists a cointegration relationship between the foreign exchange rate and the fundamentals but the coefficients may or may not be exactly those suggested by the monetary model. They find that the proportionality of the exchange rate to relative money supplies is valid for the German mark only. Later on, MacDonald and Taylor (1993) further examine the monetary approach to foreign exchange rate determination using monthly exchange rate data on the deutsche mark vis-à-vis the US dollar. Using the Johansen procedure for the cointegration test and the Campbell-Shiller methodology for the forward-looking model, they claim the monetary model is validated as a long-run equilibrium condition and a rational bubble is ruled out in the DM/$ exchange rate, but they reject the restrictions imposed on the VAR data by the forward-looking rational expectations monetary model. The forward-looking monetary model is also failed by the variance ratio test. MacDonald and Taylor (1994) also find long-run evidence of support for the model for the sterling-dollar exchange rate. In the similar spirit, Smith (1995) applies the forward-looking monetary model to formulate nominal exchange rates as discounted expected future fundamentals. The author rejects the validity of the model based on the findings that the discount rate obtained is statistically significantly negative.

While there is little evidence that the forward-looking monetary model can be validated by imposed restrictions, support for the monetary model in the long-run in simple cointegration analysis has been materialised to a greater extent. Empirical studies of the kind can be found in Francis et al. (2001) who examine the validity of the monetary approach to exchange rates using Canadian-US dollar data. Their evidence provides strong support for the long-run monetary model of exchange rates. Rapach and Wohar (2002) test the long-run monetary model of exchange rate determination for 14 industrialised countries using data spanning the late nineteenth or early twentieth century to the late twentieth century. Their findings are in support of a simple form of the long-run monetary model in over half of the 14 countries. In Dutt and Ghosh (1999), the monetary model in the long-run is tested for the Canadian dollar-US dollar exchange rate and their results are claimed to uphold the validity of the monetary approach. McNown and Wallace (1994) also find evidence of cointegration among the variables of the monetary model for three high inflation countries of Argentina, Chile and Israel. Examining the decline of the Iranian rial during the post-revolutionary period and using annual data over the 1959-1990 period, Bahmani-Oskooee (1995) shows that all variables that enter into the model have a long-run relationship with the exchange rate and they all follow the path outlined by the monetary approach. In addition to the simple long-run cointegration relationship, Diamandis and Kouretas (1996) also claim that proportionality of the exchange rate to relative monetary aggregates is accepted for all five investigated bilateral exchange rates of the Greek drachma vis-à-vis the US dollar, the Deutsche mark, the British pound, the French franc and the Italian lira.

Although many empirical studies support the unrestricted monetary model based on cointegration results, some other studies still fail to confirm a cointegration relationship between the foreign exchange rate and the fundamentals. Cushman (2000) scrutinises the validity of the monetary exchange rate model in the long run for the Canadian dollar-US dollar exchange rate, employing the Johansen (1991) and Johansen and Juselius (1990) cointegration technique. The author asserts that, despite the use of the longest data set, no evidence is found in favour of the monetary exchange rate model using the Johansen procedures, which is confirmed by several other cointegration procedures. Using various cointegration tests, Ghosh (1998) examines the validity of the monetary model in the long-run for the exchange rate of a developing economy experiencing chronic and accelerating inflation. The study offers no evidence of long-run equilibrium relationship among the variables of the monetary model. It is claimed that the monetary model is not a valid framework for analysing the long-run movements of the rupee-US dollar exchange rate.

More recently, with the development of the panel data method, the majority of the empirical research in that category is in favour of the monetary model using panel data and, at the same time, rejects the monetary model when individual bilateral exchange rates are considered separately. For example, Oh (1999) uses data from seven countries during the recent float period and finds evidence of support for the monetary model in the panel; whereas there is no cointegration relationship for the individual exchange rate time series and their respective fundamentals. Similarly, Groen and Kleibergen (2003) find evidence for the validity of the monetary model within a panel for three major European countries, while the results based on individual models for each of these countries separately are less supportive. In a panel framework, Husted and MacDonald (1998) analyse three panel data sets constructed for the US dollar, the German mark and the Japanese yen exchange rates using annual data for the recent floating period. Cointegrating relationships in all three panels are confirmed. Moreover, the mark denominated panel produces point estimates of monetary model coefficients close to their priors. Groen (2002) also reports that the panel vector error correction approach provides evidence for the validity of both the cointegration restriction as well as the long-run parameter restrictions of the monetary model.

Interestingly, the original context of German hyperinflation in Frenkel (1976) has been re-examined by a few studies. Taking into consideration of the nonstationarity of the data, the results of Engsted (1996) are claimed to be very supportive of the monetary model. Burdekin and Burkett (1996) re-examine the case by extending Frenkel's (1976) original monetary model to incorporate endogeneity of the money supply with respect to government debt, expected inflation, and money wages; the direct impact of exchange rate depreciation on the domestic price level; and endogenous wage determination. The results support each extension of the monetary model. They suggest that government deficit finance, the collapse of the exchange rate, and the monetary transmission of the wage-price spiral crucial to the price explosion.

# 8 The Dornbusch Model

The Dornbusch model has the mixed features of the Mundell-Fleming model and the monetary model, though it stems from the former and, is sometimes called the Mundell-Fleming-Dornbusch model. The Dornbusch model is prominently featured by the sticky price assumption and overshooting. The sticky price assumption suggests that prices are neither totally flexible nor totally fixed. With this assumption, the aggregate supply curve is flat in the short term, the slope of the aggregate supply curve gradually becomes steeper and steeper with the time horizon, and the curve is vertical in the long run. In the short term, increases in output are induced by shifts in aggregate demand; in the medium term, increases in output are caused by shifts in aggregate demand or shifts in aggregate supply or both; and in the long run, only a shift in aggregate supply changes output. Other assumptions of the Dornbusch model include that the exchange rate is flexible, agents have perfect foresight and UIRP holds.

This chapter first presents the building blocks of the Dornbusch model and demonstrates the evolution paths of the exchange rate in conjunction with the price, followed by an examination of exchange rate dynamics and overshooting of the exchange rate. The chapter then argues that exchange rate dynamics and the evolution path of the exchange rate are sensitive to changes in the setting and parameter assumptions – not only undershooting, but also reverse shooting, may take place. Finally the real interest rate differential model by Frankel (1979) is introduced as an attempt to bridge the opposite results and conflicting policy implications often produced by the flexible monetary model and the Dornbusch model.

## 8.1 The Building Blocks of the Model and the Evolution Paths of the Exchange Rate and the Price

The model proposed by Dornbusch (1976) has three basic building blocks: uncovered interest rate parity and expectations, demand for money or the money market equilibrium and aggregate demand the goods market equilibrium. The model is for a small open economy, so the foreign interest rate is exogenous and the long-run equilibrium interest rate for the domestic interest rate. The exchange rate and exchange rate expectations involve the interest rate differential between the foreign country and the domestic country, or in other words for an open small economy, between the long-run equilibrium interest rate and the domestic interest rate prevailing at the time. The exchange rate and exchange rate expectations therefore enter the demand for money equation where the domestic interest rare is determined by the conditions for the domestic money market to be in equilibrium or to clear. Further, the aggregate demand for domestic goods depends on the relative price of domestic goods, a relativity of the exchange rate, the foreign price and the domestic price, so the exchange rate and exchange rate expectations enter the aggregate demand equation where the relative price of domestic goods is determined by the conditions for the domestic goods market to be in equilibrium or to clear.

The first relationship in the model is UIRP, that the expected change in the foreign exchange rate is equal to the interest rate differential between the domestic country and the foreign country. In the case of a small open economy, the expected change in the foreign exchange rate is equal to the difference between the prevailing domestic interest rate and its long-run equilibrium rate:

$$E_t(\Delta e_{t+1}) = r_t - r^*$$
(8.1)

where $e_t$ is the exchange rate in logarithms, $\Delta(e_{t+1}) = e_{t+1} - e_t$, $r_t$ is the domestic interest rate, and $r^*$ is the long-run equilibrium interest rate where a time subscript is not relevant.

The second building block of the model, the demand for money equation, is the standard version:

$$m_t - p_t = \phi y_t - \lambda r_t$$
(8.2)

where $m_t$ is demand for money, $p_t$ is the price level, $y_t$ is real income, all are domestic variables and are in logarithms; and $\phi > 0$ and $\lambda > 0$ are coefficients representing the income elasticity of demand for money, and the interest rate semi-elasticity of money demand respectively.

The third element of the model is the price adjustment process through analysing aggregate demand and excess demand[1]. If we leave this part out and let the

---

[1] A simpler way proceeds as follows. Aggregate demand is:
$y_t^d = \bar{y} + \delta[(e_t + p^* - p_t) - (\bar{e} + p^* - \bar{p})] - \sigma(r_t - r^*)$, i.e., aggregate demand is its long-run equilibrium level plus the effects caused by the discrepancy between the real exchange rate and the long-run real exchange rate and the discrepancy between the prevailing interest rate and the long-run equilibrium interest rate. The price adjusts in proportion to the discrepancy between aggregate demand and its long-run equilibrium level:

price move freely, what have been derived so far are indeed a flexible price monetary model and its analytical framework. The aggregate demand function is:

$$d_t = \mu + \delta(e_t + p^* - p_t) + \gamma y_t - \sigma r_t \qquad (8.3)$$

where $d_t$ is the logarithm of the aggregate domestic demand, $p^*$ is the logarithm of the foreign price, and $\mu$ is a shift parameter, i.e., a change in $\mu$ will shift the IS curve on the Y–r plane. $e_t + p^* - p_t$, the relative price of the domestic goods, is also known as the real exchange rate denoted by $q_t$.

The domestic price, which is sticky, adjustment is proportional to excess demand, $d_t - y_t$:

$$\Delta p_{t+1} = \pi(d_t - y_t) = \pi\left[\mu + \delta(e_t + p^* - p_t) + (\gamma - 1)y_t - \sigma r_t\right] \qquad (8.4)$$

Now, let us consider exchange rate expectations that are formed in the following way:

$$E_t(\Delta e_{t+1}) = \theta(\bar{e} - e_t) \qquad (8.5)$$

where $\bar{e}$ is the long-run exchange rate and $\theta > 0$ is a coefficient. Equation (8.5) states that the expected change in the exchange rate follows a dynamic adjustment process that the exchange rate will revert to its long-run rate, with the speed of adjustment being decided by the value of $\theta$. The domestic currency is expected to depreciate when the exchange rate is below its long-run level and is expected to appreciate when it is above its long-run level. The adjustment is swift with $\theta$ is large and slow when $\theta$ is small. Exchange rate expectations in equation (8.5) crucially link the three parts of the model.

Combining equation (8.1) with equation (8.5) yields:

$$r_t - r^* = \theta(\bar{e} - e_t) \qquad (8.6)$$

or

$$r_t = r^* + \theta(\bar{e} - e_t) \qquad (8.6')$$

---

$\Delta p_{t+1} = \pi(y_t^d - \bar{y}) = \pi\delta\left[(e_t + p^* - p_t) - (\bar{e} + p^* - \bar{p})\right] - \pi\sigma(r_t - r^*)$, which is equation (8.11).
$= \pi\delta\left[(e_t - \bar{e}) - (p_t - \bar{p})\right] - \pi\sigma(r_t - r^*)$

The last term $\pi\sigma(r_t - r^*)$, can also be removed without having an effect on the outcome qualitatively, e.g., when equation (8.11) progresses to equation (8.12).

Equation (8.6) or equation (8.6') establishes a relationship for the interest rate differential and the discrepancy between the long-run exchange rate and the prevailing exchange rate. Bringing equation (8.6') into equation (8.2), the demand for money equation, we obtain:

$$m_t - p_t = \phi y_t - \lambda r^* - \lambda \theta(\bar{e} - e_t) \qquad (8.7)$$

and in equilibrium, $e_t = \bar{e}$, $p_t = \bar{p}$, where $\bar{p}$ is the long-run equilibrium price level, the above equation becomes:

$$\bar{p} = m_t - \phi y_t + \lambda r^* \qquad (8.8)$$

Equation (8.7) and equation (8.8) imply that:

$$e_t - \bar{e} = -\frac{1}{\lambda \theta}(p_t - \bar{p}) \qquad (8.9)$$

or

$$e_t = \bar{e} - \frac{1}{\lambda \theta}(p_t - \bar{p}) \qquad (8.9')$$

Equation (8.9) or equation (8.9') establishes a relationship for the discrepancy between the long-run exchange rate and the current exchange rate and the discrepancy between the long-run equilibrium price level and the current price level. It can be observed that the discrepancy between the current domestic interest rate and the long-run equilibrium interest rate is also proportional to the discrepancy between the long-run equilibrium price level and the current price level through equation (8.6) and equation (8.9).

Setting $\Delta p_{t+1} = 0$, then $p_t = \bar{p}$ and $r_t = r^*$ in equation (8.4), we obtain the aggregate demand in equilibrium:

$$0 = \pi\left[\mu + \delta(\bar{e} + p^* - \bar{p}) + (\gamma - 1)y_t - \sigma r^*\right] \qquad (8.10)$$

Except the exchange rate, the domestic price level and the domestic interest rate, which are replaced by their respective long-run equilibrium counterparts, all other variables remain the same in equation (8.10) as those in equation (8.4) and, therefore, can be cancelled out when the former is subtracted from the latter, leaving in the relationship three differential terms for the exchange rate, the domestic price and the domestic interest rate only:

$$\Delta p_{t+1} = \pi\left[\delta(e_t - \bar{e}) - \delta(p_t - \bar{p}) + \sigma(r^* - r_t)\right] \qquad (8.11)$$

Equation (8.11) suggests that changes in the domestic price is a dynamic adjustment process and is proportional to the discrepancy between the prevailing exchange rate and the long-run exchange rate, the discrepancy between the current domestic price and the long-run equilibrium price level, and the discrepancy between the domestic interest rate and the long-run equilibrium interest rate.

Nevertheless, we would like to express all the terms on the right hand side of equation (8.11) as some kind function of the price, so the dynamic path for price evolution can be solved. Notice that the second term on the right hand side of the equation is already the discrepancy between the current domestic price and the long-run equilibrium price level, the first term can be expressed as a function of the discrepancy between the current domestic price and the long-run equilibrium price level through equation (8.9), and the third term can be expressed as a function of the discrepancy between the current domestic price and the long-run equilibrium price level through equation (8.6) and equation (8.9). Therefore, equation (8.11) can be expressed in a single term that is proportional to the discrepancy between the current domestic price and the long-run equilibrium price level, as follows:

$$
\begin{aligned}
\Delta p_{t+1} &= \pi \left[ -\frac{\delta}{\lambda \theta}(p_t - \bar{p}) - \delta(p_t - \bar{p}) - \frac{\sigma}{\lambda}(p_t - \bar{p}) \right] \\
&= -\pi \left[ \delta + \frac{\delta + \sigma \theta}{\lambda \theta} \right](p_t - \bar{p}) \qquad\qquad (8.12) \\
&= -v(p_t - \bar{p})
\end{aligned}
$$

where $v = \pi \left[ \delta + \frac{\delta + \sigma \theta}{\lambda \theta} \right]$. The evolution path of the price, represented by equation (8.12), can be derived to yield the general solution:

$$
p_t = a + be^{-vt} \qquad\qquad (8.13)
$$

Considering the boundary condition that $p_t = p_0$ at time 0, a special solution is obtained as:

$$
p_t = \bar{p} + (p_0 - \bar{p})e^{-vt} \qquad\qquad (8.14)
$$

Bringing equation (8.14) into equation (8.9') yields the evolution path of the exchange rate:

$$e_t = \bar{e} - \frac{1}{\lambda\theta}(p_t - \bar{p})$$

$$= \bar{e} - \frac{1}{\lambda\theta}(p_0 - \bar{p})e^{-vt} \qquad (8.15)$$

$$= \bar{e} + (e_0 - \bar{e})e^{-vt}$$

Finally, it is shown that the real exchange rate evolves in a similar way:

$$q_t = \bar{q} + (q_0 - \bar{q})e^{-vt} \qquad (8.16)$$

Equation (8.14) to equation (8.16) indicate that both the domestic price level and the exchange rate converge to their long-run equilibrium at the rate of $v$. Equation (8.15) effectively imposes restrictions on the expectations coefficient $\theta$ in equation (8.5). For exchange rate expectations to be formed correctly, its speed of adjustment, measured by $\theta$ in equation (8.5), must equal to the rate at which the exchange rate actually converges to its long-run equilibrium level, $v$, i.e.:

$$\theta = v = \pi\left[\delta + \frac{\delta + \sigma\theta}{\lambda\theta}\right] \qquad (8.17)$$

Since both sides of equation (8.17) contain $\theta$, re-arrangement is made, leading to a so called consistent expectations coefficient:

$$\tilde{\theta} = \frac{\pi}{2}\left(\frac{\sigma}{\lambda} + \delta\right) + \left[\frac{\pi^2}{4}\left(\frac{\sigma}{\lambda} + \delta\right)^2 + \frac{\pi\delta}{\lambda}\right]^{\frac{1}{2}} \qquad (8.18)$$

## 8.2   Adjustments of the Exchange Rate and the Price and Overshooting of the Exchange Rate

To analyse the adjustment process to the equilibrium state, we need the curves for the goods market equilibrium and the money market equilibrium. Equation (8.9) represents a line on which the money market is in equilibrium. The goods market equilibrium can be derived through inserting equation (8.6) into equation (8.11) and setting $\Delta y_{t+1}$ in equation (8.11) to zero. So the goods market equilibrium is plotted on the line represented by:

$$e_t - \bar{e} = \frac{\delta}{\delta + \sigma\theta}(p_t - \bar{p}) \qquad (8.19)$$

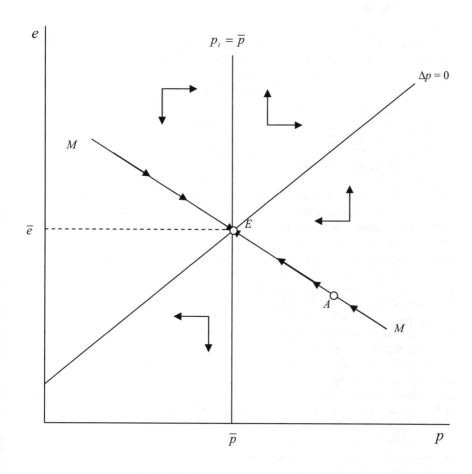

**Figure 8.1.** Adjustment paths of the Dornbusch model

The relationships shown by equation (8.9) and equation (8.19) are plotted in Figure 8.1. Equation (8.11) indicates that the line of $\Delta p = 0$ has a slope of smaller than 1. The line of $\Delta p = 0$ starts from origin if the foreign price is set to be 1, so that its logarithm is zero, i.e., $p^* = 0$ which in turn implies $\bar{e} = \bar{p}$. At the points to the left of and above the line of $\Delta p = 0$, the price will rise in response to an excess demand for goods; and at the point below and to the right of the line of $\Delta p = 0$, the price will fall due to excess supply of goods. The exchange rate will increase when $p_t > \bar{p}$, or to the right of the vertical line $p_t = \bar{p}$; and the exchanger rate will decrease when $p_t < \bar{p}$, or to the left of the vertical line $p_t = \bar{p}$. The line of $p_t = \bar{p}$ can also be labelled as $\Delta e = 0$, corresponding to the line of $\Delta p = 0$, a slightly different way to analyse the adjustment process to the equilibrium state through solving two simultaneous difference equations $\Delta p_{t+1} = 0$ and $\Delta e_{t+1} = 0$. The arrows in Figure 8.1 indicate the way the price and the exchange rate make adjustments, which is saddle–path stable. The money market is always in equilibrium and clears at every point in time. The relationship shown by equation (8.9) between the exchange rate and the price, which is plotted in Figure 8.1 as the MM line, corresponds to the situations when the money market clears. The goods market, in contrast, is not necessarily always in equilibrium, since prices do not adjust immediately in response to shocks to the economy, a feature of sticky prices. However, if the economy is not at its long-run equilibrium point $E$, it cannot be anywhere on the $p$–$e$ plane but must lie on the MM line, since the evolution path from any points other than those on the MM line will lead the exchange rate to either explode or collapse. When the economy is at a point on the MM line, the adjustment of the price and the exchange rate will bring the economy back to its long-run equilibrium position, as indicated by the arrows. For example, at point $A$ the economy has departed from its long-run equilibrium. There is an excess of supply of goods since the price is above its long-run equilibrium level; the exchange rate is below its long-run equilibrium rate, which also suggests that the domestic price is relatively too high. Therefore, prices will be falling to induce more demand for goods, the domestic currency will depreciate in the meantime and the interest rate will fall. This process of joint dynamic adjustments will continue until the economy is back at its long-run equilibrium point $E$.

Probably one of the most famous features of the Dornbusch model is overshooting. Overshooting may be readily observed by simply combining the two equations at the very beginning of this chapter, the UIRP equation and the demand for money equation, so long as it is conditioned on that the price is sticky or sluggish to adjust. In other words, the price can be considered as fixed in the short-term but flexible in the long-run, implying aggregate supply is exogenous and slow to respond to a shock to the demand equation. Nevertheless, as the dynamic adjustment mechanism of the price to excess demand is one of the building blocks of the model and is crucial to analysing exchange rate behaviour, it is helpful to work explicitly on this adjustment process. Figure 8.2 demonstrates how overshooting happens with a one time permanent increase in the nominal quantity of money.

As exhibited in Figure 8.2, the MM line shifts rightwards and the money market attains a new equilibrium and clears on the M'M' line after the shock. The long-run equilibrium price ought to be $\bar{p}'$ when the goods market clears too, accompanied by a corresponding long-run equilibrium exchange rate $\bar{e}'$, at the cross point $C$ for both the money market equilibrium and the goods market equilibrium. However, since the price is sluggish to adjust and is fixed in the short-term, the economy will move to point $B$ initially in the short-term and the exchange rate must overshoot to reach $e'$ that is higher than the long-run equilibrium exchange rate $\bar{e}'$. Over time, the price rises gradually and the domestic currency appreciates from its overshooting level; the goods market clears and the economy attains a new equilibrium at point $C$. That is, the initial depreciation of the domestic currency is more than proportional to the increase in the nominal quantity of money, followed by a kind of appreciation of the currency, the extent of which offsets exactly the magnitude of the overshooting, $e'-\bar{e}'$. The mechanism is as follows.

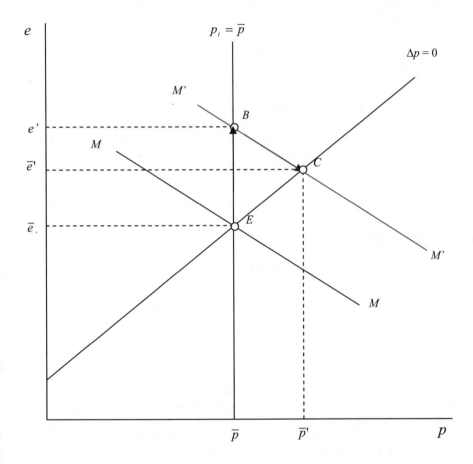

**Figure 8.2.** Overshooting of the exchange rate

Upon the increase in the nominal quantity of money, the price is fixed and does not respond to the increase in the short term, then the supply of real balances $m_t - p_t$ rises. Since aggregate supply or output is exogenous and fixed in the short-term too, the only way for the money market to clear is that the domestic interest rate must fall. Then the domestic currency is expected to appreciate consistent with UIRP. It is this expected appreciation of the domestic currency that results in the depreciation of the currency to be larger than that proportionate to the increase in the nominal quantity of money supply, the initial excess or overshooting being necessary for the expected appreciation of the currency. The initial impact of a permanent increase in the nominal quantity of money is therefore to induce immediate depreciation of the domestic currency in excess of the long-run depreciation, so the expected appreciation consistent with UIRP can materialise later to compensate for the reduced attractiveness of the domestic assets arising from both of the lowered domestic interest rate and over depreciated domestic currency.

The reader may still not be convinced why do we need all of these since the above analysis can be and are to a large extent explained by a joint examination of the UIRP equation and the demand for money equation, with an additional assumption that the price is fixed in the short-term. Now, let us formally study quantitatively the extent of overshooting so the model is of empirical use to the determination of the exchange rate and its evolution path in both the short-term and long-run. In the long-run, changes in the equilibrium price and in the equilibrium exchange rate are all proportionate to changes in the quantity of money and three of them are equal, that is:

$$\Delta \bar{p} = \Delta \bar{e} = \Delta m_t \qquad (8.20)$$

But in the short-term and according to equation (8.7):

$$\Delta m_t = -\lambda \theta (\Delta \bar{e} - \Delta e_t) \qquad (8.21)$$

Replacing $\Delta \bar{e}$ in equation (8.21) by equation (8.20) gives rise to:

$$\Delta e_t = \left(1 + \frac{1}{\lambda \theta}\right) \Delta m_t > \Delta m_t \qquad (8.22)$$

since both $\lambda$ and $\theta$ are assumed to be positive. Equation (8.22) is a mathematical expression of overshooting and provides a qualitative as well as quantitative estimation of the magnitude of overshooting based on economic agents' exchange rate expectations parameter, $\theta$, and the semi-elasticity of the interest rate in the demand for money relationship of the economy $\lambda$. With a given $\lambda$, the magnitude of overshooting is inversely related to $\theta$. When exchange rate expectations are formed in such a way that they are sensitive to any disequilibrium in the exchange rate and, consequently, responds swiftly with a large value of $\theta$, the size of overshooting is small. Conversely, if the disequilibrium in the exchange rate does not quite influence the formation of exchange rate expectations, the magnitude of overshooting can be fairly large.

The above graphical analysis is based on the $p$–$e$ plane, i.e., the relationships between the price and the exchange rate. Analysis can also be attempted on the $q$–$e$ plane, i.e., the relationships between the real exchange rate and the nominal exchange rate. To this end, we require two simultaneous equations for the real exchange rate and the nominal exchange rate to yield to relationships between them. The money market equilibrium line can be worked out from equation (8.9) by replacing the price variable by the real exchange variable and the nominal exchange rate variable:

$$e_t - \bar{e} = \frac{q_t - \bar{q}}{1 + \lambda\theta} \qquad (8.23)$$

The line representing the goods market equilibrium can be derived as follows. Applying equation (8.6) to equation (8.11) with the price and the exchange rate being replaced by the real exchange rate, the goods market equilibrium implies:

$$e_t - \bar{e} = \frac{\delta(q_t - \bar{q})}{\sigma\theta} \qquad (8.24)$$

Figure 8.3 demonstrates the relationships represented by equation (8.23) and equation (8.24). Equation (8.23) is plotted as the MM line and equation (8.24) is plotted on the line of $g(q,e)$. The slopes of both lines are positive, with the MM line being flatter than the $g(q,e)$ line. The line of $q_t = \bar{q}$ is also plotted. Together they determine the equilibrium exchange rate $\bar{e}$ and the equilibrium real exchange rate $\bar{q}$ at point E, which implies the long-run equilibrium price $\bar{p}$ as well.

To the right of $q_t = \bar{q}$ the real exchange rate is higher than its long-run equilibrium rate, the domestic price is below its long-run equilibrium level when the extent to which the nominal exchange rate is higher than its long-run equilibrium rate is smaller than that for the real exchange rate, and the domestic price is above its long-run equilibrium level when the extent to which the nominal exchange rate is higher than its long-run equilibrium rate is greater than that for the real exchange rate. So in area 1, the price is above its long-run equilibrium level and will fall; and in area 4 the price is below its long-run equilibrium level and will rise. To the left of $q_t = \bar{q}$ the real exchange rate is lower than its long-run equilibrium rate, the domestic price is above its long-run equilibrium level when the extent to which the nominal exchange rate is higher than its long-run equilibrium rate is smaller than that for the real exchange rate, and the domestic price is below its long-run equilibrium level when the extent to which the nominal exchange rate is higher than its long-run equilibrium rate is greater than that for the real exchange rate. So in area 2, the price is below its long-run equilibrium level and will rise; and in area 3 the price is above its long-run equilibrium level and will fall.

When the economy is at a point on the MM line, the adjustment of the price and the exchange rate will bring the economy back to its long-run equilibrium position, along the route marked by the arrows. For example, at point $A$ the economy has departed from its long-run equilibrium. There is an excess of demand for goods since both the real exchange rate and the nominal exchange rate are above their respective long-run equilibrium levels but the extent to which the real exchange rate exceeds its equilibrium lave is greater than that for the nominal ex-

change rate, equivalent to saying that the domestic price is below its long-run
equilibrium level. Therefore, the exchange rate will decrease or the domestic currency will appreciate in the meantime. Since the slope of the MM line is smaller
than 1, the decrease of the real exchange rate is faster than the decrease of the
nominal exchange rate, indicating that the price will rise during the course of adjustment to induce a reduction in demand for goods. This process of joint dynamic
adjustments will continue until the economy is back at its long-run equilibrium
point $E$.

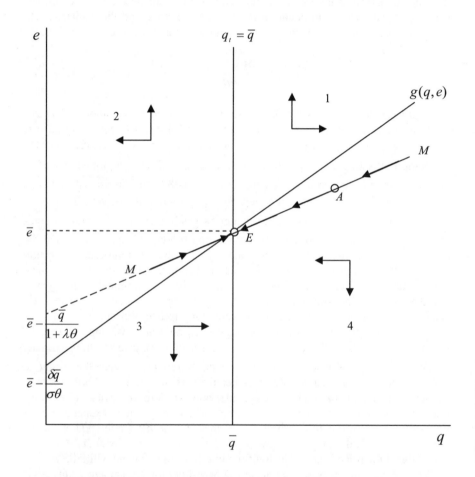

**Figure 8.3.** Adjustment paths of the Dornbusch model on the $q$–$e$ plane

Overshooting can be demonstrated on the $q$–$e$ plane too. Figure 8.4 illustrates
how overshooting happens with a one time permanent increase in the nominal
quantity of money. As demonstrated by Figure 8.4, the MM line shifts upwards

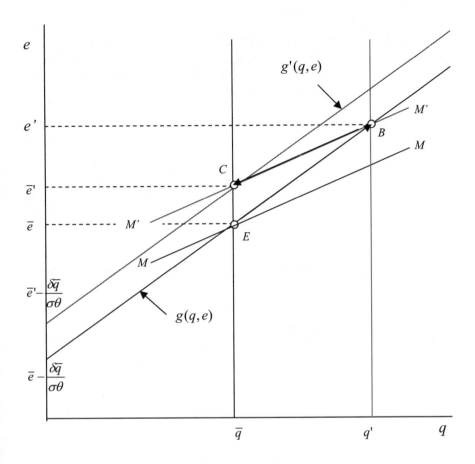

**Figure 8.4.** Illustration of overshooting on the $q$–$e$ plane

and the money market attains a new equilibrium and clears on the M'M' line after the shock. The goods market line of $g(q,e)$ shifts upwards too, reaching the new equilibrium and clearing on the new line of $g'(q,e)$. The long-run equilibrium the nominal exchange rate ought to be $\bar{e}'$ at the cross point $C$, accompanied by an un-changed real exchange rate $\bar{q}$ when both the goods market and the money market are settled down in the new equilibrium. However, since the price is fixed in the short-term, the goods market adjustment is slow. That is, it takes time for the goods market to shift from the pre-expansion equilibrium on the line of $g(q,e)$ to the new equilibrium on the line of $g'(q,e)$. The economy will move to point $B$ initially in the short-term with an increased real exchange rate, which implies an overshooting nominal exchange rate $\bar{e}'$. Over time, the price rises and the goods

market adjusts to the new equilibrium gradually. The domestic currency appreciates from its overshooting level as the real exchange rate reverts to its long-run
equilibrium level $\bar{q}$. It is observed that the both the MM line and the $g(q,e)$ line
have moved upwards by $\bar{e}'-\bar{e}$, which is equal to the amount of increase in the
nominal quantity of money. The joint dynamic adjustment process continues until
the economy attains its new long-run equilibrium point $C$.

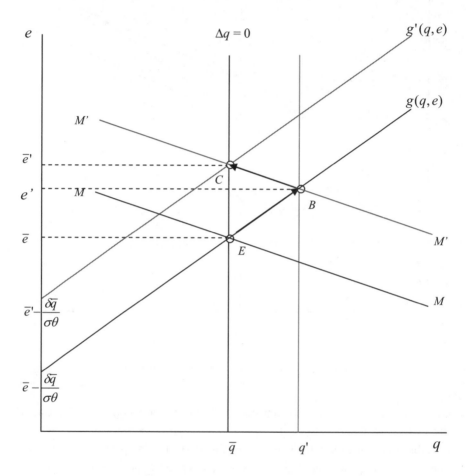

**Figure 8.5.** A case of undershooting

A common phenomenon to contrast overshooting is undershooting, demonstrated in Figure 8.5. This happens when the slope of the MM line becomes nega-

tive[2], i.e., when $\lambda\theta < -1$. Since $\lambda$ is almost certain to be positive and smaller than 1, only a negative $\theta$, with its absolute value being greater than 1, can satisfy the condition. The implication, obvious through equation (8.5), is that exchange rate expectations are formed in such a way that when the exchange rate is above its long-run equilibrium level, the exchange rate is expected to decrease or the currency is expected to appreciate; and when the exchange rate is below its long-run equilibrium level, the exchange rate is expected to increase or the currency is expected to depreciate. That is, when the currency is perceived to be stronger than that suggested by its long-run equilibrium rate, the currency is not expected to depreciate as usually will be, but instead, the currency is expected to appreciate and become even stronger. Under such circumstances, upon the impact of the money supply increase, the exchange rate will neither overshoot, nor adjust fully proportionately to the monetary expansion, but undershoot at $e'$ that is lower than the should be new long-run equilibrium exchange rate, when the economy moves initially to point B in the short-term. Over time, the price rises and the goods market adjusts to the new equilibrium gradually. The domestic currency continues to depreciate from its undershooting level as the real exchange rate reverts to its long-run equilibrium level $\bar{q}$. This process of joint dynamic adjustments will continue until the economy attains its new long-run equilibrium point $C$.

## 8.3   A Tale of Reverse Shooting and the Sensitivity of Exchange Rate Behaviour

Depending on the circumstances, the exchange rate cal also reversely shoots. Figure 8.6 shows a case when the goods market equilibrium line is flatter than the money market equilibrium line, i.e., $\delta(1+\lambda\theta) < \sigma\theta$. This implies that $\delta$, the price sensitivity to real exchange rate changes, is low; $\lambda$, the interest rate semi-elasticity of money demand, is low; and $\theta$, the exchange rate expectations coefficient, is high. Under such circumstances, upon the impact of an increase in the nominal quantity of money, since the price is even more sluggish than in the previous case the supply of real balances $m_t - p_t$ rises more than in the previous case. Moreover, the interest rate semi-elasticity of money demand is low. Both a relatively large increase in real balances and a relatively low interest rate semi-elasticity of money demand cause the domestic interest rate to fall more than that in the previous case. Accompanied by more sensitive and swift exchange rate expectations, UIRP materialises and the domestic currency appreciates upon the impact. Therefore, the economy will move to point $B$ initially in the short-term with a reduced real exchange rate and an appreciated nominal exchange rate that re-

---

[2] In Rogoff (2002), this happens when the slopes of both curves that are similar to but not exactly the same as ours here are negative, though it does not state the negative slope for the money market line, which requires a negative $\theta$, in its analysis.

versely shoots and reaches point $e'$. Since the long-run effect of a permanent increase in the nominal quantity of money is to depreciate the domestic currency, the price rises gradually over time. It follows that the domestic currency then depreciates from its reverse shooting position to settle down at the new equilibrium level $\bar{e}'$, the real exchange rate reverts to its long-run equilibrium level $\bar{q}$, the goods market clears, and the economy attains a new equilibrium at point $C$. This analysis shows how sensitive exchange rate behaviour can be, which changes the order of the over adjustment and the UIRP effect. Sluggish prices can mean an overshooting nominal exchange rate, accompanied by an increase in the real exchange rate of a comparable magnitude. Sluggish prices can also lead to a reverse shooting nominal exchange rate, together with a decrease in the real exchange rate of a similar size.

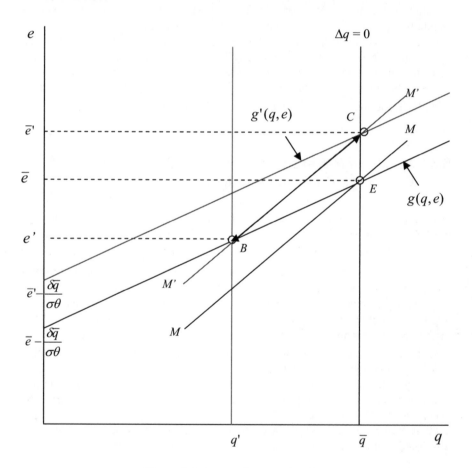

**Figure 8.6.** A case of reverse shooting

Comparing Figure 8.4, Figure 8.5 and Figure 8.6 it is observed that the exchange rate behaviour changes from over shooting, to reverse shooting and to under shooting when the slope of the line for money market equilibrium changes relative to that for the line for goods market equilibrium. Exchange rates overshoot if the slope of the MM line is positive but flatter than that of the $g(q,e)$ line. The magnitude of overshooting increases when the slope of the MM line becomes steeper and steeper. There is no overshooting when the slope of the MM line is zero or the line is horizontal; and the size of overshooting would be mathematically infinite when the slope of the MM line equalises the slope of the $g(q,e)$ line or the two lines overlap. Exchange rates reversely shoot if the slope of the MM line is positive but steeper than that of the $g(q,e)$ line. The magnitude of reverse shooting increases when the slope of the MM line becomes flatter and flatter. There is no reverse shooting when the slope of the MM line is infinite or the line is vertical; and the size of reverse shooting would be mathematically infinite when the slope of the MM line equalises the slope of the $g(q,e)$ line or the two lines overlap. The rest is the area where the slope of the MM line is negative and exchange rates under shoot. The size of undershooting increases when the slope of the MM line becomes steeper and steeper. There is no undershooting when the slope of the MM line is zero or the line is horizontal.

Let us define the slope of the MM line as SM and the slope of the $g(q,e)$ line as SG, measured in the degree of their angle with the horizontal axis, then the exchange rate overshoots if:

$$0 < SM < SG \tag{8.25}$$

the exchange rate reversely shoots if:

$$SG < SM < \frac{\pi}{2} \tag{8.26}$$

and the exchange rate under shoots if:

$$\frac{\pi}{2} < SM < \pi \tag{8.27}$$

There is neither overshooting nor undershooting when $SM = 0 = \pi$, with $SM = 0^+$ for zero overshooting and $SM = \pi^-$ for zero undershooting. The exchange rate initially does not change at all when $SM = \frac{\pi}{2}$, which is the case for zero reverse shooting $SM = \frac{\pi^-}{2}$ as well as for maximum undershooting

$SM = \dfrac{\pi^+}{2}$ . Figure 8.7 shows the boundaries and areas where exchange rates over shoot, reversely shoot and under shoot respectively.

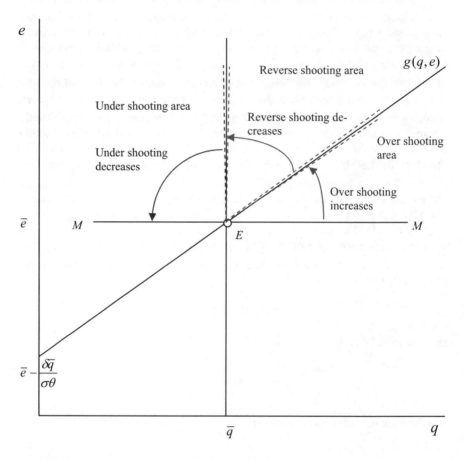

**Figure 8.7.** Overshooting, undershooting and reverse shooting

   The above analysis suggests that while overshooting sounds most common, reverse shooting is more likely to happen than undershooting since the latter requires diverging exchange rate expectations instead of a commonly accepted converging exchange rate expectations. However, converging exchange rate expectations with which overshooting and reverse shooting are associated tend to cause larger swings or higher volatility in exchange rates. On the contrary, diverging expectations in exchange rates smooth the path of exchange rate evolution and appear to generate lower volatility in exchange rates.

## 8.4   The Real Interest Rate Differential Model

It may have been noticed that the sticky price Dornbusch model introduced in this chapter and the flexible price monetary model discussed in the previous chapter often produce opposite results and offer conflicting policy implications. The starkest difference amongst is in the implications of interest rate changes for the exchange rate. The real interest rate differential model of exchange rate determination by Frankel (1979) is an attempt to reveal how and why the differences arise as well as to reconcile the two approaches. To briefly summarise, the difference may, to a certain extent, arise from the fact that both of the two approaches do not distinguish whether an interest rate increase or decrease is real or nominal, or whether the interest rate differential is real or nominal. So, the focus of Frankel's (1979) study is on real interest rate differentials.

The model is based on two assumptions. The first is that interest rate parities hold, which is equation (8.1) at the beginning of this chapter. Though similar to Frenkel (1976) the forward premium is used in place of expected appreciation/depreciation of the exchange rate that is later substituted by expected spot exchange rate changes conditional on zero risk premia. The second assumption about the formation of exchange rate expectations is a modification of equation (8.5) to include the effect of inflation differentials and is stated as follows:

$$E_t(\Delta e_{t+1}) = \theta(\bar{e} - e_t) + (\bar{\pi} - \bar{\pi}^*)$$
(8.28)

where $\bar{\pi}$ and $\bar{\pi}^*$ are the expected long-run inflation rates in the domestic and foreign countries respectively. Substituting equation (8.1) into equation (8.28), a relationship between the way in which the exchange rate adjusts to its long-run equilibrium level and the real interest rate is established[3]:

$$(\bar{e} - e_t) = \frac{1}{\theta}\left[(r_t - \bar{\pi}) - (r_t^* - \bar{\pi}^*)\right]$$
(8.29)

Together with the demand for money function for the domestic country, equation (8.2) and its counterpart for the foreign country:

$$m_t^* - p_t^* = \phi y_t^* - \lambda r_t^*$$
(8.2')

Notice that when $e_t = \bar{e}$, $p_t = \bar{p}$, $p_t^* = \bar{p}^*$, $r_t = \bar{r}_t$, $r_t^* = \bar{r}_t^*$, and $\bar{r}_t - \bar{r}_t^* = \bar{\pi} - \bar{\pi}^*$, it can be easily worked out that:

$$\bar{e} = \bar{p} - \bar{p}^* = (m_t - m_t^*) - \phi(y_t - y_t^*) + \lambda(\bar{\pi} - \bar{\pi}^*)$$
(8.30)

---

[3] Here the foreign country variables are neither the long-run equilibrium target for the domestic variables nor always in equilibrium themselves.

Bringing equation (8.30) into equation (8.29) yields:

$$e_t = (m_t - m_t^*) - \phi(y_t - y_t^*) - \frac{1}{\theta}(r_t - r_t^*) + \left(\frac{1}{\theta} + \lambda\right)(\bar{\pi} - \bar{\pi}^*) \quad (8.31)$$

Recall that in the flexible price monetary model, the third and the last term on the right hand of the exchange rate equation is $\lambda(r_t - r_t^*)$ or $\lambda[E_t(\pi_{t+1}) - E_t(\pi_{t+1}^*)]$, the differences are obvious and the implications straightforward. Let us rewrite equation (8.31) in a way similar to that in Chapter 7:

$$e_t = (m_t - m_t^*) - \alpha(y_t - y_t^*) + \beta_r(r_t - r_t^*) + \beta_\pi(\bar{\pi} - \bar{\pi}^*) \quad (8.32)$$

Equation (8.32) encompasses the standard flexible price monetary model and the Dornbusch model to a certain extent. A full real interest rate differential model implies $\beta_r < 0$ and $\beta_\pi > 0$. It is claimed to reduce to a standard flexible price monetary model when either set of parameter restrictions $\beta_r > 0, \beta_\pi = 0$ and $\beta_r = 0, \beta_\pi > 0$ is valid, though the differential in the long-run expected inflation in the two countries can be quite different from the expected inflation differential in the near future. It produces the Dornbusch model effect when $\beta_r < 0$ and $\beta_\pi = 0$. As equation (8.31) indicates that if $\beta_r = -\frac{1}{\theta} < 0$ is upheld, $\beta_\pi = \frac{1}{\theta} + \lambda = 0$ is unlikely to be satisfied. So the validity of the real interest rate differential model implies an omission of the inflation effect in the Dornbusch model. On the other hand, when the restrictions $\beta_r = 0, \beta_\pi > 0$ are valid, the real interest rate differential model reconcile the inflation version of a standard flexible price monetary model, conditional on that expected changes in the exchange rate do not respond to the discrepancy between the current exchange rate and the long-run equilibrium exchange rate, but only respond to inflation differentials. Nevertheless, the two types of inflation differentials used in the two models are different. Finally, diverging expectations in exchange rates can satisfy the restriction $\beta_r = -\frac{1}{\theta} > 0$, which makes $\beta_\pi = \frac{1}{\theta} + \lambda = 0$ possible. Therefore, the real interest rate differential model may fit the interest rate version of a standard flexible price monetary model when exchange rate expectations are formed in a diverging way.

## 8.5  Empirical Evidence on the Dornbusch Model and Some Related Developments

The first significant empirical studies of the Dornbusch model include Driskill (1981) on the issues of short-term overshooting, intermediate-term dynamics and long-run proportionality of the exchange rate, all the features of the Dornbusch model. The Swiss franc vis-à-vis the US dollar exchange rate, with 19 quarterly observations resulted from averaging three month-ends figures for the period 1973–1977, is used in the study. The empirical evidence appears to verify the overshooting hypothesis. With the pre-shock exchange rate and price level being set to zero, the exchange rate is simulated to depreciate initially to 2.30 following a monetary shock, equivalent to saying that the exchange rate overshoots by a factor of more than two in the short-term. Subsequent to overshooting, the currency appreciates to the exchange rate of 0.88, below the level of one and more than what is required to reduce the excess depreciation, in the first quarter. The appreciation continues for three quarters to an exchange rate of 0.21. Then the currency depreciates again for the next seven quarters to 0.73. So, the currency does not steadily appreciate to its long-run equilibrium exchange rate from the overshooting point. In contrast, the exchange rate fluctuates or oscillates in the adjustment process. In the meantime, the price steadily rises and becomes almost proportionate to the size of the monetary shock in about three years.

Findings in Frankel (1979) reject both the flexible price monetary model and Dornbusch's stick price monetary model based the results of coefficient restrictions. However, although the coefficient on the long-run expected inflation differential is significantly positive based on which Frankel rejects the Dornbusch model, the coefficient on the nominal interest rate differential is significantly negative, which is consistent with the Dornbusch model but contradictory to the flexible price monetary model. Moreover, in a test including the current as well as lagged nominal interest rate differentials, it is found that the coefficient on the current interest rate differential is still significantly negative but that on the lagged interest rate differential is significantly positive in one of the four test procedures, showing some weak evidence of overshooting in depreciation following a fall in the nominal interest rate differential and the subsequent appreciation.

Mussa (1982) also works on exchange rate dynamics in the early days of the recent float, which can produce the results of the Dornbusch model almost exactly if the exogenous monetary factor is assumed to be observable and follow a random walk and expectations about the behaviour of this factor is assumed to be formed and revised rationally. In Mussa's model, the exchange rate also overshoots in response to monetary shocks, when the domestic price of goods is sticky. The unexpected change in the actual exchange rate upon shocks, in response to new information about the monetary factors, is always greater than the unexpected change in the long-run equilibrium exchange rate.

Obstfeld and Rogoff (1995), inheriting much of the Mundell-Fleming-Dornbusch approach to foreign exchange rate behaviour, develop an intertemporal model of international policy transmission incorporating short-term nominal price rigidities and microeconomic foundations of aggregate supply. The model offers direct welfare implications of international monetary and macroeconomic policies and institutions. Regarding exchange rate dynamics, it produces an equation almost identical to that of the flexible monetary model of exchange rates despite that the sticky nominal price is assumed, when the output differential is replaced by the consumption differential in the equation. Since all shocks have permanent effects on the difference of domestic and foreign per capita consumption, real interest rates have the same effect on domestic and foreign consumption growth, relative consumptions follow a random walk whatever patterns the consumptions in the two countries possess, which removes the sticky price effect so the model behaves as though the model worked under a flexible price environment. It follows that the exchange rate, upon an unexpected permanent increase in money stock in the domestic country, jumps immediately to its new post-shock long-run equilibrium level despite the inability of the price to adjust in the short-term, in contrast to the exchange rate behaviour predicted by the Dornbusch model. It is because both consumption differentials and money supply differentials follow random walks, implying a one-jump to the right level feature in any adjustment processes. In other words, since consumption differentials and money supply differentials are expected to be constant, the exchange rate is expected to be constant – it adjusts only once and stops making any further adjustments immediately after the money supply shock. Chang and Lai (1997) also bring the claim that the transactions demand for money should depend on consumer expenditure rather than national income, into the Dornbusch model. It is found that whether the domestic currency will depreciate or appreciate following a balanced-budget fiscal expansion is sensitive to plausible specification in the money demand function. In addition, it is also found that the mis-adjustment pattern of exchange rate can be observed in response to a balanced fiscal expansion, even if the system displays the saddle point stability rather than the global instability.

Meese and Rogoff (1988) develop a modified version of the models by Dornbusch (1976), Frankel (1979) and others to investigate the relationship between real exchange rates and real interest rate differentials between the US, Germany, Japan and the UK. Adopting the assumptions of Dornbusch and Frankel including the sticky price assumption, they derived a function for real exchange rates and real interest rate differentials that real exchange rates are negatively associated with real interest rate differentials and changes in real exchange rates are less than proportionate to changes in real interest rate differentials. Then they use the derived functional relationship implied by the Dornbusch and Frankel models in empirical investigations by regressing real exchange rates on real interest rate differentials. Although the coefficient on the real interest rate differential variable is negative and smaller than one in its absolute value, the coefficient is statistically insignificant in all the three exchange rates of the German mark, the Japanese yen and the British pound vis-à-vis the US dollar. Further, due to near unit root properties of the real exchange rate and the real interest rate differential, a stable relationship between real exchange rates and real interest rate differentials requires that the two series be cointegrated. They find little evidence of such a long-run relationship between the real exchange rate and the real interest rate differential.

Based on these results that fail to support the model and contradict the joint hypothesis that the domestic price is sticky and monetary disturbances are predominant, they claim that real disturbances may be a source of exchange rate volatility.

A few of more recent studies are application based. Hwang (2003) employs the Dornbusch model and Frankel's real interest rate differential to forecast the US-Canadian dollar exchange rate and claims that the random walk model outperforms the Dornbusch-Frankel model at every forecasting horizon. Verschoor and Wolff (2001) investigate expectations formation using the Mexican peso – US dollar exchange rate and a survey dataset containing market participants' forecasts of the exchange rate and of the interest differential between the peso and the dollar. Their findings suggest that the survey expectations were in the wrong by a large and significant constant. Regarding the expectations formation mechanism, market participants tended to react to the current unanticipated depreciation by expecting future depreciation at the 3-, 6-, and 12-month horizons, and the overshooting effect was present in the Mexican data. However, "news" about the interest differential could be replaced by a risk premium term. Kim (2001) examines the international transmission of US monetary policy shocks in a VAR model. The paper claims that US expansionary monetary policy shocks lead to booms in the other G-7 countries. In this transmission, changes in trade balance seem to play a minor role while a decrease in the world real interest rate seems more important. On the other hand, US expansionary monetary policy shocks worsen the US trade balance in about a year, but the trade balance subsequently improves. The results suggest that the basic versions of Mundell-Flemming-Dornbusch and the sticky price intertemporal models are not found to be consistent with the details of the transmission mechanism, and appropriate modification and extensions are necessary to fit the data.

The extent to which exchange rate overshoot or possibly undershoot has been under scrutiny. Akiba (1996) investigates the rebalancing effect on exchange rate overshooting, accommodating different degrees of capital mobility and emphasising gradual adjustment of commodity prices so that purchasing power parity holds as a long-run proposition. The paper demonstrates that the rebalancing effect unambiguously reduces exchange rate volatility regardless of the degree of capital mobility, by reducing the extent of exchange rate overshooting. Examining permanent and transitory components in real exchange rates, Cavaglia (1991) demonstrates that rational agents will price the real exchange rate as the sum of three unobservable components of future expected one period real interest differentials, future expected risk premia, and the infinite horizon forecast of the real exchange rate. The study applies a multivariable Kalman filter technique obtain estimates of these unobserved components and to compute a variance decomposition of changes in real exchange rates into their permanent and transitory components. The findings of the paper contrast with the exchange rate overshooting hypothesis, since its empirical analysis for three currencies over the period 1979-1987 shows that exchange rate risk premia represent a large transitory and short lived component of real exchange rate movements, but expected real interest differentials only represent a relatively small component. Levin (1994) develops a model of exchange rate dynamics that incorporates sluggish output adjustment. In this more complex system, monetary expansion initially lowers interest rates because of sluggish output adjustment but can still produce either overshooting or under-shooting of the exchange rate as in the basic Dornbusch model. In an earlier study, Levin (1989) introduces output adjustment lags and trade flow lags into Dorn-busch model in order to analyse the dynamic effects of monetary and fiscal policy under floating exchange rates. Despite the fact that monetary expansion initially lowers interest rates, the exchange rate may undershoot its new long-run equilib-rium level. In addition, fiscal expansion always causes the exchange rate to over-shoot its new long-run equilibrium level. Finally, the system converges with oscil-lations if the output and trade-flow lags are relatively long. Kiguel and Dauhajre (1988) also incorporate sluggish output adjustment into the Dornbusch model and consider the cases of expansionary and contractionary real depreciation of the ex-change rate. They show that the exchange rate is likely to overshoot in both cases. It is claimed that when the real depreciation is expansionary, the model generates comovements in prices and output that are opposite to those presented by Dorn-busch. In the contractionary depreciation case, there is a unique stable equilibrium path and the economy is likely to experience cycles in output and the real ex-change rate. Natividad-Carlos (1994) considers intervention, imperfect capital substitution, and sluggish aggregate demand in the framework of the Dornbusch model. The paper imposes perfect foresight directly in solving the model. Results show that intervention may eliminate overshooting arising from monetary expan-sion but may only dampen overshooting resulting from fiscal expansion.

In a recent Mundell-Fleming lecture, Rogoff (2002) presents the ideas, in-sights, building blocks and workings of the Dornbusch model exhaustively. We conclude this section with the remarks of the paper that summarise the contribu-tions of the Dornbusch model as follows. First, it has breathed new life into the Mundell-Fleming model. Second, Dornbusch's 1976 paper has been the first in in-ternational finance to combine sticky prices with rational expectations. Finally, the Dornbusch model has defined a high-water mark of theoretical simplicity and ele-gance in international finance, which remains relevant for today's policy analysis.

# 9 Global Derivatives Markets

Before the proliferation of financial derivatives, foreign exchange forwards might be the only derivative instrument active in the foreign exchange market. The pair of the spot foreign exchange and the forward foreign exchange has established or led to some fundamental, significant and seemingly straightforward doctrines, such as CIRP. Over the decade, however, various financial derivative instruments have emerged and been transacted in the foreign exchange markets in enormous volumes. In contrast to foreign exchange forwards, the working of these newly emerged derivatives seem to be technical, trivial, and on the face of it, sophisticated. The widespread use of derivatives makes the market more complete and competitive on the one hand, and creates vast and complicated new financial management tasks and techniques on the other hand. Using available and relevant derivative financial instruments to manage and hedge against the exposure to foreign exchange and input and output markets has developed into a mandate, enforced upon the management of the firm by various market and corporate governance mechanisms.

Against this background, this chapter first reviews the recent, rapid, development in global derivatives market, illustrating the current state and examining the trends and changing patterns. It then introduces major derivatives exchanges in the world, together with the products, contract specifications and trading on these derivatives exchanges. Finally, the ways in which derivatives use shapes investor behaviour, risk management concept and risk management methods are discussed, leading to the study of major currency derivatives in the next three chapters.

## 9.1 Global Use of Derivatives – Current State, Trends and Changing Patterns

A phenomenal proliferation of derivative securities and their widespread use in trading and risk management is perhaps one of the most significant developments in the financial world in recent time. This section presents a survey on the current state of derivatives use and provides preliminary statistical analysis of trends and changing patterns in the data drawn from BIS (Bank for International Settlement)

Quarterly Review's derivatives statistics (various issues) and Triennial Surveys 1995, 1998 and 2001.

In response to such momentous increases of derivatives activity worldwide, the triennial Central Bank Survey of Foreign Exchange Market Activity was significantly expanded in the 1995 exercise to include the first attempt to estimate global activity in the world's derivatives markets - particularly the over-the-counter (OTC) markets, and was renamed the Central Bank Survey of Foreign Exchange and Derivatives Market Activity. Data on derivatives outstanding were collected for the first time for four market risk categories of foreign exchange, interest rate, equity and commodity derivatives, as well as turnover data on the full range of foreign exchange and interest rate derivatives. The following instrument breakdown was given in each market risk category: OTC forward contracts, OTC swaps, OTC options, Other OTC products, Futures, Exchange-traded options.

The information obtained in the surveys was compiled by pooling data provided by the central banks or monetary authorities in 26 countries with large or medium-sized derivatives markets. The counter party data were classified by "other (reporting) dealers", "other financial institutions" and "non-financial customers" for all foreign exchange and single-currency interest rate derivatives transactions. The counter party data were reduced to a breakdown by "other dealers" and "others" for equity and commodity derivatives. "Other dealers" were defined as other dealers either in the same country or in another country participating in the survey; they mainly include commercial and investment banks and securities houses which play a role as market-makers or intermediaries and other entities which are active dealers, such as subsidiaries of insurance companies. "Other financial institutions" were defined as organisations which did not participate in the survey but which provide financial services to independent companies or other economic agents. They include banks, funds and non-bank financial institutions which may be considered as financial end-users, such as mutual funds, pension funds, hedge funds, building societies, insurance companies. Transactions with central banks and monetary authorities were also placed under this heading. A "non-financial customer" was any counter party other than those described above, in practice mainly corporate firms and governments. As our main attention is on foreign exchange and interest rate derivatives, and the portions involved by non-financial corporations, we group "other dealers" and "other financial institutions" into one category of "financial institutions", and the rest, i.e., "non-financial customers", is called "non-financial firms", in our summary analysis. Since it is rare that a non-financial entity enters into a derivatives position without involving a financial institution, the "non-financial customers" figures measure non-financial firms' derivative activities fairly well.

Understandably, it is easier to collect the data of exchange-traded derivatives than OTC derivatives. Taking the availability and quality of data into account, we report, use, and analyse the statistics of exchange-traded derivatives for the period of 1992 – 2002, and those of OTC derivatives for the period of 1998 – 2001. Table 1 summarises overall derivatives market activity as in year 2001. It concentrates on foreign exchange derivatives and interest rate derivatives since they are concerned with the two most significant market risk categories; while the other two

risk categories of equity and commodity risks will be covered by detailed categorised tables. OTC derivatives by far exceed those of traded on organised exchanges in terms of notional amounts – the notional amount outstanding of OTC
foreign exchange and interest rate derivatives, with a value of $96206 billions, is
4.4 times of that of their exchange-traded counterparts at $21851 billions. Never-
theless, exchange traded derivatives are more liquid and have a much larger turnover relative to the notional amount – the daily turnover of exchange-traded foreign exchange and interest rate derivatives, with a value of $7006 billions, is much
greater than that of their OTC counterparts at $1342 billions. These figures lead to
a much higher turnover to notional amounts ratio for the exchange-traded derivatives. The last two columns of Table 9.1 indicate that an OTC foreign exchange
derivative instrument would be changed hands for 4.2 times in 100 working days,
while an exchanged-traded foreign exchange derivative instrument would be
changed hands for 38.7 time in the same period. An OTC interest rate derivative
instrument would be exchanged for less than one time and an exchange-traded interest rate derivative instrument would be exchanged for 32 times in 100 working
days. Overall, an OTC derivative instrument would be traded for 1.4 times and an
exchange-traded derivative instrument would be traded for 32.1 time in 100 working days, and the turnover ratio of exchange-traded derivatives is 23 times of that
of OTC derivatives. So the relative importance of OTC and exchange-traded derivatives cannot simply be judged by notional amounts outstanding.

**Table 9.1.** Derivatives market activity summary 2001 (in $ billions)

|  | Notional amount out-standing | | Turnover (daily averages) | | (TO/Ntn amnt outstdg)×100 | |
|---|---|---|---|---|---|---|
|  | OTC | Exchange | OTC | Exchange | OTC | Exch |
| FX | 20394 | 93 | 853 | 36 | 4.2 | 38.7 |
| Int rate | 75812 | 21758 | 489 | 6970 | 0.6 | 32.0 |
| Total | 96206 | 21851 | 1342 | 7006 | 1.4 | 32.1 |

It can be observed from Table 9.2, Figure 9.1, Table 9.3 and Figure 9.2 that
notional amounts outstanding of both OTC and exchange-traded derivatives have
been more than doubled in the six years period of 1995-2001. Derivatives traded
on organised exchanges, where longer period data are available, have been quad-
ruplicated in the last 15 years. Inspecting foreign exchange derivatives and interest
rate derivatives separately, it is revealed that these great increases have been
mainly associated with interest rate derivatives. Notional amounts of OTC foreign
exchange derivatives have merely increased by 56% in the six years period since
1995, and notional amounts of exchange-traded currency derivatives have almost
been halved in this period. Nevertheless, the spot market for foreign exchange has
been less active in this period - daily average turnover was $529 billions[1] in 2001
against a higher value of $680 billions in 1995; while daily average turnover of all
OTC foreign exchange derivatives has increased from $687 billions in 1995 to

---

[1]  Figures of non-derivatives are also from BIS to preserve consistency.

$853 billions in 2001. In the same period, notional amounts of OTC interest rate derivatives have increased from $26789 billions in 1995 to $75812 billions in 2001, which almost exactly matches the increase in total debt securities outstanding from $2803 billion in 1995 to $7511 billions in 2001. These figures suggest that the world derivatives market has entered a mature stage of stabilised growth matching the activity in the underlying securities market.

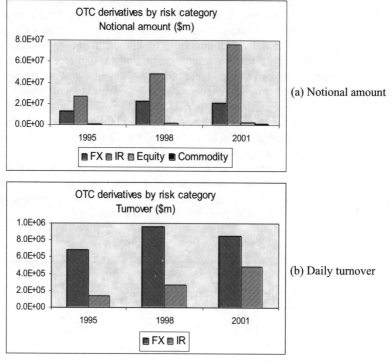

(a) Notional amount

(b) Daily turnover

**Figure 9.1.** Growing trends in OTC derivatives by risk category

**Table 9.2.a.** Notional amounts outstanding of OTC derivatives by risk category (in $ billions)

|                   | 1995  | 1998  | 2001  |
|-------------------|-------|-------|-------|
| Foreign exchange  | 13035 | 22022 | 20394 |
| Interest rate     | 26789 | 48092 | 75812 |
| Equity            | 579   | 1341  | 2039  |
| Commodity         | 318   | 278   | 674   |
| Total             | 40720 | 71733 | 98919 |

**Table 9.2.b.** OTC FX and IR derivatives turnover (daily averages in $ billions)

|                  | 1995 | 1998 | 2001 |
|------------------|------|------|------|
| Foreign exchange | 687  | 961  | 853  |
| Interest rate    | 138  | 265  | 489  |

**Table 9.3.a.** Notional amounts outstanding of exchange-traded derivatives by risk category (in $ billions)

| Year | Currency | Interest rate | Equity index | Total |
|------|----------|---------------|--------------|---------|
| 1986 | 49.4  | 514.0   | 52.3   | 615.7   |
| 1987 | 74.1  | 610.3   | 45.5   | 729.9   |
| 1988 | 60.1  | 1174.4  | 70.0   | 1304.5  |
| 1989 | 66.2  | 1587.0  | 112.0  | 1765.2  |
| 1990 | 73.5  | 2050.2  | 162.8  | 2286.5  |
| 1991 | 81.2  | 3227.0  | 213.0  | 3521.2  |
| 1992 | 98.1  | 4296.9  | 243.6  | 4638.6  |
| 1993 | 110.6 | 7321.8  | 342.5  | 7774.9  |
| 1994 | 96.1  | 8430.8  | 370.5  | 8897.4  |
| 1995 | 154.2 | 8618.0  | 510.7  | 9282.9  |
| 1996 | 171.1 | 9256.8  | 590.7  | 10018.6 |
| 1997 | 160.9 | 11226.6 | 1021.2 | 12408.7 |
| 1998 | 80.9  | 12654.9 | 1199.8 | 13935.6 |
| 1999 | 59.1  | 11680.3 | 1864.6 | 13604.0 |
| 2000 | 95.8  | 12642.0 | 1531.9 | 14269.7 |
| 2001 | 93.0  | 21758.1 | 1946.6 | 23797.7 |

**Table 9.3.b.** Exchange-traded derivatives turnover by risk category (daily averages in $ billions)

| Year | Currency | Interest rate | Equity index | Total |
|------|----------|---------------|--------------|--------|
| 1986 | 94.7  | 1452.7 | 339.8 | 1887.2 |
| 1987 | 131.7 | 2602.3 | 346.9 | 3080.9 |
| 1988 | 142.0 | 2899.1 | 267.3 | 3308.4 |
| 1989 | 156.4 | 4504.1 | 504.8 | 5165.3 |
| 1990 | 185.9 | 5064.3 | 537.4 | 5787.6 |
| 1991 | 185.0 | 5330.4 | 646.0 | 6161.4 |
| 1992 | 177.7 | 7850.3 | 550.9 | 8578.9 |
| 1993 | 48.9  | 2525.8 | 165.7 | 2740.3 |
| 1994 | 50.9  | 3590.8 | 216.2 | 3857.8 |
| 1995 | 48.7  | 2892.0 | 230.1 | 3170.8 |
| 1996 | 41.3  | 3123.5 | 273.6 | 3438.4 |
| 1997 | 40.4  | 3939.1 | 344.5 | 4324.0 |
| 1998 | 31.8  | 3937.2 | 399.7 | 4368.7 |
| 1999 | 31.2  | 3027.9 | 475.9 | 3535.0 |
| 2000 | 28.1  | 3672.3 | 478.3 | 4178.6 |
| 2001 | 35.9  | 6970.0 | 611.9 | 7617.9 |

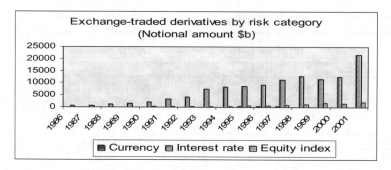

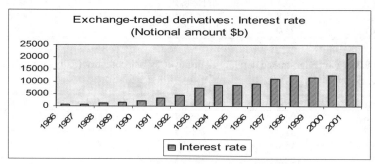

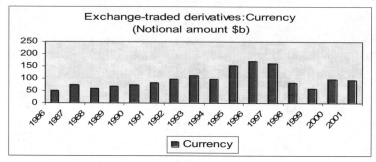

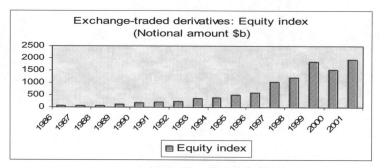

**Figure 9.2.a.** Growing trends in exchange-traded derivatives by risk category:
Notional amount

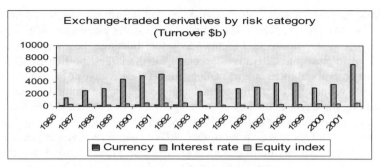

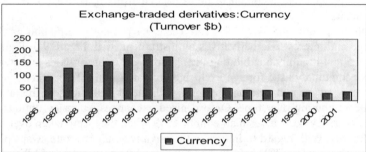

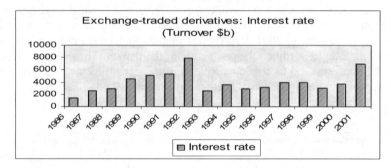

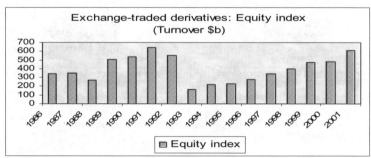

**Figure 9.2.b.** Growing trends in exchange-traded derivatives by risk category: Daily turnover

Table 9.2 and Table 9.3 also provide detailed information on the composition of OTC derivatives markets and organised derivatives exchanges with regard to risk categories. Figure 9.1 and Figure 9.2 further illustrate the compositions. The amount of interest rate derivatives accounts for the largest portion of all derivatives, which is about three quarters among all OTC derivatives of four risk categories, namely, interest rate, foreign exchange, equity and commodity, and about 90% among three risk categories of exchange-traded derivatives, interest rate, currency and equity index. In both OTC and exchange cases, interest rate and foreign exchange derivatives make up more than 90% of all derivatives in terms of notional amounts. We pay more attention to these two types of risk, since they are the most relevant and common to non-financial firms in risk exposure and risk management.

Table 9.4, Table 9.5, Table 9.6 and Table 9.7 present information on foreign exchange and interest rate derivatives by instrument, with Figure 9.3, Figure 9.4, Figure 9.5 and Figure 9.6 exhibiting the features. Outright forwards and swaps are the most commonly used foreign exchange derivatives on OTC markets, followed by currency swaps and currency options, with the contributions of the latter two instruments altering over time. On organised exchanges, currency options dominate the currency derivatives market until 1999 when they were taken over by currency futures. With regard to interest rate derivatives, interest rate swaps play the most important role in OTC trading, and the amounts outstanding of FRAs and interest rate options are more or less the same over years. Gradual increases in the use of interest rate options relative to interest rate futures have been witnessed on organised exchanges. In 2001, interest rate options took over interest rate futures for the first time to become a largest player in the market. These figures indicate that OTC markets tend to employ simple and linear instruments, whereas organised exchanges trade a substantial portion of complex and non-linear ones.

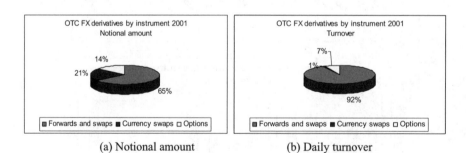

(a) Notional amount                (b) Daily turnover

**Figure 9.3.** OTC FX derivatives by instrument

**Table 9.4.a.** Notional amounts outstanding of OTC FX derivatives by instrument (in $ billions)

|                    | 1995  | 1998  | 2001  |
|--------------------|-------|-------|-------|
| Forwards and swaps | 8699  | 14658 | 13268 |
| Currency swaps     | 1957  | 2324  | 4302  |
| Options            | 2379  | 5040  | 2824  |
| FX total           | 13035 | 22022 | 20394 |

**Table 9.4.b.** OTC FX derivatives turnover by instrument (daily averages in $ billions)

|                    | 1995 | 1998 | 2001 |
|--------------------|------|------|------|
| Forwards and swaps | 643  | 864  | 786  |
| Currency swaps     | 4    | 10   | 7    |
| Options            | 41   | 87   | 60   |
| FX total           | 687  | 961  | 853  |

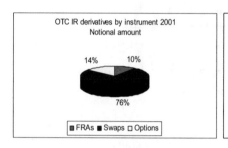 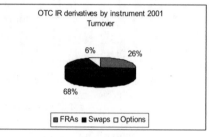

(a) Notional amount                    (b) Daily turnover

**Figure 9.4.** OTC IR derivatives by instrument

**Table 9.5.a.** Notional amounts outstanding of OTC interest rate derivatives by instrument (in $ billions)

|          | 1995  | 1998  | 2001  |
|----------|-------|-------|-------|
| FRAs     | 4957  | 6601  | 7679  |
| Swaps    | 18283 | 32962 | 57219 |
| Options  | 3548  | 8528  | 10913 |
| IR total | 26789 | 48092 | 75812 |

**Table 9.5.b.** OTC interest rate derivatives turnover by instrument (daily averages in $ billions)

|          | 1995 | 1998 | 2001 |
|----------|------|------|------|
| FRAs     | 66   | 74   | 129  |
| Swaps    | 63   | 155  | 331  |
| Options  | 10   | 36   | 29   |
| IR total | 138  | 265  | 489  |

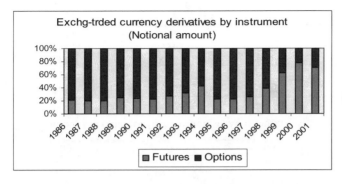

(a) Notional amount

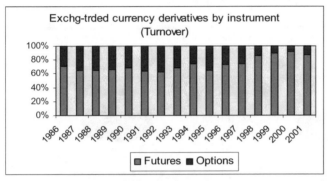

(b) Daily turnover

**Figure 9.5.** Exchange-traded FX derivatives by instrument

**Table 9.6.a.** Notional amounts outstanding of exchange-traded currency derivatives by instrument (in $ billions)

| Year | Futures | Options | Currency total |
|------|---------|---------|----------------|
| 1986 | 10.2 | 39.2 | 49.4 |
| 1987 | 14.6 | 59.5 | 74.1 |
| 1988 | 12.1 | 48.0 | 60.1 |
| 1989 | 16.0 | 50.2 | 66.2 |
| 1990 | 17.0 | 56.5 | 73.5 |
| 1991 | 18.3 | 62.9 | 81.2 |
| 1992 | 26.5 | 71.6 | 98.1 |
| 1993 | 34.7 | 75.9 | 110.6 |
| 1994 | 40.4 | 55.7 | 96.1 |
| 1995 | 33.8 | 120.4 | 154.2 |
| 1996 | 37.7 | 133.4 | 171.1 |
| 1997 | 42.3 | 118.6 | 160.9 |
| 1998 | 31.7 | 49.2 | 80.9 |
| 1999 | 36.7 | 22.4 | 59.1 |
| 2000 | 74.4 | 21.4 | 95.8 |
| 2001 | 65.6 | 27.4 | 93.0 |

**Table 9.6.b.** Exchange-traded currency derivatives turnover by instrument (daily averages in $ billions)

| Year | Futures | Options | Currency total |
|------|---------|---------|----------------|
| 1986 | 67.5 | 27.2 | 94.7 |
| 1987 | 85.3 | 46.3 | 131.7 |
| 1988 | 92.2 | 49.8 | 142.0 |
| 1989 | 102.8 | 53.6 | 156.4 |
| 1990 | 127.7 | 58.3 | 185.9 |
| 1991 | 118.6 | 66.5 | 185.0 |
| 1992 | 111.6 | 66.1 | 177.7 |
| 1993 | 33.3 | 15.6 | 48.9 |
| 1994 | 37.8 | 13.1 | 50.9 |
| 1995 | 31.6 | 17.1 | 48.7 |
| 1996 | 30.5 | 10.9 | 41.3 |
| 1997 | 29.8 | 10.5 | 40.4 |
| 1998 | 27.5 | 4.3 | 31.8 |
| 1999 | 28.1 | 3.1 | 31.2 |
| 2000 | 25.7 | 2.4 | 28.1 |
| 2001 | 31.4 | 4.5 | 35.9 |

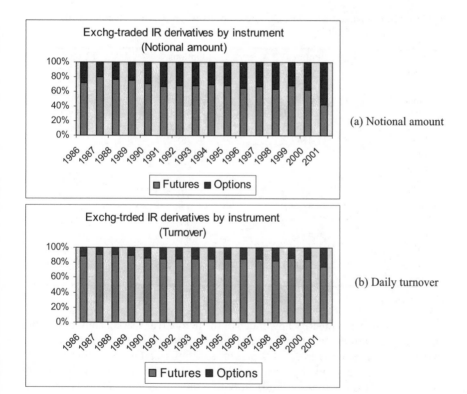

(a) Notional amount

(b) Daily turnover

**Figure 9.6.** Exchange-traded IR derivatives by instrument

**Table 9.7.a.** Notional amounts outstanding of exchange-traded interest rate derivatives by instrument (in $ billions)

| Year | Futures | Options | IR total |
|------|---------|---------|----------|
| 1986 | 370.0 | 144.0 | 514.0 |
| 1987 | 487.7 | 122.6 | 610.3 |
| 1988 | 895.4 | 279.0 | 1174.4 |
| 1989 | 1201.0 | 386.0 | 1587.0 |
| 1990 | 1454.8 | 595.4 | 2050.2 |
| 1991 | 2157.4 | 1069.6 | 3227.0 |
| 1992 | 2913.1 | 1383.8 | 4296.9 |
| 1993 | 4960.4 | 2361.4 | 7321.8 |
| 1994 | 5807.6 | 2623.2 | 8430.8 |
| 1995 | 5876.2 | 2741.8 | 8618.0 |
| 1996 | 5979.0 | 3277.8 | 9256.8 |
| 1997 | 7586.7 | 3639.9 | 11226.6 |
| 1998 | 8031.4 | 4623.5 | 12654.9 |
| 1999 | 7924.8 | 3755.5 | 11680.3 |
| 2000 | 7907.8 | 4734.2 | 12642.0 |
| 2001 | 9265.3 | 12492.8 | 21758.1 |

**Table 9.7.b.** Exchange-traded interest rate derivatives turnover by instrument (daily averages in $ billions)

| Year | Futures | Options | IR total |
|------|---------|---------|----------|
| 1986 | 1278.5 | 174.2 | 1452.7 |
| 1987 | 2358.6 | 243.7 | 2602.3 |
| 1988 | 2632.3 | 266.7 | 2899.1 |
| 1989 | 4042.1 | 462.0 | 4504.1 |
| 1990 | 4353.3 | 711.0 | 5064.3 |
| 1991 | 4542.2 | 788.2 | 5330.4 |
| 1992 | 6647.7 | 1202.5 | 7850.3 |
| 1993 | 2142.9 | 382.9 | 2525.8 |
| 1994 | 3042.5 | 548.2 | 3590.8 |
| 1995 | 2450.3 | 441.7 | 2892.0 |
| 1996 | 2647.6 | 475.9 | 3123.5 |
| 1997 | 3357.9 | 581.3 | 3939.1 |
| 1998 | 3255.3 | 681.8 | 3937.2 |
| 1999 | 2592.3 | 435.6 | 3027.9 |
| 2000 | 3100.1 | 572.2 | 3672.3 |
| 2001 | 5169.0 | 1801.0 | 6970.0 |

It is of interest to identify how much of the derivatives market activity involves financial institutions and non-financial firms respectively for risk management purposes. Table 9.8 and Figure 9.7 present such information. It is shown that derivatives activity engaged by non-financial firms account approximately for 10% of total derivatives activity in 2001 in both terms of notional amounts and turnover, declining from around 15-17% in 1995. Though derivatives activity involving non-financial firms increases at a much slower pace relative to that between financial institutions, these portions still represent a significant venture by non-financial firms, especially taking into account the fact that these firms are not primarily involved in trading that may proceed rather detached from the underlying securities.

**Table 9.8.a.** Notional amounts outstanding of OTC derivatives by counter party (in $ billions)

|  | 1995 | 1998 | 2001 |
|---|---|---|---|
| With financial institutions | 35727 | 64854 | 92051 |
| With non-financial customers | 7434 | 11444 | 12311 |

**Table 9.8.b.** OTC FX and IR derivatives turnover by counter party (daily averages in $ billions)

|  | 1995 | 1998 | 2001 |
|---|---|---|---|
| With financial institutions | 701 | 1096 | 1246 |
| With non-financial customers | 124 | 195 | 110 |

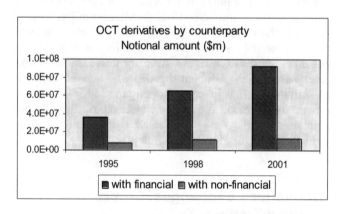

(a) Notional amount

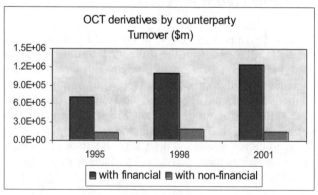

(b) Daily turnover

**Figure 9.7.** OTC derivatives by counterpart

**Table 9.9.** OTC FX and IR derivatives turnover by major country/region (daily averages in $ millions)

|  | Foreign exchange | Interest rate |
|---|---|---|
| UK | 390,313 | 237,752 |
| US | 169,076 | 115,668 |
| Germany | 65,218 | 94,030 |
| Japan | 115,946 | 15,761 |
| France | 40,925 | 65,096 |
| Singapore | 69,528 | 3,193 |
| Switzerland | 52,951 | 9,615 |
| Hong Kong | 49,388 | 2,641 |
| Australia | 40,852 | 9,811 |
| Canada | 33,379 | 9,916 |
| Total | 1,186,071 | 676,105 |

Chicago Board of Trade is the world's oldest derivatives exchange and Chicago Board of Options Exchange has pioneered the derivatives revolution of the modern time, reinforced by the developments in derivatives pricing theories and models in the surrounding academic institutions. Chicago Mercantile Exchange is the second largest exchange in the world for the trading of futures and options on futures. Moreover, the size of the US market means that the largest proportion of world derivatives trading on organised exchanges takes place in the US. Nevertheless and despite of these facts, it is the UK, not the US, who houses the world largest OTC derivatives activity. Table 9.9 reports these figures. UK OTC derivatives activity is almost twice as enormous as that in the US, and exceeds all other major economies to a great extent. These facts make a UK case study, such as ours, particularly appealing and in demand.

## 9.2 Organised Derivatives Exchanges, Contract Specifications and Trading

The most renowned financial derivatives exchanges in the world include the Chicago Mercantile Exchange (CME), the Chicago Board of Options Exchange (CBOE), the Chicago Board of Trade (CBOT), the Philadelphia Board of Trade of the Philadelphia Stock Exchange (PHLX), the Euronext, the London International Financial Futures and Options Exchange (LIFFE), and the Tokyo International Financial Futures Exchange (TIFFE). Among them, the CME is the largest organised futures market and the PHLX is the largest organised options market for foreign exchange. In addition to currency futures, the CME also trades options on currency futures. We briefly introduce these derivatives exchanges with a specific emphasis on foreign exchange.

*The Chicago Mercantile Exchange* was founded in 1898 initially as the Chicago Butter and Egg Board. At that time, futures were limited to agricultural products, especially butter and eggs. It developed quickly and, in 1919, became the Chicago Mercantile Exchange. On May 16, 1972, the CME creates the world's first financial futures contracts on seven foreign currencies. No June 26, 1992, the CME introduced GLOBEX, a global electronic trading platform offering trading approximately 23 hours a day, five days a week. In 2000, the CME was converted into a corporation from its mutual status, and in 2002, the Chicago Mercantile Exchange Holdings Inc, the parent company of the exchange, was listed on the New York Stock Exchange, becoming the first publicly traded US financial exchange.

The CME's products range from derivatives on commodity, equity indexes, foreign exchange, interest rates to derivatives on weather and TRAKRS. TRAKRS$^{SM}$ denote Total Return Asset Contracts and are designed to enable customers to track an index of stocks, bonds, currencies or other financial instruments. TRAKRS are futures contracts based on an index that is calculated on a total return basis; therefore, declared dividends and other distributions are included in the calculation of the index. Euro Currency TRAKRS$^{SM}$ are non-traditional futures contracts designed to provide customers with an effective way to gain exposure to the euro/US dollar exchange rate. Euro Currency TRAKRS futures are designed to track the Euro Currency TRAKRS Index, a total return index designed by Merrill Lynch. The Euro Currency TRAKRS Index is designed to track the total return performance of the euro relative to the US dollar.

Trading activity on the CME is shown in Table 9.10 for monthly trading volumes in October 2003 for exchange total, product group totals and currency product group details. Since the subject is foreign exchange here, details of other product groups are omitted. It can be observed from the top panel of the table that trading volume of futures is five times larger than that of options. The middle panel indicates that, among four product groups of agricultural products, currency products, equity & index products and interest rate products, the currency product group is the second smallest. Its trading volume is less than 1/10 of that for the interest rate product group, the largest product group in terms of trading volumes. The relative activity of the four product groups remains largely unchanged when trading volume is broken down into futures and options on futures. Trading volumes of a number of currency futures are presented in the lower panel of the table. The most active market is that for euros, followed by Japanese yen, Canadian dollars, Swiss francs and British pounds.

Table 9.11 lists the contract sizes of currency futures on the Australian dollar, the Brazilian real, the British pound, the Canadian dollar, the euro, the Japanese yen, the Mexican peso, the New Zealand dollar, the Norwegian kroner, the Russian ruble, the South African rand, the Swedish kronor and the Swiss franc traded on the CME. The contract size of the option on currency futures is one currency futures contract of the corresponding currency.

**Table 9.10.** Trading volume on CME October 2003

## EXCHANGE OVERALL, PRODUCT GROUPS AND FUTURES PRODUCTS

| | |
|---|---:|
| TOTAL | 57,287,504 |
| FUTURES | 48,155,737 |
| OPTIONS ON FUTURES | 9,131,767 |

### PRODUCT GROUP VOLUME TOTALS

| | |
|---|---:|
| FUTURES & OPTIONS COMBINED - | |
| AGRICULTURAL PRODUCTS | 948,458 |
| CURRENCY PRODUCTS | 2,718,568 |
| EQUITY & INDEX PRODUCTS | 25,151,200 |
| INTEREST RATE PRODUCTS | 28,469,278 |
| | |
| FUTURES ONLY - | |
| AGRICULTURAL FUTURES | 822,104 |
| CURRENCY FUTURES | 2,549,771 |
| EQUITY & INDEX FUTURES | 24,678,308 |
| INTEREST RATE FUTURES # | 20,105,554 |
| | |
| OPTIONS ON FUTURES ONLY - | |
| AGRICULTURAL OPTIONS * | 126,354 |
| CURRENCY OPTIONS | 168,797 |
| EQUITY & INDEX OPTIONS | 472,892 |
| INTEREST RATE OPTIONS | 8,363,724 |

### CURRENCY FUTURES

| | |
|---|---:|
| AUSTRALIAN DLR FUT # | 142,706 |
| BRITISH POUND FUT | 212,596 |
| BRAZILIAN REAL FUT | 13 |
| CANADIAN DLR FUT # | 285,682 |
| E- MINI EURO FX | 2,077 |
| EUROFX FUT # | 1,069,590 |
| E- MINI J- YEN FUT # | 511 |
| JAPANESE YEN FUT | 396,636 |
| MEXICAN PESO FUT | 172,189 |
| NZ DOLLAR FUT # | 9,925 |
| NOK FUT | --- |
| RUSSIAN RUBLE FUT # | 593 |
| SA RAND FUT 4, 373 | 4,373 |
| SEK FUT * | 4 |
| SWISS FRANC FUT | 237,163 |

\# denotes record volume month
\* denotes all time record volume month

**Table 9.11.** Contract sizes of currency futures traded on CME

| Currency | Contract size |
|---|---|
| Australian dollar (A$) | 100,000 Australian dollars |
| Brazilian real (BR) | 100,000 Brazilian reals |
| British pound (£) | 62,500 British pounds |
| Canadian dollar (C$) | 100,000 Canadian dollars |
| Euro (€) | 125,000 euros |
| Japanese yen (¥) | 12,500,000 Japanese yen |
| Mexican peso (MP) | 500,000 Mexican pesos |
| New Zealand dollar (NZ$) | 100,000 New Zealand dollars |
| Norwegian kroner (NKr) | 2,000,000 Norwegian kroner |
| Russian ruble (RU) | 2,500,000 Russian rubles |
| South African rand (RA) | 500,000 South African rand |
| Swedish kronor (SKr) | 2,000,000 Swedish kronor |
| Swiss franc (SFr) | 125,000 Swiss francs |

Source: Chicago Mercantile Exchange

**Table 9.12.** CME contract specifications

(a) Euro currency futures

| Euro FX Futures | | |
|---|---|---|
| Trade Unit | 125,000 Euro | |
| Point Descriptions | 1 point = $.0001 per Euro = $12.50 per contract | |
| Contract Listing | Six months in the March Quarterly Cycle. Mar, Jun, Sep, Dec. See notes +++ ** | |
| Strike Price Interval | N/A | |
| Product Code | Clearing=EC<br>Ticker=EC<br>GLOBEX=6E<br>AON=UG<br>(100 Threshold)& | |
| **Trading Venue: Floor** | | |
| Hours | 7:20 a.m.-2:00 p.m. LTD(9:16 a.m.)^ | |
| Listed | All listed series | |
| Strike | N/A | |
| Limits | No limits | |
| Minimum Fluctuation | Regular | 0.0001=$12.50 |
| | Calendar Spread | 0.00005=$6.25 |
| | All or None | 0.00005=$6.25 |
| **Trading Venue: GLOBEX®** | | |
| Hours | Mon/Thurs 5:00 p.m.-4:00 p.m. Sun & Hol 5:30 p.m.-4:00 p.m. | |
| Listed | All listed series plus 3 calendar spreads | |
| Strike | N/A | |
| Limits | No limits | |
| Minimum Fluctuation | Regular | 0.0001=$12.50 |
| | Calendar Spread | 0.00005=$6.25 |

**Table 9.12.** (cont.)

(b) Options on euro currency futures

| Euro FX Options | | |
|---|---|---|
| Trade Unit | | One Euro futures contract |
| Point Descriptions | | 1 point = $.0001 per Euro = $12.50 per contract |
| Contract Listing | | Four months in the March cycle, Mar, Jun, Sep, Dec and two months not in the March cycle (serial months), plus four weekly expirations. + |
| Strike Price Interval | | $.005 per Euro, e.g. $1.055, $1.060, $1.065, etc. Initial put and call strike prices listed at nearest strike to previous day's settlement price and 24 strikes higher and lower. New strikes added next day at next unlisted level higher or lower as underlying futures prices occur within a half-strike interval of the 24th higher or lower strike prices. |
| Product Code | | Clearing Calls/Puts=EC Ticker Calls=EC Ticker Puts=EC Weekly Expiration Options: Calls=1XC/5XC Puts=1XP/5XP AON=UG (100 Threshold)& |
| Trading venue: floor | | |
| Hours | | 7:20 a.m.-2:00 p.m. LTD(2:00 p.m.)^ |
| Listed | | All listed series |
| Strike | | All listed intervals |
| Limits | | No limits |
| Minimum Fluctuation | Regular | 0.0001=$12.50 |
| | Cab | 0.00005=$6.25 |
| | Special "Half Tick" | 0.00005=$6.25 for premium <0.0005, spreads w/net premium <0.0005, non-generic combos with total premium<0.0010. |
| Trading venue: GLOBEX® | | |
| Hours | | Mon/Thurs 2:30 p.m.-7:05 a.m. Sun & Hol 5:30 p.m.-7:05 a.m. |
| Listed | | 2 Quarterly and 2 Serial Months |
| Strike | | 16 strikes up & down, and including, the strike nearest the money. |
| Limits | | No limits |
| Minimum Fluctuation | Regular | 0.0001=$12.50 |
| | Cab | 0.00005=$6.25 |
| | Special "Half Tick" | 0.00005=$6.25 for premium <0.0005, spreads w/net premium <0.0005, non-generic combos with total premium<0.0010. |

Source: Chicago Mercantile Exchange

**Table 9.13.** Trading hours at CME

| Product | RTH Hours Mon.-Fri.* (CST) | GLOBEX Hours (CT) (Scheduled maintenance 4:00 – 5:00 p.m.) | | |
| --- | --- | --- | --- | --- |
| | | Weekday Openings | Sunday / Holiday Openings | All Closings |
| Australian Dollar | 7:20-14:00 | 17:00 | 17:30 | 16:00 |
| Australian Dollar Options | 7:20-14:00 | | | |
| Brazilian Real | 7:20-14:00 | 17:00 | 17:30 | 16:00 |
| Brazilian Real Options | 7:20-14:00 | 14:30 | 17:30 | 7:05 |
| British Pound | 7:20-14:00 | 17:00 | 17:30 | 16:00 |
| British Pound Options | 7:20-14:00 | 14:30 | 17:30 | 7:05 |
| British Pound / Japanese Yen | 7:20-14:00 (AON Only) | 17:00 | 17:30 | 16:00 |
| British Pound / Swiss Franc | 7:20-14:00 (AON Only) | 17:00 | 17:30 | 16:00 |
| Canadian Dollar | 7:20-14:00 | 17:00 | 17:30 | 16:00 |
| Canadian Dollar Options | 7:20-14:00 | 14:30 | 17:30 | 7:05 |
| E-Mini Euro FX | | 17:00 | 17:30 | 16:00 |
| E-Mini Japanese Yen | | 17:00 | 17:30 | 16:00 |
| Euro FX | 7:20-14:00 | 17:00 | 17:30 | 16:00 |
| Euro FX Options | 7:20-14:00 | 14:30 | 17:30 | 7:05 |
| Euro FX / British Pound | 7:20-14:00 (AON Only) | 17:00 | 17:30 | 16:00 |
| Euro FX / British Pound Cross Options | 7:20-14:00 | 14:30 | 17:30 | 7:05 |
| Euro FX / Japanese Yen | 7:20-14:00 (AON Only) | 17:00 | 17:30 | 16:00 |
| Euro FX / Japanese Yen Options | 7:20-14:00 | 14:30 | 17:30 | 7:05 |
| Euro FX / Swiss Franc | 7:20-14:00 (AON Only) | 17:00 | 17:30 | 16:00 |
| Euro FX / Swiss Franc Options | 7:20-14:00 | 14:30 | 17:30 | 7:05 |
| Japanese Yen | 7:20-14:00 | 17:00 | 17:30 | 16:00 |
| Japanese Yen Options | 7:20-14:00 | 14:30 | 17:30 | 7:05 |
| Mexican Peso | 7:20-14:00 | 17:00 | 17:30 | 16:00 |
| Mexican Peso Options | 7:20-14:00 | 14:30 | 17:30 | 7:05 |
| New Zealand Dollar | 7:20-14:00 | 17:00 | 17:30 | 16:00 |
| New Zealand Dollar Options | 7:20-14:00 | | | |
| Norwegian Krone | 7:20-14:00 (AON Only) | 17:00 | 17:30 | 16:00 |
| Russian Ruble | 7:20-14:00 | 17:00 | 17:30 | 16:00 |
| Russian Ruble Options | 7:20-14:00 | 14:30 | 17:30 | 7:05 |
| South African Rand | 7:20-14:00 | 17:00 | 17:30 | 16:00 |
| South African Rand Options | 7:20-14:00 | | | |
| Swiss Franc Futures | 7:20-14:00 | 17:00 | 17:30 | 16:00 |
| Swiss Franc Options | 7:20-14:00 | 14:30 | 17:30 | 7:05 |
| Swiss Franc / Japanese Yen | 7:20-14:00 (AON Only) | 17:00 | 17:30 | 16:00 |

AON – All Or None. At order entry, if the order can execute in total, then it executes. Otherwise it stays in the order book until it can execute in total.
RTH – Reference Regular Trading Hours

Source: Chicago Mercantile Exchange

In addition to the standard currency futures on the euro and the Japanese yen, the CME also offers E-mini Euro FX futures and E-mini Japanese yen futures. The E-mini Euro FX futures contract has a size of 62,500 euros, half of that of the Euro FX futures contract; and the E-mini Japanese yen futures' contract size, at the value of 6,250,000 Japanese yen, is also half of that of the standard Japanese yen futures. Both E-minis trade on the GLOBEX electronic trading system only and do not have their options counterparts.

Table 9.12a is an example of contract specifications for euro currency futures and Table 9.12b is an example of contract specification for options on euro currency futures on the CME. These futures and options are traded on both the CME floor and the electronic trading platform of GLOBEX and are quoted almost identically except the trading hours. Table 9.13 provides trading hour information on major currency futures and futures options traded on the CME. It can be seen that GLOBEX trades currency futures for 23 hours on weekdays, commencing at 17:00pm and continuing into the next day at 16:00pm, and for 22.5 hours between 17:30pm and 16:00pm on Sundays. While trading hours for options on futures are shorter for approximately 16.5 hours between 14:30pm and 7:05am on weekdays and for approximately 13.5 hours between 17:30pm and 7:05am on Sundays.

***The Philadelphia Stock Exchange***, founded in 1790, was the oldest securities exchange in the United States. The PHLX is reputed for its invention of exchange traded currency options in 1982. By 1988, currency options were trading in volumes as high as $4 billion per day in underlying value. Currency options put the Exchange on international maps, bringing trading interest from Europe, Pacific Rim and the Far East, and leading the Exchange to be the first securities exchange to open international offices in money centres overseas. Currency options made the Philadelphia Stock Exchange around-the-clock operation. In September 1987, Philadelphia was the first securities exchange in the United States to introduce an evening trading session, chiefly to accommodate increasing demand for currency options in the Far East, and the exchange responded to growing European demand by adding an early morning session in January 1989. In September 1990, The PHLX became the first exchange in the world to offer around-the-clock trading by bridging the gap between the night session and the early morning hours. Although the exchange subsequently scaled back its trading hours, its current currency option trading hours from 2:30 a.m. to 2:30 p.m. (the Philadelphia time) are longer than any other open outcry auction marketplace.

The PHLX trades more than 2,200 stocks, over 1,180 equity options, 15 index options, and multiple currency pairs. The PHLX offers high flexibility in currency option trading – both standardised and customised currency options are available. Customised currency options offer choice of expiration date, strike price and premium payment. Contract specifications for major currency futures traded on the PHLX are illustrated in Table 9.14a and contract specifications for major standardised currency options traded on the PHLX are shown in Table 9.14b. The contract size of currency options, both standardised and customised, is half of the contract size of their respective currency futures.

**Table 9.14.** PHLX contract specifications

## (a) Currency futures traded on PHLX

| Currency Futures | | | | | | |
|---|---|---|---|---|---|---|
| | Australian Dollar | British Pound | Canadian Dollar | Euro | Japanese Yen | Swiss Franc |
| Symbol | ZA | ZB | ZC | OZ | ZJ | ZS |
| Contract size | 100,000 | 62,500 | 100,000 | 125,000 | 12,500,000 | 125,000 |
| Quotation | USD per AUD | USD per GBP | USD per CAD | USD per EUR | USD per JPY×100 | USD per CHF |
| Minimum premium change | $.0001 =$10.00 | $.0001 =$6.25 | $.0001 =$10.00 | $.0001 =$12.50 | $.000001 =$12.50 | $.0001 =$12.50 |
| Contract month | March, June, September, December and two additional near-term months | | | | | |
| Last trading day | Friday before the third Wednesday of month | | | | | |
| Settlement | Cash (USD) | | | | | |
| Delivery settlement date | The first day on which The Options Clearing Corporation (OCC) is open for settlement following the last day of trading | | | | | |
| Daily price limits | None | | | | | |
| Position accountability limits | None | | | | | |
| Trading hours | 2:30 a.m. to 2:30 p.m., Eastern Time (Trading Hours for the Canadian dollar are 7: 00 a. m. to 2: 30 p. m., Eastern Time) | | | | | |
| Contract month Symbols | JAN F | BEF G | MAR H | APR J | MAY K | JUN M |

| Contract month | JAN | BEF | MAR | APR | MAY | JUN | JUL | AUG | SEP | OCT | NOV | DEC |
|---|---|---|---|---|---|---|---|---|---|---|---|---|
| Symbols | F | G | H | J | K | M | N | Q | U | V | X | Z |

## (b) Standardised currency options traded on PHLX

| Standardised Currency Options | | | | | | |
|---|---|---|---|---|---|---|
| | Australian Dollar | British Pound | Canadian Dollar | Euro | Japanese Yen | Swiss Franc |
| Ticker symbols (American/European) | | | | | | |
| Mid-month Options | XAD/CAD | XBP/CBP | XCD/CCD | XEU/ECU* XEB/ECB** | XJY/CJY | XSF/CSF |
| (Three near-term months only) | | | | | | |
| Half-point Strike | XAZ/CAZ | n.a./n.a. | XCD/CCD | n.a./n.a. | XJZ/CJZ | XSZ/CSZ |
| Alternate Symbols | XAY/CAY | XBX/CBX XBY/CBY | XCV/CCV | XEV/ECY | XJJ/CJJ XJV/CJV | XSY/CSY |
| Month-end Options | ADW/EDA | BPW/EPO | CDW/ECD | XEW/ECW* XEN/ECN** | JYW/EJY | SFW/ESW |
| Half-point Strike | AZW/EAW | n.a./n.a. | CDW/ECD | n.a./n.a. | JYZ/EJZ | SFZ/ESZ |
| Alternate Symbols | n.a./n.a. | BPU/EPU BPX/EPX | n.a./n.a. | XEZ | JYX/EJX | SFU/ESU |
| Contract size | 50,000 | 31,250 | 50,000 | 62,500 | 6,250,000 | 62,500 |
| Position & exercise limits | 200,000 | 200,000 | 200,000 | 200,000 | 200,000 | 200,000 |
| Base currency | USD | USD | USD | USD | USD | USD |
| Underlying currency | AUD | GBP | CAD | EUR | JPY | CHF |
| Exercise price intervals | | | | | | |
| Three Nearest Months | 1¢ | 1¢ | .5¢ | 1¢ | .005¢ | .5¢ |
| 6, 9 and 12 Months | 1¢ | 2¢ | .5¢ | 1¢ | .01¢ | 1¢ |
| Premium quotations | Cents per unit | Cents per unit | Cents per unit | Cents per unit | Hundredths of a cent per unit | Cents per unit |
| Minimum premium change | $.(00)01 per unit = $5.00 | $.(00)01 per unit = $3.125 | $.(00)01 per unit = $5.00 | $.(00)01 per unit = $6.25 | $.(0000)01 per unit = $6.25 | $.(00)01 per unit = $6.25 |

Source: Philadelphia Stock Exchange

*The Tokyo International Financial Futures Exchange* was established in April 1989 under the Financial Futures Trading Law of Japan. Unlike most futures exchanges in the US, the TIFFE trades exclusively in foreign exchange derivatives and primarily in currency futures and options on currency futures. Its products are limited to three-month Euroyen futures, three-month Euroyen LIBOR futures, Dollaryen currency futures, options on three-month Euroyen futures, and five-year and ten-year swapnotes. Table 9.15 provides contract specifications for the three month Euroyen futures and options on three month Euroyen futures traded on the TIFFE. The contract size for the three month Euroyen futures is ¥100,000,000, eight times of ¥12,500,000, the contract size of the yen futures traded on the CME and the PHLX. The contract size of the options on three month Euroyen futures is one unit of the futures contract. The monthly trading volume of the three month Euroyen futures on the TILLE is 652,860 units for the month of October 2003, much larger than the trading volume of 396,636 units of Japanese yen futures on the CME in the same period, taking into account the difference in contract size. However, trading in Dollaryen futures on the TIFFE is almost negligible. Call and put options on three month Euroyen futures are American options.

**Table 9.15.** TIFFE contract specifications

(a) Euroyen futures on TIFFE

| Three-month Euroyen Futures | |
|---|---|
| Trading unit | ¥100,000,000 (Notional principal amount) |
| Price quotation | 100 minus rate of interest |
| Tick size & value | 0.005<br>¥1,250 |
| Contract months | 20 quarterly months and 2 serial months (Serial months are the months other than March, June, September and Decem- |
| Last trading day | Two business days prior to the third Wednesday of the contract month |
| Final settlement date | The first business day following the last trading day |
| Final settlement | Cash settlement |
| Trading hours (JST) | 8:45 - 18:00 |
| Trading hours for the contract on its last trading day (JST) | 8:45 - 9:00   Pre-open period<br>9:00 - 11:00 Day session |

**Table 9.15.** (cont.)

(b) Options on Euroyen futures on TIFFE

| Options on Three-month Euroyen Futures | |
|---|---|
| Underlying asset | Three-month Euroyen futures |
| Trading unit | One unit of Three-month Euroyen futures ("Euroyen futures") <br> ¥100,000,000 (Notional principal amount) |
| Price quotation | Quoted in Euroyen futures points (0.005) |
| Strike price interval | 0.125 |
| Tick size & value | 0.005 <br> ¥1,250 |
| Contract months | 5 contract quarterly months <br> (March, June, September, December) |
| Exercise style | American type |
| Last trading day | Two business days prior to the third Wednesday of the contract month |
| Final settlement date | The first business day following the last trading day |
| Trading hours (JST) | 8:45 – 18:00 |
| Trading hours for the contract on its last trading day (JST) | 8:45 - 9:00   Pre-open period <br> 9:00 - 11:00 Day session |

Source: Tokyo International Financial Futures Exchange

Alongside Euroyen futures and options on Euroyen futures, the TIFFE is heavily involved in swapnote trading. The yen swapnote has been devised in cooperation with Euronext.liffe, the combined derivatives operations of the Euronext, and is traded on the TIFFE under licence from the LIFFE, with the permission of ICAP plc group, the inter-dealer broker. Brief information about swapnotes is provided in the introduction to the LIFFE underneath.

***Euronext*** was formed on 22 September 2000 when the exchanges of Amsterdam, Brussels and Paris merged. The Euronext group expanded through the mergers with the LIFFE and with the Portuguese exchange BVLP (Bolsa de Valores de Lisboa e Porto) in 2002. At present, Euronext consists of ***Euronext Paris***, ***Euronext Brussels***, ***Euronext Amsterdam***, ***Euronext Lisbon*** and ***Euronext.liffe***. Since its inception, Euronext has implemented a single trading platform (NSC) and a set of common trading rules for the cash markets in Amsterdam, Brussels and Paris, allowing investors at different business locations to access these markets in the same way. The migration of the Brussels and Paris markets to LIFFE CONNECT in 2003 and the changeover to Clearing 21®, which had already been used in Paris and Brussels, have been the first steps towards the harmonisation of the trading and clearing systems of the derivative markets. The integration process will continue to move the Portuguese markets to Euronext's cash trading platform, and complete the migration of the derivative markets to LIFFE CONNECT and the harmonisation of their clearing systems.

*Euronext.liffe*, legendarily known as the *LIFFE, the London International Financial Futures and Options Exchange*, was created in 1992 when the original LIFFE, the London International Financial Futures Exchange established in 1982, merged with the London Traded Options Market. In 1996, the LIFFE merged with the London Commodity Exchange, incorporating soft and agricultural commodity contracts into its product range. Notice that the acronym does not include the first letter of Options though Options is with the full name. LIFFE products include short term interest rates (STIRs), bonds, swapnotes, equities and commodities derivatives, with a focus on STIRs. In 1998, the LIFFE embarked on a programme to transfer all its contracts from the traditional method of trading to an electronic platform, LIFFE CONNECT, claimed to be the most sophisticated electronic derivatives trading platform in the world. In February 1999, the LIFFE's shareholders voted unanimously for a corporate restructuring, which progressed the LIFFE further towards becoming a profit-oriented commercial organisation. With effect from April 1999, the restructuring split the right to trade and membership from shareholding, simplified a complex share structure and enabled non-members to purchase shares in LIFFE (Holdings) plc. In 2002, the LIFFE was taken over by Euronext and the new Euronext.liffe is the pan-European derivatives business of Euronext, comprising the Amsterdam, Brussels, LIFFE, Lisbon and Paris derivatives markets. Consequently, currency futures and options previously traded on the Amsterdam Exchanges are now accessible through Euronext.liffe. Currently, these currency derivatives are primarily Euro/US dollar futures, US dollar/Euro futures, Euro/US dollar options and US dollar/Euro options. The contract size of €/$ currency futures and $/€ currency futures is €20,000 and $20,000 respectively; and the contract size of €/$ currency options and $/€ currency options, with the value being €10,000 and $10,000 respectively, is half of that for their corresponding futures counterpart. Table 9.16 summarises trading volume information on the currency futures and options traded on Euronext.liffe/ Euronext Amsterdam. Comparing with Table 9.10, it can be observed that trading volume of currency futures and options on Euronext.liffe is substantially lower than that on the CME.

In March 2001, the LIFFE launched swapnote products. The swapnote is a bond future referenced to the swap market, so it can be viewed as a bond futures contract that is priced in line with the swaps curve. Swapnotes are exchange-traded and centrally cleared. "Swapnote$^{TM}$" is a trade mark of the ICAP plc group and is exclusively licensed to the LIFFE. Swapnote contracts are denominated in euros and US dollars at the LIFFE. In each of the currencies, there are swapnote contracts on bonds with two-, five- and ten-year maturities. However, the bond on which the swapnote is written does not exist; it is a "notional bond". The swapnote contract is cash settled against a value calculated by the Exchange, requiring no delivery of a bond chosen from a specified list. This value is calculated as the present value of the notional bond's cash flows of the coupon and principal payments, using zero coupon discount factors derived from the ISDA (International Swaps and Derivatives Association) swaps fixings on the contract's last trading day. Using ISDA swaps fixings in this way ensures that the swapnote contract is valued in line with the swap market in that the notional bond has the credit risk of the inter bank swaps market. The notional principal is $200,000 for the two-year $ swapnote futures contract and $100,000 for five- and ten- year $ swapnote futures contracts. The notional principal is €100,000 for all of the two-, five- and ten- year € swaptnote futures contracts. A notional fixed rate of 6% applies to all of them. Table 9.17 shows two examples of contract specifications for ten-year € swapnote futures and two-year $ swapnote futures. In March 2004, the LIFFE launched its three month Eurodollar futures and options contracts, the most advanced and widely distributed electronic derivatives trading system in the world. Table 9.18 presents examples of contract specifications for three month Eurodollar interest rate futures contract, options on three month Eurodollar futures contract, and one year mid-curve options on three month Eurodollar futures.

**Table 9.16.** Trading volume of currency futures and options on Euronext.liffe, 2003

|      | Futures | | | | Options | | | |
|------|--------|-----------|-----------|-----------|--------|-------------|--------|-------------|
|      | €/$ (FED) | | $/€ (FDE) | | €/$(EDX) | | $/€(DEX) | |
|      | Units | Value (€) | Units | Value (€) | Units | Value (€) | Units | Value (€) |
| Jan  | 59  | 1,180,000 | 39  | 736,458   | 3,054  | 30,540,000  | 3,792  | 35,622,019  |
| Feb  | 32  | 640,000   | 19  | 351,028   | 2,022  | 20,220,000  | 1,659  | 15,396,323  |
| Mar  | 204 | 4,080,000 | 124 | 2,279,594 | 3,645  | 36,450,000  | 8,955  | 83,876,307  |
| Apr  | 8   | 160,000   | 84  | 1,557,350 | 1,832  | 18,320,000  | 2,184  | 20,061,129  |
| May  | 65  | 1,300,000 | 82  | 1,426,526 | 7,054  | 70,540,000  | 6,187  | 53,520,011  |
| Jun  | 246 | 4,920,000 | 70  | 1,203,966 | 4,998  | 49,980,000  | 3,927  | 33,636,862  |
| Jul  | 71  | 1,420,000 | 59  | 1,043,078 | 4,028  | 40,280,000  | 2,328  | 20,500,890  |
| Aug  | 90  | 1,800,000 | 30  | 546,222   | 4,380  | 43,800,000  | 2,746  | 24,769,663  |
| Sep  | 134 | 2,680,000 | 84  | 1,481,608 | 6,586  | 65,860,000  | 3,970  | 34,973,211  |
| Aug  | 222 | 4,440,000 | 52  | 885,920   | 10,006 | 100,060,000 | 5,423  | 46,283,209  |
| Nov  | 138 | 2,760,000 | 49  | 836,374   | 10,433 | 104,330,000 | 7,191  | 61,264,097  |
| Dec  | 136 | 2,720,000 | 396 | 6,361,808 | 16,241 | 162,410,000 | 15,683 | 127,375,528 |

**Table 9.17.** LIFFE contract specifications of € swapnote futures

(a) Ten-year € swapnote futures on LIFFE

| Ten-Year € Swapnote® Futures | |
|---|---|
| Unit of Trading[1] | €100 000 notional principal amount with 6.0% notional fixed rate |
| Maturities[2] | Notional principal amount due ten years from the delivery day |
| Delivery Months | March, June, September and December such that the nearest two delivery months are always available for trading |
| Quotation | Per €100 nominal |
| Minimum Price Movement (Tick Size & Value) | 0.01 (€10) |
| Last trading day | 10:00 Two business days prior to the delivery day |
| Delivery Day | Third Wednesday of the delivery month |
| Trading Hours | 07:00 – 18:00 |

(b) Two-year $ swapnote futures on LIFFE

| Two-Year $ Swapnote® Futures | |
|---|---|
| Unit of Trading[1] | $200 000 notional principal amount Notional Fixed Rate 6.0% |
| Maturities[2] | Notional principal amount due two years from the delivery day |
| Delivery Months | March, June, September and December such that the nearest two delivery months are always available for trading |
| Quotation | Per $100 nominal value |
| Minimum Price Movement (Tick Size & Value) | 0.005 ($10) |
| Last Trading Day | 11:00 New York time Two business days prior to the delivery day |
| Delivery Day | Third Wednesday of the delivery month |
| Trading Hours | 07:00 – 20:00 |

Source: Euronext.liffe

**Table 9.18.** LIFFE contract specifications for $ swapnote futures

(a) Three month Eurodollar interest rate futures on LIFFE

| Three Month Eurodollar Interest Rate Futures Contract | |
|---|---|
| Unit of Trading | Interest rate on three month deposit of $1,000,000 |
| Delivery Months | March, June, September, December and four serial months, such that 24 delivery months are available for trading, with the nearest six delivery months being consecutive calendar months |
| Quotation | 100.000 minus rate of interest |
| Minimum Price Movement (Tick Size & Value) | 0.005 ($12.50) for all delivery months |
| Last Trading Day | 11:00 London time – Two London business days prior to the third Wednesday of the delivery month |
| Delivery Day | First business day following the Last Trading Day |
| Trading Hours | 07:00 to 21:00 London time |
| Daily Settlement | Positions settled to nearest 0.005<br>20:00 London time |

(b) Options on three month Eurodollar interest rate futures on LIFFE

| Options on Three Month Eurodollar Futures Contract | |
|---|---|
| Unit of Trading | One Three Month Eurodollar Futures Contract |
| Expiry Months | March, June, September and December and two serial months, such that ten expiry months are available for trading, with the nearest three expiry months being consecutive calendar months (serial options relate to the following quarterly delivery month of the futures contract) |
| Quotation | Percentage points |
| Minimum Price Movement (Tick Size & Value) | 0.005<br>$12.50 for all expiry months |
| Exercise Day | Exercise by 20:00 London time on any business day prior to the Last Trading Day<br>Exercise by 11:45 London time on the Last Trading Day |
| Last Trading Day | 11:00 London time Two London business days prior to the third Wednesday of the expiry month |
| Delivery Day | First business day following Exercise |
| Trading Hours | 07:02 to 21:00 London Time |
| Daily Settlement | Positions settled to the nearest 0.005<br>20:00 London time. |

**Table 9.18.** (cont.)

(c) One year mid-curve options on three month Eurodollar interest rate futures on LIFFE

| One Year Mid-Curve Options on Three Month Eurodollar Futures | |
|---|---|
| Unit of Trading | One Three Month Eurodollar Futures Contract |
| Expiry Months | March, June, September and December and two serial months, such that six expiry months are available for trading, with the nearest three expiry months being consecutive calendar months (quarterly options relate to future with delivery month one year further than the option's expiry month; serial options relate to future with delivery month one year further than the following quarterly delivery month) |
| Quotation | Percentage points |
| Minimum Price Movement (Tick Size & Value) | 0.005 on all expiry months ( $12.50 on all expiry months) |
| Exercise Day | Exercise by 20:00 hours London time on any business day prior to the Last Trading Day Exercise by 11:45 London time on the Last Trading Day |
| Last Trading Day | Two London business days prior to the third Wednesday of the expiry month at 11:00 hours London time for both serial expiry months and quarterly expiry months. |
| Delivery Day | Delivery on the first business day after the exercise day |
| Trading Hours | 07:02 – 21:00 hours London time |
| Daily Settlement | Positions settled to the nearest 0.005 20:00 hours London time |

Source: Euronext.liffe

## 9.3    Use of Derivatives Shapes Investor Behaviour, Risk Management Concept and Risk Management Methods

Introduction of new securities to a complete market is unnecessary. Any new types of securities can be formed using a selection of the existing securities, with the exactly same payoffs. When the market is incomplete as it is the case in reality, a new security will have some kind of role to play in the financial market, it may or may not make the market more complete, depending on the degree to which the payoff of the new security defers from that of a combination of the existing ones. In the last three decades, derivative securities have rapidly found a significant role in the incomplete market, which makes the market more complete and competitive on the one hand, and creates vast and complicated new financial management tasks and techniques on the other hand.

Before the emergence and widespread applications of derivatives, the portfolio theory based on mean-variance diversification of Markowitz, the Capital Asset

Pricing Model and its variations have dominated the approaches to institutional investment in the equity market. The use of derivatives has added an additional dimension to equity investment strategies, e.g., by entering into a put option contract on an equity index, one could insure an equity portfolio that mimics the index against dropping below a certain level of its market value, which is not attainable by CAPM portfolios. In the management of risk exposure of interest rate products, such as bonds and bond portfolios, derivatives use has taken some attention away from those traditionally used strategies based on duration, timing and interest rate forecasts, through alternating the cash generating patterns of assets and liabilities in response to interest rate changes, to achieve desirable cash flows. With regard to foreign exchange, forward contracts came into existence as early as spot transactions existed. The impact of recent developments in the derivatives market would be the use of advanced instruments such as options and currency swaps against the preliminary products of outright forwards and swaps.

In the corporate financial management arena of non-financial firms, the use of financial securities has been traditionally and mainly for the purpose of raising capital and financing projects cost-effectively. The range of financial securities involved in these corporations is rather limited. The use of derivative securities opens a new channel to corporate financial management in an era of financial innovations, to the great effect of alternating and helping achieve desirable cash flow patterns. Prudently applied, it reduces risks in operations, leading to the reduction of risk in unlevered equity; it reduces risks in liabilities, leading to the reduction of risk in levered equity. Traditional financial performance measures, such as leverage and the interest coverage ratio, can no longer stand on their own to serve as debt management criteria without having considered derivatives. Sensible and effective use of derivatives in the debt management area by corporate financial managers has almost become a legitimate requirement of investors, shareholders and creditors alike, upon which financial and managerial performance is formally or informally evaluated. Not only financial figures, but also cash flows from operations, have increasingly been under the scrutiny of financial analysts and investors, impacted by the development of derivative securities and derivatives markets. Using available and relevant derivative financial instruments to manage and hedge against the exposure to foreign exchange and input/output markets has developed into a mandate, enforced upon the management by various market and corporate governance mechanisms, even if it were not required by financial regulatory authorities.

Financial management in general and risk management in particular must be a dynamic process due to the widespread availability of derivative financial instruments and an easy access to the derivatives market, replacing the past practice of setting static goals or targets in financial planning, which, no matter how perfect they look, cannot be maintained in a changing environment. The next three chapters will introduce major financial derivatives – futures, options and swaps, with a focus on foreign exchange. Managing foreign exchange exposure with foreign exchange derivatives will be addressed in Chapter 13 and Chapter 14 after discussions of foreign exchange exposure and types of foreign exchange exposure.

# 10 Currency Futures

This chapter and the next two chapters introduce major financial derivatives used for financial risk management and, in particular, for foreign exchange risk management. Futures are in many ways similar to forwards, the primary distinction being that the former is exchange traded standardised contract and the latter is an OTC product that may be negotiated or tailored to meet the specific needs of the parties involved. However, there is no such contrast for other major derivatives, such as options and swaps – they can be exchange traded and OTC. e.g., an exchange traded option does not distinguish from its OTC counterpart with a different name, unlike futures and forwards, they are both called options.

Futures and forwards are the most straightforward derivatives products. So straightforward that their price and price movement are almost identical to that in their corresponding spot market, with a time lag. The difference in the futures or forward market and the spot market arises primarily from interest accrual, whether the trading activity is confined to the domestic market or across borders. Due to this nature, forwards and futures command the largest trading volume in derivatives markets, on OTC markets and derivatives exchanges.

## 10.1 Futures Contracts and Trading

Similar to forwards, a futures contract specifies that a certain amount of an asset, a financial asset or a commodity, will be purchased or sold at a predetermined price at a predetermined future time. Unlike forwards, futures are standardised contracts trading on organized exchanges with daily resettlement through a clearinghouse. Futures contracts are standardised in contract size and delivery time, and are marked-to-market. That is, gains or losses are credited or debited daily from a margin account that must be opened prior to trading, so losses are not possible to accumulate. Whereas a forward is a private agreement between a buyer and a seller for the future delivery of an asset at an agreed price, with the negotiated contract size, delivery time and delivery method, being settled at the end of the contract period. Table 10.1 contrasts a futures contract with a forward contract. Replacing in the above the general term "an asset" by a specific one "a currency", currency futures emerge. A currency futures contract is then an agreement specifying that a certain amount, multiple of the contract size, of a currency will be exchanged for another currency at a predetermined price, i.e., the exchange rate between the two currencies, at a predetermined future time. Contract sizes of major currency futures products traded on the CME and other major derivatives exchanges have been presented in Chapter 10 and require no further discussion, so we start with the trading process with a focus on daily resettlement, the most important mechanism of futures trading, and progress to the more technical aspects of futures contracts.

**Table 10.1.** Futures versus forwards

| Forwards | Futures |
|---|---|
| OTC/ Private contracts between two parties | Exchange traded involving a clearing house |
| Customised | Standardised |
| Usually one specified delivery date | A range of delivery dates |
| Settled at maturity | Daily resettlement |
| Delivery or final cash settlement usually takes place | Contracts usually closed out prior to maturity |

To begin with, the buyer or the seller of a futures contact opens a *margin account* with a broker. The *margin*, also referred to as *performance bond*, providing financial safeguards to ensure that clearing members perform on their customers' open futures contracts, is the amount of money or collateral deposited by individual buyers or sellers of futures contracts with their brokers, or by clearing members with a clearinghouse, which is referred to as *custom margin* in the former and *clearing margin* in the latter. The amount of margin per contract required to be deposited into the margin account at the time a customer places an order to buy or sell a futures contract is called *initial margin*, also referred to as *original margin* or *initial performance bond*. Since the futures price fluctuates during trading sessions, gains or losses are made and are credited or debited daily from the margin account, so the level of the margin account may change every day. A set minimum margin that a customer must maintain in the margin account is *maintenance margin*. When adverse price movements cause the margin account to drop below the maintenance margin, the customer receives a call from the broker, or a clearing member receives a call from a clearinghouse, to deposit more money into the margin account and bring the account back to the initial margin level. Such calls are termed as *margin call*, or *performance bond call*. The maintenance margin is always smaller than the initial margin; otherwise a margin call would have been triggered even before the trading session had started. Table 10.2 lists the initial margin and maintenance margin required for major currency futures traded on the PHLX. Margins are determined on the basis of market risk and contract value.

Recall the contract sizes of these currency futures presented in Chapter 9, the initial margin is about 2% of the respective contract value and the maintenance margin is about 1/2 to 2/3 of the respective initial margin.

**Table 10.2.** PHLX customer margins

|  | Initial margin | Maintenance margin |
|---|---|---|
| Australian Dollar (ZA$^*$) | $1,350 | $1,000 |
| British Pound (ZB) | $1,823 | $1,350 |
| Canadian Dollar (ZC) | $1,350 | $1,000 |
| Euro (OZ) | $2,400 | $1,100 |
| Japanese Yen (ZJ) | $1,755 | $1,300 |
| Swiss Franc (ZS) | $1,800 | $1,300 |

\* Product symbol at PHLX

It has been noticed in the above that in futures trading and daily resettlement, clearinghouses, clearing members and brokers are involved, alongside buyers and sellers of futures contracts. A *broker* is an individual or a firm paid a fee or commission for executing the futures order for the customer. A *clearinghouse* is an agency or separate corporation of a futures exchange that is responsible for settling trading accounts, clearing trades, collecting deposits, maintaining margins, regulating delivery, and reporting trading data, such as closing prices. A clearinghouse acts as the third party to all futures contracts, as a buyer to every clearing member seller and a seller to every clearing member buyer. A *clearing member* refers to the membership of an exchange clearinghouse and is a firm qualified to clear trades through clearinghouses.

The following example demonstrates how daily resettlement works. Suppose Clare entered into ten euro currency futures contacts traded on the CME on January 2, 2004 to sell euros in June 2004 at the price of $1.2546 for one euro or at the exchange rate of $1.2546/€. The contract size is €125,000 per contract, the initial margin is set at $3,240 and the maintenance margin is $2,400. The second column in Table 10.3 is the settlement price at the closing of each of the trading days based on which daily gains or losses are calculated. The third column records daily losses made during the trading session where negatives figures represent trading gains and the fourth column records cumulative losses or gains. The fifth column is margin account balance, which was $3,240 per contract when the account was opened on January 2, 2004, as though there were no margin calls. On the second trading day of January 5, 2004 the settlement price was $1.2621 and Clare made a loss of $937.5 per contract, calculated as $(1.2621-1.2546)\times125,000$. According to the contract, Clare could exchange €125,000 for $156,825 (€125,000×$1.2546/€) in June but on January 5 the same amount of euros was worth $157762.5 (€125,000×$1.2621/€) in June. So she was worse off by $937.5 per contract and her total loss in ten contracts was $9,375. This loss brought down

**Table 10.3.** Daily resettlement example – June 2004 euro currency futures

| Date | Settlement price | Daily losses/ gains | Cumulative losses/gains | Margin account balance without margin calls | Margin call | Margin account balance |
|---|---|---|---|---|---|---|
| Jan 02, 04 | 1.2546 | | | 3,240.0 | | |
| Jan 05, 04 | 1.2621 | 937.5 | 937.5 | 2,302.5 | 937.5 | 3,240.0 |
| Jan 06, 04 | 1.2708 | 1,087.5 | 2,025.0 | 1,215.0 | 1,087.5 | 3,240.0 |
| Jan 07, 04 | 1.2593 | -1,437.5 | 587.5 | 2,652.5 | | 4,677.5 |
| Jan 08, 04 | 1.2710 | 1,462.5 | 2,050.0 | 1,190.0 | | 3,215.0 |
| Jan 09, 04 | 1.2789 | 987.5 | 3,037.5 | 202.5 | 1,012.5 | 3,240.0 |
| Jan 12, 04 | 1.2700 | -1,112.5 | 1,925.0 | 1,315.0 | | 4,352.5 |
| Jan 13, 04 | 1.2699 | -12.5 | 1,912.5 | 1,327.5 | | 4,365.0 |
| Jan 14, 04 | 1.2617 | -1,025.0 | 887.5 | 2,352.5 | | 5,390.0 |
| Jan 15, 04 | 1.2529 | -1,100.0 | -212.5 | 3,452.5 | | 6,490.0 |
| Jan 16, 04 | 1.2328 | -2,512.5 | -2725.0 | 5,965.0 | | 9,002.5 |

**Table 10.4.** Summary of transactions in June 2004 euro currency futures

| Initial margin account balance (1) | Margin call deposits (2) | Total deposits (3) =(1)+(2) | Final margin account balance (4) | Trading loss/gain (5) =(4)-(3) |
|---|---|---|---|---|
| $3,240.0 | $3037.5 | $6,277.5 | $9,002.5 | -2,725.0 |

her margin account to $2,302.5 (3,240-937.5), which was lower than the maintenance margin of $2,400, triggering a margin call to deposit $937.5 per contract into the margin account so the margin account balance was brought back to its initial level of $3,240. The sixth column in Table 10.3 shows all the margin calls Clare received from her broker when the contracts remained open and the seventh column of Table 10.3 is the actual margin account balance that was always higher than or equal to $2,400, the maintenance margin. The US dollar continued to weaken and the settlement price became $1.2708 on January 6, 2004. As a result, Clare made an additional loss of $1087.5, which was calculated as (1.2708-1.2621)×125,000 and the cumulative loss was $2,025. Due to the loss made on the day, the margin account once again dropped to a level below the maintenance margin (2152.5 = 3,240-1870.5), so a margin call was received to deposit $1,087.5 into the margin account and the margin account was brought back to $3,240 on January 6, 2004. On January 7, 2004, the settlement price changed in favour of Clare and she made a substantial trading gain of $1,437.5, which brought down her cumulative loss to $587.5 and her margin account balance to $4,677.5. For the sake of convenience in discussion as well as in practice let us keep the extra money in the margin account. The exchange rate continued to fluctuate and she made a large trading loss of $1,462.5 the next day. However, the margin account balance, at $3,215, was above the level of maintenance margin, so no margin call was necessary and made. On January 9, an additional loss of $987.5 made her margin account drop to $2227.5 and an extra amount of $1,012.5 was deposited. The settlement price fell in all five days in the next week Clare made trading gains every day in the week. She decided to close to contracts on Friday, January 16, 2004. Her cumulative gain was $2,725 per contract. The final margin account balance per contract was $9,002.5, which Clare got back from her broker. During this period, three margin calls were made and an extra amount of $3,037.5 was deposited per contract. Together with the initial margin requirement of $3,240, Clare put a total $6,277.5 per contract as deposit with her broker. The difference of the final margin account balance of $9,002.5 and the total deposit of $6,277.5, which was $2,725, was her trading gain per contract in this period. Her total trading gain in ten contracts was $27,250. Table 10.4 summarises the transactions.

## 10.2 Futures Quotes

In the above example, we have used settlement prices in the calculation of daily losses or gains. The settlement price is among the most important and relevant information in futures quotes. This section introduces and discusses how currency futures are quoted and the associated terminology for futures quotes. Table 10.5, daily bulletin of January 15, 2004 for euro currency futures trading, is used an example for discussion. The table is an extraction of a range of futures products of foreign currencies vis-à-vis the US dollar  The first column, beginning with EUROFX, is the product type, e.g., JUN04 stands for euro currency futures that matures in June 2004, MAR05 for euro currency futures maturing in March 2005. In the second column is *opening range*, the range of prices at which buy and sell transactions took place during the opening of the market, e.g., for March 2004 futures it was quoted as 1.26190@1.26180. Whereas the first price of a contract at the beginning of the trading session is *opening price*, e.g., it was 1.25870, 1.25400 and 1.24950 for June 2004, September 2004 and December 2004 futures respectively. *High* is the highest price for a futures contract during the trading session, e.g., it was 1.25930 and 1.25600 for the June 2004 futures contract and the September 2004 futures contract respectively. A letter B affixed to the price indicates that it is a bid price, e.g., 1.25600B for September 2004 futures. Since the bid price is usually lower than its corresponding ask price, so figures in the column for High are usually ask price and an indication is made when it is not an ask price. *Low* is the lowest price at which a contract was traded during the trading session, e.g., it was 1.25500 for March 2004 futures and 1.25220 for June 2004 futures. The letter A affixed to the price indicates that it is ask price, e.g., 1.25220A for June 2004 futures, for the same reason given earlier. The last price paid for a

**Table 10.5.** Sample daily bulletin of CME

CURRENCY FUTURES
INDIVIDUAL CONTRACT PRICE DATA FOR OPEN, HIGH, LOW, CLOSE AND SETTLEMENT PLUS CLEARED VOLUME
FIGURES REFLECT CME REGULAR
NUMBER 010 PG07
THU, JAN 15, 2004

TRADING HOURS SESSION ONLY. RTH VOLUME REFLECTS PIT TRADING AND CASH-FOR-FUTURES ONLY. VOLUME OR OPEN INTEREST (BOTH BEFORE AND AFTER THE LAST DAY OF TRADING) MAY BE AFFECTED BY: CASH FOR FUTURES, SPREADS, PRIOR DAYS' CLEARED TRADES (OUT-TRADES), POSITION ADJUSTMENTS, OPTIONS EXERCISES, POSITIONS IN DELIVERY, OR POSITIONS IN A CASH SETTLEMENT CYCLE. B=BID A=ASK N=NOMINAL P=POST SETTLEMENT SESSION #=NEW CONTRACT HIGH PRICE *=NEW CONTRACT LOW PRICE R=RECORD VOL OR OPN INT. SETTLEMENT PRICE DETERMINED BY CME RULE 813. B=BID A=ASK N=NOMINAL P=POST SETTLEMENT. PRODUCT LISTINGS REPRESENT CONTRACTS WITH PRICE/VOLUME ACTIVITY AND/OR HAVE ESTABLISHED OPEN INTEREST. PRODUCTS ELIGIBLE TO TRADE BUT ARE INACTIVE DO NOT APPEAR IN THIS REPORT.

| | OPEN RANGE | HIGH | LOW | CLOSING RANGE | SETT. PRICE & RECIPROCAL | PT. CHGE | VOLUME TRADES CLEARED | OPEN INTEREST | CONTRACT HIGH | CONTRACT LOW |
|---|---|---|---|---|---|---|---|---|---|---|
| EUROFX | | | | | | | | | | |
| MAR04 | 1.26190@1.26180 | 1.26250 | 1.25500 | 1.25580 @1.25570 | 1.25580 (.7963) | - 88 | 13548 | 124733 - 3005 | 1.28750 | 1.04250 |
| JUN04 | 1.25870 | 1.25930 | 1.25220A | 1.25270 | 1.25290 (.7981) | - 88 | 205 | 995 - 46 | 1.28370 | 1.05700 |
| SEP04 | 1.25400 | 1.25600B | 1.24950 | 1.24950 | 1.25020 (.7999) | - 88 | 17 | 179 - 17 | 1.27800 | 1.05000 |
| DEC04 | 1.24950 | 1.24950 | 1.24700 | 1.24700 | 1.24800 (.8013) | - 88 | 2 | 182 UNCH | 1.27550 | 1.07350 |
| MAR05 | ---- | ---- | ---- | 1.25520N | 1.24640 (.8023) | - 88 | ---- | 16 UNCH | 1.13630 | 1.13630 |
| TOTAL EUROFX | | | | | | | 13772 | 126105 - 3068 | | |
| EURO FX INTERBANK SPOT: | 1.2672 | | 1.2571 | | 1.2575 | ------ - 78 | | | | |

Source: Chicago Mercantile Exchange

**Table 10.6.** Contract month symbols

| January  | F | July      | N |
|----------|---|-----------|---|
| February | G | August    | Q |
| March    | H | September | U |
| April    | J | October   | V |
| May      | K | November  | X |
| June     | M | December  | Z |

contract or instrument at the end of the trading session is ***closing price***, e.g., it was 1.24700 for December 200 futures. The high and low prices or bids and offers recorded during the period designated by the exchange as the official close, which, for example, is the final 60 seconds of trading in currencies on the CME, are referred to as ***closing range***, e.g., it was 1.25580 @1.25570 for March 2004 futures. The letter N affixed to a figure indicates that the price is nominal, e.g., 1.25520N for March 2005 future. It is largely for recording purposes and it can be observed that there was no trading in March 2005 futures during that trading session. ***Settlement price*** is usually the official daily closing price; if there is a closing range of prices, the settlement price is typically set at the midpoint or average of the closing range, e.g., it was 1.25290 for March 2004 futures at the close of January 15, 2004, a figure appeared in Table 10.3 and used in the daily settlement example. Nevertheless, the rule for determining the settlement price can be sophisticated, e.g., the explanatory notes in Table 10.5 states that the settlement price is determined by CME rule 813, which contain six paragraphs with nearly 500 wards. ***Net change*** is the amount of increase or decrease from the previous trading period's settlement price. ***Life-of-contract high*** and ***life-of-contract low*** are the highest price and the lowest price reached in the lifetime of a futures contract or a specific delivery month. ***Volume*** is the number of contracts traded (one side of each trade only) for each delivery month during the trading period. ***Open interest*** is the accumulated total of all currently outstanding contracts (one side only), which refers to unliquidated purchases and sales. Futures contracts are settled in one of two ways: cash-settled or delivered. However, most traders offset their positions before cash settlement or delivery. If the contract is not offset prior to the contract's maturity, it is settled either by physical delivery or in cash. For currency futures traded on the CME, delivery shall be made on the third Wednesday of the ***delivery month***, also called ***contract month***, which identifies the month and year in which a futures contract expires. If that day is not a business day in the countries/locations involved, then delivery shall be made on the next day which is a business day in the countries/locations. These days are referred as to ***delivery days***. Abbreviations or symbols are often used to identify products and contract months on quote boards and in publications. They are useful as a type of shorthand when writing down prices from the radio, television, or your broker. The order is to list the product first, then the month. The contract month symbols are listed in Table 10.6.

## 10.3 Pricing of Futures Products

The pricing of currency futures is almost the same as that of foreign exchange forwards. We use the phrase "almost the same" to imply that there can be minor differences between these two types of currency derivatives in their pricing, arising from their differences as listed in Table 10.1, mainly in trading platforms, which may result in their difference in risk premium requirement, and delivery dates, which may lead to their difference in the calculation of accrued interest or interest rate differentials. Ignoring these differences, they are treated identically in their pricing in the rest of this section.

Covered interest rate parity introduced in Chapter 3 is also a pricing formula for the foreign exchange forward. We adapt it slightly as follows:

$$F_{t,T} = \frac{(1+r_h)^{T-t}}{(1+r_f)^{T-t}} S_t \qquad (10.1)$$

where $F_{t,t+1}$ the forward exchange rate or the price of the currency futures at time $t$ and to be delivered at time $T$, $S_t$ the currently prevailing spot exchange rate at time $t$, $r_h$ the annualised interest rate in the home country, and $r_f$ the annualised interest rate in the foreign country during the period $t$ to $T$. Equation can be approximated by:

$$F_{t,T} \approx S_t (1+r_h)^{T-t} (1-r_f)^{T-t}$$
$$\approx S_t (1+r_h - r_f)^{T-t} \approx S_t e^{(T-t)\times(r_h - r_f)} \qquad (10.2)$$

The last step is due to the fact that futures or forward contracts usually mature within a year, typically in three, six, nine, or twelve months, so continuous compounding is applied. The interest rates used in the calculation are usually risk free Treasury bill rates for two reasons. First, since the contract period is short, the currency at hand, the domestic currency, can only be invested in the domestic money market to earn interest at the money market rate that is default free, so the delivery of the currency can be guaranteed when the contract matures; similarly, the trader or contract holder misses the interest on the currency forgone, the foreign currency that is accrued at the foreign money market risk free rate. Second, derivatives pricing follows a so called risk neutral valuation principle, which will be discussed in the next chapter with a more complicated type of derivatives - options, implying all relevant interest rates must be risk free.

Equation (10.2) suggests that the futures price is the spot price adjusted by the benefit from not exchanging the domestic currency for the foreign currency now, i.e., to earn interest in the domestic money market, and the cost of not exchanging the domestic currency for the foreign currency now, i.e., missing out the opportunity to earn interest in the foreign money market. This is generally applicable to

all futures pricing. That is, the futures price is the spot price adjusted for any benefit retained and any benefit forgone during the contract period. It is a comparison
between the delivery of the asset now and the delivery of the asset in the future.

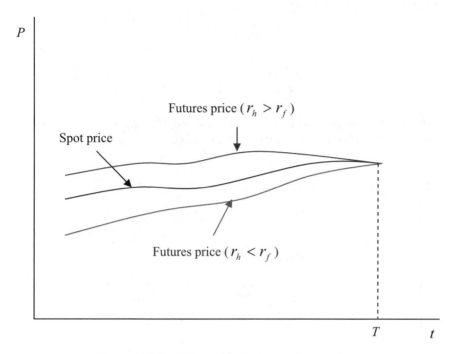

**Figure 11.1.** Evolution paths of currency futures prices

If a futures contract is confined to the domestic country, such as futures on a
domestically listed stock, then it is priced as:

$$F_{t,T} = S_t e^{(T-t)r} \qquad\qquad (10.3)$$

where $r$ is the risk free interest rate, assuming that the stock does not pay dividends during the period. If the stock pays dividends in the contract period, the futures price is given as:

$$F_{t,T} = S_t e^{(T-t)\times(r-d)} \qquad\qquad (10.4)$$

or

$$F_{t,T} = (S_t - D)e^{(T-t)r} \qquad\qquad (10.4')$$

where $d$ is the dividend yield and $D$ is the present value of the dividend paid per contract size. The pricing is similar for futures on other securities, e.g., bonds, where dividend yields can be replaced by coupon rates and the present value of the dividend paid can be replaced by the present value of the interest income.

Commodities involve storage costs, which should be taken into account in the pricing of commodity futures:

$$F_{t,T} = S_t e^{(T-t)\times(r+c)} \tag{10.5}$$

or

$$F_{t,T} = (S_t + C)e^{(T-t)r} \tag{10.5'}$$

where $c$ is the storage cost measured in rates, and $C$ is the present value of the storage cost per contract size for the contract period.

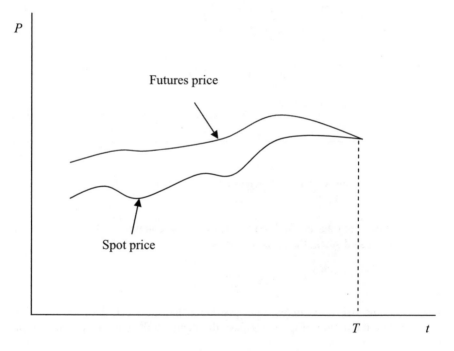

**Figure 11.2.** Evolution path of stock futures price

It can be observed that, for an asset or product that does not provide income or incur costs during the futures contract period, such as that represented by equation (10.2) or equation (10.3), the futures price of the asset, product or underlying financial instrument will move closer and closer to the spot price of the same asset, product or underlying financial instrument over time. In theory the futures price equals the spot price on the delivery day, though trading in a futures product usually comes to a close several days prior to the delivery day, customarily the last Friday before the delivery day. Figure 11.1 plot the typical evolution paths of futures prices over time for currency futures. Depending on the interest rate differential, the curve for the futures price /exchange rate may be above that for the spot price / exchange rate or below that for the spot price / exchange rate. Figure 11.2 shows a typical evolution path for the price of futures on non dividend paying stocks where the curve for the futures price is above that for the spot price. In both cases, the futures price and the spot price converge on the delivery day.

The term **basis** is commonly used to stand for the difference between the spot price and the futures price of the same asset, product or underlying financial instrument. Hedging is usually designed based on basis but the basis of an asset or product may changes. The unexpected variation in basis is called **basis risk**, which may lead to losses of expected income when a futures contract is liquidated and the asset or product is sold on the spot market.

We conclude this section with several examples of futures pricing, two for currency futures and one for futures on stocks.

*Example 1*: Suppose the spot exchange rate of the British pound vis-à-vis the euro was quoted as £0.7027/€ in Chicago on January 5, 2004; the risk free interest rate in the UK was 4.00% and that in the euroland was 3.25%, and they would remain unchanged for the next six months. What should be the price/exchange rate for the June 2004 euro-pound futures traded on the CME?

*Solutions*:

It is about 5.5 months or 0.4583 year from January 5, 2004 to the third Wednesday of June 2004. The numerate currency is the British pound and the denominator currency is the euro in this case. So, $r_h$ is for the British pound and $r_f$ is for the euro. Applying the formula with the figures yield:

$$F_{t,T} = S_t (1 + r_h - r_f)^{T-t}$$
$$= 0.7027 \times (1 + 0.04 - 0.0325)^{0.4583} = 0.70511$$

Or if continuous compounding is assumed:

$$F_{t,T} = S_t e^{(T-t) \times (r_h - r_f)}$$
$$= 0.7027 e^{0.4583 \times (0.04 - 0.0325)} = 0.70512$$

If the fifth decimal point is omitted, then the two results are the same. So the June 2004 euro-pound futures should be priced at £0.7051/€ on January 5, 2004.

*Example 2*: On February 12, 2004, the stock of Kingfisher was traded at 276 pence on the London Stock Exchange, what would be the price of the June and September 2004 Kingfisher stock futures traded on the LIFFE, assuming no dividends were expected to be paid and the risk free interest rate was expected to remain 4.00% in the period?

*Solutions*:

Suppose the delivery would be made around the middle of the delivery month, then it is about 4 months or 0.3333 year for the June 2004 futures to mature and 7 months or 0.5833 year for the September 2004 futures to mature. So the June 2004 futures would be priced as:

$$F_{t,T} = S_t e^{(T-t)r}$$
$$= 276 e^{0.3333 \times 0.04} = 280$$

and the September futures price would be:

$$F_{t,T} = S_t e^{(T-t)r}$$
$$= 276 e^{0.5833 \times 0.04} = 283$$

So, the June 2004 Kingfisher stock futures would trade at 280 pence on the LIFFE and the September 2004 Kingfisher stock futures would trade at 283 pence on the LIFFE on February 2004.

*Example 3*: The spot exchange rate of the US dollar vis-à-vis the British pound was $1.8287/£ and the spot exchange rate of the US dollar vis-à-vis the euro was $1.2152/€ on April 2, 2004. The following table provides the settlement price information for the pound and euro currency futures traded on the PHLX on April 2, 2004. Suppose the British risk free interest rate was expected to remain 4.00% in the whole year that follows, what risk free interest rate was implied by the futures price in the US? What risk free interest rate was implied by the futures price in the euroland from the US rate?

Currency futures on PHLX, April 2, 2004

| British Pound | | | Euro | | |
|---|---|---|---|---|---|
| Contract* | Month | Settle-ment | Contract | Month | Settle-ment |
| ZB U | Sep | 1.8037 | OZ U | Sep | 1.2097 |
| ZB Z | Dec | 1.7875 | OZ Z | Dec | 1.2080 |
| ZB H | Mar | 1.7793 | OZ H | Mar | 1.2072 |

\* ZB is the currency code/symbol for the British pound and OZ is the currency code/symbol for the euro at the PHLX.
Source: Philadelphia Board of Trade

*Solutions*:

In the first part, the numerate currency is the US dollar and the denominator currency is the British pound in this case. So, $r_h$ is for the US dollar and $r_f$ is for the British pound. From:

$$F_{t,T} = S_t e^{(T-t)\times(r_h-r_f)}$$

the US (domestic) risk free interest rate is derived as:

$$r_h = \frac{Ln(F_{t,T}/S_t)}{T-t} + r_f$$

It is about 5.5 months for the September 2004 futures to mature, 8.5 months for the December 2004 futures to mature and 11.5 months for the March 2005 futures to mature. Bringing the figures into the above formula yields the average US risk free interest rate for the following periods.

Between April and September 2004:

$$r_h = \frac{Ln(F_{t,T}/S_t)}{T-t} + r_f$$
$$= \frac{Ln(1.8037/1.8287)}{0.4583} + 0.0400 = 0.0100$$

Between April and December 2004:

$$r_h = \frac{Ln(F_{t,T}/S_t)}{T-t} + r_f$$

$$= \frac{Ln(1.7875/1.8287)}{0.7083} + 0.0400 = 0.0078$$

Between April 2004 and March 2005:

$$r_h = \frac{Ln(F_{t,T}/S_t)}{T-t} + r_f$$

$$= \frac{Ln(1.7793/1.8287)}{0.9583} + 0.0400 = 0.0114$$

Therefore, the risk free interest rate in the US was expected to be 1.00% between April and September 2004, 0.78% (notice this is not the rate in any particular month, so it is not bound by the 0.25% incremental grid) between April and December 2004, and 1.14% between April 2004 and March 2005.

In the second part, the numerate currency is the US dollar and the denominator currency is the euro in this case. So, $r_h$ is for the US dollar and $r_f$ is for the euro. From:

$$F_{t,T} = S_t e^{(T-t) \times (r_h - r_f)}$$

the euroland (foreign) risk free interest rate is derived as:

$$r_f = r_h - \frac{Ln(F_{t,T}/S_t)}{T-t}$$

Bringing the figures into the above formula yields the average US risk free interest rate for the following periods.

Between April and September 2004:

$$r_f = r_h - \frac{Ln(F_{t,T}/S_t)}{T-t}$$

$$= 0.0100 - \frac{Ln(1.2097/1.2152)}{0.4583} = 0.0200$$

Between April and December 2004:

$$r_f = r_h - \frac{Ln(F_{t,T}/S_t)}{T-t}$$

$$= 0.0127 - \frac{Ln(1.2080/1.2152)}{0.7083} = 0.0162$$

Between April 2004 and March 2005:

$$r_f = r_h - \frac{Ln(F_{t,T}/S_t)}{T-t}$$

$$= 0.0150 - \frac{Ln(1.2072/1.2152)}{0.9583} = 0.0183$$

Therefore, the risk free interest rate in the euroland was expected to be 2.00% between April and September 2004, 1.62% between April and December 2004, and 1.83% between April 2004 and March 2005.

It should be noted that spot exchange rates are very volatile, so are futures/forward rates. Changes in exchange rates are usually much larger than what can be explained by interest rate differentials or changes in interest rate expectations. So the above exercises should only be considered indicative. Other relevant factors, as well as noise trading, have not been and are difficult to be dealt with by these formulae and calculations.

# 11    Currency Options

Continued from the previous chapter on currency futures, this chapter introduce options, arguably the most innovative, complicated and publicised class of derivative instruments ever developed, with a focus on currency options. Options can be traded on OTC markets and organised exchanges. Options are not as straightforward as forwards and futures and, consequently, option pricing is much more complicated than the pricing of a forward product or futures product and warrants more discussion. Therefore, this chapter also devotes one section to the risk neutral valuation principle in options pricing in particular and in derivatives pricing in general, which covers the binomial tree method and the Black-Scholes model.

## 11.1 Option Basics

An option gives the option contract holder the right, but not the obligation, to buy or sell a given quantity of an underlying asset, commodity or financial security at a pre determined price at or prior to a specified time in the future. An option is a currency option where the underlying asset is a currency. The primary difference between futures or forwards and options is that an option contract dose not involves obligations for the contract holder to buy or sell the asset. This leads to a second difference between futures and options that there is no margin requirement for exchange traded options for option holders, since "no obligation" implies that the maximum loss of the option holder is the price, also known as option premium, paid for having the option, which has already been paid at the beginning when the contract comes into effect. Nevertheless, no obligation applies only to the option holder, not to the option writer or seller. So, there is still margin requirement for option writers or sellers. The right of an option holder to buy a given quantity of an asset at a pre determined price corresponds to the obligation of the option seller to sell the given quantity of the asset at that price; and the right of an option holder to sell a given quantity of an asset at a pre determined price corresponds to the obligation of the option seller to buy the given quantity of the asset at that price. Unlike forwards or futures, options are asymmetric for the two parties involved, i.e., the buying activity is not mirrored by the selling activity.

There are two types of options arising from the asymmetric features of options, namely, *call* options that the holder has the right but no obligation to buy a given quantity of an asset at a pre determined price, at or prior to a specified time in the future, and **put** options that the holder has the right but no obligation to sell a given quantity of an asset at a pre determined price, at or prior to a specified time in the future. The action to buy or sell is called strike or exercise. The pre determined price at which the underlying asset may be sold or bought is call the **strike price** or **exercise price**. Depending on whether the option can be exercised at a specified time, i.e., the expiration date, only, or can be exercised at any time up to and including the expiration date, options are classified into two categories. The former, which can only be exercised on the expiration date, is **European** options; and the latter, which can be exercised at any time prior to and including the expiration date, is **American** options. Since an American option includes everything a European option has and, additionally, may offer some extras, the value of American options is usually worth more than, or at least equal to, that of European options, other things equal.

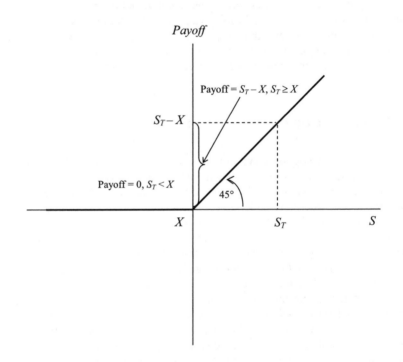

**Figure 11.1.** Gross payoff of a stock call option (long)

Options are best illustrated by their payoffs. We work with stock options where the underlying asset is a corporate stock first, then progress to the case of currency options, since stock options are most intuitive. Let $S$ be the stock price, $S_T$ be the stock price at maturity or on the expiration date and $X$ be the strike or exercise price. Figure 11.1 shows the gross payoff of a call option, i.e., the payoff excluding the cost of the option, from the option holder's perspective. In other words, it is the gross payoff of a long position in the call. The horizontal axis is for the stock price and the vertical axis is for the gross payoff corresponding to the level of the stock price. The gross payoff is $S_T - X$ when $S_T \geq X$ at maturity or zero when $S_T < X$ at maturity, as being demonstrated in the figure. When $S_T \geq X$ at maturity, the option holder exercises the option by buying the stock at the pre determined exercise price $X$ that is lower than the prevailing market price of the stock at the time $S_T$, so she or he makes a gross profit that is the difference between the prevailing market price of the stock and the exercise price. However, when $S_T < X$ at maturity, the option holder does not make a loss, since she or he does not have the obligation to buy the stock with an exercise price that is higher than the prevailing market price of the stock. The option holder can simply walk away. If the option holder wants to buy that stock, she or he can simply buy the stock on the stock market at the prevailing market price without resorting to the option. So the payoff is a 45° line to the right of the exercise price $X$ and overlaps with the horizontal axis to the left of the exercise price $X$.

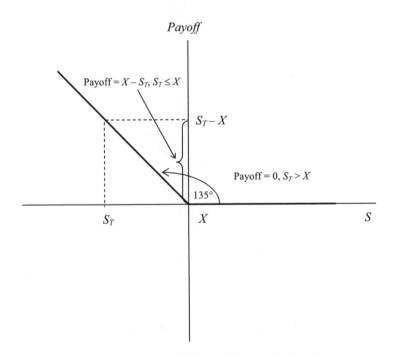

**Figure 11.2.** Gross payoff of a stock put option (long)

Figure 11.2 shows the gross payoff for a long put option on a corporate stock. Since the option holder has the right but no obligation to sell the stock at the exercise price $X$, the lower the prevailing market price of the stock at maturity, the higher the payoff. The gross payoff is $X - S_T$ when $S_T \leq X$ at maturity or zero when $S_T > X$ at maturity, as being exhibited by the figure. When $S_T \leq X$ at maturity, the option holder exercises the option by selling the stock at the pre determined exercise price $X$ that is higher than the prevailing market price of the stock at the time $S_T$, so she or he makes a gross profit that is the difference between the exercise price and the prevailing market price of the stock. However, when $S_T > X$ at maturity, the option holder does not make a loss, since she or he does not have the obligation to sell the stock with an exercise price that is lower than the prevailing market price of the stock. The option holder can simply walk away, leaving the option expired unexercised. If the option holder wants to sell that stock, she or he can simply sell it on the stock market at the prevailing market price without resorting to the option. So the payoff is a 135° line to the left of the exercise price $X$ and overlaps with the horizontal axis to the right of the exercise price $X$.

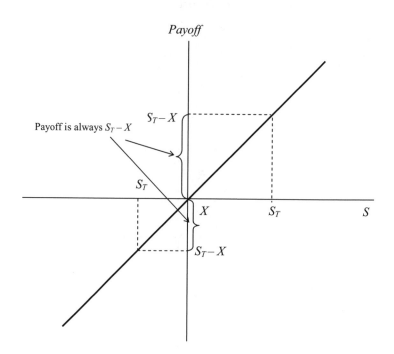

**Figure 11.3.** Gross payoff of futures/forwards on stocks (long)

The payoff of options can be contrasted with that of forwards or futures to demonstrate their difference with regard to obligations. Figure 11.3 draws the payoff of a long a position in futures or forwards written on the corporate stock, which is a 45° straight line crossing the origin and on the both sides of the origin. A long position in futures involves both the right and the obligation to buy the stock, whatever the prevailing market price of the stock might be at maturity. So the futures holder makes a profit of the size of $S_T - X$ when the prevailing market price of the stock is greater than the exercise price, i.e., $S_T > X$, at maturity; and makes a loss of the size of $X - S_T$ when the prevailing market price of the stock is lower than the exercise price, i.e., $S_T < X$, at maturity.

Finally it is of interest to compare the payoffs of the above options and futures/forwards with that of their underlying asset, the corporate stock. There is no exercise price and time to maturity in this case, so the payoff is a comparison of the current stock price $S$ and the stock price at which the stock was purchased $S_0$ at an earlier time. Figure 11.4 demonstrates its payoff, which is simply the gain or loss made during the period when the stock has been held, or the holding period capital gain. When the stock price rises, the holder of the stock, or the shareholder, if chooses to sell the stock, makes a capital gain of the size of $S - S_0$, the difference between the current prevailing market price of the stock and the stock price at which the stock was purchased before. When the stock price falls, the shareholder, makes a capital loss of the size of $S_0 - S$, the difference between the stock price at which the stock was purchased before and the current prevailing market price of the stock, imagining she or he sells the stock now.

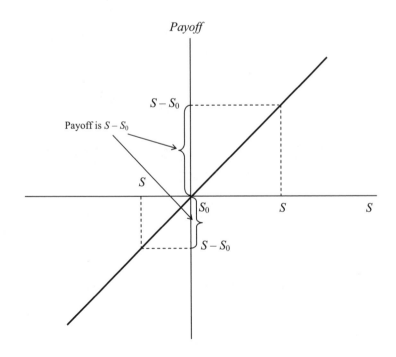

**Figure 11.4.** Gross payoff of the stock (long)

Now let us take costs into account, which include the option price, or the premium paid when the contract is established, and the accrued interest. Same as in Chapter 11, interest is calculated at the continuous compounding basis, since most options mature within a year, typically in three, six, nine, or twelve months. Denote $c$ as the price or premium of a European call option, $p$ as the price or premium of a European put option, $C$ as the price or premium of an American call option, $P$ as the price or premium of an American option, and $r$ as the risk free interest rate. Then the cost at maturity is $e^{r(T-t)}c$ for holding a European stock call option contracted at time $t$ and expires at time $T$. Similarly, the cost at maturity is $e^{r(T-t)}p$ for holding a European stock put option contracted at time $t$ and expires at time $T$. For American type options, the interest may or may not be accrued for the whole contract period $T$-$t$, since the option may be exercised prior to the expiration date. Figure 11.5 and Figure 11.6 demonstrate the net payoffs of a European stock call option and a European stock put option respectively. Compared with Figure 11.1 and Figure 11.2, the whole payoff curve is moved down by $e^{r(T-t)}c$ for the call option and by $e^{r(T-t)}p$ for the put option.

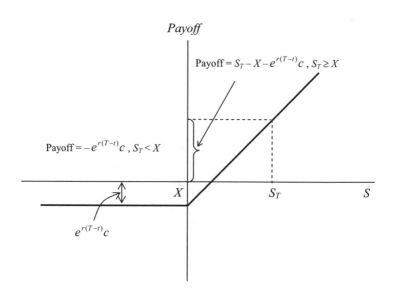

**Figure 11.5.** Net payoff of a European stock call option (long)

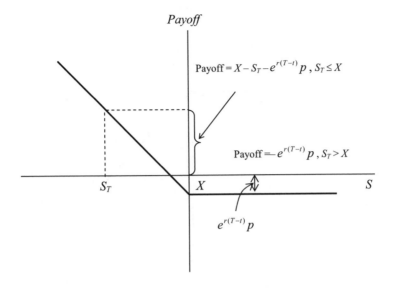

*Payoff*

$\text{Payoff} = X - S_T - e^{r(T-t)}p \ , \ S_T \le X$

$\text{Payoff} = -e^{r(T-t)}p \ , \ S_T > X$

$S_T$

$X$

$S$

$e^{r(T-t)}p$

**Figure 11.6.** Net payoff of a European stock put option (long)

Due to the cost incurred, the option holder may still make a loss even if the option is worthwhile exercising. The option holder only makes a net profit when the gross payoff made from exercising the option is more than offsetting the incurred cost. Nevertheless, as shown in Figure 11.5 and Figure 11.6, the loss is limited to the option premium plus lost interest, whereas the gain from holding options appears to be unlimited, at least for call options in theory. In the case of put options on stocks, since the stock price is bound to be at least zero, the maximum gain is the exercise price minus the cost, which can also be extraordinarily large in theory. Since the payoff for an option writer or seller is exactly the opposite of that for an option holder or buyer, the gain is limited and the loss may be unlimited for option writers or sellers. Figure 11.7 and Figure 11.8 exhibit such net payoffs for call option writer and put option writer respectively. It is for these reasons of limited and unlimited losses for the different parties in the game that margin requirement is applied to option writers but not to option holders.

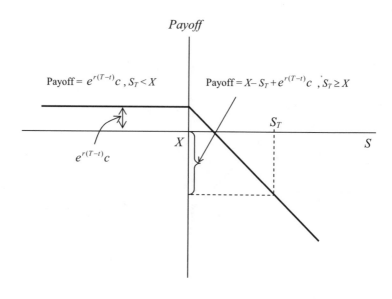

**Figure 11.7.** Net payoff of a European stock call option (short)

It should be clear now that buying a call option is not equivalent or similar to selling a put option. Nonetheless, there are some relationships between calls and puts in long and short positions. Let us assume that the underlying stock is the same for all these options, so is the exercise price, time to maturity and risk free interest rate. A long call mirrors a short call exactly and they are symmetric against the horizontal axis. A long put mirrors a short put exactly and they are symmetric against the horizontal axis. A long call and a long put are about to mirror each other against the vertical axis when the premium of the call option is not the same as that of the put and may mirror each other exactly against the vertical axis when the premium of the call option equals that of the put. A short call and a short put are about to mirror each other against the vertical axis when the premium of the call option is not the same as that of the put and may mirror each other exactly against the vertical axis when the premium of the call option equals that of the put.

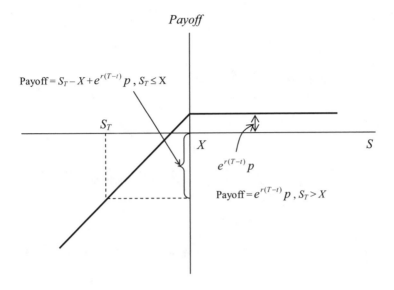

*Payoff*

$\text{Payoff} = S_T - X + e^{r(T-t)} p, \; S_T \leq X$

$S_T$

$X$

$S$

$e^{r(T-t)} p$

$\text{Payoff} = e^{r(T-t)} p, \; S_T > X$

**Figure 11.8.** Net payoff of a European stock put option (short)

The following are two examples of stock options. The first is a long call and the second is a short put.

*Example 1*: Consider a call option on the BAE Systems stock traded on the LIFFE: the current stock price, $S_0$, is £2.15, the exercise price, $X$, is £2.00, the option price, $c$, is £0.30, it is a European call maturing in six months, i.e., $T=0.5$, the risk free interest rate is 4.00% per annum, and the contract size for UK stocks is 1000 shares per contract on the LIFFE. Suppose, on the expiration date, the BAE stock is traded at £2.60, what is the profit from having one contract of the option?

*Solution*:

Relevant figures are given as $X=2.00$, $S_T=2.60$, $c=0.30$, $T=0.5$, $t=0$, $r=0.04$. The cost per option at maturity $= e^{r(T-t)} c = e^{0.04 \times 0.5} \times 0.30 = £0.3061$. Since $S_T > X$, the option is exercised and the gross payoff per option from exercising the option $= S_T - X = 2.60 - 2.00 = £0.60$. The net payoff per option $=$ gross payoff $-$ costs $= 0.60 - 0.3061 = £0.2939$, as shown in the graph below. So the net payoff or profit per option contract is £0.2939$\times$1000 $=$ £293.90.

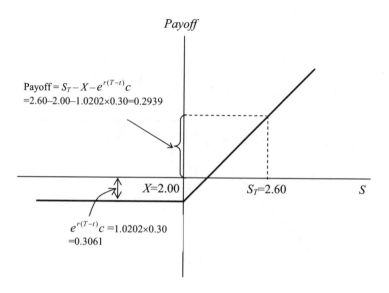

*Payoff*

$$\text{Payoff} = S_T - X - e^{r(T-t)}c$$
$$= 2.60 - 2.00 - 1.0202 \times 0.30 = 0.2939$$

$X=2.00$

$e^{r(T-t)}c = 1.0202 \times 0.30$
$= 0.3061$

$S_T = 2.60$

$S$

*Example 2*: The stock of Apple Computer Inc is currently traded at $27.53 per share. A three month European put option on the stock with an exercise price of $30.00 is traded on the PHLX at $3.90, the contract size is 100 shares per option contract and the risk free interest rate is 1.00% per annum. Suppose, on the expiration date, the stock of Apple Computer Inc is traded at $28.00, what is the profit from selling one contract of the put option?

*Solution*:

Relevant figures are given as $X=30.00$, $S_T=28.00$, $p = 3.90$, $T=0.25$, $t=0$, $r = 0.01$. The cost per option at maturity $= e^{r(T-t)}p = e^{0.01 \times 0.25} \times 3.90 = \$3.9098$. *Since $S_T < X$, the option is exercised* and gross payoff per option from exercising the put $= X - S_T = 30.00 - 28.00 = \$2.00$. The net payoff per option for the option holder $= X - S_T - e^{r(T-t)}p = 30.00 - 28.00 - 3.9098 = -\$1.9098$. For the option seller, the net payoff is just the opposite and is equal to $1.9098, as shown in the above graph. So the net payoff or profit per contract is $1.9098 \times 100 = \$190.98$. In this case, although $S_T < X$ and the put option holder strikes, she or he still makes a loss. It is because the price or premium paid for the option, together with the interest accrued, is greater than the gross payoff from exercising the option. However, she or he must exercise the option, since otherwise the loss would be even greater.

*Payoff*

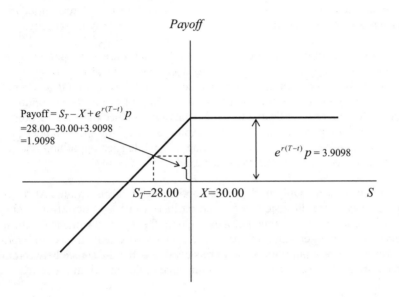

$$\text{Payoff} = S_T - X + e^{r(T-t)}p$$
$$=28.00 - 30.00 + 3.9098$$
$$=1.9098$$

$$e^{r(T-t)}p = 3.9098$$

$S_T=28.00$    $X=30.00$    $S$

## 11.2 Option Terminology and Quotes

Options are generally more complicated than futures or forwards, there are more terms in the glossary of options than futures or forwards. This section briefly discusses some commonly referred option terminology and option quotes, without repeating those considered in the previous chapter.

*At-the-money*: An option is said to be at-the-money if the exercise price or strike price of the option is equal to the prevailing market price of the underlying security. It means that, ignoring the cost, the option holder would make neither gain nor loss if you exercise the option now. Then *near-the-money* options are options with their exercise price and the market price of the underlying security being fairly close to each other.

*In-the-money*: An in-the-money option is an option that would generate gross profit for the option holder if exercised now. A call option is in-the-money if the exercise price or strike price is lower than the prevailing market price of the underlying security. A put option is in-the-money if the exercise price or strike price is greater than the prevailing market price of the underlying security

*Out-of-the-money*: An option is out-of-the-money when the option holder would make a gross loss if exercised now. A call option is out-of-the-money if the exercise price or strike price is greater than the prevailing market price of the underlying security. A put option is out-of-the-money if the exercise price or strike price is lower than the prevailing market price of the underlying security.

It should be noted that a currently in-the-money European option may end up out-of-the-money when it expires, and a currently out-of-the-money or at-the-money European option may be in-the-money on the expiration date. So not only in-the-money options, but also at-the-money and out-of-the-money options, have values. It is more complicated for American options since they can be exercised at any time leading to and including the expiration date. An option holder may lose the opportunity to strike on the expiration date while such opportunity has existed at some points of time in the contract period.

*Intrinsic value*: Only in-the-money options have intrinsic value. At-the-money options have zero intrinsic value or no intrinsic value, and out-of-the money options have no intrinsic value. For a call option, the intrinsic value is the difference between the market value of the underlying security and the exercise price or strike price. For a put option, the intrinsic value is the difference between the exercise price or strike price and the market value of the underlying security.

*Time value*: The amount by which an option's premium exceeds the intrinsic value of the option is time value of the option. It is the portion of the option price that is not intrinsic value or the amount option buyers are willing to pay over intrinsic value, given the amount of time left to expiration for the market price of the underlying security to rise in the case of calls, or the market price of the underlying security to fall in the case of puts. The relationship between option premium, intrinsic value and time value is: option premium – intrinsic value = time value.

*Cabinet price*: The lowest possible tradable price for an option. It is the nominal price for liquidating deep out-of-the-money options contracts. Trades on options done at a price equal to zero are considered cabinet trades.

*Delta*, *Gamma*, *Vega*, and *Theta*: Delta is a measurement of the rate of change of an option premium with respect to the change in the price of the underlying security. Delta is confined between -1 and +1. Gamma is the measure of the change in an option's delta with respect to the change in the price of the underlying security. Vega measures the change in an option's premium with respect to the change in the volatility of the price of the underlying security. Theta measures the change in an option's premium with respect to the option's time to maturity.

*Implied volatility*: A measure of the volatility in the underlying security's price implied by the option's price, while historical volatility is the actual, observed, volatility of the underlying security's price in the past.

The above discussed terms often appear, or are relevant, in option quotes. For example and as evident in the following cases, one may be interested in near-the-money options only. Unlike futures trading where there is usually just one futures product for one underlying asset in a particular contract month, numerous exercise or strike prices can be listed for an option on the same underlying asset in a particular contract month, many of them involving infrequent trading or no trading at all. Depending on the circumstances, some may only buy in-the-money or at-the-money options for hedging purposes, while some others may be specialised in out-of-the-money options. Moreover, it is of interest to know how the various aspects of an option may change in relation to the change in the various aspects of the underlying assets represented by those Greek letters, which are regularly provided too.

Table 11.1 and Table 11.2 show a case of option quotes for Apple Computer Inc. Table 11.1 lists a range of call and put options written on the Apple Computer stock traded on April 12, 2004. These are American options. Only near-the-money options expiring in July and October 2004 and January 2005 are selected. It can be observed that there are quite a few option products in any particular months. On the top the underlying security's information is provided. The left half panel is for calls and the right half panel is for puts, with the exercise or strike price being listed in the middle. The first column in both of the call section and the put section is ticker or product symbol, including information on strike prices and expiration months. It is clear that the premium of call options, either the last settlement price (second column), bid price (fourth column) or ask price (fifth column), is a decreasing function of the strike price; while the premium of put options is an increasing function of the strike price (second, fourth and fifth columns). The reason is that, holding the stock price constant, the intrinsic value of a call is a decreasing function of the strike price and the intrinsic value of a put is an increasing function of the strike price for in-the-money options. Out-of-money options only have time value that decreases with the strike price for calls and increases with the strike price for puts, holding the stock price constant. The option premium also increases with the length of time to expiration, other things being equal, e.g., the premium of the October 2004 call with a strike price of $25 is higher than the premium of the July 2004 call with the same strike price. For out-of-money options, since their intrinsic value is zero, their premium is all derived from their time value. The longer the time to expiration, the higher is the time value, and the higher is the option premium. The last two columns are trading volume and open interest. It can be observed that both figures are larger for calls than for puts and are higher for out-of-the money options than for in-the-money options in this case, reflecting, among other things, investor expectations about the future price movement of the Apple Computer stock. Table 11.2 quotes the Greek letters and implied volatility of the July 2004 options on the Apple Computer Inc stock traded on April 13, 2004.

**Table 11.1.** Option quotes – Apple Computer Inc

| APPLE COMPUTER INC(AAPL ) | | | | | | | | | | 28.0400 | 0.0000 |
|---|---|---|---|---|---|---|---|---|---|---|---|
| Symbol | Last | Time | Net | Bid | Ask | Open | High | Low | Close | | Vol |
| AAPL | 28.0400 | 04/12 | 0.0000 | 16.7400 | 39.2000 | 0.0000 | 0.0000 | 0.0000 | 28.0400 | | 0 |

| | | Calls | | | | Jul 2004 | | | Puts | | | | |
|---|---|---|---|---|---|---|---|---|---|---|---|---|---|
| Ticker | Last | Net | Bid | Ask | Vol | Open Interest | Strike | Ticker | Last | Net | Bid | Ask | Vol | Open Interest |
| .AAQGD | 7.40 | 0.00 | 8.20 | 8.40 | | 695 | 20 | .AAQSD | 0.25 | 0.00 | 0.15 | 0.30 | 110 | 6073 |
| .AAQGT | 6.20 | +0.10 | 6.00 | 6.30 | 20 | 9064 | 22.5 | .AAQST | 0.50 | 0.00 | 0.45 | 0.55 | 505 | 10928 |
| .AAQGE | 4.10 | +0.30 | 4.10 | 4.30 | 1128 | 12883 | 25 | .AAQSE | 1.10 | -0.15 | 1.05 | 1.15 | 175 | 5413 |
| .AAQGA | 2.75 | +0.47 | 2.70 | 2.75 | 516 | 14225 | 27.5 | .AAQSA | 2.15 | -0.10 | 2.05 | 2.20 | 588 | 3089 |
| .AAQGF | 1.70 | +0.30 | 1.70 | 1.75 | 9362 | 19286 | 30 | .AAQSF | 3.90 | 0.00 | 3.50 | 3.70 | | 218 |
| .AAQGZ | 1.05 | +0.35 | 1.00 | 1.10 | 17868 | 3122 | 32.5 | .AAQSZ | 7.20 | 0.00 | 5.30 | 5.50 | | 96 |

| | | Calls | | | | Oct 2004 | | | Puts | | | | |
|---|---|---|---|---|---|---|---|---|---|---|---|---|---|
| Ticker | Last | Net | Bid | Ask | Vol | Open Interest | Strike | Ticker | Last | Net | Bid | Ask | Vol | Open Interest |
| .AAQJD | 8.20 | +0.40 | 8.50 | 8.80 | 4 | 165 | 20 | .AAQVD | 0.80 | 0.00 | 0.40 | 0.55 | | 242 |
| .AAQJT | 5.90 | 0.00 | 6.50 | 6.70 | | 142 | 22.5 | .AAQVT | 1.05 | 0.00 | 0.90 | 1.00 | | 1698 |
| .AAQJE | 4.30 | 0.00 | 4.80 | 5.00 | | 1316 | 25 | .AAQVE | 1.65 | -0.25 | 1.65 | 1.80 | 34 | 1736 |
| .AAQJA | 3.00 | 0.00 | 3.40 | 3.60 | | 3244 | 27.5 | .AAQVA | 2.85 | -0.15 | 2.75 | 2.85 | 6 | 607 |
| .AAQJF | 2.40 | +0.35 | 2.35 | 2.40 | 636 | 674 | 30 | .AAQVF | 4.50 | 0.00 | 4.10 | 4.30 | | 299 |
| .AAQJZ | 1.55 | +0.27 | 1.60 | 1.65 | 44 | 1223 | 32.5 | .AAQVZ | 7.10 | 0.00 | 5.80 | 6.00 | | 20 |
| .AAQJG | 1.05 | +0.10 | 1.00 | 1.05 | 23 | 793 | 35 | .AAQVG | 8.50 | 0.00 | 7.70 | 7.90 | | 54 |

| | | Calls | | | | Jan 2005 | | | Puts | | | | |
|---|---|---|---|---|---|---|---|---|---|---|---|---|---|
| Ticker | Last | Net | Bid | Ask | Vol | Open Interest | Strike | Ticker | Last | Net | Bid | Ask | Vol | Open Interest |
| .ZAAAD | 8.50 | 0.00 | 8.90 | 9.20 | | 8750 | 20 | .ZAAMD | 0.80 | -0.10 | 0.75 | 0.80 | 2 | 25655 |
| .ZAAAT | 7.10 | +0.60 | 7.00 | 7.10 | 55 | 3409 | 22.5 | .ZAAMT | 1.35 | 0.00 | 1.30 | 1.40 | | 1665 |
| .ZAAAE | 5.40 | +0.50 | 5.40 | 5.60 | 40 | 16506 | 25 | .ZAAME | 2.40 | 0.00 | 2.15 | 2.25 | | 5753 |
| .ZAAAA | 4.00 | +0.20 | 4.10 | 4.20 | 10 | 6407 | 27.5 | .ZAAMA | 3.40 | 0.00 | 3.20 | 3.40 | | 508 |
| .ZAAAF | 3.00 | +0.36 | 2.95 | 3.00 | 222 | 29522 | 30 | .ZAAMF | 4.80 | 0.00 | 4.60 | 4.80 | | 639 |
| .ZAAAG | 1.55 | 0.00 | 1.45 | 1.60 | 79 | 6657 | 35 | .ZAAMG | 10.1 | 0.00 | 8.00 | 8.30 | | 223 |

**Table 11.2.** Greek letters and implied volatility – Apple Computer Inc options

| APPLE COMPUTER INC(AAPL ) | | | | | | | | 26.9300 | -1.1100 |
|---|---|---|---|---|---|---|---|---|---|
| Symbol | Last | Time | Net | Bid | Ask | Reference price | Div freq | Div amt | Historical Volatility |
| AAPL | 26.9300 | 04/13 | -1.1100 | 16.0500 | 37.8300 | 26.93 | 0 | 0 | 25.340% |

| Calls | | | | | Jul 2004 | | Puts | | | |
|---|---|---|---|---|---|---|---|---|---|---|
| Ticker | Last | Delta | Gamma | Theta | Implied Volatility | Strike | Ticker | Last | Delta | Gamma | Theta | Implied Volatility |

| Ticker | Last | Delta | Gamma | Theta | Implied Volatility | Strike | Ticker | Last | Delta | Gamma | Theta | Implied Volatility |
|---|---|---|---|---|---|---|---|---|---|---|---|---|
| .AAQGY | 16.50 | 1.00 | 0.000 | -0.000 | 0.00% | 7.5 | .AAQSY | 0.00 | 0.00 | 0.000 | -0.000 | 108.16% |
| .AAQGB | 17.70 | 1.00 | 0.000 | -0.000 | 0.00% | 10 | .AAQSB | 0.00 | -0.00 | 0.000 | -0.000 | 84.94% |
| .AAQGR | 14.10 | 1.00 | 0.000 | -0.000 | 0.00% | 12.5 | .AAQSR | 0.00 | -0.00 | 0.000 | -0.000 | 73.97% |
| .AAQGC | 11.60 | 1.00 | 0.000 | -0.000 | 62.11% | 15 | .AAQSC | 0.05 | -0.00 | 0.000 | -0.000 | 58.00% |
| .AAQGS | 9.20 | 1.00 | 0.000 | -0.001 | 51.95% | 17.5 | .AAQSS | 0.10 | -0.00 | 0.000 | -0.000 | 47.60% |
| .AAQGD | 7.40 | 0.99 | 0.006 | -0.001 | 48.76% | 20 | .AAQSD | 0.30 | -0.01 | 0.006 | -0.000 | 47.11% |
| .AAQGT | 6.20 | 0.93 | 0.038 | -0.003 | 45.87% | 22.5 | .AAQST | 0.65 | -0.07 | 0.038 | -0.002 | 45.08% |
| .AAQGE | 3.49 | 0.75 | 0.092 | -0.006 | 45.16% | 25 | .AAQSE | 1.40 | -0.25 | 0.092 | -0.006 | 44.22% |
| .AAQGA | 2.15 | 0.47 | 0.115 | -0.008 | 44.85% | 27.5 | .AAQSA | 2.60 | -0.53 | 0.115 | -0.007 | 44.14% |
| .AAQGF | 1.35 | 0.23 | 0.087 | -0.006 | 45.29% | 30 | .AAQSF | 3.90 | -0.77 | 0.087 | -0.005 | 44.20% |
| .AAQGZ | 0.80 | 0.08 | 0.045 | -0.003 | 44.57% | 32.5 | .AAQSZ | 7.20 | -0.92 | 0.045 | -0.002 | 44.60% |

## 11.3 Currency Options

Having studied option basics, terminology and quotes in general, it is straightforward to progress to a specific type of options relevant in this book, currency options. Currency options are options where the underlying asset or security is currencies. A currency option can be written on currencies directly or on currency futures. While both are currency options the latter is usually referred as to currency futures options. Table 11.3 and Table 11.4 list a range of call and put options on euros traded on the PHLX on April 14, 2004, expiring in the mid-month of July 2004. Table 11.3 is for European options while Table 11.4 is for American options.

**Table 11.3.** Currency option quotes on PHLX – European options

| PHLX EURO MID-MONTH (EURO)(ECU ) | | | | | | | | | 1.1914 | -0.0049 |
|---|---|---|---|---|---|---|---|---|---|---|
| Symbol | Last | Time | Net | Bid | Ask | Open | High | Low | Close | Vol |
| ECU | 1.1914 | 07:00 | -0.0049 | 0.0000 | 0.0000 | 1.1955 | 1.1991 | 1.1898 | 1.1963 | 0 |

| | Calls | | | | | Jun 2004 | | Puts | | | | | |
|---|---|---|---|---|---|---|---|---|---|---|---|---|---|
| Ticker | Last | Net | Bid | Ask | Vol | Open Interest | Strike | Ticker | Last | Net | Bid | Ask | Vol | Open Interest |
| .ECUFT (*) | 5.14 | 0.00 | 1.75 | 1.85 | | | 74 | .ECURT (*) | 1.95 | 0.00 | 2.66 | 2.81 | | 153 |
| .ECUFN (*) | 2.21 | 0.00 | 0.10 | 0.15 | | 11 | 84 | .ECURN (*) | 0.00 | 0.00 | 0.00 | 0.00 | | |
| .ECBFG (*) | 0.00 | 0.00 | 0.00 | 0.00 | | | 111 | .ECBRG (*) | 0.00 | 0.00 | 0.00 | 0.00 | | |
| .ECUFK (*) | 5.27 | 0.00 | 0.00 | 0.00 | | | 112 | .ECURK (*) | 0.92 | 0.00 | 0.00 | 0.00 | | |
| .ECBFO (*) | 0.00 | 0.00 | 0.00 | 0.00 | | | 113 | .ECBRO (*) | 0.00 | 0.00 | 0.00 | 0.00 | | |
| .ECUFS (*) | 3.88 | 0.00 | 0.00 | 0.00 | | | 114 | .ECURS (*) | 0.56 | 0.00 | 0.51 | 0.61 | | 7 |
| .ECBFW (*) | 0.00 | 0.00 | 0.00 | 0.00 | | | 115 | .ECBRW (*) | 0.48 | 0.00 | 0.71 | 0.81 | | |
| .ECUFD (*) | 2.30 | 0.00 | 0.00 | 0.00 | | | 116 | .ECURD (*) | 0.35 | 0.00 | 0.97 | 1.07 | | |
| .ECBFH (*) | 1.41 | 0.00 | 0.00 | 0.00 | | | 117 | .ECBRH (*) | 0.70 | 0.00 | 1.29 | 1.32 | | 18 |
| .ECUFL (*) | 0.15 | 0.00 | 2.72 | 2.87 | | | 118 | .ECURL (*) | 1.45 | +0.70 | 1.65 | 1.75 | 32 | 196 |
| .ECBFP (*) | 0.00 | 0.00 | 2.19 | 2.34 | | | 119 | .ECBRP (*) | 1.44 | 0.00 | 2.12 | 2.27 | | 33 |
| .ECBFA (*) | 0.00 | 0.00 | 1.38 | 1.48 | | | 121 | .ECBRA (*) | 2.46 | 0.00 | 3.27 | 3.42 | | 4 |
| .ECUFE (*) | 2.63 | 0.00 | 1.05 | 1.15 | | 6 | 122 | .ECURE (*) | 1.65 | 0.00 | 3.94 | 4.09 | | 16 |
| .ECBFI (*) | 2.15 | 0.00 | 0.81 | 0.91 | | 15 | 123 | .ECBRI (*) | 2.45 | 0.00 | 4.67 | 4.82 | | 2 |
| .ECUFM (*) | 1.35 | 0.00 | 0.60 | 0.70 | | 80 | 124 | .ECURM (*) | 3.75 | 0.00 | 5.46 | 5.61 | | 38 |
| .ECBFQ (*) | 1.30 | 0.00 | 0.47 | 0.52 | | | 125 | .ECBRQ (*) | 3.23 | 0.00 | 0.00 | 0.00 | | |
| .ECUFU (*) | 3.71 | 0.00 | 0.00 | 0.00 | | 16 | 126 | .ECURU (*) | 0.00 | 0.00 | 0.00 | 0.00 | | |
| .ECBFB (*) | 1.48 | 0.00 | 0.27 | 0.32 | | 16 | 127 | .ECBRB (*) | 0.00 | 0.00 | 0.00 | 0.00 | | |
| .ECUFF (*) | 0.63 | 0.00 | 0.20 | 0.25 | | 37 | 128 | .ECURF (*) | 0.00 | 0.00 | 0.00 | 0.00 | | |
| .ECBFJ (*) | 0.00 | 0.00 | 0.00 | 0.00 | | | 129 | .ECBRJ (*) | 0.00 | 0.00 | 0.00 | 0.00 | | |
| .ECBFR (*) | 1.97 | 0.00 | 0.06 | 0.11 | | 6 | 131 | .ECBRR (*) | 0.00 | 0.00 | 0.00 | 0.00 | | |
| .ECUFV (*) | 0.00 | 0.00 | 0.00 | 0.00 | | | 132 | .ECURV (*) | 0.00 | 0.00 | 0.00 | 0.00 | | |
| .ECBFC (*) | 0.00 | 0.00 | 0.00 | 0.00 | | | 133 | .ECBRC (*) | 0.00 | 0.00 | 0.00 | 0.00 | | |
| .ECUFG (*) | 0.00 | 0.00 | 0.00 | 0.00 | | | 134 | .ECURG (*) | 0.00 | 0.00 | 0.00 | 0.00 | | |
| .ECBFK (*) | 0.00 | 0.00 | 0.00 | 0.00 | | | 135 | .ECBRK (*) | 0.00 | 0.00 | 0.00 | 0.00 | | |

**Table 11.4.** Currency option quotes on PHLX – American options

| PHLX EURO MID-MONTH (AMER)(XEU ) | | | | | | | | 1.1914 | -0.0049 |
|---|---|---|---|---|---|---|---|---|---|

| Symbol | Last | Time | Net | Bid | Ask | Open | High | Low | Close | Vol |
|---|---|---|---|---|---|---|---|---|---|---|
| XEU | 1.1914 | 07:10 | -0.0049 | 0.0000 | 0.0000 | 1.1955 | 1.1991 | 1.1898 | 1.1963 | 0 |

| Calls | | | | | | Jun 2004 | Puts | | | | | |
|---|---|---|---|---|---|---|---|---|---|---|---|---|
| Ticker | Last | Net | Bid | Ask | Vol | Open Interest | Strike | Ticker | Last | Net | Bid | Ask | Vol | Open Interest |
| .XEBFB (*) | 0.40 | 0.00 | 0.27 | 0.32 | | 20 | 81 | .XEBRB (*) | 6.54 | 0.00 | 8.06 | 8.21 | | 30 |
| .XEBFG (*) | 3.97 | 0.00 | 0.00 | 0.00 | | | 111 | .XEBRG (*) | 0.00 | 0.00 | 0.00 | 0.00 | | |
| .XEUFK (*) | 6.20 | 0.00 | 0.00 | 0.00 | | | 112 | .XEURK (*) | 0.40 | 0.00 | 0.00 | 0.00 | | |
| .XEBFO (*) | 0.00 | 0.00 | 0.00 | 0.00 | | | 113 | .XEBRO (*) | 0.76 | 0.00 | 0.00 | 0.00 | | |
| .XEUFS (*) | 3.67 | 0.00 | 0.00 | 0.00 | | | 114 | .XEURS (*) | 0.46 | 0.00 | 0.51 | 0.61 | | |
| .XEBFW (*) | 11.08 | 0.00 | 0.00 | 0.00 | | | 115 | .XEBRW (*) | 0.72 | 0.00 | 0.71 | 0.81 | | |
| .XEUFD (*) | 1.13 | 0.00 | 0.00 | 0.00 | | | 116 | .XEURD (*) | 0.68 | 0.00 | 0.97 | 1.07 | | |
| .XEBFH (*) | 3.12 | 0.00 | 0.00 | 0.00 | | | 117 | .XEBRH (*) | 0.52 | 0.00 | 1.29 | 1.39 | | |
| .XEUFL (*) | 5.61 | 0.00 | 2.75 | 2.90 | | 2 | 118 | .XEURL (*) | 1.30 | 0.00 | 1.66 | 1.76 | | 19 |
| .XEBFP (*) | 3.16 | 0.00 | 2.21 | 2.36 | | | 119 | .XEBRP (*) | 1.75 | 0.00 | 2.12 | 2.27 | | |
| .XEUFT (*) | 5.22 | 0.00 | 1.77 | 1.87 | | | 120 | .XEURT (*) | 2.64 | +0.28 | 2.67 | 2.82 | 25 | 39 |
| .XEBFA (*) | 4.50 | 0.00 | 1.39 | 1.49 | | | 121 | .XEBRA (*) | 2.33 | 0.00 | 3.28 | 3.43 | | 10 |
| .XEUFE (*) | 3.07 | 0.00 | 1.07 | 1.17 | | 5 | 122 | .XEURE (*) | 2.15 | 0.00 | 3.95 | 4.10 | | 13 |
| .XEBFI (*) | 3.78 | 0.00 | 0.82 | 0.92 | | | 123 | .XEBRI (*) | 2.75 | 0.00 | 0.00 | 0.00 | | |
| .XEUFM (*) | 1.24 | 0.00 | 0.61 | 0.71 | | 46 | 124 | .XEURM (*) | 2.90 | 0.00 | 5.46 | 5.61 | | 32 |
| .XEBFQ (*) | 2.16 | 0.00 | 0.48 | 0.53 | | 16 | 125 | .XEBRQ (*) | 5.11 | 0.00 | 6.29 | 6.44 | | 25 |
| .XEUFU (*) | 1.40 | 0.00 | 0.35 | 0.40 | | 120 | 126 | .XEURU (*) | 0.00 | 0.00 | 0.00 | 0.00 | | |
| .XEUFF (*) | 0.35 | 0.00 | 0.20 | 0.25 | | 75 | 128 | .XEURF (*) | 7.06 | 0.00 | 8.99 | 9.14 | | 11 |
| .XEBFJ (*) | 0.61 | 0.00 | 0.14 | 0.19 | | 10 | 129 | .XEBRJ (*) | 0.00 | 0.00 | 0.00 | 0.00 | | |
| .XEUFN (*) | 0.77 | 0.00 | 0.10 | 0.15 | | 10 | 130 | .XEURN (*) | 0.00 | 0.00 | 0.00 | 0.00 | | |
| .XEBFR (*) | 0.00 | 0.00 | 0.00 | 0.00 | | | 131 | .XEBRR (*) | 0.00 | 0.00 | 0.00 | 0.00 | | |
| .XEUFV (*) | 0.00 | 0.00 | 0.00 | 0.00 | | | 132 | .XEURV (*) | 0.00 | 0.00 | 0.00 | 0.00 | | |
| .XEBFC (*) | 0.00 | 0.00 | 0.00 | 0.00 | | | 133 | .XEBRC (*) | 0.00 | 0.00 | 0.00 | 0.00 | | |
| .XEUFG (*) | 0.00 | 0.00 | 0.00 | 0.00 | | | 134 | .XEURG (*) | 0.00 | 0.00 | 0.00 | 0.00 | | |
| .XEBFK (*) | 0.00 | 0.00 | 0.00 | 0.00 | | | 135 | .XEBRK (*) | 0.00 | 0.00 | 0.00 | 0.00 | | |

**Table 11.5.**  euro currency futures options traded on the CME
– American options

PIT-TRADED OPTIONS
**Euro Fx Options**                              **Pit-Traded prices as of 04/14/04 04:10 pm (cst)**

| MTH/ | | --- SESSION --- | | | | PT | EST | ---- PRIOR | DAY | ---- |
| STRIKE | OPEN | HIGH | LOW | LAST | SETT | CHGE | VOL | SETT | VOL | INT |
|---|---|---|---|---|---|---|---|---|---|---|
| ZC JUN04 EURO FX OPTIONS CALL | | | | | | | | | | |
| 1000 | ---- | ---- | ---- | ---- | .19390 | +16 | | .19230 | | |
| 1170 | ---- | ---- | ---- | ---- | .03490 | +10 | | .03390 | | 169 |
| 1180 | ---- | ---- | ---- | ---- | .02860 | +8 | | .02780 | | 26 |
| 1190 | .01880 | .02150 | .01880 | .02150 | .02290 | +6 | 60 | .02230 | 350 | 355 |
| 1200 | .01480 | .01680 | .01480 | .01680 | .01810 | +5 | 135 | .01760 | 5 | 112 |
| 1205 | ---- | ---- | ---- | ---- | .01600 | +5 | | .01550 | 5 | 8 |
| 1210 | .01230 | .01370 | .01230 | .01370 | .01410 | +4 | 20 | .01370 | 4 | 113 |
| 1215 | .01020 | .01190 | .01020 | .01190 | .01240 | +4 | 35 | .01200 | | 124 |
| 1220 | .00880 | .01010B | .00880 | .00990B | .01090 | +5 | 10 | .01040 | 8 | 112 |
| 1225 | ---- | ---- | ---- | ---- | .00950 | +4 | | .00910 | 10 | 15 |
| 1230 | ---- | ---- | .00770A | .00770A | .00830 | +4 | | .00790 | 24 | 286 |
| 1235 | ---- | ---- | ---- | ---- | .00720 | +3 | | .00690 | | 504 |
| 1240 | .00500 | .00580B | .00480A | .00560 | .00620 | +3 | 25 | .00590 | 98 | 642 |
| 1245 | .00460 | .00460 | .00460 | .00460 | .00540 | +3 | 5 | .00510 | 4 | 299 |
| 1250 | .00400 | .00430 | .00350 | .00430 | .00460 | +2 | 100 | .00440 | 421 | 2233 |
| 1255 | .00310 | .00310 | .00310 | .00310 | .00400 | +2 | 5 | .00380 | | 22 |
| 1260 | .00270 | .00310 | .00270 | .00280 | .00340 | +2 | 40 | .00320 | 53 | 826 |
| 1265 | ---- | ---- | ---- | ---- | .00290 | +1 | | .00280 | 10 | 37 |
| 1270 | .00210 | .00240 | .00210 | .00240 | .00250 | +1 | 30 | .00240 | 175 | 506 |
| 1275 | .00180 | .00180 | .00180 | .00180 | .00210 | +1 | 5 | .00200 | 17 | 34 |
| 1280 | .00120 | .00170 | .00120 | .00170 | .00180 | +1 | 20 | .00170 | 73 | 2374 |
| 1285 | ---- | ---- | ---- | ---- | .00160 | +1 | | .00150 | | 70 |
| 1290 | .00100 | .00100 | .00100 | .00100 | .00140 | +1 | 5 | .00130 | 2 | 334 |
| 1295 | ---- | ---- | ---- | ---- | .00120 | +1 | | .00110 | | 80 |
| 1300 | .00080 | .00100 | .00080 | .00100 | .00100 | +1 | 20 | .00090 | 22 | 767 |
| 1305 | ---- | ---- | ---- | ---- | .00090 | +1 | | .00080 | | 27 |
| 1310 | ---- | ---- | .00060A | .00060A | .00080 | +1 | 1 | .00070 | 5 | 677 |
| 1315 | ---- | ---- | ---- | ---- | .00070 | +1 | | .00060 | | 59 |
| 1320 | .00050 | .00050 | .00050 | .00050 | .00060 | +1 | 5 | .00050 | 1 | 572 |
| 1340 | .00020 | .00020 | .00020 | .00020 | .00020 | UNCH | 5 | .00020 | | 486 |
| 1350 | ---- | ---- | ---- | ---- | .00010 | UNCH | 2 | .00010 | | 619 |
| 1355 | ---- | ---- | ---- | ---- | .00005 | UNCH | | .00005 | | 24 |
| 1360 | .00010 | .00010 | .00010 | .00010 | CAB | ---- | 5 | CAB | | 502 |
| 1365 | ---- | ---- | ---- | ---- | CAB | ---- | | CAB | | 54 |
| | | | | | | | | | | |
| ZC JUN04 EURO FX OPTIONS PUT | | | | | | | | | | |
| 1050 | ---- | ---- | ---- | ---- | CAB | ---- | | CAB | | 8 |
| 1070 | ---- | ---- | ---- | ---- | .00010 | UNCH | | .00010 | | 20 |
| 1090 | ---- | ---- | ---- | ---- | .00050 | +1 | | .00040 | | 60 |
| 1100 | ---- | ---- | ---- | ---- | .00080 | +1 | | .00070 | | 222 |
| 1110 | ---- | ---- | ---- | ---- | .00130 | UNCH | | .00130 | | 125 |
| 1120 | .00240 | .00240 | .00240 | .00240 | .00200 | -1 | 27 | .00210 | | 242 |
| 1130 | .00330 | .00380 | .00330 | .00340 | .00290 | -2 | 45 | .00310 | 10 | 233 |
| 1135 | .00410 | .00410 | .00340 | .00340 | .00340 | -3 | 15 | .00370 | 42 | 46 |
| 1140 | .00500 | .00540 | .00450 | .00450 | .00410 | -4 | 57 | .00450 | 91 | 1285 |
| 1145 | ---- | ---- | ---- | ---- | .00490 | -4 | | .00530 | | 18 |
| 1150 | .00730 | .00760 | .00580 | .00580 | .00590 | -4 | 122 | .00630 | 33 | 550 |
| 1155 | ---- | ---- | ---- | ---- | .00690 | -5 | | .00740 | 4 | 58 |
| 1160 | .00970 | .01000B | .00810 | .00810 | .00820 | -4 | 76 | .00860 | 365 | 1313 |
| 1165 | ---- | ---- | ---- | ---- | .00950 | -6 | | .01010 | | 19 |
| 1170 | .01320 | .01370 | .01110 | .01110 | .01110 | -6 | 41 | .01170 | 70 | 853 |
| 1175 | .01530 | .01530 | .01510 | .01510 | .01280 | -7 | 10 | .01350 | 4 | 11 |
| 1180 | .01590 | .01790 | .01500A | .01520 | .01470 | -8 | 165 | .01550 | 14 | 892 |
| 1190 | .02150 | .02290 | .01890 | .01890 | .01900 | -10 | 84 | .02000 | 368 | 649 |
| 1200 | .02740 | .02800 | .02530A | .02530A | .02420 | -11 | 30 | .02530 | 45 | 1183 |
| 1205 | ---- | ---- | ---- | ---- | .02710 | -11 | | .02820 | | 7 |
| 1210 | ---- | ---- | ---- | ---- | .03020 | -12 | | .03140 | 9 | 301 |
| 1215 | .03810 | .03810 | .03490A | .03490A | .03340 | -12 | 5 | .03460 | 350 | 805 |
| 1220 | .04030 | .04030 | .03800 | .03800 | .03690 | -11 | 16 | .03800 | 8 | 334 |
| 1225 | ---- | ---- | ---- | ---- | .04050 | -12 | | .04170 | | 6 |
| 1230 | .04560 | .04560 | .04560 | .04560 | .04430 | -12 | 5 | .04550 | 2 | 349 |
| 1235 | ---- | ---- | ---- | ---- | .04820 | -13 | | .04950 | 125 | 575 |

Only selected products or options with selected strike prices are shown in these tables. On the top the underlying security's information can be observed, which is the spot exchange rate between the US dollar and the euro at $1.1914/€ at close. It can be seen that there is low or no open interest in deep out-of-the-money options, though there are some exceptions. Most of them are rarely traded. It can be further found out from the PHLX that a regular daily trading volume for all euro currency options is 220 contracts and the open interest in all euro currency options is 3,741 contracts. The combined daily trading volume is 369 contracts for all American mid-month currency options and is 183 contracts for all European mid-month currency options. There is very little trading in month end currency options. In theory, an American option has a higher value than a European option, other things being equal. This may be observed by contrasting Table 11.3 and Table 11.4. Nevertheless, since there is no trading activity in most of these options during the session, these figures do not always reflect the features and differences in these two types of options, at least for the reason that these figures were taken at different times. Table 11.5 lists selected euro currency futures options traded on the CME. These are American type options. Trading activity is evidently much more intensive in options on currency futures on the CME.

We conclude this section by presenting two examples to illustrate how currency options and currency futures options work and the payoffs from holding and exercising these options.

*Example 3*: The current spot exchange rate between the US dollar and the euro, or the price of one euro in terms of the US dollar, $S_0$, is 1.1914 ($1.1914/€) on April 14, 2004. Information on a currency option on the euro traded on the PHLX on the day is as follows: the exercise price, $X$, is 118 ($1.1800/€), the option price, $c$, is 2.75 (as can be found in Chapter 11, the figure is cents per unit, i.e., $0.0275 per euro), it is an American call expires in mid June 2004, the risk free interest rate is 1.00% per annum, and the contract size for euro currency option on the PHLX is 62,500 euros. Suppose Ken buys one contract of the option on April 14, 2004 and decides to exercise the option in mid May when the exchange rate, at $1.2758/€, reaches, in his view, the peak before its expiration in mid June. What is the profit made by Ken from having one contract of the option?

*Solution*:

Relevant figures are given as $X$=1.1800, $S_T$=1.2758, $c$ = 0.0275, $T$=1/12, $t$=0, $r$ = 0.01. The cost per euro at maturity $= e^{r(T-t)}c = e^{0.01 \times 1/12} \times 0.0275 =$ $0.027523. Since $S_T > X$, the option is exercised and the gross payoff per euro from exercising the option $= S_T - X$ =1.2758-1.1800 =$0.0958. The net payoff per euro = gross payoff − costs =0.0958–0.027523=$0.068277, as shown in the graph below. The net payoff or profit per option contract is $0.068277 \times 62,500 = \$4267.32$. So Ken makes a net profit of $4267.32 from the option trading.

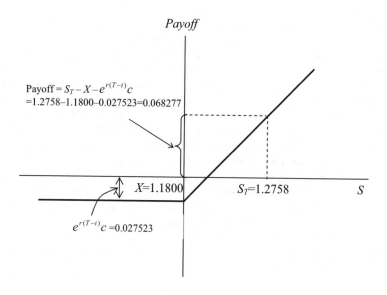

*Example 4*: The British pound is currently traded for the US dollar at an exchange rate $S_0 = 1.7823/£$ and the six month British pound futures is currently traded at $F_0 = 1.7497$ ($\$1.7497/£$) on the CME. Information on a European currency put option on the British pound futures is given: the exercise price, $X$, is $\$1.7900/£$, the option price, $p$, is 3.72 cents per pound, the risk free interest rate is 1.00% per annum, and the contract size for currency options on British pound futures on the CME is 62,500 pounds. Suppose Lisa buys one contract of the option now, and on the expiration date, the futures price, $F_T$, is 1.7475. What is the profit made by Lisa from having one contract of the put option?

*Solution*:

Relevant figures are given as $X=1.7900$, $F_T=1.7475$, $p = 0.0372$, $T=0.5$, $t=0$, $r = 0.01$. The cost per pound at maturity $= e^{r(T-t)}c = e^{0.01 \times 0.5} \times 0.0372 = \$0.037386$. Since $F_T < X$, the option is exercised and the gross payoff per pound from exercising the option $= X - F_T = 1.7900 - 1.7475 = \$0.0425$. The net payoff per pound $=$ gross payoff $-$ costs $= 0.0425 - 0.037386 = \$0.005114$, as shown in the graph below. The net payoff or profit per option contract is $\$0.005114 \times 62,500 = \$319.60$. So Lisa makes a net profit of $4267.32 from exercising the put option on British pound futures.

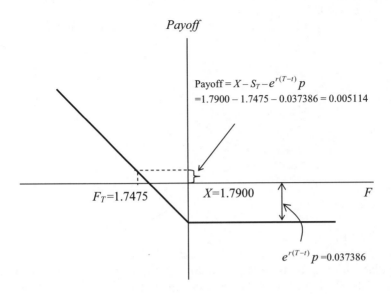

*Payoff*

$$\text{Payoff} = X - S_T - e^{r(T-t)}p$$
$$= 1.7900 - 1.7475 - 0.037386 = 0.005114$$

$F_T = 1.7475$

$X = 1.7900$

$F$

$$e^{r(T-t)}p = 0.037386$$

## 11.4 Option Pricing – *the Binomial Tree Approach*

Option pricing follows the so called risk neutral valuation principle. The valuation or pricing of options, which in general can be extended to all derivative securities such as futures, works as follows. Construct a portfolio consisting one option and several units or a fraction of one unit of the underlying security or asset. The proportions of the option and the underlying in the portfolio are chosen in such a way that the values of the portfolio at the option's expiration date under all different circumstances, i.e., given any prices of the underlying security on the day, are always the same. Therefore, there is no risk in the portfolio and the portfolio will grow at the risk free interest rate. It is reasonable to form such a portfolio, since the primary role of a derivative security is to manage or hedge the risk in the underlying security and, consequently, the derivative security is usually, if not always, used along with the underlying security.

In this section the binomial tree approach to option pricing is introduced. A binomial tree model is not accurate, especially if it involves only one or two steps in the modelling process. However, it is sufficient to demonstrate the valuation principle, which is the same in more complicated methods, such as the Black-Scholes model.

Consider an option on the Apple Computer stock first. Suppose the stock is currently traded at $28.00. In six months time the stock price will be either $32.00 or $24.00. A European call option on the stock expiring in six months has an exercise price of $30.00. The risk free interest rate is 2.00% per annum. How much should be paid for the option's premium?

First we sketch the payoffs for the stock and the option with the following binomial tree:

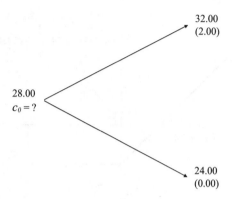

Since the exercise price is $30.00, the option payoff is $2.00 on the expiration date if the stock price is $32.00 and the option payoff is zero on the expiration date if the stock price is $24.00. What is unknown and to be solved is $c_0$, the current option price or premium.

Let us buy several shares or a fraction of one share of the stock and short one call option to form a portfolio. Designating the number of shares as $\Delta$, the payoffs of the portfolio are shown as follows:

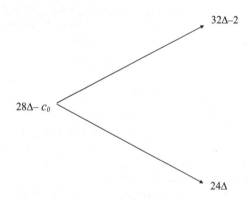

A risk free portfolio means that the two outcomes are the same:

$$32\Delta - 2 = 24\Delta \tag{11.1}$$

Therefore, $\Delta$ is solved to be 0.25. $\Delta$ is the hedge ratio as shown in Table 11.2. The portfolio value at maturity is:

$$32\Delta - 2 = 32 \times 0.25 - 2 = 6 \qquad (11.2)$$

or

$$24\Delta = 24 \times 0.25 = 6 \qquad (11.3)$$

Since the portfolio is risk free, the present value of the portfolio can be obtained through discounting the portfolio value at maturity by the risk free interest rate:

$$PV(portfolio) = 6e^{-0.02 \times 0.5} = 5.94 \qquad (11.4)$$

We also know than the present value of the portfolio is:

$$28\Delta - c_0 = 28 \times 0.25 - c_0 = 7 - c_0 \qquad (11.5)$$

Comparing the above two equations leads to:

$$5.94 = 7 - c_0 \qquad (11.6)$$

$$c_0 = 1.06 \qquad (11.7)$$

Therefore the option price is solved as $c_0 = \$1.06$, i.e., a premium of $1.06 should be paid for holding this option.

Now we develop the general binominal tree formulae for the pricing of derivatives, such as calls, puts and futures. Define the relevant variables as follows:

$S_0$:    current price of an asset, such as stocks, bonds, commodities and foreign currencies

$u$:    scale of upward movement of the asset price on the expiration date of the derivative, $u > 1$

$S_u$:    the asset price when it goes up on the expiration date of the derivative, $S_u = S \cdot u$

$d$:    scale of downward movement of the asset price on the expiration date of the derivative, $d < 1$

$S_d$:    the asset price when goes down on the expiration date of the derivative, $S_d = S \cdot d$

$v_0$:    current price of the derivative written on the asset

$v_u$:    the value of the derivative when the asset price goes up on the expiration date of the derivative

$v_d$:    the value of the derivative when the asset price goes down on the expiration date of the derivative

$T$:    time to maturity of the derivative

$r$:    risk free interest rate

The payoffs for the stock and the derivative are shown with the following binomial tree:

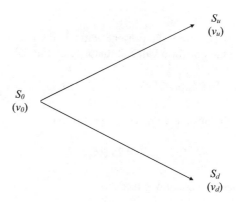

Let us long $\Delta$ units of the asset and short one unit of the derivative to form a portfolio. The payoffs of the portfolio are given as follows:

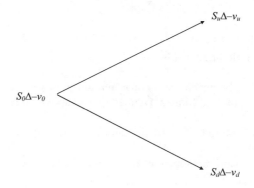

A risk free portfolio means that the two outcomes are the same:

$$S_u \Delta - v_u = S_d \Delta - v_d \qquad (11.8)$$

which is the portfolio value at maturity. $\Delta$, the hedge ratio, is solved as:

$$\Delta = \frac{v_u - v_d}{S_u - S_d} \qquad (11.9)$$

With this hedge ratio, the ratio of the units of the stock to the units of the derivative, the portfolio is risk free. Since the portfolio is risk free, it should grow at the risk free interest rate. We know than the present value of the portfolio is:

$$PV(portfolio) = S_0\Delta - v_0 \tag{11.11}$$

So another expression of the portfolio value at maturity is:

$$PV(portfolio) = (S_0\Delta - v_0)e^{rT} \tag{11.12}$$

Comparing the above equation (11.8) and equation (11.12) leads to:

$$v_0 = S_0\Delta - (S_u\Delta - v_u)e^{-rT} \tag{11.12}$$

or:

$$v_0 = S_0\Delta - (S_d\Delta - v_d)e^{-rT} \tag{11.13}$$

Substituting equation (11.9) into equation (11.12) yields:

$$
\begin{aligned}
v_0 &= S_0\frac{v_u - v_d}{S_u - S_d} - S_u e^{-rT}\frac{v_u - v_d}{S_u - S_d} + v_u e^{-rT} \\
&= \frac{S_0 - S_d e^{-rT}}{S_u - S_d}v_u - \frac{S_0 - S_u e^{-rT}}{S_u - S_d}v_d = \left(\frac{S_0 e^{rT} - S_d}{S_u - S_d}v_u - \frac{S_0 e^{rT} - S_u}{S_u - S_d}v_d\right)e^{-rT} \\
&= \left(\frac{S_0 e^{rT} - dS_0}{uS_0 - dS_0}v_u - \frac{S_0 e^{rT} - uS_0}{uS_0 - dS_0}v_d\right)e^{-rT} = \left(\frac{e^{rT} - d}{u - d}v_u - \frac{e^{rT} - u}{u - d}v_d\right)e^{-rT} \\
&= \left[\frac{e^{rT} - d}{u - d}v_u + \left(1 - \frac{e^{rT} - d}{u - d}\right)v_d\right]e^{-rT} \\
&= [pv_u + (1 - p)v_d]e^{-rT}
\end{aligned}
\tag{11.14}
$$

where

$$p = \frac{e^{rT} - d}{u - d} \tag{11.15}$$

is the risk neutral probability of upward movement of the asset price, and $1 - p$ is the risk neutral probability of downward movement of the asset price. The current price or the present value of the derivative can now be intuitively interpreted as its expected value at maturity discounted by the risk free interest rate over the contract period, where the expected value of the derivative at maturity is the weighted average of its value when the asset price goes up and its value when the asset price goes down, with the weightings being the risk neutral probabilities. This implies that the value of the derivative is expected to grow at the risk free rate. Moreover, the underlying asset price is also expected to grow at the risk free rate, given the risk neutral probabilities of upward and downward movements of the asset price:

$$S_0 e^{rT} = [pS_u + (1-p)S_d]$$  (11.16)

So the payoffs of the asset and the derivative can be illustrated by the following binomial tree:

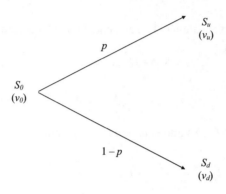

Let us re-examine the above case.

$$\Delta = \frac{v_u - v_d}{S_u - S_d} = \frac{2-0}{32-24} = 0.25$$

$$p = \frac{e^{rT} - d}{u - d} = \frac{e^{rT} - S_d / S_0}{S_u / S_0 - S_d / S_0} = \frac{e^{0.02 \times 0.5} - 24/28}{32/28 - 24/28}$$

$$= \frac{1.01005 - 0.587143}{1.142857 - 0.587143} = 0.535176$$

So:

$$v_0 = [pv_u + (1-p)v_d]e^{-rT}$$
$$= [0.535176 \times 2 + (1 - 0.535176) \times 0]e^{-0.02 \times 0.5}$$
$$= 1.06$$

Since $p$ and $1-p$ are risk neutral probabilities, we have more intuitive way to find out their values from the asset prices, bringing figures into equation (2.16)

$$28e^{0.02 \times 0.5} = [32p + 24(1-p)]$$

$p$ can also be solved to be equal to 0.535176.

For an asset price to have only two states at a future time is not realistic. So, a two step binomial model, which divides time to maturity into two periods, is examined in the following. The study of the two step binomial model indicates the way in which more and more states or outcomes of the price at a future time can be introduced. In the first step, the price of the asset either moves up with a risk neutral probability of $p$ or moves down with a risk neutral probability of $1-p$. If the state of the price is $S_u$ at the first period, the price may continue to move up with the same risk neutral probability of upward movement of the price, $p$, to $S_{uu}$, or it may move down with the same risk neutral probability of downward movement of the price, $1-p$, to $S_{ud}$, in the second period Similarly, if the state of the price is $S_d$ at the first period, the price may move up with the same to risk neutral probability of upward movement of the price, $p$, to $S_{du} (= S_{ud})$, or it may continue to move down with the same risk neutral probability of downward movement of the price, $1-p$, to $S_{dd}$, in the second period. It can be easily sensed that the probability for the price to be $S_{ud}$ is higher than the probability for the price to be $S_{uu}$ or $S_{dd}$. When more and more steps are introduced, more and more states of the price can be considered. Moreover, in such binomial models, the probability for the price in a state closer to the centre point is greater than the probability for the price to be in a state that is less close to the centre point, which is sensible.

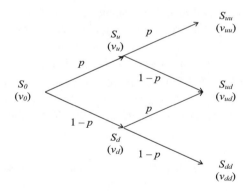

We work backwards from the end of the second sub-period to find the solution.

$$v_u = \left[pv_{uu} + (1-p)v_{ud}\right]e^{-rT} \tag{11.17}$$

$$v_d = \left[pv_{ud} + (1-p)v_{dd}\right]e^{-rT} \tag{11.18}$$

$$v_0 = [pv_u + (1-p)v_d]e^{-rT}$$
$$= [p^2v_{uu} + 2p(1-p)v_{ud} + (1-p)^2v_{dd}]e^{2rT} \qquad (11.19)$$

where the risk neutral probability of upward movement of the asset price is given in equation (2.16).

Equation (11.17), equation (11.18) and equation (11.19) are for derivatives that cannot be exercised before maturity, e.g., European options. For American options than can be exercised prior to the expiration date, $v_u$ or $v_d$ from exercising the option earlier at the end of the first period can be higher than that given by equation (11.17) or equation (11.18). In that case, $v_u$ or $v_d$ from exercising the option earlier at the end of the first period should replace that given by equation (11.17) or equation (11.18) and be used in equation (2.19).

We re-examine the above case in the two step model with some adaptations as two examples in the following.

> *Example 5*: Suppose the stock of Apple Computer Inc is currently traded at $28.00. In six months time the stock price will be either $32.00 or $24.00. A European call option on the stock expiring in six months has an exercise price of $30.00. The risk free interest rate is 2.00% per annum. Solve the option's premium with a two step binomial model.
>
> *Solution*:
>
> Since the option expires in six months, so $T$=0.25 for the length of one period. The scale of upward movement of the stock price in six months is $uu = 32/28 = 1.142857$, so at the end of the first period in three months, the scale of upward movement of the stock price is $u = (32/28)^{0.5} = 1.069045$, and $S_u$=29.93. The scale of downward movement of the stock price in six months is $dd = 24/28 = 0.857143$, the scale of downward movement of the stock price at the end of the first period in three months is $d = (24/28)^{0.5} = 0.92583$, and $S_d$=25.92.
>
> The risk neutral probability of upward movement of the asset price is:
>
> $$p = \frac{e^{rT} - d}{u - d} = \frac{e^{0.02 \times 0.25} - 0.92583}{1.069045 - 0.92583} = 0.552924$$
>
> The value of the option at the end of the first period when the stock price goes up is:

$$v_u = [pv_{uu} + (1-p)v_{ud}]e^{-rT}$$
$$= [0.552924 \times 2 + (1 - 0.552924) \times 0]e^{-0.02 \times 0.25}$$
$$= 1.100332$$

The value of the option at the end of the first period when the stock price goes down is zero. So the value of the option now is:

$$v_0 = [pv_u + (1-p)v_d]e^{-rT}$$
$$= [p^2 v_{uu} + 2p(1-p)v_{ud} + (1-p)^2 v_{dd}]e^{2rT}$$
$$= 0.552924 \times 1.100332 \times e^{-0.02 \times 0.25} = (0.552924)^2 \times 2 \times e^{-0.05 \times 0.5}$$
$$= 0.61$$

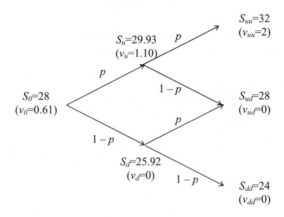

Therefore, the option premium paid now should be $0.61. The figure is lower than that from the one step model. The reason is simple. The situation that the stock price will be $32 in six months is now one of the three states, while it is one of the two states in the one step model. Consequently, the probability of the stock price goes up to $32 at the time when the option expires is smaller.

*Example 6*: Suppose the stock of Apple Computer Inc is currently traded at $28.00. A European call option on the stock expiring in twelve months has an exercise price of $30.00. In six months time the stock price will be either $32.00 or $24.00 and the stock price will continue to rise or fall with the same patterns in the next six months. The risk free interest rate is 2.00% per annum. Solve for the option's premium with a two step binomial model.

*Solution*:

Since the option expires in twelve months, so $T=0.5$ for the length of one period. The scale of upward movement of the stock price in six months is $u = 32/28 = 1.142857$, $S_u=32$, and $S_{uu}=36.57$. The scale of downward movement of the stock price in six months is $d = 24/28 = 0.857143$, $S_d=25.92$, and $S_{dd}=20.57$. Since $S_{uu}$ in twelve months is higher at \$36.57 in this example than that in the previous one, $v_{uu}$ is also higher at \$6.57 instead of \$2.00 previously.

The risk neutral probability of upward movement of the asset price is:

$$p = \frac{e^{rT} - d}{u - d} = \frac{e^{0.02 \times 0.5} - 0.857143}{1.142857 - 0.857143} = 0.535176$$

The value of the option at the end of the first period when the stock price goes up is:

$$v_u = \left[ p v_{uu} + (1-p) v_{ud} \right] e^{-rT}$$
$$= \left[ 0.535176 \times 6.571429 + (1 - 0.535176) \times 0 \right] e^{-0.02 \times 0.5}$$
$$= 3.481877$$

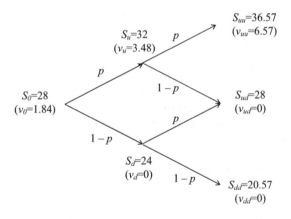

The value of the option at the end of the first period when the stock price goes down is zero. So the value of the option now is:

$$v_0 = [pv_u + (1-p)v_d]e^{-rT}$$
$$= [p^2 v_{uu} + 2p(1-p)v_{ud} + (1-p)^2 v_{dd}]e^{2rT}$$
$$= 0.535176 \times 3.481877 \times e^{-0.02 \times 0.5} = (0.535176)^2 \times 6.51429 \times e^{-0.05 \times 1}$$
$$= 1.84$$

Therefore, the option price now should be $1.84, which is higher than that in Example 5. It is because the stock price rises more, as well as falls more, in a longer period. While the payoff of the option, with the exercise price being unchanged, increases when the stock price goes up, the payoff of the option does not decrease when the stock price goes down. This suggests that the benefit of holding an option that expires in a longer period is greater than that of holding an option that expires in a shorter period, other things equal. Compared with Example 5, the option holder has the same chance to have a larger gain and has the same chance to incur the same loss, so the option premium must be higher.

Finally, the binomial models are applied to currency options in this section. The foreign exchange rate is the relative price of two currencies, which suggests that the risk free interest rates of the two countries or two currency zones will be involved in the calculation of currency options' prices or premia. Notice that the left hand side of equation (2.16) is the futures price for a domestically traded asset, i.e.:

$$F_{0,T} = [pS_u + (1-p)S_d] \qquad (11.16')$$

For currencies, equation (2.16') takes the form of:

$$S_0 e^{(r_h - r_f) \times T} = [pS_u + (1-p)S_d] \qquad (11.16'')$$

The risk neutral probability of upward movement of the exchange rate is given as:

$$p = \frac{e^{(r_h - r_f) \times T} - d}{u - d} \qquad (11.15')$$

Then the option's premium is:

$$v_0 = [pv_u + (1-p)v_d]e^{-(r_h - r_f) \times T} \qquad (11.14')$$

For the two step binomial model, the option premium is obtained as:

$$v_u = [pv_{uu} + (1-p)v_{ud}]e^{-(r_h - r_f) \times T} \qquad (11.17')$$

$$v_d = \left[pv_{ud} + (1-p)v_{dd}\right]e^{-(r_h-r_f)\times T} \qquad (11.18')$$

$$v_0 = \left[pv_u + (1-p)v_d\right]e^{-(r_h-r_f)\times T}$$
$$= \left[p^2 v_{uu} + 2p(1-p)v_{ud} + (1-p)^2 v_{dd}\right]e^{2(r_h-r_f)T} \qquad (11.19')$$

The following two examples demonstrate how to determine options' prices using the binomial model

> *Example 7*: The current spot exchange rate between the US dollar and the euro, $S_0$, is 1.1900 ($1.1900/€) on April 15, 2004. A European currency call option on the euro traded on the PHLX expiring in two months has an exercise price $X=118$ ($1.1800/€). In two months time the exchange rate will be either $1.2100/€ or $1.1700/€. The risk free interest rate is 1.00% per annum in the US and 2.00% per annum in the euroland. The contract size for euro currency option on the PHLX is 62,500 euros. Solve the option premium per contract with the one step binomial model.

> *Solution*:

> Since the option expires in two months, so $T=1/6$. The scale of upward movement of the exchange rate in two months is $u = 1.1210/1.1900 = 1.016807$. The scale of downward movement of the exchange rate in two months is $d = 1.1700/1.1900 = 0.983193$. The payoff of the option at maturity when the exchange rate rises is $v_u = S_u - X = 1.2100 - 1.1800 = 0.03$. The payoff of the option at maturity when the exchange rate decreases is zero

> The risk neutral probability of upward movement of the asset price is:

$$p = \frac{e^{(r_h-r_f)T} - d}{u-d} = \frac{e^{(0.01-0.02)\times 0.1667} - 0.983193}{1.016807 - 0.983193} = 0.450458$$

> The present value or the premium of the option is:

$$v_0 = \left[pv_u + (1-p)v_d\right]e^{-(r_h-r_f)T}$$
$$= 0.450458 \times 0.03 \times e^{-(0.01-0.02)\times 0.1667}$$
$$= 0.013491$$

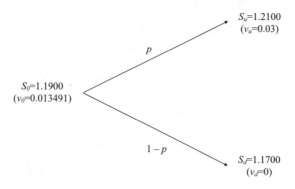

$S_u$=1.2100
($v_u$=0.03)

$p$

$S_0$=1.1900
($v_0$=0.013491)

$1-p$

$S_d$=1.1700
($v_d$=0)

Therefore the premium per contract is 0.013491×62500=$843.20.

*Example 8*: The British pound is currently traded for the US dollar at an exchange rate $S_0 = 1.7800/\pounds$. The scale of upward movement of the exchange rate in three months, $u$, is 1.15; and scale of downward movement of the exchange rate in three months, $d$, is 0.85. A currency put option on the British pound has an exercise price of $X = \$1.9000/\pounds$ and expires in six months. The risk free interest rate is 1.00% per annum in the US and 4.00% per annum in the UK. The contract size is £31,250. Solve the premium of a European put option per contract with a two step binomial model. What should be the option premium per contract if the option is American?

*Solution*:

Each of the two period is three months, so $T$=1/4=0.25.
In three months, $S_u$= 1.78×1.15= 2.047, $S_d$= 1.78×0.85= 1.513.
In six months, $S_{uu}$= 2.047×1.15=2.35405, $S_{dd}$= 1.513×0.85=1.28605, $S_{ud}$= 1.7800.
The payoffs of the option at maturity are $v_{dd}$= $X - S_{dd}$= 1.9000 –1.28605 = 0.61395, $v_{du}$= $v_{ud}$ = $X - S_{ud}$= 1.9000 –1.7800 = 0.12, and $v_{uu}$=0.
The risk neutral probability of upward movement of the asset price is:

$$p = \frac{e^{(r_h - r_f)T} - d}{u - d} = \frac{e^{(0.01-0.04)\times0.25} - 0.85}{1.15 - 0.85} = 0.475094$$

The value of the option at the end of the first period when the exchange rate increases is:

$$v_u = \left[pv_{uu} + (1-p)v_{ud}\right]e^{-(r_h - r_f)\times T}$$
$$= \left[0.475094 \times 0 + (1-0.475094) \times 0.12\right]e^{-(0.01-0.04)\times 0.25}$$
$$= 0.063463$$

The value of the option at the end of the first period when the exchange rate decreases is:

$$v_d = \left[pv_{ud} + (1-p)v_{dd}\right]e^{-(r_h - r_f)\times T}$$
$$= \left[0.475094 \times 0.12 + (1-0.475094) \times 0.61395\right]e^{-(0.01-0.04)\times 0.25}$$
$$= 0.382133$$

The option premium per pound is:

$$v_0 = \left[pv_u + (1-p)v_d\right]e^{-(r_h - r_f)\times T}$$
$$= \left[0.475094 \times 0.063464 + (1-0.475094) \times 0.382133\right]e^{-(0.01-0.04)\times 0.25}$$
$$= 0.232472$$

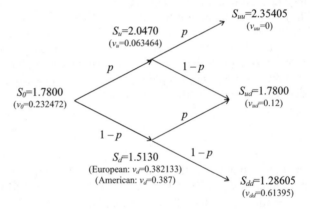

Therefore the premium per contract is 0.232472×31250=$7264.75 for the European put option on the British pound.

If the option is American that can be exercised prior to expiration in three months, then $v_d = 1.900-1.513 = 0.387$, which is higher than 0.382133 if exercised on the expiration date in six months. So the option premium per pound is:

$$v_0 = \left[ pv_u + (1-p)v_d \right] e^{-(r_h - r_f) \times T}$$
$$= \left[ 0.475094 \times 0.063464 + (1-0.475094) \times 0.387 \right] e^{-(0.01-0.04) \times 0.25}$$
$$= 0.235064$$

The premium per contract is 0.235064×31250=$7345.19 for the American put option on the British pound, which is higher than the premium of its European counterpart.

## 11.5 Option Pricing – *the Black-Scholes Model*

The binomial models in the previous section are intuitive and indicative with regard to how options should be priced, but they are rough estimates concerning option premia. In practice, the Black-Scholes model and its various variations and extensions are used in the pricing of options and other derivatives. The Black-Scholes model also adopts the risk neutral valuation principle where the price of the derivatives security, as well as the price of its underlying asset or security, follows stochastic processes. The price of the option or other derivatives securities is modelled in such a fashion that there is no stochastic component in a portfolio consisting one unit (several units) of the option and several units (one unit) of the underlying security. The stochastic components in the option price and the price of the underlying security have been cancelled out, so there are only deterministic elements in the portfolio that is risk free.

In this section the Black-Scholes model for stock options is introduced first, followed by the adaptation for currency options. The mathematical derivation of the model, which is beyond the scope of this book, is not provided. Nevertheless we explain the role of relevant variables and parameters in the model intuitively to make them as financially meaningful as possible. Finally several examples are presented to demonstrate the application of the model.

The basic Black-Scholes model for a European call option on a stock that does not pay a dividend in the option contract period is as follows:

$$c_0 = S_0 N(d_1) - X e^{-rT} N(d_2)$$
$$= \left[ F_{0,T} N(d_1) - X N(d_2) \right] e^{-rT}$$

(11.20)

where $c_0$ is the current price of the option, $S_0$ is the current price of the stock, $F_{0,T}$ is the price of a futures product on the stock at time 0 for delivery at time $T$. at the time when the option expires, $X$ is the exercise or strike price, $r$ is the risk free interest rate, $T$ is time to maturity, and $N(d_1)$ and $N(d_2)$ are cumulative normal distributions. $F_{0,T} N(d_1) - X N(d_2)$ can be viewed as the option payoff at maturity, having taken the statistical distribution of the stock price into consideration. Following the risk neutral valuation principle, this payoff is discounted by the risk free interest rate to derive the present value or the current price of the option.

The parameters in the normal distribution, $d_1$ and $d_2$, are given by:

$$d_1 = \frac{Ln(S_0 / X) + (r + \sigma^2 / 2)T}{\sigma\sqrt{T}} \qquad (11.21)$$

and

$$d_2 = \frac{Ln(S_0 / X) + (r - \sigma^2 / 2)T}{\sigma\sqrt{T}} = d_1 - \sigma\sqrt{T} \qquad (11.22)$$

where $\sigma^2$ is the volatility of the stock.

The Black-Scholes model for a European put option on a non divided paying stock is:

$$
\begin{aligned}
p_0 &= X\,e^{-rT}\,N(-d_2) - S_0\,N(-d_1) \\
&= \left[X\,N(-d_2) - F_{0,T}\,N(-d_1)\right]e^{-rT}
\end{aligned}
\qquad (11.23)
$$

where $p_0$ is the current price of the option. Similar to the call option case, $X\,N(-d_2) - F_{0,T}\,N(-d_1)$ can be viewed as the put option payoff at maturity, with some probabilities.

Currency options involve the risk free interest rates in both the domestic country and the foreign country. However, if we choose to use the futures price, the formulae are almost the same in appearance. The current price of a European call option is as follows:

$$
\begin{aligned}
c_0 &= S_0 e^{-r_f T} N(d_1) - X\,e^{-r_h T} N(d_2) \\
&= \left[F_{0,T} N(d_1) - X\,N(d_2)\right]e^{-r_h T}
\end{aligned}
\qquad (11.24)
$$

The current price of a European put option is given by the formula:

$$
\begin{aligned}
p_0 &= X\,e^{-r_h T} N(-d_2) - S_0 e^{-r_f T} N(-d_1) \\
&= \left[X\,N(-d_2) - F_{0,T} N(-d_1)\right]e^{-r_h T}
\end{aligned}
\qquad (11.25)
$$

where $S_0$ is the current spot exchange rate, $F_{0,T}$ is the current price of a currency futures product, $X$ is the exercise price or the exercise exchange rate, $r_h$ is the risk free interest rate in the domestic country, $r_f$ is the risk free interest rate in the foreign country, and $T$ is time to maturity. $d_1$ and $d_2$ are also slightly different from those in equation (11.21) and equation (11.22).

$$d_1 = \frac{Ln(S_0/X)+(r_h-r_f+\sigma^2/2)T}{\sigma\sqrt{T}}$$
$$= \frac{Ln(F_{0,T}/X)+\sigma^2T/2}{\sigma\sqrt{T}}$$

(11.26)

and

$$d_2 = \frac{Ln(S_0/X)+(r_h-r_f-\sigma^2/2)T}{\sigma\sqrt{T}}$$
$$= \frac{Ln(F_{0,T}/X)-\sigma^2T/2}{\sigma\sqrt{T}} = d_1 - \sigma\sqrt{T}$$

(11.27)

where $\sigma^2$ is the volatility of the exchange rate.

In the second row of equation (11.24), the term in brackets is the call option payoff at maturity in terms of domestic currency, so it is discounted at the risk free interest rate in the domestic country. The risk free interest rate is implied by the futures price, $F_{0,T}$. Similarly, in the second row of equation (11.25), the term in brackets is the put option payoff at maturity in terms of domestic currency, so it is discounted at the risk free interest rate in the domestic country. Also, the differential between the domestic and foreign risk free interest rates $r_h - r_f$ appears in parameters $d_1$ and $d_2$ for currency options, replacing the domestic risk free interest rate in the expression for a stock option. Since $Ln(F_{0,T}) = Ln(S_0) + (r_h - r_f) \times T$, both the domestic risk free interest rate and the foreign risk free interest rate disappear in the second row of equation (11.26) and in the second row of equation (11.27), but they are implicitly contained in $F_{0,T}$.

From the above analysis and formulae, it is observed that there are five factors to influence the price of non dividend paying stock options, and there are six factors that determine the price of currency options. Table 11.6 and Table 11.7 summarise how these factors influence the option price. The influence of some factors is straightforward, such as that the exercise price is negatively related to the price of a call option and positively related to the price of a put option. The influence of some other factors is subtle and requires detailed analysis beyond the scope of this book. Interested readers may refer to specialised books on options and derivatives, such as Hull (2003).

**Table 11.6.** Factors and ways of influence on stock options

|  | Call | Put |
|---|---|---|
| Stock price | + | − |
| Exercise price | − | + |
| Risk free interest rate | + | − |
| Volatility of the stock | + | + |
| Time to maturity | + | + |

**Table 11.7.** Factors and ways of influence on currency options

|  | Call | Put |
|---|---|---|
| Exchange rate | + | − |
| Exercise price | − | + |
| Domestic risk free interest rate | + | − |
| Foreign risk free interest rate | + | − |
| Volatility of the exchange rate | + | + |
| Time to maturity | + | + |

Now we present three examples to demonstrate the application of the Black-Scholes model.

*Example 9*: Suppose the stock of Apple Computer Inc is currently traded at $28.00. The volatility of the stock is 25% per annum. A European call option on the stock expiring in six months has an exercise price of $30.00. The risk free interest rate is 2.00% per annum. Apply the Black-Scholes model to solve the option's premium.

*Solution*:

$$d_1 = \frac{Ln(S_0/X) + (r + \sigma^2/2)T}{\sigma\sqrt{T}}$$

$$= \frac{Ln(28/30) + (0.02 + 0.25^2/2) \times 0.5}{0.25\sqrt{0.5}} = -0.24533$$

$$d_2 = d_1 - \sigma\sqrt{T} = -0.15694 - 0.25\sqrt{0.5} = -0.4221$$

$$c_0 = S_0 N(d_1) - X e^{-rT} N(d_2)$$
$$= 28\, N(-0.24533) - 30\, e^{-0.02 \times 0.5} N(-0.4221)$$
$$= 28\, N \times 0.403102 - 30\, e^{-0.02 \times 0.5} \times 0.336475$$
$$= 1.29$$

Therefore the option premium is $1.29 per share of the Apple Computer stock.

*Example 10*: The current spot exchange rate between the US dollar and the euro, $S_0$, is 1.1900 ($1.1900/€) on April 15, 2004. A European currency call option on the euro traded on the PHLX expiring in two months has an exercise price $X$=118 ($1.1800/€). The volatility of the exchange rate is 35% per annum. The risk free interest rate is 1.00% per annum in the US and 2.00% per annum in the euroland. The contract size for euro currency option on the PHLX is 62,500 euros. Solve the option premium per contract with the Black-Scholes model.

*Solution*:

$$d_1 = \frac{Ln(S_0 / X) + (r_h - r_f + \sigma^2 / 2)T}{\sigma\sqrt{T}}$$

$$= \frac{Ln(1.1900 / 1.1800 + (0.01 - 0.02 + 0.35^2 / 2) \times 1/6}{0.35\sqrt{1/6}} = 0.118839$$

$$d_2 = d_1 - \sigma\sqrt{T} = 0.118839 - 0.35\sqrt{1/6} = -0.02405$$

$$c_0 = S_0 e^{-r_f T} N(d_1) - X e^{-r_h T} N(d_2)$$
$$= 1.1900 e^{-0.02/6} N(0.118839) - 1.1800 e^{-0.01/6} N(-0.02405)$$
$$= 1.1900 e^{-0.02/6} \times 0.547299 - 1.1800 e^{-0.01/6} \times 0.490407$$
$$= 0.071401$$

Therefore, the option premium per contract is $0.071401 \times 62500 =$ $4462.58.

*Example 11*: The British pound is currently traded for the US dollar at an exchange rate $S_0 = 1.7800/£$. A currency put option on the British pound has an exercise price of $X = $1.9000/£$ and expires in six months. The volatility of the exchange rate is 30% per annum. The risk free interest rate is 1.00% per annum in the US and 4.00% per annum in the UK. The contract size is £31,250. Apply the Black-Scholes model to solve the premium of a European put option per contract.

*Solution*:

$$d_1 = \frac{Ln(S_0 / X) + (r_h - r_f + \sigma^2 / 2)T}{\sigma\sqrt{T}}$$

$$= \frac{Ln(1.7800 / 1.9000) + (0.01 - 0.04 + 0.30^2 / 2) \times 0.5}{0.30\sqrt{0.5}} = -0.27219$$

$$d_2 = d_1 - \sigma\sqrt{T} = -0.27219 - 0.30\sqrt{0.5} = -0.48432$$

$$p_0 = X\,e^{-r_h T}\,N(-d_2) - S_0 e^{-r_f T}\,N(-d_1)$$
$$= 1.9000\,e^{-0.01 \times 0.5}\,N(0.48432) - 1.7800\,e^{-0.04 \times 0.5}\,N(0.27219)$$
$$= 1.9000\,e^{-0.01 \times 0.5} \times 0.685922 - 1.7800\,e^{-0.04 \times 0.5} \times 0.607263$$
$$= 0.237228$$

Therefore, the option premium per contract is $0.237228 \times 31250 =$ $7413.38.

# 12    Currency Swaps

A swap is an agreement between two counterparties to exchange cash flows of different features at specified future times or at specific periodic intervals. It has been observed in Chapter 10 that the swap is one of the three major types of derivatives securities widely used in risk management, with the other two being forwards/futures and options. A swap with which exchange of cash flows is all made in one currency is simply called swaps or interest rate swaps. A swap involving exchange of cash flows denominated in two currencies is commonly referred to as the currency swap, which, though, includes exchange of principals as well. Obviously, there is no need to exchange principals where all cash flows are denominated in the same currency. When the exchange of cash flows made in two currencies involve interest only, the instrument is close to being one or several forward rate agreements and is therefore classified in the category of forwards and swaps by the BIS. Chapter 10 indicates that the interest rate swap is the largest group in OTC derivatives securities in terms of both notional amount and daily turnover, and the currency swap is the second largest group in OTC foreign exchange derivatives measured by notional amounts. If swaps in the category of forwards and swaps are taken into consideration, swaps are also the largest group in OTC foreign exchange derivatives in terms of notional amount and daily turnover. This chapter first introduces what swaps are and how swaps work in a simple context of interest rate swaps. Then it progresses to discuss currency swaps. Finally cases of a new class of products called swapnotes mentioned in Chapter 10 are presented and examined.

## 12.1 Basics of Swaps

Swaps look much simpler than options, which is one of the reasons why swaps are more popular in terms of usage whereas options are more popular in terms of theory and pricing models. Therefore, it is perhaps the best way to begin with the study of swaps with an example.

The simplest swap is to convert fixed rate interest cash flows to floating rate interest cash flows for one party of the swap and to convert floating rate interest cash flows to fixed rate interest cash flows for the other party of the swap, commonly referred to plain vanilla interest rate swaps, as illustrated below.

Suppose two firms plan the raise €1,000,000 to finance their investment projects respectively. Firm A can issue 10-year fixed-rate euro bonds at 10 percent per annum; alternatively, it can issue floating-rate euro bonds at LIBOR + 1 percent. Firm B can issue 10-year fixed-rate euro bonds at 12 percent per annum; alternatively, firm B can raise the money by issuing 10-year floating-rate euro bonds at LIBOR + 1.5 percent. The borrowing profiles of the two firms are summarised below:

**Table 12.1.** The borrowing opportunities of the two firms

|  | Firm A | Firm B |
| --- | --- | --- |
| Fixed rate | 10% | 12% |
| Floating rate | Libor + 1% | Libor + 1.5% |

Suppose the two firms agree to swap as follows:

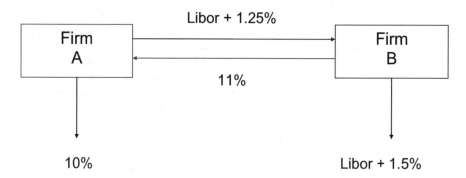

**Figure 12.1.** Interest rate swap – floating ↔ fixed rates

Firm A issues euro bonds or borrows at the fixed rate of 10%. Firm B issues euro bonds or borrows at a floating rate of LIBOR + 1.5%. The arrows indicate cash outflows from the two firms. Then the two firms carry out a swap in which firm A receives interest payment from firm B at the fixed rate of 11.25% and, in return, pays interest at the floating rate of LIBOR + 1.25% to firm B. The cash flows from and to firm B are just the opposite, i.e., firm B receives interest payment from firm A at the floating rate of LIBOR + 1.25% and, in return, pays interest at the fixed rate of 11.25% to firm A.

The net borrowing position of firm A from the above illustration is:

$$10\% - 11\% + (LIBOR + 1.25\%) = LIBOR + 0.25\%$$

which is 0.75% better off than firm A can borrow at the floating rate without the swap. There are three elements involved in this swap for firm A: it borrows through the financial market by issuing euro bonds at a fixed rate of 10% per annum, it lends to firm B at a fixed rate of 11% per annum, and it borrows from firm B at a floating rate of LIBOT+1.25% per annum. The net borrowing position of firm B is:

$$(LIBOR + 1.5\%) - (LIBOR + 1.25\%) + 11\% = 11.25\%$$

which is 0.75% better off than firm B can borrow at the fixed rate without the swap. The swap involves three elements of action for firm B: it borrows through the financial market by issuing euro bonds at a floating rate of LIBOR+1.5% per annum, it borrows from firm A at a fixed rate of 11% per annum, and it lends to firm A at a floating rate of LIBOR+1.25% per annum. For a principal of €1,000,000, the savings on interest are €7,500 per annum for ten years for both of the two firms.

Through this swap, firm A effectively borrows at a floating rate of LIBOR+0.25%, and firm B effectively borrows at a fixed rate of 11.25%. For firm A, it is a fixed to floating rate swap; and for firm B, it is a floating to fixed rate swap. That is, the interest payment at a fixed rate has been converted to the interest payment at a floating rate for firm A, and the interest payment at a floating rate has been converted to the interest payment at a fixed rate for firm B. If firm A prefers a floating rate to a fixed rate and firm B prefers a fixed rate to a floating rate, then both firms benefit from the above swap. The reason for both counterparties to engage in a swap and benefit in a swap lies in comparative advantages in fixed rate or floating rate borrowing. It has been observed that the borrowing cost of firm B is always higher than that of firm A whether the interest payment is made at the fixed rate or the floating rate. However, firm B's cost of fixed rate borrowing is 2% higher than firm A's, while firm B's cost floating borrowing is 0.5% higher than firm A's. Consequently, firm B enjoys a comparative advantage in floating rate borrowing, though it has disadvantages in both fixed rate borrowing and floating rate borrowing. So firm B borrows or issues euro bands on the financial market at the floating rate of LIBOR+1.5%. With regard to firm A, although it enjoys advantages in both fixed rate borrowing and floating rate borrowing, it has a comparative advantage in fixed rate borrowing in that the gap in fixed rate borrowing is wider than that in floating rate borrowing. So firm A borrows or issues euro bands on the financial market at the fixed rate of 10%. Both firms decide the way of raising money from the financial market according to their respective comparative advantages based on which a swap can be possibly conducted.

The above swap not only has benefited both firm A and firm B, but also changed the risk profiles of the two firms. The fixed rate risk profile of firm A has been changed to a floating rate risk profile while the floating rate risk profile of firm B has been changed to a fixed rate risk profile in the meantime through the swap. This is the second main reason for firms to enter into swap agreements.

The benefit of the swap is equally divided between the two firms in the above case for the reason of simplicity. Nevertheless how to carve the benefit may be negotiated depending on the circumstances. Moreover, a third party, usually a financial institution or a bank, may be brought into the process as financial intermediation, which reduces the benefit of the swap to the two counterparties but reduces risks, e.g., credit risk, as well. For example, if LIBOR increases significantly, firm A may default on the agreement due to the increased cost of financing. On the other hand, if LIBOR falls to a large extent, firm B may not oblige the agreement since it can pay much less at the fixed rate of 10% without entering into the swap. So, let us reconsider the above case when a financial institution is involved.

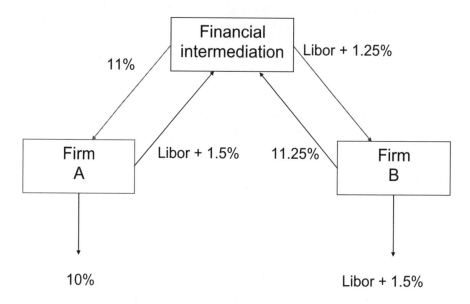

**Figure 12.2.** Interest rate swap with financial intermediation

The net borrowing position of firm A from the above illustration is:

$$10\% - 11\% + (LIBOR + 1.5\%) = LIBOR + 0.5\%$$

which is 0.5% better off than firm A can borrow at the floating rate without the swap. The savings on interest are €5,000 per annum for ten years for a principal of €1,000,000 with this swap. The net borrowing position of firm B is:

$$(LIBOR + 1.5\%) - (LIBOR + 1.25\%) + 11.25\% = 11.5\%$$

which is also 0.5% better off than firm B can borrow at the fixed rate without the swap. The savings on interest for firm B are also €5,000 per annum for ten years for a principal of €1,000,000 with this swap.

The benefit for the financial institution is:

$$(LIBOR+1.5\%)-(LIBOR+1.25\%)+11.25\%-11\% = 0.5\%$$

The profit made out of this swap transaction agreement is €5,000 per annum for ten years for the financial institution for its services and intermediation. With the involvement of the financial institution, the swap agreement is not directly between firm A and firm B. Instead, there are swap agreements, one between firm A and the financial institution and one between firm B and the financial institution. Firm A and firm B may or may not know each other and the financing requirements of the counterpart. For firm A, it is a swap agreement with the financial institution for converting fixed rate borrowing to floating rate borrowing; and for firm B, it is a swap agreement with the financial institution for converting floating rate borrowing to fixed rate borrowing. Nevertheless, the financial institution, while performing a floating to fixed rate swap deal with firm B, knows that there is fixed to floating rate swap requirement from firm A, and vice versa.

## 12.2 Currency Swaps

This section discusses currency swaps in a similar way as in the previous section, i.e., using examples to illustrate how currency swaps work. Suppose a German corporation, firm A, plans to raise £10,000,000 to finance an investment project in the UK. At the same time, a British corporation, firm B, plans to finance a €15,000,000 investment project in France. Both firms can borrow relatively cheaply in the home country and more expensively in the foreign country. Their borrowing opportunities are as follows:

**Table 12.2.** The borrowing opportunities of the two firms in Euroland and England

|     | Firm A | Firm B |
| --- | --- | --- |
| € | 5% | 6% |
| £ | 9% | 8% |

The principals of the borrowing of both firm A and firm B will be paid back in five years. The exchange rate between the pound and the euro is €1.5/£. Suppose the two firms decide to borrow in their respective home countries, and then swap the currencies to meet their investment needs. The principals are swapped at the beginning, and then swapped back at the end of the period. Since firm A has advantages in borrowing in the euro and firm B has advantages in borrowing in sterling, the interest payments are swapped as follows:

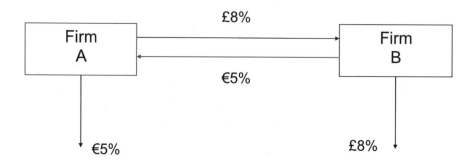

**Figure 12.3.** Currency swap – the workings

The net borrowing position of firm A is:

$$€5\% - €5\% + £8\%$$

There is a one percent point gain in its borrowing position in pound sterling for firm A through this swap. The net borrowing position of firm B is:

$$£8\% - £8\% + €5\%$$

There is a one percent point gain in its borrowing position in the euro for firm B through this swap. Through this swap, firm A effectively finances its British investment project at a cost of 8% to service the debt in sterling, and firm B effectively finances its French project at a cost of 5% to service the debt in euros. Table 12.3 shows cash flow conversions between the two firms. Look at the cash flows from and to firm A, the second and third columns in Table 12.3, first. At the beginning, firm A lends €15,000,000 to firm B at an interest rate of 5% per annum, and at the same time, receives £10,000,000 from firm B, which is the swap of principals. In the subsequent year-ends, interest is paid on its sterling borrowing at the rate of 8% and interest is received on its euro lending at the rate of 5%, which is the swap of interest payments. At the end of year five, the euro principal of €15,000,000 is paid back from firm B to firm A, and the sterling principal of £10,000,000 is paid back to firm B from firm A, which is again the swap of principals. The cash flows to and from firm B mirror those of firm A exactly, shown in the fourth and fifth columns in the table.

**Table 12.3.** Cash flow conversions

| Year | Firm A: € to £ | | Firm B: £ to € | |
|---|---|---|---|---|
| | € | £ | £ | € |
| 0 | -15,000,000 | +10,000,000 | -10,000,000 | +15,000,000 |
| 1 | +750,000 | -800,000 | +800,000 | -750,000 |
| 2 | +750,000 | -800,000 | +800,000 | -750,000 |
| 3 | +750,000 | -800,000 | +800,000 | -750,000 |
| 4 | +750,000 | -800,000 | +800,000 | -750,000 |
| 5 | +15,750,000 | -10,800,000 | +10,800,000 | -15,750,000 |

Similar to the case of same currency interest rate swaps, financial intermediation may be involved in currency swaps as well. The illustration below extends the
above example to demonstrate a currency swap intermediated by a financial institution. Instead of swapping cash flows with each other, both firm A and firm B
deal with the financial institution for swap transaction agreements. It is agreed that
firm A swaps its euro borrowing at the cost of 5% for sterling borrowing at the
cost of 8.5% with the financial institution; and that firm B swaps its sterling borrowing at the cost of 8% for euro borrowing at the cost of 5.5% with the financial
institution. The second and third columns in Table 12.4 show cash flows to and
from firm A. Compared with Table 12.3, its sterling cash outflows increase by
0.5% per annum, or by £50,000 per annum due to the involvement of the financial
institution. However, its euro cash inflows from its euro lending are secure since
the counterparty credit risk is removed or reduced due to the same reason of financial intermediation. The fourth and fifth columns in Table 12.4 show cash flows to
and from firm B. Compared with Table 12.3, its euro cash outflows increase by
0.5% per annum, or by €75,000 per annum due to financial intermediation. Nevertheless, its sterling cash inflows from its sterling lending are secure since the counterparty credit risk is removed or reduced due to this financial intermediation.

**Table 12.4.** Cash flow conversions with financial intermediation

| Year | Firm A: € to £ | | Firm B: £ to € | |
|---|---|---|---|---|
| | € | £ | £ | € |
| 0 | -15,000,000 | +10,000,000 | -10,000,000 | +15,000,000 |
| 1 | +750,000 | -850,000 | +800,000 | -825,000 |
| 2 | +750,000 | -850,000 | +800,000 | -825,000 |
| 3 | +750,000 | -850,000 | +800,000 | -825,000 |
| 4 | +750,000 | -850,000 | +800,000 | -825,000 |
| 5 | +15,750,000 | -10,850,000 | +10,800,000 | -15,825,000 |

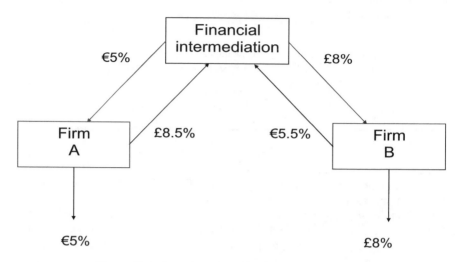

**Figure 12.4.** Currency swap with financial intermediation

The financial institution also makes profit by providing the service of financial intermediation to the two firms. On the one hand, the financial institution borrows euros from firm A at the rate of 5% per annum while lends euros to firm B at the rate of 5.5% per annum. So, the profit margin is 0.5% for the financial institution in the euro transaction. On the other hand, the financial institution borrows sterling from firm B at the rate of 8% per annum while lends sterling to firm A at the rate of 8.5% per annum. So, the profit margin is also 0.5% for the financial institution in the sterling transaction. Table 12.5 summarises the profit made by the financial institution in these swaps. The profit is €75,000 per annum for five year from the euro transactions and £50,000 per annum for five years from the sterling transactions. If the exchange rate is taken as €1.5/£ for the whole period, then the profit is either £100,000 or €150,000 per annum for five years in total.

**Table 12.5.** Profits made by financial institution for providing financial intermediation

| Year | Euro transactions | | | Sterling transactions | | |
|---|---|---|---|---|---|---|
| | In | Out | Net | In | Out | Net |
| 1 | +825,000 | -750,000 | +€75,000 | +850,000 | -800,000 | +£50,000 |
| 2 | +825,000 | -750,000 | +€75,000 | +850,000 | -800,000 | +£50,000 |
| 3 | +825,000 | -750,000 | +€75,000 | +850,000 | -800,000 | +£50,000 |
| 4 | +825,000 | -750,000 | +€75,000 | +850,000 | -800,000 | +£50,000 |
| 5 | +825,000 | -750,000 | +€75,000 | +850,000 | -800,000 | +£50,000 |

## 12.3 Swapnotes

Swapnotes are exchange traded derivatives based on interest rate swap curves. Specifically, the ¥ swapnote of the TIFFE is a kind of swap futures based on the yen interest rate swap curve and the € swapnote at the LIFFE is a kind of swap futures based on the euro swap curve. Swapnotes are standardised in size and delivery time. Since swapnotes are exchange traded, counterparty credit risk is removed. Customarily, the swapnote contract is an agreement that one party pays interest at a fixed rate and receives interest at a floating rate on a nominal principal, while the counterparty pays interest at a floating rate and receives interest at a fixed rate on the same nominal principal, over a certain time period. No principals change hand in transactions. The floating rate is usually some kind of reference interest rates, such as LIBOR. The fixed rate is referred to as the swap rate.

The price of a ¥ swapnote contract is based on the value of the notional cash flows equivalent to a 3% semi-annual coupon and the principal repayment at the notional maturity date. Whereas the price of a € swapnote contract is based on the value of the notional cash flows equivalent to a 6% annual coupon and the principal repayment at the notional maturity date. These notional cash flows are discounted to their present values, using a zero coupon discount curve that is derived from yen swap rates or euro swap rates as quoted in the OTC swap market. Therefore, the price of swapnote contracts traces and reflects the rates quoted in the OTC swap market.

The pricing of swapnotes means to create a standardised exchange traded futures contract with price sensitivity of interest rate swaps. Up to expiry of the contract, the price of a swapnote contract reflects underlying supple and demand. At expiry, the price is fixed by the exchange using the Exchange Delivery Settlement Price (EDSP) algorithm. The EDSP is the sum of the discounted notional cash flows, each of which has been given a present value using zero coupon discount factors derived from the ISDA Benchmark Swap Rates at 10.00hrs (London time for € swapnotes at the LIFFE and Tokyo time for ¥ swapnotes at the TIFFE) on the last trading day. For these purposes, the zero coupon discount factors are calculated using a standard bootstrapping technique.

We introduce the EDSP algorithm as follows. The EDSP price is calculated on the last trading day from the euro swap rate fixings in accordance with the following equation:

$$EDSP = 100d_m + F\sum_{i=1}^{m} A_i d_i \qquad (12.1)$$

In the above formula, $F$ is the notional coupon per 100 nominal of the swapnote contract and is 6 for € swapnotes for all contract expiries at the LIFFE where the coupon is annual and 3 ¥ swapnotes for all contract expiries at the TIFFE where the coupon is semi-annual. $m$ is the maturity of the swapnote contract in years. $A_i$ is the accrual factor between the notional cash flows, defined as the number of days between the dates of the $(i-1)^{th}$ and the $i^{th}$ notional cash flows, calculated on a 30/360 day count basis and divided by 360 at the LIFFE and calculated on an actual/365 (fixed) day count basis and divided by 365 at the TIFFE. $d_i$ indicates the zero coupon discount factor calculated from the swap rate fixings applicable for the period between the commencement day and the date the $i^{th}$ notional cash flow occurs. The zero coupon discount factors are constructed from the ISDA Benchmark Swap Rates fixings, $C_i$, available on the last trading day using a standard bootstrapping method.

The first discount factor, $d_1$, is calculated as follows according to the above definition:

$$d_1 = \frac{1}{1 + A_1 C_1} \qquad (12.2)$$

Subsequent discount factors, $d_i$ $(i \geq 2)$, is given by the following formula:

$$d_i = \frac{1 - C_i \sum_{j=1}^{i-1} A_j d_j}{1 + A_i C_i} \qquad (12.3)$$

At any point in time prior to expiry, the price discovery process and daily settlement prices are established by the market. A theoretical arbitrage-free "fair price" can be calculated in the same way as the EDSP. The "fair price" is the sum of the present values of notional cash flows valued to the trade date which are then forward valued (equivalent to financing the position) to the contract commencement date. In this instance, the discount factors derived from the current swap rates ruling on the trade date will not coincide with the notional cash flow dates. Accordingly, an interpolation of either the rates or the discount factors will be required. As such, the fair price will depend on what interpolation approach has been adopted.

The following is an example of the EDSP calculation for a ten-year € swapnote. Let us assume that the ISDA Benchmark Swap Rates on the last trading day of the September 2002 contract are given in panel (a) of Table 12.6. The notional cash flows and adjusted cash flows are provided in panel (b) of Table 12.6.

Based on information given in Table 12.6, discount factors can be calculated as follows:

$$d_1 = \frac{1}{1 + A_1 C_1} = \frac{1}{1 + 1.00000000 \times 0.03408} = 0.96704317$$

$$d_2 = \frac{1 - C_2 \sum_{j=1}^{1} A_j d_j}{1 + A_2 C_2} = \frac{1 - C_2 A_1 d_1}{1 + A_2 C_2}$$

$$= \frac{1 - 0.03638 \times 1.00000000 \times 0.96704317}{1 + 1.00555556 \times 0.03638} = 0.93076946$$

$$d_3 = \frac{1 - C_3 \sum_{j=1}^{2} A_j d_j}{1 + A_3 C_3} = \frac{1 - C_3 (A_1 d_1 + A_2 d_2)}{1 + A_3 C_3}$$

$$= \frac{1 - 0.03900(1.00000000 \times 0.96704317 + 1.00555556 \times 0.93076946)}{1 + 0.99722222 \times 0.03900}$$

$$= 0.89112626$$

Repeating the procedure yields the subsequent discount factors as follows:

$$d_4 = 0.85058392, \quad d_5 = 0.80956480, \quad d_6 = 0.76898135,$$
$$d_7 = 0.72960367, \quad d_8 = 0.69173761, \quad d_9 = 0.65584476,$$
$$d_{10} = 0.62184917$$

**Table 12.6.** Rates and cash flows of € swapnote contract

(a) Rates of ten-year € swapnote contract

| Term (years) | 1 | 2 | 3 | 4 | 5 | 6 | 7 | 8 | 9 | 10 |
|---|---|---|---|---|---|---|---|---|---|---|
| Rate (%) | 3.408 | 3.638 | 3.900 | 4.105 | 4.280 | 4.427 | 4.546 | 4.640 | 4.716 | 4.776 |

(b) Cash flows from ten-year € swapnote

| Term | Commence-ment and pay-ment date | Day of week | Days to next pay-ment | Accrual factor | Notional cash flow | Adjusted cash flow |
|---|---|---|---|---|---|---|
| Start | 18 Sept 02 | Wed | | | | |
| 1 | 18 Sept 03 | Thurs | 360 | 1.00000000 | 6 | 6.00000000 |
| 2 | 20 Sept 04 | Mon | 362 | 1.00555556 | 6 | 6.03333336 |
| 3 | 19 Sept 05 | Mon | 359 | 0.99722222 | 6 | 5.98333332 |
| 4 | 18 Sept 06 | Mon | 359 | 0.99722222 | 6 | 5.98333332 |
| 5 | 18 Sept 07 | Tue | 360 | 1.00000000 | 6 | 6.00000000 |
| 6 | 18 Sept 08 | Thurs | 360 | 1.00000000 | 6 | 6.00000000 |
| 7 | 18 Sept 09 | Fri | 360 | 1.00000000 | 6 | 6.00000000 |
| 8 | 20 Sept 10 | Mon | 362 | 1.00555556 | 6 | 6.03333336 |
| 9 | 19 Sept 11 | Mon | 359 | 0.99722222 | 6 | 5.98333332 |
| 10 | 18 Sept 12 | Tue | 359 | 0.99722222 | 106 | 5.98333332 |

Finally, information and elements involved in the derivation of the EDSP price are presented in Table 12.7. The last column is the discounted cash flows. In terms 1 to 9, the discounted cash flow is the notional coupon of 6 being adjusted by the accrual factor and the discount factor. In term 10, the discounted cash flow is the sum of the notional coupon of 6 and the notional principal of 100, which is 106, being adjusted by the accrual factor and the discount factor. The EDSP price of the ten-year € swapnote is the sum of the present values of all these cash flows, which is 109.69.

**Table 12.7.** Components and derivation of EDSP price – ten-year € swapnote

| Term | Rate (%) | Commence- ment and payment date | Day of week | Accrual factor | Discount factor | Notional cash flow | PV of cash flow |
|------|------|------|------|------|------|------|------|
| Start | | 18 Sept 02 | Wed | | | | |
| 1 | 3.408 | 18 Sept 03 | Thurs | 1.00000000 | 0.96704317 | 6 | 5.80225901 |
| 2 | 3.638 | 20 Sept 04 | Mon | 1.00555556 | 0.93076946 | 6 | 5.61564242 |
| 3 | 3.900 | 19 Sept 05 | Mon | 0.99722222 | 0.89112626 | 6 | 5.33190542 |
| 4 | 4.105 | 18 Sept 06 | Mon | 0.99722222 | 0.85058392 | 6 | 5.08932714 |
| 5 | 4.280 | 18 Sept 07 | Tue | 1.00000000 | 0.80956480 | 6 | 4.85738882 |
| 6 | 4.427 | 18 Sept 08 | Thurs | 1.00000000 | 0.76898135 | 6 | 4.61388811 |
| 7 | 4.546 | 18 Sept 09 | Fri | 1.00000000 | 0.72960367 | 6 | 4.37762202 |
| 8 | 4.640 | 20 Sept 10 | Mon | 1.00555556 | 0.69173761 | 6 | 4.17348357 |
| 9 | 4.716 | 19 Sept 11 | Mon | 0.99722222 | 0.65584476 | 6 | 3.92413779 |
| 10 | 4.776 | 18 Sept 12 | Tue | 0.99722222 | 0.62184917 | 106 | 65.90564832 |
| | | | | | | EPSD = | 109.69130262 |

The above information can be readily used for the EPSD price of the five- and two- year € swapnote contracted at the same time. The procedure is repeated for these swapnotes and the results are presented in Table 12.8 and Table 12.9 respectively. For the five-year € swapnote, only cash flows in terms 1 to 5 are included, and the cash flow in term 5 is 106, which is the sum of the coupon and the principal. The EPSD price for the five-year € swapnote is derived as 107.65. Similarly, for two-year € swapnote, only cash flows in terms 1 and 2 are included, and the cash flow in term 2 is the sum of the coupon and the principal. The EPSD price for the two-year € swapnote is therefore 105.01.

**Table 12.8.** Derivation of five-year € swapnote EDSP price

| Term | Rate (%) | Com- mencement and payment date | Day of week | Accrual factor | Discount factor | Notional cash flow | PV of cash flow |
|------|------|------|------|------|------|------|------|
| Start | | 18 Sept 02 | Wed | | | | |
| 1 | 3.408 | 18 Sept 03 | Thurs | 1.00000000 | 0.96704317 | 6 | 5.80225901 |
| 2 | 3.638 | 20 Sept 04 | Mon | 1.00555556 | 0.93076946 | 6 | 5.61564242 |
| 3 | 3.900 | 19 Sept 05 | Mon | 0.99722222 | 0.89112626 | 6 | 5.33190542 |
| 4 | 4.105 | 18 Sept 06 | Mon | 0.99722222 | 0.85058392 | 6 | 5.08932714 |
| 5 | 4.280 | 18 Sept 07 | Tue | 1.00000000 | 0.80956480 | 106 | 85.81386880 |
| | | | | | | EPSD = | 107.65300279 |

**Table 12.9.** Derivation of two-year € swapnote EDSP price

| Term | Rate (%) | Commencement and payment date | Day of week | Accrual factor | Discount factor | Notional cash flow | PV of cash flow |
|------|----------|-------------------------------|-------------|----------------|-----------------|--------------------|-----------------|
| Start |         | 18 Sept 02                    | Wed         |                |                 |                    |                 |
| 1    | 3.408    | 18 Sept 03                    | Thurs       | 1.00000000     | 0.96704317      | 6                  | 5.80225901      |
| 2    | 3.638    | 20 Sept 04                    | Mon         | 1.00555556     | 0.93076946      | 106                | 99.20968299     |
|      |          |                               |             |                |                 | EPSD =             | 105.01194200    |

The LIFFE has provided an EDSP calculator for interested investors or learn-
ers to find out the EDSP price of a swapnote product. What is required is simply
inputting the swap rate fixings into relevant cells and the EDSP price for ten-, five,
and two-yeas € swapnotes will display. The following is a case for all the three
expiries of ten-, five-, and two-year € swapnotes of March 2003 contracts.

Panel (a) of Table 12.10 provides information of ISDA swap rate fixings and
the calculated accrual factors and discount factors, while panel (b) of Table 12.10
presents discounted cash flows and the EDSP price as the sum of these discounted
cash flows.

**Table 12.10.** Application of EDSP calculator

(a) ISDA swap rate fixings

| Term /yrs | ISDA fix | Modified Following Maturity | Accrual Factor 30/360 | Zero Coupon Discount Factor |
|-----------|----------|------------------------------|------------------------|------------------------------|
| 0         | #N/A     | 19-Mar-03                    |                        |                              |
| 1         | 2.446    | 19-Mar-04                    | 1.00000000             | 0.97612401                   |
| 2         | 2.621    | 21-Mar-05                    | 1.00555556             | 0.94939393                   |
| 3         | 2.890    | 20-Mar-06                    | 0.99722222             | 0.91775078                   |
| 4         | 3.163    | 19-Mar-07                    | 0.99722222             | 0.88215612                   |
| 5         | 3.404    | 19-Mar-08                    | 1.00000000             | 0.84443270                   |
| 6         | 3.609    | 19-Mar-09                    | 1.00000000             | 0.80597625                   |
| 7         | 3.784    | 19-Mar-10                    | 1.00000000             | 0.76752491                   |
| 8         | 3.938    | 21-Mar-11                    | 1.00555556             | 0.72918874                   |
| 9         | 4.070    | 19-Mar-12                    | 0.99444444             | 0.69209931                   |
| 10        | 4.183    | 19-Mar-13                    | 1.00000000             | 0.65610581                   |

**Table 12.10.** (cont.)
(b) cash flows and EDSP prices – ten-year, five-year and two-year swapnotes

| 10yr Swapnote | |
|---|---|
| **Cash Flow** | **Discounted** |
| 6.00000000 | 5.85674406 |
| 6.03333336 | 5.72801007 |
| 5.98333332 | 5.491208821 |
| 5.98333332 | 5.278234106 |
| 6.00000000 | 5.0665962 |
| 6.00000000 | 4.8358575 |
| 6.00000000 | 4.60514946 |
| 6.03333336 | 4.399438751 |
| 5.96666664 | 4.129525865 |
| 106.00000000 | 69.54721586 |
| **EDSP =** | **114.94** |

| 5yr Swapnote | |
|---|---|
| **Cash Flow** | **Discounted** |
| 6.00000000 | 5.85674406 |
| 6.03333336 | 5.72801007 |
| 5.98333332 | 5.491208821 |
| 5.98333332 | 5.278234106 |
| 106.00000000 | 89.5098662 |
| **EDSP =** | **111.86** |

| 2yr Swapnote | |
|---|---|
| **Cash Flow** | **Discounted** |
| 6.00000000 | 5.85674406 |
| 106.03333336 | 100.6674031 |
| **EDSP =** | **106.525** |

# 13    Transaction Exposure

This chapter and the next chapter introduce and discuss foreign exchange exposure in the context of firms' exposure to foreign exchange rate fluctuations. The types of foreign exchange exposure, the measurement of foreign exchange exposure, and the management of foreign exchange exposure will be examined, which will utilise the knowledge acquired in the previous chapters on foreign exchange rate determination, international parities, and foreign exchange derivatives. In particular, the use of foreign exchange derivatives in managing foreign exchange exposure or hedging foreign exchange rate risks will be discussed and different approaches to managing foreign exchange exposure will be compared.

In an efficient foreign exchange market where PPP, CIRP and IFE hold, there is no need for foreign exchange exposure management since it makes no difference between different strategies for international investments. Firms expose to some kind of foreign exchange risk when one or more of these international parity conditions are violated, which may affect the transaction gain or loss, the economic value of a firm or a project, or the consolidated accounts of multinational corporations. Under such circumstances, foreign exchange rate forecasts based on the exchange rate theory and models of exchange rate determination would be helpful, and the use of foreign exchange derivatives in foreign exchange risk management would be of practical relevance and importance.

Changes and uncertainties caused by foreign exchange rate fluctuations in transaction outcomes, in the economic value of firms or projects, and in the consolidated accounts items of multinational corporations give rise to three types of foreign exchange exposure – transaction exposure, economic exposure, and accounting or translation exposure. This chapter studies transaction exposure. The next two chapters study economic exposure and accounting exposure respectively.

## 13.1 Introduction to Transaction Exposure and Its Management

Transaction exposure measures how the home currency value of a firm's foreign currency denominated contractual cash flows would be affected by exchange rate fluctuations. Transaction exposure arises from the possibility of incurring exchange gains or losses on transactions already entered into which is denominated in a foreign currency. Management of transaction exposure is to control and reduce the risk of exchange rate fluctuations involved in these contractual transactions.

**Table 13.1.** Major approaches to hedging foreign exchange risk

|  | Cash inflows/ receivables | Cash outflows/ payables | Features | Advantages/ disadvantages |
|---|---|---|---|---|
| Forward/ futures | Long position | Short position | Right and obligations | Forward market gains offset spot market losses exactly; spot market gains may also be offset by forward market losses |
| Options | Lon in put | Long in call | Right but no obligations | No contractual obligation to exercise, only (small) part of the spot market gain may be offset by the option loss; the option gain is always less than offsetting the spot market loss entirely. |
| Money market | Borrow the foreign currency | Borrow the domestic currency | Borrow, save and repay | CIRP may not hold and there can be shortfall or excess in payables or receivables |

Foreign currency denominated contractual cash flows take two forms, cash inflows or receivables and cash outflows or payables. In the former, there is uncertainty in the value of cash inflows measured in the domestic currency when cash inflows denominated in a foreign currency are received and converted to the domestic currency, though there is no uncertainty in the value of cash inflows in terms of the foreign currency. That is, a firm may receive less or more in terms of the domestic currency in a transaction involving a foreign currency, depending on how the exchange rate changes. In the latter, there is uncertainty in the amount of the domestic currency units to pay a given and certain amount of the foreign currency units. That is, a firm may pay more or pay less in terms of the domestic currency in a transaction involving a foreign currency due to foreign exchange rate fluctuations.

To manage transaction exposure or to control and reduce the above described uncertainties in transactions, a number of approaches have been developed and various derivatives instruments are used. Commonly adopted approaches to managing transaction exposure include forward hedge, futures hedge, money market hedge, and option hedge, most of them resorting to currency derivatives. Table 13.1 summarises the use and features of these approaches and instruments in managing transaction exposure, which are discussed respectively in the following sections.

## 13.2 Forward Hedge and Futures Hedge

A forward hedge involves the use of foreign exchange forwards. A futures hedge is the same except that the forward gain or loss is settled at the end of the contract period while the futures gain or loss is settled daily with the exchange. We only discuss forward hedges here since the analysis and results apply to futures hedges in the same way. To hedge future foreign currency cash outflows, the firm may enter into a long position in a forward contract, to secure the right amount of foreign currency at a pre determined exchange rate. To hedge future foreign currency cash inflows, the firm may enter into a short position in a forward contract to sell the foreign currency at a pre determined exchange rate. Let us examine two cases of hedging transaction cash inflows and cash outflows respectively.

Suppose a British car dealer specialised in importing German cars has made orders for the coming year. Payment of €30 million in euros is due in twelve months. In line with common knowledge the importer is concerned with the effect of changes in the euro-sterling exchange rate on accounts payables. For instance, the cash outflow in pounds would be £21.74 million according to the current prevailing exchange rate of €1.48/£. But if the exchange rate is dropped to €1.38/£, the payment in pounds would be £20.27 million, a 1.47 million extra of pound sterling or 7% more than the payment if the exchange rate were kept unchanged.

Therefore, the importer decides to enter into a forward contract with a forward exchange rate being €1.4423/£. The importer has effectively fixed the amount of payables or cash outflows in sterling at £20.80 = €30/€1.4423/£, no matter what the exchange rate will be in twelve months. In other words, the uncertainty in, or the effect of spot exchange rate fluctuations on, the sterling payables is removed, which, though, is not necessarily always desirable. Figure 13.1 shows the forward gain or loss given the spot exchange rate at the expiry of the forward contract. The importer makes a forward gain if the future spot exchange rate at the time when the forward contract matures falls below the forward exchange rate of €1.4423/£, or the euro turns out to be stronger than the forward exchange rate has suggested. The importer makes a forward loss if the future spot exchange rate at the time when the forward contract matures rises above the forward exchange rate of

€1.4423/£, or the euro turns out to be weaker than the forward exchange rate has suggested.

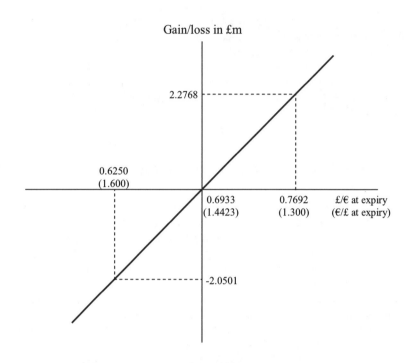

**Figure 13.1.** Forward hedge for payables – gains and losses

Put it more formally, the forward gain is $(S_1 - F_{0,1}) \times €30m$, where $S_1$ is the spot exchange rate at the end of the contract period, $F_{0,1}$ is the forward exchange rate contracted at the beginning of the period for the delivery at the end of the period, and the exchange rate is measured by the units of the domestic currency per foreign currency unit, which is £/€ in this case. So, the forward exchange rate is £0.6933/€ in this expression. If the spot exchange rate in twelve months is €1.3/£ or £0.7692/€, the forward gain is therefore (£0.7692/€ – £0.6933/€) × €30 = £2.2768m. If the spot exchange rate in twelve months ends up €1.6/£ or £0.6250/€, then the forward gain is (£0.6250/€ – £0.6933/€) × €30 = –£2.0501m, or there is a forward loss of £2.0501 million.

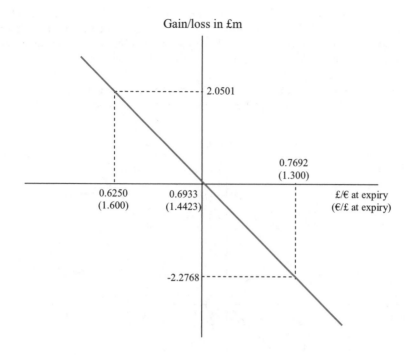

**Figure 13.2.** Un-hedged position of payables – gains and losses

If the importer does not resort to the forward contract, then the un-hedged po-sition is just the opposite to that of the forward hedge. When the euro strengthens and is stronger than the forward exchange rate has suggested, the importer makes a spot market loss relative to the value based on the forward contract. That is, the importer would have been worse off if it had not entered into the forward contract. When the euro weakens and is weaker than the forward exchange rate has sug-gested, the importer makes a spot market gain relative to the value based on the forward contract and the importer would have been better off without the forward contract. The size of the gain (loss) is exactly the same as that of the loss (gain) made in the forward market. Figure 13.2 demonstrates the spot gain or loss, against the benchmark of the forward contract and given the spot exchange rate at the expiry of the forward contract. The spot gain is derived as $(F_{0,1} - S_1) \times €30m$, exactly the opposite to that of the forward gain. For instance, if the spot exchange rate in twelve months is €1.3/£ or £0.7692/€, the spot gain is (£0.6933/€ – £0.7692/€) × €30 = –£2.2768m, or the loss in the spot market is £2.2768 million. If the spot exchange rate in twelve months turns out to be €1.6/£ or £0.6250/€, then the spot gain is (£0.6933/€ – £0.6250/€) × €30 = £2.0501m.

Figure 13.3 combines forward market gains/losses and spot market gains/losses. It is obvious to observe that forward market gains (losses) will be ex-actly offset by spot market losses (gains). So, one may be better off without entering into a forward contract if the forward transaction means a loss in the end. This situation may be avoided if one chooses to hedge a spot market position with an options contract, since an option holder has right but involves no obligation to exercise the option, which will be discussed in Section 14.4. Nevertheless, a forward contract at least ensures a certainty in future cash flows or accounts payables/receivables and, moreover, it is straightforward and simple to operate, which makes forwards a popular risk management tool in foreign exchange markets.

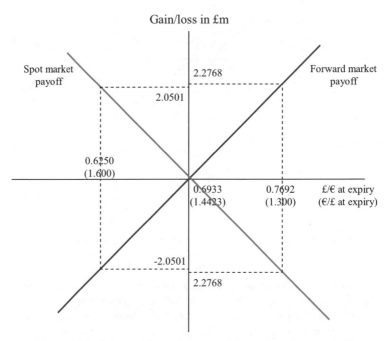

**Figure 13.3.** Gains and losses in spot and forward markets – payables

The next case examines how to hedge cash inflows or receivables. As indicated in Table 13.1, the hedger will enter a short position in a forward contract to hedge cash inflows. Suppose a Japanese firm doing business in the US will receive a payment of $100 million in US dollars in six months and intends to convert the payment into the Japanese yen upon the payment is made. The current prevailing exchange rate between the US dollar and the Japanese yen is ¥110.355/$. There are signs of weakening in the US dollar and the firm fears that cash receivables measured in the Japanese yen will be substantially reduced when the US dollar payment is received in six months. The firm decides to hedge its exposure to foreign exchange risk by shorting in a forward contract to sell the US dollar at an exchange rate of ¥109.000/$. The forward exchange rate is lower than the prevailing spot exchange rate, but the firm considers it acceptable since the future spot exchange rate in six months might be even lower.

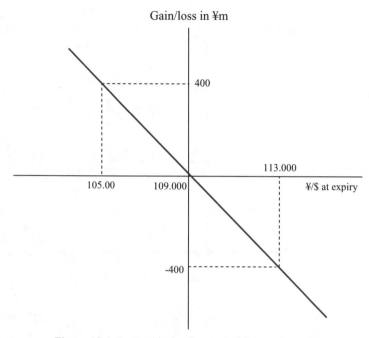

**Figure 13.4.** Forward hedge for receivables – gains and losses

Figure 13.4 illustrates the forward gain or loss given the spot exchange rate at the time when the forward contract matures. The firm makes a forward gain if the future spot exchange rate in six months does falls below the forward exchange rate of ¥109.00/$, or the firm's fear of a weakening dollar that has weakened beyond the forward exchange rate has implied is confirmed. However, the firm makes a forward loss if the US dollar does not depreciate substantially and the spot exchange rate in six months is above the forward exchange rate of ¥109.000/$.

Since the firm has shorted a forward contract to sell the US dollar, the forward gain is $-(S_1 - F_{0,1}) \times \$100m$ or $(F_{0,1} - S_1) \times \$100m$. For example, if the future spot exchange rate in six months is ¥105.000/$, the forward gain is $(F_{0,1} - S_1) \times \$100m$ = (¥109.000/$ – ¥105.000/$) × \$100m = ¥400m. If the spot exchange rate in six months turns out being ¥113.000/$, then the firm makes a forward loss, which is $(F_{0,1} - S_1) \times \$100m$ = (¥109.000/$ – ¥113.000/$) × \$100m = –¥400m.

Gain/loss in ¥m

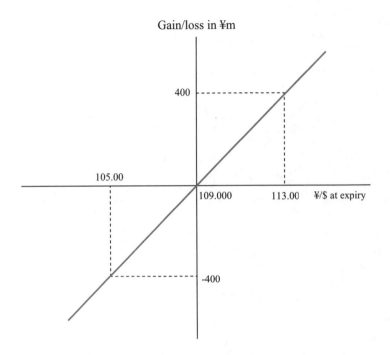

**Figure 13.5.** Un-hedged position of receivables – gains and losses

Since the spot market transaction is to convert the US dollar to the Japanese yen, the payoff in that market is opposite to the spot market payoff in the car import case, as illustrated in Figure 13.5. When the US dollar strengthens beyond the level as suggested by the forward exchange rate, the firm makes a spot market gain relative to the value based on the forward contract. That is, the firm would have been better off if it had not entered into the forward contract. When the US dollar weakens and is weaker than the forward exchange rate has suggested, the firm makes a spot market loss relative to the value based on the forward contract and the firm would have been worse off without the forward contract. The size of the gain (loss) is exactly the same as that of the loss (gain) made in the forward market. Figure 13.5 shows the spot gain or loss as against the benchmark of the forward contract and given the spot exchange rate at the time when the forward contract matures. The spot gain is $(S_1 - F_{0,1}) \times \$100\text{m}$, exactly the opposite to that of the forward gain. If the spot exchange rate in six months is ¥113.000/$, the spot market gain is (¥113.000/$ – ¥109.000/$) × $100m = ¥400m. If the spot exchange rate in six months turns out to be ¥105.000/$, then spot market gain is (¥105.000/$ – ¥109.000/$) × $100m = –¥400m, or the firm makes a spot market loss of ¥400m. Figure 13.6 shows the gains and losses made in both the forward market and the spot market. Again, they offset each other and the net gain is zero.

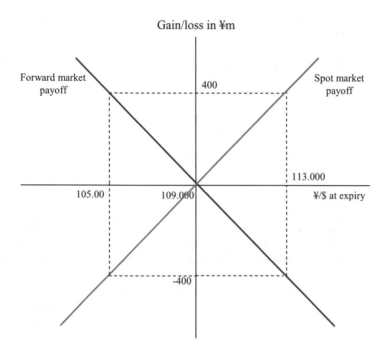

**Figure 13.6.** Gains and losses in spot and forward markets – receivables

## 13.3 Money Market Hedge

The theory and idea behind money market hedge is interest rate parity and non arbitrage conditions. To hedge future foreign currency outflows/ payables, a firm may resort to money market hedge in the following steps:

Step 1:  Borrow the domestic currency in the domestic money market – the amount is the domestic currency equivalent to the present value of the payable.

Step 2:  Convert the borrowed domestic currency into the foreign currency now at the current prevailing spot exchange rate.

Step 3:  Let the money grow at the foreign interest rate to the amount that equals the payable in the foreign currency at the time the payable is made.

Step 4:  Repay the borrowed domestic currency plus interest – the exactly same amount as in the forward contract case when CIRP holds.

To hedge future foreign currency inflows/ receivables in the money market, the following steps are taken by the firm:

Step 1:  Borrow the foreign currency – the amount equals the present value of the receivable.

Step 2:  Convert the foreign currency to the domestic currency now at the current prevailing spot exchange rate.

Step 3:  Let the money grow at the domestic interest rate – the exactly same amount as in the forward contract case when CIRP holds.

Step 4:  Repay the borrowed foreign money plus interest with the receivable.

We use the same cases as in the previous section to illustrate how money market hedge works. In the car import case, we further suppose that the interest rate (the money market rate) is effectively 1.50% per annum in the Euroland and is effectively 4.153% per annum in the UK in the coming year. The present value of €30 million payable is therefore €30m/(1+0.015) = €29.5567m. According to the current prevailing exchange rate of €1.48/£, the importer need to borrow €29.5567m/€1.48/£ = £19.9707m in the domestic currency. The domestic currency borrowing incurs interest so the amount of repayment in twelve months is the principal plus the interest, being £19.9707m ×(1+0.04153) = 20.8001. This is the same amount the importer pays with the forward hedge, since CIRP holds in this case, which can be verified as follows:

$$1.0261 = \frac{1/1.4423}{1/1.48} = \frac{F_{0,1}}{S_0} = \frac{1+r_h}{1+r_f} = \frac{1+0.04153}{1+0.015} = 1.0261$$

When CIRP holds, forward hedge and money market hedge render the same payoff for hedging payables, and all the analysis in the forward hedge case can apply to the money market hedge case by substituting the forward market payoff by the money market payoff, shown by Figure 13.7. When CIRP does not hold, then money market hedge may be superior or inferior to forward hedge, depending on the circumstances. Applying the knowledge gained in Chapter 3, money market hedge is preferred in hedging payables if

$$\frac{F_{0,1}}{S_0} > \frac{1+r_h}{1+r_f}$$

Otherwise, forward hedge would be a better choice.

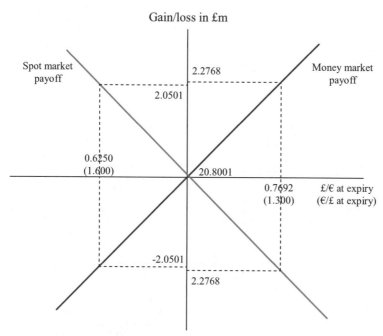

**Figure 13.7.** Gains and losses in spot and money markets – payables

In the receivable hedge case, let us assume the interest rate is effectively 0.25% per annum in Japan and is effectively 1.5 % in the US for the next six months. The present value of the receivable, which is to be paid in six months, is $100m/(1+0.015/2) = $99.2556m. This amount of US dollars is exchanged for the Japanese yen at the prevailing exchange rate of ¥110.355/$ at the beginning of the period, yielding $99.2556m×¥110.355/$ = ¥10953.35m. The amount of ¥10953.35m is then invested in the domestic money market, reaching ¥10953.35m×(1+0.0025/2) = ¥10967.04m in six months, which is the receivable in the domestic currency, the Japanese yen. In the meantime, the US dollar borrowing of $99.2556m has grown to $100m in six months, which is exactly paid for by the receivable at the time. Compared with the forward hedge results, the figure of the receivable denominated in the Japanese yen in the money market hedge case is greater than ¥10900m in the forward hedge case, so money market hedge is preferred.

Again, when CIRP holds, forward hedge and money market hedge render the same payoff for hedging receivables, and all the analysis in the forward hedge case can apply to the money market hedge case by substituting the forward market payoff by the money market payoff. When CIRP does not hold, then money market hedge and forward hedge may or may not be the same. Analysis of CIRP tells us that money market hedge is superior in hedging receivables if

$$\frac{F_{0,1}}{S_0} < \frac{1+r_h}{1+r_f}$$

Otherwise, forward hedge is preferred.

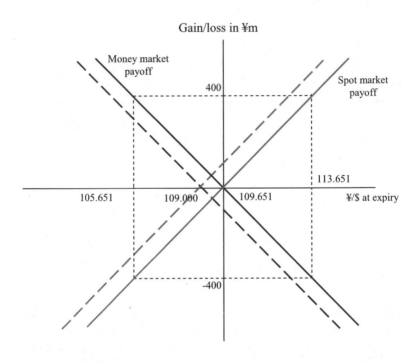

**Figure 13.8.** Gains and losses in spot and money markets – receivables

Compared with the forward hedge results, the figure of the receivable denominated in the Japanese yen in the money market hedge case, ¥10967.04m, is greater than ¥10900m in the forward hedge case, so money market hedge is preferred. It is because

$$0.9879 = \frac{109.000}{110.335} = \frac{F_{0,1}}{S_0} < \frac{1+r_h}{1+r_f} = \frac{1+0.0025/2}{1+0.015/2} = 0.9938$$

CIRP indicates a forward rate of ¥109.651/$ in this case. Figure 13.8 illustrates the money market payoff and the corresponding spot market payoff. The dashed lines are the forward market payoff and the spot market payoff with the previous reference forward exchange rate of ¥109.000/$.

## 13.4 Option Hedge

Although forward hedging is simple to use, there may be some cases where payables can be lower and receivable can be higher without a forward contract. Options provide some flexibility in hedging transaction exposure since they do not involve obligations to exercise. In the following, we use options to hedge the same payable and receivable examined in the previous two sections, so comparison can be made between them.

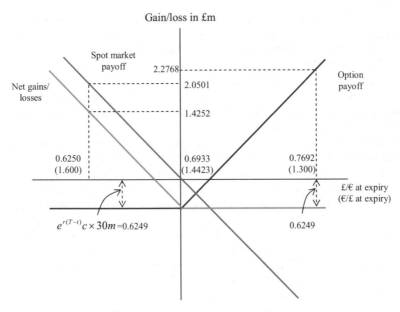

**Figure 13.9.** Option hedge – payables

   A long position in a currency call is taken to hedge foreign currency payables. Suppose the car importer buys euro currency call options to hedge the €30m payable due in twelve months with an exercise price of £0.6933/€, the same exercise price as in the forward contract. The effective interest rate is 4.153% per annum in the UK in the next twelve months. The option price is £0.02 per euro. The cost of option at maturity is £0.02×(1+0.04153) = £0.0208306 per euro or £624,918 for the total amount of the payable of €30m. If the future spot exchange rate in twelve months is £0.6933/€ or lower including £0.6250/€, the currency option will not exercised, and the option payoff is –£624,918. If the future spot exchange rate in twelve months is greater than £0.6933/€, the option will be exercised. e.g., if the future spot exchange rate in twelve months is £0.7690/€, the option will be exercised and the net option payoff is (£0.7690/€ – £0.6933/€)×€30,000,000 –

£624,918 = £1,651,894. Nevertheless, there is a spot market loss whenever the option is exercised, as illustrated in Figure 13.9. Moreover, the option gain is always smaller in size than the spot market loss by the amount that is equal to the cost of these currency options. On the other hand, when the option is not exercised, which means there is a loss incurred in the option transaction, there is always a spot market gain. Unlike the forward hedge case, the spot market gain will not be exactly and totally offset by the option loss, as demonstrated by Figure 13.9. e.g., if the future spot exchange rate is £0.6250/€ in twelve months, the spot market gain is (£0.6933/€ − £0.6250/€)×€30,000,000 = £2,050,111. Offset by a fixed option loss of £624,918, the net payoff is £1,425,193 instead of zero in the forward hedge case.

To hedge foreign currency receivables involves taking a long position in a currency put option. For example the Japanese firm is long in US dollar currency put options to hedge the $100m receivable to be realised in six months with an exercise price of ¥109.000/$, the same exercise price as in the forward hedge case. The effective interest rate is 0.25% per annum in Japan for the next six months. The option price is ¥3 per US dollar. Then the cost of put option at maturity is ¥3×(1+0.0025/2) = ¥3.00375 per US dollar or ¥300,375,000 for the total amount of the receivable of $100m.

Figure 13.10 illustrates the payoffs and net gains/losses of this option hedge. If the future spot exchange rate at maturity is smaller than ¥109.000/$, the put option will be exercised. e.g., when the future spot exchange rate in six months is ¥105.000/$, the net put option payoff is (¥109.000/$ − ¥105.000/$)×$100m = ¥99.625m. This will partly offset the spot market loss of ¥400m and the overall loss is ¥300.375m. As can be observed in Figure 13.10, the loss is always confined to ¥300.375m whatever the future spot exchange will be. When the future spot exchange rate is greater than ¥109.000/$, the option will not be exercised, incurring a fixed loss of ¥300.375m whatever the spot market gain will be. That is, unlike forward hedge, the spot market gain will not be exactly and totally offset by the option loss. For instance, when the future spot exchange rate in six months is ¥113.000/$, the spot market gain is ¥400, which, offset by the option loss of ¥300.375m, yields a net gain of ¥99.625m.

From the above cases it can be concluded that option hedge provides more flexibility than forward hedge but is more complicated as well. The net payoff can either be a positive figure or a negative figure of a fixed size in option hedge, whereas the payoff of the forward contract and the payoff in the spot foreign exchange market always offset each other. Moreover, the variety of option hedge may in theory be considerably extended when the range of exercise prices is taken into account. The choice among these hedging approaches, and indeed, between hedging and non-hedging, will depend on the circumstances in which firms are exposed to foreign exchange risk and economic conditions evolve.

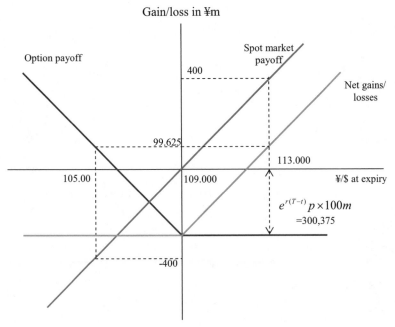

**Figure 13.10.** Option hedge – receivables

# 14 Economic Exposure and Accounting Exposure

This chapter examines firms' economic exposure and accounting exposure to foreign exchange risk. Economic exposure measures how the value of a firm, the present value of all future cash flows, will be affected by changes in foreign exchange rates. While future foreign currency receivables/cash inflows or payables/cash outflows give rise to the transaction exposure of a firm to foreign exchange market uncertainties individually and respectively, these future foreign currency cash inflows and cash outflows give rise to the economic exposure of a firm to foreign exchange market uncertainties collectively and as a whole, accompanied by a changing economic environment that affects, among others, the discount rate applied to the firm. Yet, firms with economic exposure do necessarily have transaction exposure. Domestic cash flows can also be affected by foreign exchange risk, due to the effect on foreign competition in the domestic market of foreign exchange rate changes. Activities in managing transaction exposure contribute in part to the objectives of managing economic exposure. Indeed, a substantial portion of empirical research in foreign exchange risk management investigates firms' transaction exposure hedging activities to assess their effectiveness in economic exposure management. However, economic exposure has implications beyond the reach of transaction exposure – the scope of economic exposure management is wide and the horizon of economic exposure management is distant. If transaction exposure management is tactical and technical, then economic exposure management is strategic and fundamental.

Accounting exposure or translation exposure measures how a multinational company's (MNC) consolidated financial statements /accounts will be affected by foreign exchange rate fluctuations. Accounting exposure does not directly affect cash flows and is regarded as less relevant or irrelevant in some cases. Managing accounting exposure, which is concerned with the potential impact and stock market implications of consolidated financial accounts arising from the translation of the accounts items of the MNC, is therefore less important than managing transaction exposure and economic exposure and has a lower priority among all foreign exchange risk management activities. Moreover, accounting exposure may differ under different translation methods. If the adoption of the translation methods is not mandatory, accounting exposure can be arbitrary.

## 14.1 Measuring Economic Exposure

Economic exposure measures how the value of a firm, the present value of all future cash flows, will be affected by changes in foreign exchange rates. Management of economic exposure is the effort to control and reduce the adverse effect of exchange rate fluctuations on firm value.

Changes or fluctuations in exchange rates have effect on cash flows/value of firms engaged in international activities as well as firms of domestic nature. The value of a pure domestic firm may be affected by economic exposure through foreign competition in the domestic and local market. Firms with more foreign costs than foreign revenues will be unfavourably affected by stronger foreign currencies; while firms with more foreign revenues than foreign costs will be unfavourably affected by weaker foreign currencies. Table 14.1 describes the effects on firms' activity of currency appreciation/depreciation, which affect the present value of future cash flows and firm value. Currency depreciation or appreciation is in real terms when relevant, though depreciation or appreciation in terms of nominal exchange rates can also be, and in many cases is, real. However, nominal depreciation/appreciation matters where cash flows are bound by contractual agreements.

When the domestic currency appreciates, foreign goods become cheaper and more competitive, so domestic sales of a firm may fall in the relevant domestic market where domestic goods compete with imported foreign goods, reducing the firm's cash inflows. When the domestic currency depreciates, foreign goods become dearer and less competitive, so domestic sales as well as cash inflows of a firm may increase in the relevant domestic market since domestic goods become better positioned compared with imported foreign goods.

A firm's foreign sales will be affected by changes in the relative currency value in a similar way. If the domestic currency appreciates, goods for foreign sales denominated in the domestic currency become more expensive in terms of the foreign currency in the foreign market and they become less competitive. Consequently, foreign sales fall and cash flows decline as a result of domestic currency appreciation. In contrast, depreciation of the domestic currency makes goods for foreign sales cheaper and more competitive and, consequently, foreign sales increase. The competitiveness of goods for foreign sales denominated in the foreign currency remains unchanged in the foreign market whether the domestic currency appreciates or depreciates, so sales, as well as cash flows measured in the foreign currency will not be affected. However, the amount of cash flows denominated in the domestic currency will decrease as a result of domestic currency appreciation, and will increase as a result of domestic currency depreciation. Therefore, the effect on foreign sales of currency appreciation/depreciation would be the same whether foreign sales are denominated in the domestic currency or foreign currency.

**Table 14.1.** Effects of currency appreciation and depreciation

| Activity | Effect on firm value of | |
|---|---|---|
| | Domestic currency appreciation | Domestic currency depreciation |
| Domestic sales | Decrease | Increase |
| Foreign sales denominated in domestic currency | Decrease | Increase |
| Foreign sales denominated in foreign currency | Decrease | Increase |
| Importing goods for domestic sales denominated in domestic currency | No change/ Decrease | No change/ Increase |
| Importing goods for domestic sales denominated in foreign currency | Increase | Decrease |
| Importing production materials/ input denominated in domestic currency | No change | No change |
| Importing production materials/ input denominated in foreign currency | Decrease | Increase |
| Dividends received from foreign direct investment and portfolio investment abroad | Decrease | Increase |
| Interest received from portfolio investment abroad | Decrease | Increase |
| Interest payments on bonds, loans and other funds denominated in foreign currency | Increase | Decrease |

Imported production materials or input to production denominated in the domestic currency will not be affected by currency depreciation or appreciation. Imported production materials or input denominated in the foreign currency, however, will decrease in value of the domestic currency when the domestic currency appreciates and increase in value of the domestic currency when the domestic currency depreciates. Therefore, the firm's cash inflows will increase when the domestic currency appreciates as its cash outflows decrease, and the firm's cash inflows will decrease when the domestic currency depreciates as its cash outflows increase under the circumstances.

The activity of importing goods for domestic sales will compete in the domestic market. Imported goods for domestic sales denominated in the domestic currency will not be affected in their competition with domestically manufactured goods when the domestic currency appreciates. But, imported goods for domestic sales denominated in the foreign currency become cheaper and more competitive as a result. Consequently, sales of imported goods denominated in the domestic currency, along with domestically manufactured goods, may fall and cash flows from the sales decline, if the same goods are imported in the foreign currency denomination at the same time by other competitors. On the other hand, imported goods for domestic sales denominated in the domestic currency become cheaper and more competitive in the domestic market relative to the same imported goods denominated in the foreign currency when the domestic currency depreciates, so sales may go up and cash inflows increase. Imported goods for domestic sales denominated in the foreign currency become more competitive when the domestic currency appreciates, and increased volume of goods may be imported with the same domestic currency value before the appreciation. As a result, sales go up and cash flows from the sales increase. In contrast, sales fall and cash inflows decline when the domestic currency depreciates.

Proceeds received from foreign investment abroad, such as dividends from direct investment and portfolio investment and interest payments, will decrease when the domestic currency appreciate and increase when the domestic currency depreciates. Interest payments on bonds, loans and other funds denominated in the foreign currency will also decrease when the domestic currency appreciate, leading to reduced cash outflows, which tends to have a positive effect on the value of the firm. When the domestic currency depreciates, interest payments increase, which tends to have a negative effect on the value of the firm.

Table 14.1 identifies the areas where a firm may incur economic exposure and the way in which the value of the firm may be affected. Overall, the economic exposure of a firm can be illustrated by the following formula:

$$\Delta PV_t = a + b\Delta FX_t + \varepsilon_t \qquad (14.1)$$

where $\Delta PV_t$ is changes in the present value of the firm in period $t$, $\Delta FX_t$ is changes in foreign exchange rates in period $t$, $a$ is an intercept, $b$ is a coefficient, and $\varepsilon_t$ is the residual term. $\Delta FX_t$ can be an individual exchange rate between the pair of the domestic currency and a foreign currency, or a foreign exchange rate index, such as the effective exchange rate. Equation (14.1) tells how the present value of the firm is affected by foreign exchange risk, with coefficient $b$ measuring the sensitivity of changes in the present value of the firm to changes in foreign exchange rates. If $b$ is positive, then depreciation of the domestic currency will lead to an increase in the present value of the firm overall, or domestic currency depreciation is favourable and domestic currency appreciation is unfavourable for the firm. If $b$ is negative, then depreciation of the domestic currency will result in a fall in the present value of the firm and, under such circumstances, domestic currency depreciation is unfavourable and domestic currency appreciation is favourable for the firm. If, however, $b$ is indifferent to zero, then the firm does not involve economic exposure as exchange rate fluctuations do not have an effect on the firm's present value.

A commonly adopted formula for measuring economic exposure is an asset pricing equation, which is usually the market model, a variation of the Capital Asset Pricing Model (CAPM), augmented by the foreign exchange rate variable, as follows:

$$R_{i,t} = \alpha_i + \beta_i R_{m,t} + \gamma_i \Delta FX_t + \varepsilon_{i,t} \qquad (14.2)$$

where $R_{i,t}$ is rate of return on firm $i$ in period $t$, $R_{m,t}$ is rate of return on the market in period $t$, $\alpha_i$ is an intercept, $\beta_i$ is the sensitivity of the return on firm $i$ to the market return, $\gamma_i$ is the sensitivity of the return on firm $i$ to foreign exchange rate changes or return on foreign exchange, and $\varepsilon_{i,t}$ is residual. Equation (14.2) says that firms' return is a function of the return on the market and the return on foreign exchange. In an ideal CAPM world, firms' return is exclusively explained by the market return, and there is no role left for other variables, including the foreign exchange rate, to play, so $\gamma_i$ must be zero. Yet, empirically, firms do expose to foreign exchange risk, over and above market risk. So $\gamma_i$ can be a figure different from zero, though the size of $\gamma_i$ might be smaller than that of $b$ in equation (14.1). The above interpretations of $b$ apply to $\gamma_i$ in principle.

## 14.2 Managing Economic Exposure

Since the scope of economic exposure is wider than transaction exposure and economic exposure management more strategic than transaction exposure management, many areas of firms' activity fall into the ring of economic exposure management, with some strategic implications to firm value and way in which firm value may be increased. These include production strategy, marketing strategy, product strategy, R&D strategy, and financial strategy, almost every area in the management of business firms.

Market strategy is concerned with the control and management of the exposure of sales to foreign exchange risk. It involves demand elasticity analysis, pricing, market selection and targeting, market diversification and market promotion. It is crucial to comprehend what is the scope for price adjustment impacted by a change in foreign exchange rates. The scope for price adjustment tolerable by the firm and/or the competitors will then be scrutinised with demand elasticity analysis of the product to estimate how the market share for domestically manufactured product and imported product is to change. A corresponding pricing strategy will be developed that increases the market share as much as desired due to a favourable change in foreign exchange rates, or shrink the market share as less as possible under unfavourable foreign exchange conditions. A firm may also select a market or market segment where it enjoys competitive and comparative advantages, which may alternate due to currency appreciation or depreciation. That is, a market analysis may reveal that a reasonable market share in one of its traditional markets may be no longer sustainable due to an unfavourable change in exchange rates but the changed situation may create a new opportunity for the firm in another product market or market segment that did not exist previously. Moreover, the firm may target a certain clientele proactively and adjust its products and production correspondingly to maximise its cash flows or maintain an acceptable level of cash flows whenever there is a change in exchange rates. In line with financial diversification, a firm may pursue market diversification as well so its overall sales and cash flows will remain stable under various foreign exchange conditions.

Production strategy pays attention to the control and management of the exposure of production costs to foreign exchange risk. Approaches include product sourcing, input mix and shift, and site rotation. With flexible product sourcing, the firm may avoid high costs by shifting the production or service to a place that is not affected by the exchange rate change. An input mix serves to diversify the risk in production costs in a passive way and an input shift attempts to control costs proactively. Site rotation means that the production of a few types of products, whenever possible, will be arranged in a way that the combination of the product and the plant site is optimal after a change in foreign exchange conditions. Product strategy is not necessarily confined to the foreign exchange sphere and aims to generate more cash flows by product differentiation, product innovation, and product upgrading. R&D strategy is to invent and raise productivity fundamentally and in the long run, making it possible for product differentiation and product innovation at the time when they are demanded by a marketing strategy or in a production process.

Financial strategy aims to reduce the cost of capital of the firm and maintain a certain level of future cash flows. Hedging transaction exposure is much but not all of it. Hedging stabilises firms' contractual cash flows, and reduces uncertainties in firms' return. A firm engaged in risk management with foreign exchange derivatives is therefore perceived in the financial market and by investors as less risky, compared with a firm that is identical in all aspects except that it does not use foreign exchange derivatives for risk management. Consequently the cost of capital in the former can be lower than that in the latter and, with the same amounts of cash inflows, the value of the former is greater than that of the latter. Hedging transaction exposure discussed in the previous chapter is mostly in the short term. Yet, hedging can also be carried out in the long run, such as the use of currency swaps to alter a firm's foreign exchange risk profile. As having been observed in the previous chapter, there are many financial risk management tools at the technical level. Financial strategy requires a strategic use of these risk management tools in managing economic exposure of the firm.

## 14.3 Measuring Accounting Exposure

Accounting exposure or translation exposure measures how the consolidated financial statements /accounts of an MNC will be affected by exchange rate fluctuations. Accounting exposure does not directly affect cash flows, however. Management of accounting exposure is concerned with the potential impact and stock market implications of consolidated financial accounts arising from the translation of the accounts items of the MNC.

The use of accounting methods has an effect on the degree of accounting exposure, as well as the size and activity of foreign subsidiaries. In the following we introduce four accounting methods for translating the accounts and accounts items of a foreign subsidiary of a MNC and their effects on the consolidated accounts of the MNC – the current rate method, the temporal method, the monetary/non-monetary method and the current/non-current method.

The current rate method is the simplest – all financial statement items are translated at the current exchange rate except equity items. Assets and liabilities are translated at the rate of exchange in effect on the balance sheet date. Income statement[1] items are translated at either the actual exchange rate on the dates the various revenues, expenses, gains and losses were incurred or at a weighted average exchange rate for the period. Distributions of dividends are translated at the rate in effect on the date of payment. Equity items are translated at the historical rate in effect when the item was first recorded on the account. Gains or losses from translation are closed to an equity reserve account called the cumulative translation adjustment (CTA), and will not appear in the MNC's consolidated income statement, unless the foreign subsidiary incurring the gain or loss is liquidated. The balance sheet will always be balanced by the CTA with this translation method.

Under the current/non-current method, assets and liabilities are categorised by their maturity and are translated accordingly. It is because the value of current account items, or items mature in short periods, is most likely to change when the exchange rate changes. That is, all current account items are translated at the current exchange rate and non-current account items are translated at the historical rate in effect when the item was first recorded entered the book. Income statement items are translated at either the actual exchange rate on the date when the item was incurred or at a weighted average exchange rate for the period. There may be translation gains or translation losses adopting this method, which appears in the consolidated income statement of the MNC.

The monetary/non-monetary method deems that only the value of monetary items will change when the exchange rate changes, whereas the value of non-

---

[1] The income statement refers to the profit/loss account in the UK.

monetary items will not be affected. So maturity is not an appropriate criterion under certain circumstances regarding the currency translation of a subsidiary's accounts. With the monetary/non-monetary methods, monetary balance sheet items, e.g., cash, accounts receivable, accounts payable, and long-term debt are translated at current exchange rates; and non-monetary balance sheet items, e.g., inventory[2], plant and equipment, long-term investments, are translated at the historical exchange rate. Income statement items are translated at the average exchange rate for the period except for depreciation and cost of goods sold which are associated with non-monetary items, these items are translated at their historical rate. Distributions of dividends are translated at the exchange rate in effect the date of payment. Equity items are translated at the historical rate. Similar to the current/non-current method, there may be translation gains or translation losses appearing in the consolidated income statement.

Under the temporal method, specific assets and liabilities are translated at exchange rates consistent with the timing of these items' creation. That is, assets and liabilities should be translated based on how they are carried on the accounts. Balance sheet items are translated at the current exchange rate if they are carried on the accounts at their current value. Items that are carried on the accounts at historical costs are translated at the historical exchange rates in effect at the time the items were recorded on the accounts. This treatment means that in most cases the temporal method of currency translation is similar to the monetary/non-monetary method except that the translation of inventory is the same as under the current/non-current method.

The differences in these translation methods lie in how to determine which foreign currency denominated assets and liabilities will be translated at the current exchange rate and which will be translated at the historical exchange rate. The current exchange rate is post-change exchange rate and the historical exchange rate is pre-change exchange rate. So, items translated at the current exchange rate are exposed to foreign exchange risk in the accounting concept and measure, whereas items translated at the historical exchange rate are not exposed to foreign exchange risk. Accounting exposure is indeed the net exposure of assets and liabilities, i.e., the difference between exposed assets and exposed liabilities, which varies with the translation method adopted. Under the current rate method, all assets and liabilities as regarded as exposed. Under the current/non-current method, only current assets and liabilities are exposed. Under the monetary/non-monetary method, only monetary assets and liabilities are exposed. Under the temporal method, assets and liabilities valued at the current cost are exposed and assets and liabilities valued at the historical cost are not exposed.

Following is a case illustrating the four translation methods. Table 14.2 is the balance sheet of a US subsidiary of a Dutch MNC. Fixed assets, long-term debt and common stock were acquired at the historical exchange rate of $0.9/€. Inventory was purchased over a period when the average exchange rate was $1.0/€. The average exchange rate in 2003 was also $1.0/€. However, to keep the case simply, retained earnings in the local currency of US dollars are assumed to be zero.

---

[2] Stock is used in place of inventory in the UK.

Therefore, the retained earnings in the consolidated income statement are all due to translation gains or losses. The US dollar depreciated on January 2, 2004. The exchange rate was $1.1/€ before the depreciation on December 31, 2003 and became $1.2/€ after the depreciation on January 2, 2004.

**Table 14.2.** Balance sheet of subsidiary (in $ thousand)

| Assets | | Liabilities and shareholders equity | |
| --- | --- | --- | --- |
| Cash | 1,100 | Accounts payable | 1,500 |
| Accounts receivable | 2,400 | Short-term loans | 500 |
| Inventory | 3,000 | Long-term debt | 6,000 |
| Net fixed assets | 9,000 | Equity/ common stock | 7,500 |
| Total assets | 15,500 | Total liabilities and equity | 15,500 |

Table 14.3 is the translated balance sheet adopting the current rate method, in which all account items are translated at the current exchange rate except equity. So, only equity/common stock was not exposed to foreign exchange risk in the accounting concept and measure, which remained €8.333m after the depreciation of the US dollar. The accounting exposure was $7.500m (cash 1.1 + accounts receivable 2.4 + inventory 3.0 + bet fixed assets 9.0 – accounts payable 1.5 – short-term loans 0.5 – long-term debt 6.0) in the local function currency of the US dollar, €6.818m before the depreciation of the US dollar, and €6.250m after the depreciation of the US dollar. Both assets and liabilities were reduced in € value after the depreciation, with the reduction in the value of the assets being larger than that in the value of the liabilities. There was a translation loss in the consolidated balance sheet under the current rate method as indicated by a negative CTA. The CTA was –€1.515m before the depreciation and became –€2.083m after the depreciation, suggesting the € value of the translated assets dropped more than the € value of the translated liabilities due to the depreciation.

Table 14.4 shows the translated balance sheet items under the current/non-current method, where all current account items are translated at the current exchange rate and non-current account items are translated at the historical exchange rate. So, equity/common stock, net fixed assets and long-term debt were not exposed, which remained €8.333m, €10.000m and €6.667m respectively after the depreciation of the US dollar. The rest, i.e., cash, accounts receivable, inventory, accounts payable and short-term loans, were exposed. The accounting exposure was $4.500m (cash 1.1 + accounts receivable 2.4 + inventory 3.0 – accounts payable 1.5 – short-term loans 0.5) in the local function currency of the US dollar, €4.091m before the depreciation of the US dollar, and €3.750m after the depreciation of the US dollar. Again, the reduction in the value of the assets was larger

**Table 14.3.** Current rate method (in thousand)

| | Value in local currency ($) | Before depreciation | | After depreciation | |
|---|---|---|---|---|---|
| | | $/€ | Value in € | $/€ | Value in € |
| Cash | 1,100 | 1.1 | 1,000 | 1.2 | 917 |
| Accounts receivable | 2,400 | 1.1 | 2,182 | 1.2 | 2,000 |
| Inventory | 3,000 | 1.1 | 2,727 | 1.2 | 2,500 |
| Net fixed assets | 9,000 | 1.1 | 8,182 | 1.2 | 7,500 |
| Total assets | 15,500 | | 14,091 | | 12,917 |
| | | | | | |
| Accounts payable | 1,500 | 1.1 | 1,364 | 1.2 | 1,250 |
| Short-term loans | 500 | 1.1 | 455 | 1.2 | 417 |
| Long-term debt | 6,000 | 1.1 | 5,455 | 1.2 | 5,000 |
| Equity/common stock | 7,500 | 0.9 | 8,333 | 0.9 | 8,333 |
| Retained earnings | 0 | | 0 | | 0 |
| CTA | | | (1,515) | | (2,083) |
| Total liabilities and equity | 15,500 | | 14,091 | | 12,917 |

**Table 14.4.** Current/non-current method

| | Value in local currency ($) | Before depreciation | | After depreciation | |
|---|---|---|---|---|---|
| | | $/€ | Value in € | $/€ | Value in € |
| Cash | 1,100 | 1.1 | 1,000 | 1.2 | 917 |
| Accounts receivable | 2,400 | 1.1 | 2,182 | 1.2 | 2,000 |
| Inventory | 3,000 | 1.1 | 2,727 | 1.2 | 2,500 |
| Net fixed assets | 9,000 | 0.9 | 10,000 | 0.9 | 10,000 |
| Total assets | 15,500 | | 15,909 | | 15,417 |
| | | | | | |
| Accounts payable | 1,500 | 1.1 | 1,364 | 1.2 | 1,250 |
| Short-term loans | 500 | 1.1 | 455 | 1.2 | 417 |
| Long-term debt | 6,000 | 0.9 | 6,667 | 0.9 | 6,667 |
| Equity/common stock | 7,500 | 0.9 | 8,333 | 0.9 | 8,333 |
| Retained earnings | 0 | | (909) | | (1,250) |
| Total liabilities and equity | 15,500 | | 15,909 | | 15,417 |

than that in the value of the liabilities. There was also a translation loss in the consolidated balance sheet under the current/non-current, which entered the income statement as a negative figure as retained earnings adjustment. The translation loss under this method was smaller than that under the current rate method, which was –€0.909m before the depreciation and –€1.250m after the depreciation, indicating a larger drop in the € value of the assets than in the € value of the liabilities due to the depreciation.

The case for the monetary/non-monetary method is presented in Table 14.5. In this case, inventory, fixed assets and equity were not exposed to foreign exchange rate fluctuations, which remained €3.000m, €10.000m and €8.333m respectively after the depreciation of the US dollar. The rest, i.e., cash, accounts receivable, accounts payable, both short-term loans and long-term debt, were exposed. The accounting exposure was –$4.500m (cash 1.1 + accounts receivable 2.4 – accounts payable 1.5 – short-term loans 0.5 – long-term debt 6.0) in the local function currency of the US dollar, –€4.091m before the depreciation of the US dollar, and –€3.750m after the depreciation of the US dollar. In this case, both assets and liabilities were reduced in € value due to the depreciation, with the reduction in the value of the assets being smaller than that in the value of the liabilities. There was a translation gain under the monetary/non-monetary method, which entered the income statement as retained earnings adjustment. The depreciation resulted in an increase in translation gains, indicating the fall in the € value of the assets is smaller than the fall in the € value of the liabilities due to the depreciation.

**Table 14.5.** Monetary/non-monetary method

| | Value in local currency ($) | Before depreciation | | After depreciation | |
|---|---|---|---|---|---|
| | | $/€ | Value in € | $/€ | Value in € |
| Cash | 1,100 | 1.1 | 1,000 | 1.2 | 917 |
| Accounts receivable | 2,400 | 1.1 | 2,182 | 1.2 | 2,000 |
| Inventory | 3,000 | 1.0 | 3,000 | 1.0 | 3,000 |
| Net fixed assets | 9,000 | 0.9 | 10,000 | 0.9 | 10,000 |
| Total assets | 15,500 | | 16,182 | | 15,917 |
| | | | | | |
| Accounts payable | 1,500 | 1.1 | 1,364 | 1.2 | 1,250 |
| Short-term loans | 500 | 1.1 | 455 | 1.2 | 417 |
| Long-term debt | 6,000 | 1.1 | 5,455 | 1.2 | 5,000 |
| Equity/common stock | 7,500 | 0.9 | 8,333 | 0.9 | 8,333 |
| Retained earnings | 0 | | 576 | | 917 |
| Total liabilities and equity | 15,500 | | 16,182 | | 15,917 |

Finally, Table 14.6 demonstrates the translation with the temporal method. All the items are translated in the same way as with the monetary/non-monetary method except that inventory is translated at the current rate. Therefore, inventory was exposed to foreign exchange rate fluctuations, along with cash, accounts receivable, accounts payable, short-term loans and long-term debt. The accounting exposure was –$1.500m (cash 1.1 + accounts receivable 2.4 + inventory 3.0 – accounts payable 1.5 – short-term loans 0.5 – long-term debt 6.0) in the local function currency of the US dollar, –€1.364m before the depreciation of the US dollar, and –€1.250m after the depreciation of the US dollar. Both assets and liabilities were reduced in € value due to the depreciation, with the reduction in the value of the assets being smaller than that in the value of the liabilities. There was a translation gain as well under the temporal method, which entered the income statement as retained earnings adjustment. The translation gain was smaller than that in the monetary/non-monetary case, both before the depreciation and after the depreciation of the US dollar.

**Table 14.6.** Temporal method

| | Value in local currency ($) | Before depreciation | | After depreciation | |
|---|---|---|---|---|---|
| | | $/€ | Value in € | $/€ | Value in € |
| Cash | 1,100 | 1.1 | 1,000 | 1.2 | 917 |
| Accounts receivable | 2,400 | 1.1 | 2,182 | 1.2 | 2,000 |
| Inventory | 3,000 | 1.1 | 2,727 | 1.2 | 3,000 |
| Net fixed assets | 9,000 | 0.9 | 10,000 | 0.9 | 10,000 |
| Total assets | 15,500 | | 15,909 | | 15,417 |
| | | | | | |
| Accounts payable | 1,500 | 1.1 | 1,364 | 1.2 | 1,250 |
| Short-term loans | 500 | 1.1 | 455 | 1.2 | 417 |
| Long-term debt | 6,000 | 1.1 | 5,455 | 1.2 | 5,000 |
| Equity/common stock | 7,500 | 0.9 | 8,333 | 0.9 | 8,333 |
| Retained earnings | 0 | | 303 | | 417 |
| Total liabilities and equity | 15,500 | | 15,909 | | 15,417 |

## 14.4 Managing Accounting Exposure

While it is universally accepted that transaction exposure and economic exposure must be managed, managing accounting exposure does not appear to be as crucial as managing transaction exposure and economic exposure and may be regarded irrelevant in some cases. It is because translation gains or losses may not have any effect on cash flows, e.g., when the current rate method is adopted and the subsidiary is not going to be liquidated, so the CTA will not be realised. Translation gains or losses may have cash flow implications under some circumstances when other translation methods are adopted but the effect is usually much smaller than that of foreign exchange transaction gains or losses. Nevertheless, there is still influence of accounting exposure, real or perceived, on MNCs at times. Moreover, accounting information, including information on translation gains or losses, is often used by financial analysts, creditors and other stakeholders to assess the performance of the firm and the management, so the management of the firm may have some incentive to alter translation gains or losses to signal the market or influence the perception of investors about the firm.

There are two major approaches to managing accounting exposure: balance sheet hedge and derivatives hedge. Balance sheet hedge is to minimise accounting exposure by matching foreign currency assets and foreign currency liabilities on the balance sheet. When a change in the foreign exchange rate leads to a change in the value of the assets on the consolidated balance sheet, a change of the same size but of the opposite sign will take place in the value of the liabilities on the consolidated balance sheet as well. Since only exposed assets and exposed liabilities will be affected by foreign exchange rate fluctuations, the design of balance sheet hedge depends on which of the translation methods is adopted under the circumstances. Given a certain translation method, balance sheet hedge attempts to minimise the accounting exposure or the net exposure of an MNC, or the difference between exposed assets and exposed liabilities on the consolidated balance sheet. When net exposure cannot be reduced to zero, the net exposure can be positive, i.e., the value exposed assets is greater than the value of the exposed liabilities, or negative, i.e., the value exposed assets is smaller than the value of the exposed liabilities. A positive net exposure indicates that the translation gain (loss) will increase (decrease) when the function currency of the subsidiary appreciates, and the translation gain (loss) will decrease (increase) when the function currency of the subsidiary depreciates, and the translation gain may turn to a translation loss if the depreciation is substantial. On the other hand, a negative net exposure indicates that the translation gain (loss) will decrease (increase) when the function currency of the subsidiary appreciates, and the translation gain (loss) will increase (decrease) when the function currency of the subsidiary depreciates, and the translation loss may become a translation gain if the function currency of the subsidiary appreciates to a large extent.

Let us re-examine the above case with regard to balance sheet hedging. Under the current rate method, the accounting exposure or the net exposure was positive, indicating the value of exposed assets were greater than the value of exposed liabilities. So depreciation would reduce the value of the translated assets more than the value of the translated liabilities and the translation loss increased from €1.515 €2.083m, as revealed in Table 14.3(a). For the MNC to hedge its accounting exposure, it should reduce the amount of exposed assets or increase the amount of exposed liabilities or do both, especially when the inflation in the US was expected to be higher than that in the euroland with a prospect of US dollar depreciation. If, however, the function currency of the subsidiary is likely to appreciate, some positive exposure can be helpful since it may reduce translation losses or increase translation gains in such environments. The situation under the current/non-current method was similar, as shown in Table 14.3(b), though both the exposure and the translation loss were smaller, due to the fact that net fixed assets and long-term debt were not regarded to be exposed. Under the monetary/non-monetary method and the temporal method, the accounting exposure of the MNC was negative. Therefore, if one of such translation methods was mandatory, the MNC should attempt to increase the amount of exposed assets or reduce the amount of exposed liabilities in its balance sheet hedging exercise. Nevertheless, some negative accounting exposure would be helpful when the function currency of the subsidiary is expected to depreciate. In this case, the translation gain increased from €0.576m to €0.917 under the monetary/non-monetary method, and the translation gain increased from €0.303m to €0.417 under the temporal method, as indicated by Table 14.3(c) and Table 14.3(d) respectively.

The other common approach to managing accounting exposure is derivatives hedge, e.g., the use of forward contracts to hedge balance sheet items. Not all exposed items need to be hedged. Derivatives hedge may apply to a small amount of exposed assets and/or liabilities or to selected items only, to reduce accounting exposure or net exposure, the difference between exposed assets and exposed liabilities. Other derivatives may also be used to hedge accounting exposure under various scenarios. e.g., option hedge provides some flexibility at a small cost, though the cost may not be worthwhile, while swaps may be useful tools for hedging long-term account items.

Managing accounting exposure and managing transaction exposure can be complementary to some extent under certain circumstances or in conflict under some other circumstances. That is, reducing transaction exposure may reduce accounting exposure to a similar degree at the same time, or reducing transaction exposure may results in increased accounting exposure. The elimination of both transaction exposure and accounting exposure at the same time and over some time horizon is more by coincidence than by design. In general, MNCs trying to reduce both transaction exposure and accounting exposure should manage or reduce transaction exposure first. Since the accounting exposure of an MNC may be altered by its transaction exposure management activity, the MNC should then re-estimate its accounting exposure and implement some measures to reduce accounting exposure without creating much new transaction exposure.

# 15 Country Risk and Sovereign Risk Analysis

The previous two chapters have addressed issues in firms' exposure to foreign exchange risk – how transaction cash flows, firm value, and consolidated financial statements are subjected to foreign exchange rate fluctuations and how to manage the three types of foreign exchange exposure. Firms engaged in foreign business activities are not only exposed to uncertainties in foreign exchange markets – they are additionally susceptible to adverse events in the host country concerning the political climate, the economic environment, the financial condition, and the social institution. That a firm's financial performance and interests are adversely affected by the events and uncertainties in the political climate, the economic environment, the financial condition, and the social institution of the host country is referred to as country risk. While the factors contributing to country risk have far reaching effects on MNCs, there is little consensus in the identification and the relative importance of the factors of influence and the effects on an MNC's financial interests and performance are difficult to measure and quantify. Therefore, country risk analysis requires broad knowledge and experience in the host country's society beyond narrowly defined financial considerations. Bearing the above in mind, this chapter introduces country risk measures as a judgemental instrument that provides a structured assessment procedure with clues of a particular country risk score and country risk ranking, but not as a simple number that can be totally relied upon.

Sovereign risk refers to the risk that a host government or sovereign power will default on its payment obligations, i.e., a host government or sovereign power may unilaterally repudiate its foreign obligations or may prevent local firms from honouring their foreign obligations. Country risk can be regarded to have encompassed sovereign risk to a certain extent. That is, country risk covers most of the elements for sovereign risk analysis but country risk analysis does not elaborate these elements in great detail as sovereign risk analysis does. Although factors that determine sovereign risk are easier to quantify than those for country risk, sovereign risk analysis still involves substantial judgement based on the rating agency's knowledge and experience of the host country.

## 15.1 Factors of Influence on Country Risk

We classify factors that determine country risk into four groupings: the political climate, the economic environment, the financial condition, and the social institution. The political climate factor refers to the stability, maturity and functioning of the political system; the representativeness and collectiveness of government; the scale of domestic conflict – racial relations, civil war or insurgence; and the conditions of international relations – sanctions imposed due to political reasons, border dispute or military conflict with neighbouring countries. The economic environment is concerned with economic development stages – GDP per capita and growth in GDP; economic stability – inflation, unemployment and provision of social security; infrastructure – the communications system, skills of the labour force, the competitiveness of the industry, the maturity of the service sector and the efficiency of government departments and agencies; taxation – consistency in and levels of tax charges, and tax incentives for foreign  investment and for  certain  industries; macroeconomic management – formation, implementation and effectiveness of monetary policy and fiscal policy; and international economic relations  –  international  trade,  balance  of  payments,  foreign  exchange  rate arrangements and foreign reserves. The financial condition is related to the stability of the financial system, the functioning of the capital market, the operation of the foreign exchange market, and the maturity of the corporate sector. Finally, the social institution reveals the legal, regulative, cultural and institutional aspects of a country that may have effects on the financial interests and performance of an MNC in the country. It covers the legal system – independence, transparency and enforcement of the legal system, crime and security in the society; regulations and legislations – consistency, fairness and effectiveness; work organisation and corporate governance – compatibility, harmony and functioning; the influence of interest groups – professional bodies, trade unions and employers organisations;  the

**Table 15.1.** Country risk: factors of influence

| Factor | Factor component | Criterion |
|---|---|---|
| Political Climate | Political system | Stability<br>Maturity<br>Functioning |
| | Government | Representativeness<br>Collectiveness |
| | Domestic conflict | Racial relations<br>Civil war/unrest<br>Insurgence |
| | International relations | Economic sanctions<br>Border dispute with neighbouring countries<br>Military conflict or war against foreign countries |

**Table 15.1.** (cont.)

| | | |
|---|---|---|
| Economic Environment | Development stages | GDP per capita<br>Growth in GDP |
| | Economic stability | Inflation<br>Unemployment<br>Provision of social security |
| | Infrastructure | Functioning of communications systems<br>Skills of the labour force<br>Competitiveness of the industry<br>Maturity of the service sector<br>Efficiency of government departments and agencies |
| | Taxation | Consistency in tax charges<br>Levels of tax charges<br>Tax incentives for foreign investment<br>Tax incentives for industries |
| | Macroeconomic management | Policy formation<br>Policy implementation<br>Policy effectiveness |
| | International economic relations | International trade<br>Balance of payments<br>Foreign exchange rate arrangements<br>Foreign reserves |
| Financial condition | Financial system | Stability, regulation and supervision |
| | Capital market | Functioning, efficiency, liquidity, resilience and transparency |
| | Foreign exchange market | Stability, resilience and intervention |
| | Corporate sector | Maturity, information disclosure and corporate governance |
| Social Institution | Legal systems | Independence<br>Transparency<br>Enforcement |
| | Legislations and regulations | Consistency<br>Fairness<br>Effectiveness |
| | Work organisation and corporate governance | Compatibility<br>Harmony<br>Functioning |
| | Interest groups | Professional bodies<br>Trade unions<br>Employers organisations |
| | Emergencies and rescues | Occurrences of natural disasters and major accidents<br>Ability of handling natural disasters and emergency rescues |
| | Social attitude | Toward work and social life<br>Towards wealth distribution Towards foreign investment and national interests |

ability of handling natural disasters and emergency rescues; and social attitude towards work, social life, wealth distribution, foreign investment, and national interests. Table 15.1 lists and summarises these factors of influence for country risk analysis.

## 15.2 Country Risk Analysis and Ratings

It is clear that some of the elements for country risk analysis are not quantitatively measurable and understandably that some proxies have to be used to yield country risk ratings. In the following, we introduce two major country risk analysis models by World Markets Research Centre (WMRC) and Standard & Poor's (S&P), based on which some ratings examples will be presented and discussed. The WMRC adopts a six factor model to analyse country risk for 186 countries. These factors are political (weighting 25%), economic (weighting 25%), legal (weighting 15%), tax (weighting 15%), operational (weighting 10%), and security (weighting 10%). Each country is given a risk rating of between 1 and 5 for each of the six

**Table 15.2.** Six risk factors by WMRC for country risk analysis

*(a) Political risk*

| Criteria | Description |
|---|---|
| Institutional permanence | An assessment of how mature and well-established the political system is. It is also an assessment of how far political opposition operates within the system or attempts to undermine it from outside. A country with high institutional permanence would unquestionably survive the death or removal from power of the current leadership. A mature political system will conventionally have a clearly established relationship between the executive, legislative and judicial branches of government |
| Representativeness | How well the population and organised interests can make their voices heard in the political system. Provided representation is handled fairly and effectively, it will ensure greater stability and better designed policies. |
| Internal political consensus | Whether the country is riven by major social and political divides, and how far these are exploited by nationalist or extremist leaders. Serious divisions will frequently spill over into violence and major political instability. |
| External political consensus | The degree to which the country is seen as a menace to, or is menaced by, third countries. Poor external political consensus is generally cause for longer term, but intense risk. Strongly antagonistic foreign states may well sponsor destabilising domestic opposition movements. |

**Table 15.2.** (cont.)

## (b) Economic risk

| Criteria | Description |
| --- | --- |
| Degree of market orientation | An assessment of the economic stance of the government and economy - whether market forces can operate properly and how actively the current government encourages this. |
| Policy consistency and forward planning | How confident businesses can be of the continuity of economic policy stance - whether a change of government will entail major policy disruption, and whether the current government has pursued a coherent strategy. This factor also looks at the extent to which policy-making is far-sighted, or conversely aimed at short-term economic (and electoral) advantage. |
| Diversity and resilience of the economy | This assesses how stable the economy is - how well diversified over different sectors it is, how well-balanced is the reliance on domestic and external demand, and how likely it is to survive sectoral crashes. This will usually correspond with the level of development and maturity of the economy. |
| Macroeconomic fundamentals | An assessment of the broad economic health of the country at present - whether factors such as growth, inflation, unemployment and trade are in a good, stable state. |

## (c) Legal risk

| Criteria | Description |
| --- | --- |
| Legislation | An assessment of whether the necessary business laws are in place, and whether there any outstanding gaps. This includes the extent to which the country's legislation is compatible with, and respected by, other countries' legal systems. |
| Transparency | An assessment of how clear and intelligible the legal procedures are in the country. The definition of the legal system and the clarity of criminal and commercial law and precedents are considered. |
| Independence | An assessment of how far the state and other outside actors can influence and distort the legal system. This will determine the level of legal impartiality investors can expect. |
| Experience | How long-established the legal system is, and whether, if young, the system draws on the well-established systems and precedents of another country. This is also an assessment of the experience and quality of the legal professionals - in particular judges. |

**Table 15.2.** (cont.)

## (d) Tax risk

| Criteria | Description |
| --- | --- |
| Coherence | This factor concerns the clarity, logic and transparency of the taxation system. A highly coherent system will make sense and allow companies to calculate their likely burden and plan ahead. A less coherent system is likely to have an abundance of tax-collecting bodies that are poorly co-ordinated. |
| Fairness | How fairly the taxation burden is shared - whether certain companies are forced to pay excessive taxes while others can operate virtually tax-free. This factor is also concerned with whether the state or other bodies regularly influence and distort the taxation system. |
| Level | The relative taxation burden in the country - whether it compares well internationally and whether it represents an incentive or disincentive to investors. |
| Effectiveness | How efficient the country's tax collection system is. The rules may be clear and transparent, but whether they are enforced consistently. This factor looks at the relative effectiveness too of corporate and personal, indirect and direct taxation. |

## (e) Operational risk

| Criteria | Description |
| --- | --- |
| Attitudes to foreign investment | An assessment of the government's stance on foreign investment - whether the country is open to it, how active encouragement is and whether the government takes an interventionist stance once the investment has been made. This factor also applies to popular attitudes towards foreign investors, and whether these can impede a business' operations. For some industries this may include the level of environmental activism. |
| Infrastructural quality | Whether foreign investors stand to benefit or suffer from the quality of infrastructure in the country. This will include all forms of physical transport, as well as the quality of the communications and internet infrastructure. We also assess in this category the quality of the public utilities infrastructure, such as energy and water supplies. Major natural hazards likely to disrupt the infrastructure and business activity are taken into account. |
| Labour | A measure of the state of labour relations in the country, whether disruptive unrest/strikes are common, and the degree of disruption that can be expected. This factor also assesses the quality and availability of labour. |
| Bureaucracy and corruption | This assesses the quality and intrusiveness of the country's bureaucracy. The amount of red tape is assessed, as is the likelihood of encountering corrupt officials and other groups. The better the bureaucracy the quicker decisions are made and the more easily foreign investors can go about their business. |

**Table 15.2.** (cont.)

*(f) Security risk*

| Criteria | Description |
|---|---|
| Civil unrest | How widespread political unrest is, and how great a threat it poses to investors. Demonstrations in themselves may not be cause for concern, but they will cause major disruption if they escalate into severe violence. At the extreme, this factor would amount to civil war. |
| Crime | How much of a threat businesses face from crime such as kidnapping, extortion, street violence, burglary and so on. These problems can cause major inconvenience for foreign investors and require them to take expensive security precautions. |
| Terrorism | Whether the country suffers from a sustained terrorist threat, and from how many sources. The degree of localisation of the threat is assessed, and whether the active groups are likely to target or affect businesses. |
| External security threats | Whether the country faces major threats of physical incursion from neighbouring countries, or cross-border bomb attacks. Such threats will tend to be latent, and will only affect the Security Risk Rating if they are likely to compromise investor security in the near future. |

Source: World Markets Research Centre

factors. 1 indicates the minimum risk and 5 is the maximum risk. The minimum increment is 0.25. The overall country risk is then calculated using a geometric mean[1] of the six individual risk categories. As the geometric mean is always smaller than the arithmetic mean, and the larger the variation in the elements, the larger is the difference between the two means, this approach tends to penalise countries exhibit large variations among the six risk categories, other things being equal. Table 15.2 presents the six factors used by the WMRC for country risk analysis with the corresponding criteria and descriptions.

In line with its credit rating practice, the S&P classifies country risk factors into two categories: business risk factors and financial risk factors, primarily for so called emerging markets. Amongst the business risk category, there are 12 risk elements: macroeconomic volatility, access to imported raw materials, exchange-rate risk, government regulation, taxes/royalties/duties, legal issues, labour issues, infrastructure problems, changing tariff barriers/trade blocs/ subsidies, corruption issues, terrorism, and industry structure/operating environment. The financial risk factors include three risk areas and 12 risk elements. The three risk areas are:

---

[1] It is claimed to be the geometric mean of the six individual risk ratings but the formula is:

$$[0.25(Political\ risk)^2 + 0.25(Economic\ risk)^2 + 0.15(legal\ risk)^2 +$$

$$0.15(Tax\ risk)^2 + 0.10(Operational\ risk)^2 + 0.10(Security\ risk)^2]^{0.5}$$

**Table 15.3.** S&P risk factors for country risk analysis

*(a) Business risk factors*

| | |
|---|---|
| **Macroeconomic volatility** | Does the country's economic track record suggest high volatility in the macro environment? This may compound the constraint on credit quality typically associated with cyclical industries, since they become even more cyclical, and may experience stronger "booms" and "busts." |
| **Access to imported raw materials** | Is the company heavily dependent on imported supplies, and could the company's operations therefore be interrupted if foreign-exchange controls are imposed by the sovereign? |
| **Exchange rate risk** | Is the exchange rate subject to significant volatility, which could compress margins relative to global peers and/or affect demand for products? |
| **Government regulation** | Is there a risk of the government "changing the rules of the game," through import/export restrictions, direct intervention in service quality or levels, redefining boundaries of competition such as service areas, altering existing barriers to entry, changing subsidies, or changing antitrust legislation? For extractive industries, what is the risk of government contract renegotiation or nationalisation? Are environmental regulations expected to tighten significantly; are local lobbying groups gaining political clout in this respect? |
| **Taxes/royalties/ duties** | Does the company or its key investments enjoy tax subsidies or royalty arrangements that have renegotiation risk at the federal or regional level? Does the government have a history of micro-managing the cur rent account balance through changing taxes or duties on imports/exports/foreign borrowings? |
| **Legal issues** | What is the transparency of the legal system? Does the type of legal system create differences in contract risks or treatment of creditor rights, particularly with regard to collateral and workout/bankruptcy situations? |
| **Labour issues** | What is the potential for strikes? Is there inflexibility of regulations which may make firing workers an unrealistic or expensive option? |
| **Infrastructure problems** | Are there potential bottlenecks, poor transport, high cost/inefficient port services? Is there a need to supply own electricity or other basic services/infrastructure? |
| **Changing tariff barriers/trade blocs/ Subsidies** | Are domestic companies protected by tariffs or other industry subsidies that are likely to drop as governments liberalize their external trade regulations? Has/will the country join a local trade bloc, which could immediately drop tariffs on imports from members? |

**Table 15.3.** (cont.)

| | |
|---|---|
| **Corruption issues** | Is corruption an issue in terms of raising the cost of business or creating uncertainty about maintaining a "level playing field" for business? |
| **Terrorism** | Are there risks of attacks on the companies' facilities, kidnapping of key employees? How has the company mitigated these risks? |
| **Industry structure/ operating environment** | Industry characteristics may be favourable or and fragmented US market. Growth prospects for consumer products or new technologies and services can offer tremendous opportunities, by tracking expected population growth or increasing per capita incomes, which may be offset by other risks. |

*(b) Financial risk factors*

| | | |
|---|---|---|
| **Financial policy** | *Disclosure/ local accounting standards issues* | Does the company provide consolidated financial statements? The lack of consolidated statements, which may not be required by local regulatory/accounting standards, can hinder the analyst's ability to assess overall cash flow generation and debt service coverage. Lack of segment information may make it difficult to analyze properly profitability trends or project performance. Changes in overall accounting presentation, for example eliminating inflation accounting without requiring restatement of prior years, makes trend comparisons meaningless or difficult. Obtaining timely financial statement reporting may be an issue. |
| | *Foreign-exchange risks* | Does the company hedge foreign-exchange risks, to the extent it is within its control to do so? Does the company show a propensity to speculate with financial arbitrage opportunities? (For example, does the company borrow in U.S. dollars to invest in high interest rate local currency instruments, exposing itself to devaluation risk?) |
| | *Family/ group ownership issues* | If the issuer is part of a conglomerate or family-controlled group of companies, is the company's financial policy dictated by the group, and are there potential weaknesses at other group companies that could negatively affect the issuer? Conversely, strong group ownership and support can enhance creditworthiness. |

**Table 15.3.** (cont.)

| | | |
|---|---|---|
| **Profitability/cash flow** | *Potential price controls* | These are particularly a threat for basic local goods or services, such as telephone/electric services, or gasoline sales. At times of spiralling inflation (a risk captured in the sovereign foreign currency rating), governments often try to assuage consumers services, and under severe stress may freeze all prices in an effort to control inflation. |
| | *Inflation/currency fluctuation risk* | Where existing or potential high/accelerating inflation is an issue, does the company have the pricing flexibility, systems, and know-how to keep revenues increasing in-line with or ahead of costs? Will import prices of supplies be affected by devaluation? How well matched, by currency, are revenues and costs? Does a mismatch expose the company to devaluation or, for exporters, currency appreciation risk, which can lead to sustained reductions in profitability? |
| | *Restricted access to subsidiary cash flow* | Is access to cash flows of foreign subsidiaries constrained by potential transfer/convertibility risk? |
| **Capital structure/financial flexibility** | *Inflation accounting* | Does local accounting tend to overstate fixed asset values, which leads to understated or non-comparable leverage ratios? As a consequence of overstated fixed asset values, high depreciation charges may lead to relatively understated earnings. |
| | *Devaluation risk* | Does the currency of debt obligations expose the company to devaluation risk? How well matched by currency are revenues versus debt? |
| | *Access to capital* | This is often a key constraint for emerging market issuers, which broadly penalises their credit quality relative to those of firms in developed markets. |
| | *Debt maturity structure* | For emerging market issuers, concentration in short-term debt, whether home- or local-currency denominated, exposes the company to critical rollover risk. |
| | *Local dividend payout requirements* | Do the requirements make dividends more like a fixed cost? In Chile, public companies must pay out a minimum 30% of net income as dividends, while Brazil has a 25% minimum requirement. On the other hand, this explicit link of payments to profits gives companies more flexibility to lower dividends when profits decrease. |
| | *Liquidity restrictions* | Is the company's liquid asset position held in local government bonds, local banks, or local equities, and will the issuer have access to these assets at times of stress on the sovereign. |

Source: Standard & Poor's

**Table 15.4.** euromoney risk factors for country risk analysis

| Political risk | The risk of non-payment or non-servicing of payment for goods or services, loans, trade-related finance and dividends, and the non-repatriation of capital. Risk analysts give each country a score between 10 and zero - the higher, the better. This does not reflect the creditworthiness of individual counterparties. |
|---|---|
| Economic performance | It is based (1) on GNI (Atlas Method) figures per capita and (2) on results of euromoney poll of economic projections, where each country's score is obtained from average projections for the current year and the next year. The sum of these two factors, equally weighted, makes up this column - the higher the result, the better. |
| Debt indicators | These are calculated using these ratios from the World Bank's World Development Indicators (the most recent issue): total debt stocks to GNP (A), debt service to exports (B); current account balance to GNP (C). Scores are calculated as follows: A + (B x 2) - (C x 10). The lower this score, the better. |
| Debt in default or rescheduled | Scores are based on the ratio of rescheduled debt to debt stocks, taken from the World Bank's World Development Indicators (the most recent issue). The lower the ratio, the better. OECD and developing countries which do not report under the debtor reporting system (DRS) score 10 and zero respectively. |
| Credit ratings | Nominal values are assigned to sovereign ratings from Moody's, S&P and Fitch IBCA. The higher the average value, the better. Where there is no rating, countries score zero. |
| Access to bank finance | It is calculated from disbursements of private, long-term, un-guaranteed loans as a percentage of GNP. The higher the result, the better. OECD and developing countries not reporting under the DRS score five and zero respectively. Source: the World Bank's World Development Indicators (the most recent issue). |
| Access to short-term finance | It takes into account OECD consensus groups (source: ECGD) and short-term cover available from the US Exim Bank and NCM UK. The higher the score, the better. |
| Access to capital markets | Heads of debt syndicate and loan syndications rated each country's accessibility to international markets at the time of the survey. The higher the average rating out of 10, the better. |
| Discount on forfeiting | It reflects the average maximum tenor for forfeiting and the average spread over riskless countries such as the US. The higher the score, the better. Countries where forfeiting is not available score zero. |

Source: euromoney

**Table 15.5.** Selected country risk ratings – WMRC

| World Markets Research Centre | | | | | | | | | |
|---|---|---|---|---|---|---|---|---|---|
| Country Risk Centre | | | | | | | | | |
| Country | Current Overall Risk | 12 Month Trend | Last Risk Change | Pol: 25% | Eco: 25% | Leg: 15% | Tax: 15% | Ope: 10% | Sec: 10% |
| Luxembourg | 1.15 | No Change | 01-Nov-98 | 1 | 1 | 1 | 1.5 | 1.5 | 1 |
| Switzerland | 1.26 | Higher Risk | 24-Apr-03 | 1.5 | 1.25 | 1 | 1 | 1.5 | 1 |
| Ireland | 1.35 | Lower Risk | 24-Apr-03 | 1.5 | 1.5 | 1 | 1 | 1.75 | 1 |
| Australia | 1.47 | Higher Risk | 24-Apr-03 | 1.5 | 1.25 | 1 | 1.5 | 1.5 | 2.25 |
| Norway | 1.49 | Higher Risk | 24-Apr-03 | 1.75 | 1.25 | 1 | 2 | 1.5 | 1 |
| United States | 1.6 | Higher Risk | 04-Jul-03 | 1.5 | 1.5 | 1 | 1 | 1.5 | 3 |
| Austria | 1.62 | Higher Risk | 24-Apr-03 | 2 | 1.75 | 1 | 1.5 | 1.5 | 1.25 |
| France | 1.69 | Higher Risk | 24-Apr-03 | 1.5 | 1.75 | 1 | 1.5 | 2 | 2.5 |
| Spain | 1.69 | Higher Risk | 04-Jul-03 | 1.25 | 1.75 | 1.5 | 1.5 | 2 | 2.5 |
| Chile | 1.75 | Lower Risk | 24-Apr-03 | 1.75 | 2 | 1.5 | 1.5 | 1.5 | 2 |
| Japan | 1.86 | Higher Risk | 24-Apr-03 | 1.5 | 2.5 | 1.5 | 1.75 | 1.75 | 1.5 |
| Uruguay | 2.21 | No Change | 24-Apr-03 | 2.25 | 2.75 | 2 | 1.5 | 2 | 2 |
| South Africa | 2.22 | Lower Risk | 24-Apr-03 | 2.25 | 2.25 | 2 | 1.5 | 2 | 3.25 |
| Malaysia | 2.23 | Higher Risk | 15-May-03 | 2.5 | 2.5 | 2 | 1.5 | 1.75 | 2.5 |
| Tunisia | 2.33 | Lower Risk | 04-Jul-03 | 2.25 | 2.5 | 2.5 | 2.5 | 2.25 | 1.5 |
| Mexico | 2.48 | Lower Risk | 24-Apr-03 | 2.25 | 2.5 | 2.5 | 2 | 3 | 3 |
| Croatia | 2.56 | Higher Risk | 24-Apr-03 | 2.75 | 2.5 | 2.5 | 2.5 | 2.5 | 2.5 |
| Israel | 2.56 | Higher Risk | 24-Apr-03 | 2.75 | 3 | 1 | 1.5 | 2.25 | 3.75 |
| Brazil | 2.63 | Lower Risk | 29-May-03 | 2.5 | 2.75 | 2 | 3 | 2.5 | 3 |
| Senegal | 2.64 | Higher Risk | 24-Apr-03 | 2.5 | 2.75 | 2.5 | 3 | 2.5 | 2.5 |
| Bulgaria | 2.76 | No Change | 24-Apr-03 | 2.5 | 2.75 | 3 | 2.75 | 2.75 | 3 |
| Saudi Arabia | 2.76 | Higher Risk | 16-May-03 | 3 | 2.5 | 3 | 2.25 | 2.5 | 3.25 |
| Turkey | 2.78 | Higher Risk | 04-Jul-03 | 3 | 2.5 | 2 | 3 | 3 | 3.25 |
| Kazakhstan | 2.86 | Lower Risk | 24-Apr-03 | 2.75 | 2.75 | 3 | 3 | 3.25 | 2.5 |
| Lebanon | 2.89 | Lower Risk | 04-Jul-03 | 3 | 3 | 2.5 | 2.5 | 3.25 | 3 |
| China | 2.93 | Lower Risk | 24-Apr-03 | 3 | 2.5 | 3.25 | 3 | 3.25 | 2.75 |
| Egypt | 2.98 | Lower Risk | 04-Jul-03 | 2.75 | 3 | 3.5 | 3 | 3 | 2.5 |
| Lesotho | 3 | Lower Risk | 24-Apr-03 | 3.5 | 3 | 2.5 | 2.5 | 3 | 3 |
| Russia | 3.01 | Lower Risk | 07-Jul-03 | 2.75 | 3 | 2.75 | 2.75 | 3.5 | 3.75 |
| Syria | 3.01 | Lower Risk | 04-Jul-03 | 2.75 | 3 | 3 | 3.5 | 3.5 | 2.25 |
| Sri Lanka | 3.02 | Lower Risk | 24-Apr-03 | 3.25 | 3 | 2.5 | 3 | 3 | 3.25 |
| Argentina | 3.03 | Lower Risk | 11-Sep-03 | 3.5 | 3.5 | 2 | 2.5 | 3 | 2.5 |
| Madagascar | 3.15 | Lower Risk | 24-Apr-03 | 3.25 | 3.5 | 3 | 3 | 3 | 2.5 |
| El Salvador | 3.17 | No Change | 01-Nov-98 | 3 | 3.5 | 3 | 2.5 | 3.5 | 3.5 |
| Ethiopia | 3.27 | Higher Risk | 24-Apr-03 | 3.25 | 3.25 | 3.25 | 3 | 3.25 | 3.75 |
| Mongolia | 3.27 | No Change | 12-Jan-00 | 3.5 | 3.5 | 3 | 3 | 3.5 | 2.5 |
| Cuba | 3.31 | No Change | 01-Nov-98 | 3.5 | 3.5 | 3.5 | 3 | 3.5 | 2 |
| Colombia | 3.41 | No Change | 24-Jun-99 | 3.5 | 3.5 | 3 | 2.5 | 4 | 4 |
| Macedonia (FYR) | 3.41 | No Change | 23-Mar-01 | 3.5 | 3 | 3 | 3 | 3.5 | 4 |
| Tanzania | 3.43 | Lower Risk | 24-Apr-03 | 3 | 3.75 | 3.5 | 3.5 | 3.75 | 3 |
| Azerbaijan | 3.45 | Higher Risk | 04-Jul-03 | 3.5 | 3.25 | 3.5 | 3 | 4 | 3.75 |
| Ecuador | 3.47 | No Change | 10-Mar-99 | 3.5 | 4 | 3.5 | 3 | 3 | 3 |
| Algeria | 3.5 | Lower Risk | 24-Apr-03 | 3.75 | 3.5 | 3 | 2.5 | 4 | 4.25 |
| Mozambique | 3.5 | Higher Risk | 24-Apr-03 | 3.75 | 3.75 | 3.5 | 2.5 | 3.75 | 3.25 |
| Georgia | 3.51 | Higher Risk | 24-Apr-03 | 3.5 | 3.5 | 3.25 | 3.25 | 4 | 3.75 |
| Bangladesh | 3.52 | Higher Risk | 24-Apr-03 | 3.25 | 4.25 | 3.25 | 3 | 3.5 | 3.25 |
| Uzbekistan | 3.64 | Lower Risk | 24-Apr-03 | 3.25 | 4 | 4 | 3 | 4 | 3.5 |
| Congo | 3.73 | Lower Risk | 24-Apr-03 | 3.5 | 3.5 | 4 | 4 | 4 | 3.75 |
| Libya | 3.76 | Lower Risk | 24-Apr-03 | 3.25 | 3.5 | 4 | 4.75 | 4 | 3.25 |
| Angola | 3.8 | Lower Risk | 24-Apr-03 | 4 | 4 | 3.25 | 3.5 | 4 | 3.75 |
| Sierra Leone | 4 | Lower Risk | 24-Apr-03 | 4 | 4 | 4 | 4 | 3.75 | 4.25 |
| Zimbabwe | 4.01 | Higher Risk | 24-Apr-03 | 4.25 | 4.25 | 4 | 3.5 | 3.75 | 3.75 |
| Somalia | 4.72 | Lower Risk | 24-Apr-03 | 4.5 | 4.75 | 5 | 5 | 4.5 | 4.5 |
| Iraq | 4.88 | Higher Risk | 23-May-03 | 5 | 4.75 | 4.75 | 5 | 5 | 4.75 |

Source: World Markets Research Centre

**Table 15.6.** Selected country risk ratings in September 2003 – euromoney

| Rank | Country | Total 100 | (1) 25 | (2) 25 | (3) 10 | (4) 10 | (5) 10 | (6) 5 | (7) 5 | (8) 5 | (9) 5 |
|---|---|---|---|---|---|---|---|---|---|---|---|
| 1 | Luxembourg | 99.36 | 24.67 | 25.00 | 10.00 | 10.00 | 10.00 | 5.00 | 5.00 | 5.00 | 4.69 |
| 2 | Norway | 97.75 | 24.51 | 23.55 | 10.00 | 10.00 | 10.00 | 5.00 | 5.00 | 5.00 | 4.69 |
| 3 | Switzerland | 97.48 | 24.97 | 22.81 | 10.00 | 10.00 | 10.00 | 5.00 | 5.00 | 5.00 | 4.69 |
| 4 | United States | 96.64 | 24.95 | 21.69 | 10.00 | 10.00 | 10.00 | 5.00 | 5.00 | 5.00 | 5.00 |
| 5 | Denmark | 95.27 | 24.62 | 21.17 | 10.00 | 10.00 | 9.79 | 5.00 | 5.00 | 5.00 | 4.69 |
| 6 | United Kingdom | 93.93 | 25.00 | 19.24 | 10.00 | 10.00 | 10.00 | 5.00 | 5.00 | 5.00 | 4.69 |
| 7 | Finland | 93.82 | 24.59 | 19.54 | 10.00 | 10.00 | 10.00 | 5.00 | 5.00 | 5.00 | 4.69 |
| 8 | Sweden | 93.79 | 24.34 | 20.17 | 10.00 | 10.00 | 9.58 | 5.00 | 5.00 | 5.00 | 4.69 |
| 9 | Netherlands | 93.48 | 24.51 | 19.28 | 10.00 | 10.00 | 10.00 | 5.00 | 5.00 | 5.00 | 4.69 |
| 10 | Austria | 92.37 | 23.96 | 18.72 | 10.00 | 10.00 | 10.00 | 5.00 | 5.00 | 5.00 | 4.69 |
| 91 | Senegal | 39.58 | 8.43 | 5.86 | 8.70 | 10.00 | 1.88 | 0.25 | 2.33 | 0.00 | 2.12 |
| 92 | Seychelles | 39.21 | 9.34 | 6.16 | 9.29 | 10.00 | 0.00 | 0.00 | 3.92 | 0.50 | 0.00 |
| 93 | Honduras | 39.19 | 8.60 | 7.15 | 8.72 | 9.23 | 1.25 | 0.39 | 2.50 | 0.00 | 1.35 |
| 94 | Ukraine | 39.03 | 8.05 | 7.79 | 9.40 | 8.77 | 1.46 | 0.73 | 1.83 | 1.00 | 0.00 |
| 95 | Bhutan | 38.43 | 10.79 | 6.34 | 9.14 | 10.00 | 0.00 | 0.00 | 2.17 | 0.00 | 0.00 |
| 96 | Guyana | 38.42 | 8.90 | 10.18 | 7.17 | 10.00 | 0.00 | 0.00 | 2.17 | 0.00 | 0.00 |
| 97 | Bangladesh | 38.35 | 9.12 | 5.23 | 9.43 | 10.00 | 0.00 | 0.00 | 2.67 | 0.00 | 1.90 |
| 98 | Lebanon | 38.09 | 7.69 | 5.94 | 7.75 | 10.00 | 0.83 | 0.24 | 2.33 | 1.00 | 2.30 |
| 99 | Uganda | 37.80 | 7.34 | 7.20 | 8.66 | 10.00 | 0.00 | 0.00 | 2.33 | 0.00 | 2.27 |
| 100 | Bolivia | 37.48 | 7.34 | 6.92 | 8.48 | 10.00 | 0.94 | 0.47 | 2.33 | 1.00 | 0.00 |
| 176 | DR Congo | 18.36 | 2.60 | 4.59 | 0.00 | 10.00 | 0.00 | 0.00 | 1.17 | 0.00 | 0.00 |
| 177 | New Caledonia | 18.22 | 13.53 | 4.69 | 0.00 | 0.00 | 0.00 | 0.00 | 0.00 | 0.00 | 0.00 |
| 178 | Micronesia | 13.92 | 10.79 | 0.63 | 0.00 | 0.00 | 0.00 | 0.00 | 2.50 | 0.00 | 0.00 |
| 179 | Somalia | 13.18 | 1.86 | 0.15 | 0.00 | 10.00 | 0.00 | 0.00 | 1.17 | 0.00 | 0.00 |
| 180 | Cuba | 11.96 | 1.89 | 8.90 | 0.00 | 0.00 | 0.00 | 0.00 | 1.17 | 0.00 | 0.00 |
| 181 | Liberia | 11.57 | 0.74 | 0.00 | 0.00 | 10.00 | 0.00 | 0.00 | 0.83 | 0.00 | 0.00 |
| 182 | Marshall | 10.66 | 8.52 | 0.64 | 0.00 | 0.00 | 0.00 | 0.00 | 1.50 | 0.00 | 0.00 |
| 183 | Afghanistan | 7.81 | 2.71 | 0.68 | 0.00 | 0.00 | 0.00 | 0.00 | 0.83 | 0.00 | 3.59 |
| 184 | Iraq | 4.28 | 0.74 | 2.71 | 0.00 | 0.00 | 0.00 | 0.00 | 0.83 | 0.00 | 0.00 |
| 185 | Korea North | 3.26 | 0.00 | 2.09 | 0.00 | 0.00 | 0.00 | 0.00 | 1.17 | 0.00 | 0.00 |

Source: euromoney

financial policy, profitability/cash flow and capital structure/financial flexibility. Within the financial policy area, there are three risk elements: disclosure/local accounting standards issues, foreign exchange risks, and family/group ownership issues. The profitability/cash flow area also covers three risk elements: potential price controls, inflation/currency fluctuation risk, restricted access to subsidiary cash flow. Finally the capital structure/financial flexibility area includes six risk elements of inflation accounting, devaluation risk, access to capital, debt maturity structure, local dividend payout requirements, and liquidity restrictions. Table 15.3 presents these risk factors, together with the discussions of the ways in which each of the risks is assessed.

Euromoney is another important player in country risk analysis. In assessing the overall country risk, euromoney has identified nine risk factors: political risk (weighting 25%), economic performance (weighting 25%), debt indicators (weighting 10%), debt in default or rescheduled (weighting 10%), credit ratings (weighting 10%), access to bank finance (weighting 5%), access to short-term finance (weighting 5%), access to capital markets (weighting 5%), discount on forfeiting (weighting 5%). euromoney adopts a 0 – 100 scale for country risk ratings. In contrast to the WMRC, the higher the score, the lower is the risk with the euromoney methodology. Table 15.4 presents the risk factors and their assessment by euromoney. Selected country risk ratings by the WMRC and euromoney are listed in Table 15.6 and Table 15.7 respectively.

Other major rating agencies involved in country risk analysis include the Institutional Investor, Moody's and the Economist Intelligence Unit. While it is worth mentioning that they all provide some kinds of country risk analysis services, this chapter does not intend to cover them all and to show and explain all their similarities and differences. The classifications of the risk factors of the WMRC, the S&P and euromoney appear to differ significantly in their expression, but they all fit our four factor analytical framework one way or another. For example, the legal risk of the WMRC is largely covered by the social institution, the tax risk is covered by economic environment, the operational risk is covered partly by the economic environment and partly by the social institution, and the security risk is largely included in the political climate. The risk factors of the S&P can also fit into our four risk factor framework. Although the S&P has only two categories of the business risk factors and the financial risk factors in their country risk analysis model, some of the factors are political and social in nature. It is the convention of the S&P to assess country risk following its traditional credit rating practice.

Finally, samples of country risk ratings by the WMRC and euromoney are provided. Table 15.5 is selected country risk ratings by the WMRC. The countries in the table are ranked in an ascending way according to their risk ratings. The second column is the latest ratings available, with the fourth column giving the date of last risk change. The third column indicates whether the risk rating for a country increases or decreases in a 12 months horizon. Columns 6-10 are risk ratings in the six categories of the political risk, the economic risk, the legal risk, the tax risk, the operational risk and the security risk, which contribute to the overall risk with the assigned weightings. The WMRC assign 1 to the lowest risk and 5 to the highest risk for all of the six risk categories, as being described in the methodology part. According to the WMRC, Luxemburg enjoys the lowest country risk in the world with a country risk rating of 1.15. Inspecting the sources of risk, it is found that Luxemburg's country risk arises largely from its tax risk and operational risk. Moreover, Luxemburg is highly stable with regard to country risk – its country risk rating has not changed since November 1998. On the other hand, Iraq involves the highest country risk in the world with a country risk rating of 4.88 as in May 2003. Comparing the two countries, it can be easily imagined that country risk is not the only consideration in international investment decision making processes; it may not be the major consideration either in many cases. In the between, most western industrialised countries, such as the US, France, Norway and Japan, possess low country risk. Large developing countries like the People's Republic, Brazil, Argentina and Mexico possess medium country risk.

Table 15.6 provides a selection of country risk ratings from euromoney as in September 2003 – top ten countries with the lowest country risk, top ten countries with the highest country risk, and ten countries in the middle. euromoney's ranking scale is 0 – 100, with 100 being the lowest country risk rating and 0 the highest risk rating. Luxemburg again tops the ratings list with an almost full risk rating score of 100 (99.36). The ten lowest risk countries are exclusively in Western Europe except the US. Iraq is considered to incur the highest country risk second only to North Korea. The two countries have a country risk rating of 4.28 and 3.26 out of 100 respectively.

## 15.3 Sovereign Risk Analysis and Ratings

Sovereign risk refers to the risk that a host government or sovereign power will default on its payment obligations by unilaterally repudiating its foreign obligations or preventing local firms from honouring their foreign obligations. In a sense it is similar to the credit risk of corporations, but the entity is a sovereign state rather than a business firm, and the scope is wider, which covers the sovereign government as well as the issuers in that sovereign state. On the other hand, sovereign risk can also be regarded to have been encompassed by country risk to a certain extent. Consequently, some rating agencies use the same or similar rating grades for sovereign risk as for credit risk, such as Moody's and the S&P, while some other agencies follow the methodology similar to that for country risk analysis in their sovereign risk rating practice, such as the WMRC. In some cases, sovereign risk is simply applied to government bonds; and in some other cases, sovereign risk refers to the risk of all sort of default on payments within the jurisdiction of a sovereign state.

In assessing sovereign risk, the S&P takes the following factors into consideration: actions by the sovereign, government ownership and regulation, duration of controls, governing law, and special cases. Sovereign risk here is the risk of all sort of default on payments within the jurisdiction of a sovereign state. These factors are relevant and important for the following reasons:

> *Actions by the sovereign*: Sovereign governments in many countries act to constrain an issuer's ability to meet offshore debt obligations in a timely manner. While higher-rated sovereigns are not expected to interfere with the issuer's ability to use available funds to meet such offshore obligations, the chances of some form of intervention increase significantly for entities domiciled in lower-rated nations. At a time of local economic stress, when foreign exchange is viewed as an increasingly

scarce and valuable commodity, the likelihood of direct constraint, intervention, or interference with access to foreign exchange can be high. For this reason alone, it is unlikely that most issuers' ability to meet offshore debt obligations in a timely manner can be viewed as more probable than their sovereign's own likelihood of meeting their offshore debt obligations.

*Government ownership and regulation*: Many of the entities issuing debt that are domiciled in low-rated countries are partially, or completely, government owned. If foreign exchange controls are imposed, it is unlikely that government owned institutions would be permitted or would choose to circumvent government controls.

*Duration of controls*: When controls or restrictions are imposed, their duration cannot be predicted. In some instances, controls have lasted for only a few weeks or months, and in some others, they have been applied selectively. In still other cases, they have been much longer lasting and all encompassing.

*Governing law*: The law governing a specific debt issue, as well as other legal factors, may be relevant in evaluating whether a sovereign could affect timely payment on a debt obligation. When sovereign powers are involved, issues such as conflicts of law, waivers, and permission to hold and use funds held outside the country of domicile are confused at best and would likely be tested and resolved by the courts only after, rather than prior to, a default.

*Special cases*: In some instances, an issuer is technically domiciled in a particular country for tax or reasons other than business undertaken within that country. For example, issuers domiciled in certain specified financial centres are viewed as independent of that financial centre's sovereign risk. No substantial business is undertaken within that jurisdiction; no substantive assets are maintained in that jurisdiction; and the issuer could change its location quickly and without risk to the debt-holder should the sovereign impose any form of controls or onerous taxes. In the case of multilateral lending institutions, such as the International Bank for Reconstruction and Development (World Bank) and the International Finance Corporation (IFC), enjoy preferred creditor status. By virtue of the borrowing country's membership in the lending organization and as a condition of eligibility to receive loans, the country assures that it will not impose any currency restriction or other impairment to the repayment of such loans. In some cases, the treaty establishing the organisation also specifies such special treatment of loans by member nations.

The WMRC adopts an eight factor model for sovereign risk analysis. These factors and their weightings are listed in Table 15.7. Factors 1 – 5 are financial factors, contributing to 50% of the total score. The other three are called economic, structural and political factors, making up the rest 50% of the total score. The overall sovereign risk rating score is on a 0 – 100 scale, with 0 indicating the lowest sovereign risk and 100 the highest sovereign risk.

**Table 15.7.** Sovereign risk factors and weightings of WMRC

| Sovereign Risk Model Outline: Maximum Potential Risk Associated with Each Factor (or 'weighted factors') | |
|---|---|
| 1. Total Debt / Exports or GDP | 10% |
| 2. Debt Service Ratio | 10% |
| 3. Liquidity Gap Ratio | 10% |
| 4. Current a/c / GNP Ratio | 10% |
| 5. Import Coverage | 10% |
| 6. Commodity Reliance | 5% |
| 7. Economic Structure and Policy Management | 25% |
| 8. Political and Strategic Risk | 20% |
| **Total** | **100%** |

Two examples of sovereign risk ratings by the S&P and the WMRC are provided in Table 15.8 and Table 15.9 respectively. We can observe that the grades for sovereign risk ratings by the S&P are the same as in its credit risk ratings. Indeed, sovereigns and corporations are listed together. One can choose a filter to obtain ratings for required identities from the S&P's website, as illustrated by Table 15.8. The WMRC also provides other rating agencies' sovereign risk assessment along with its own ratings for comparison purposes.

**Table 15.8.** Selected sovereign risk ratings as of 11 September 2003 by S&P

**Results For:    Sovereigns**

Filter by:    > Region: | Europe, Middle East, Africa ▼ |

> Country: | All ▼ |

Optional > Name: [          ]                                    **FILTER** ▶

(Entity / Issuer Name)

| ▲Entity | Local Currency | Foreign Currency | National Scale | Type[a] |
|---|---|---|---|---|
| Austria (Republic of) | AAA/Stable/A-1+ | AAA/Stable/A-1+ | | ICR |
| Belgium (Kingdom of) | AA+/Stable/A-1+ | AA+/Stable/A-1+ | | ICR |
| Botswana (Republic of) | A+/Stable/A-1 | A/Stable/A-1 | | ICR |
| Bulgaria (Republic of) | BBB-/Stable/A-3 | BB+/Stable/B | | ICR |
| Caisse d'Amortissement de la Dette Sociale | AAA/Stable/A-1+ | AAA/Stable/A-1+ | | ICR |
| Central American Bank for Economic Integration | | BBB-/Positive/A-3 | | ICR |
| Corporacion de Reservas Estrategicas de Productos Petroliferos | AA+/Positive/A-1+ | AA+/Positive/A-1+ | | ICR |
| Croatia (Republic of) | BBB+/Stable/A-2 | BBB-/Stable/A-3 | | ICR |
| Cyprus (Republic of) | A+/Stable/A-1 | A/Stable/A-1 | | ICR |
| Czech Republic | A+/Stable/A-1 | A-/Stable/A-2 | | ICR |
| Denmark (Kingdom of) | AAA/Stable/A-1+ | AAA/Stable/A-1+ | | ICR |

a. ICR: Issuer Credit Ratings; FSR: Financial Strength Ratings
Source: Standard & Poor's

**Table 15.9.** Selected sovereign risk ratings in Americas as of 21 August 2003 by WMRC

| WMRC Scoreboard | | | | Sovereign Credit Risk Rating: Placings | | | | |
|---|---|---|---|---|---|---|---|---|
| Country | Outlook ▲ = Positive ▷ = Stable ▼ = Negative | DEFINES (Default probability continuum) | WMRC Risk Score Scale: 0-100 | Rating Agency's view v WMRC: | | | CONSENSUS RATING | |
| | | | | Moody's | Standard & Poor's | Fitch IBCA | Country | WMRC Score Sheet |
| US | ▶ | Highest Quality | 0 (A) | Similar Risk | Similar Risk | Similar Risk | US | 0 (A) |
| | | Very High Quality | 5 (A) | | | | Canada | 5 (A) |
| Canada | ▶ | High Quality | 10 (A) | Lower Risk | Lower Risk | Similar Risk | | 10 (A) |
| | | Good Quality | 15 (A) | | | | Bermuda | 15 (A) |
| Bahamas | ▶ | Strong Payment Capacity | 20 (B) | Higher Risk | Not Rated | Not Rated | Cayman Islands | 20 (B) |
| Bermuda | ▶ | | | Lower Risk | Lower Risk | Lower Risk | | |
| Mexico | ▶ | Credit fundamentals should absorb most market pressures | 40 (C) | Lower Risk | Similar Risk | Similar Risk | Mexico | 40 (C) |
| | | | | | | | Trinidad & Tobago | |
| INVESTMENT GRADE | | | | | | | | |
| SPECULATIVE GRADE | | | | | | | | |
| Colombia | ▶ | Likely to fulfil obligations | 45 (D) | Higher Risk | Higher Risk | Higher Risk | Martinique | 45 (D) |
| Costa Rica | ▶ | Ongoing Uncertainty | 50 (D) | Lower Risk | Similar Risk | Similar Risk | Colombia | 50 (D) |
| | | | | | | | Panama | |
| | | | | | | | Antigua & Barbuda | |
| Venezuela | ▼ | | | Higher Risk | Higher Risk | Higher Risk | Peru | |
| | | | | | | | Jamaica | |
| Peru | ▶ | Very High Risk | 60 (E) | Lower Risk | Lower Risk | Lower Risk | Venezuela | 60 (E) |
| | | | | | | | Paraguay | |

*NB: Standard and Poor's, Moody's and Fitch IBCA are not associated with this service and WMRC makes no warranty or representation about the accuracy of their ratings.*
*NB: Euro = 'euro' currency-denominated long-term currency bonds issues by Euroland Sovereigns' are risk-rated at '0' or top-draw quality, equivalent to triple 'AAA'.*
Source: World Markets Research Centre

# 16 Foreign Direct Investment and International Portfolio Investment

According to the classification of the balance of payment, there are three major channels of international economic linkages between nations around the globe – exports/imports, foreign direct investment (FDI) and international portfolio investment (IPI). The latter two channels of international economic linkages, i.e., FDI and IPI, have become increasingly important and significant in the last two decades in the name of globalisation, leading to the recommendation and installation of the international investment position statement that records primarily FDI and IPI activities. The entries to the international investment position are the same and consistent with the balance of payments financial account, so FDI and IPI activities are recorded and can be analysed both as stocks of, and as flows to/from, a country in the global economy.

This chapter examines international investment in terms of FDI and IPI. It presents the recent profiles of international investment, discusses the channels, types and strategies of international investment and makes contract between them. We analyse international investment from the viewpoint of international economic linkages revealed by the balance of payments and the international investment position statement, taking into account opportunities, returns and risks involved in investing in foreign lands.

## 16.1 Recent Profiles of Foreign Direct Investment

As discussed in Chapter 4, FDI involves a significant degree of control and/or management in a corporation or other entities located in a foreign country with a long lasting interest. Estimation of FDI figures by the IMF involves three terms: direct investment enterprises, direct investors, and direct investment capital in foreign countries. Direct investment enterprises are defined as incorporated or unincorporated enterprises in which a direct investor who resides in another country owns 10 percent or more of the ordinary shares or voting power for an incorporated enterprise or the equivalent for an unincorporated enterprise. Direct investment enterprises include subsidiaries where a non-resident investor owns more than 50 percent, associates where a non-resident investor owns between 10 to 50 percent, and branches that are unincorporated enterprises wholly or jointly owned by the direct investor directly or indirectly. Direct investors can be individuals, incorporated or unincorporated private or public enterprises, associated groups of individuals or enterprises, governments or government agencies, or other entities that own direct investment enterprises in countries where the direct investors are non-residents. If combined ownership of an associated group of individuals or enterprises equals or exceeds 10 percent of the direct investment enterprise, the group is considered to have a degree of influence on management of the enterprise

**Table 16.1.** FDI inflows in country groups (US$ millions)

| GROUP | 1998 | 1999 | 2000 | 2001 |
|---|---|---|---|---|
| TOTAL WORLD | 694,457.30 | 1,088,263.00 | 1,491,934.00 | 735,145.70 |
| Developed countries | 484,239.00 | 837,760.70 | 1,227,476.00 | 503,144.00 |
| Western Europe | 274,738.80 | 507,221.70 | 832,067.40 | 336,210.00 |
| European Union | 262,215.90 | 487,897.50 | 808,518.80 | 322,954.20 |
| Other Western Europe | 12,522.90 | 19,324.20 | 23,548.60 | 13,255.80 |
| North America | 197,243.30 | 307,811.30 | 367,529.30 | 151,899.90 |
| Other developed countries | 12,256.80 | 22,727.70 | 27,879.70 | 15,034.10 |
| Least developed countries (LDCs) | 3,947.60 | 5,428.30 | 3,704.30 | 3,837.60 |
| Oil-exporting countries | 14,441.90 | 5,461.40 | 3,510.00 | 6,557.10 |
| Developing countries | 187,610.60 | 225,140.00 | 237,894.40 | 204,801.30 |
| Africa | 9,020.90 | 12,821.20 | 8,694.00 | 17,164.50 |
| North Africa | 2,788.10 | 4,896.30 | 2,903.70 | 5,323.40 |
| Other Africa | 6,232.80 | 7,924.90 | 5,790.30 | 11,841.10 |
| Latin America and the Caribbean | 82,203.30 | 109,310.80 | 95,405.40 | 85,372.60 |
| South America | 51,885.60 | 70,879.60 | 56,837.10 | 40,111.40 |
| Other Latin America & Caribbean | 30,317.70 | 38,431.20 | 38,568.40 | 45,261.20 |
| Asia and the Pacific | 96,386.50 | 103,008.00 | 133,795.00 | 102,264.20 |
| Asia | 96,109.20 | 102,779.40 | 133,706.60 | 102,066.10 |
| West Asia | 6,704.60 | 323.6 | 688.3 | 4,132.80 |
| Central Asia | 3,152.20 | 2,466.30 | 1,895.10 | 3,568.80 |
| South, East and South-East Asia | 86,252.40 | 99,989.50 | 131,123.20 | 94,364.60 |
| The Pacific | 277.3 | 228.5 | 88.4 | 198.1 |
| Central and Eastern Europe | 22,607.70 | 25,362.80 | 26,563.10 | 27,200.40 |
| All developing countries minus China | 143,859.60 | 184,821.00 | 197,122.40 | 157,955.30 |

Source: UNCTAD

that is similar to that of an individual with the same degree of ownership. Direct investment capital is capital provided by a direct investor to a direct investment enterprise either directly or through other related enterprises, or capital received from a direct investment enterprise by a direct investor. The above analysis indicates that 10 percent of ownership is considered by the IMF as the threshold, at or above which a significant degree of control in a corporation or other entities can be exerted by the investor who is subsequently defined as direct investor and whose investment as direct investment. Within such scope of reign, there are subsidiaries, associates and branches in the classification of FDI, depending on the degree of ownership and control.

According to the latest statistics of the United Nations Conference on Trade and Development (UNCTAD), the world FDI inflows reached a peak value of 1,491,934.00 million US dollars in 2000, and then were almost halved in 2001 to 735,145.70 million US dollars. It is claimed that the fall was caused by the decline in cross border mergers and acquisitions that account for the vast majority of FDI investment and most of the FDI growth over the last decade. Table 16.1 presents FDI inflows in country groups from 1998 to 2001. It can be observed that FDI inflows to developed countries account for about three quarters of the world total FDI inflows, as exhibited in Figure 16.1. So developing countries still do not play a significant role in this fast developing area of international economic collaboration, despite decades of hard work made by developing countries and extensive measures taken by a few of international organisations.

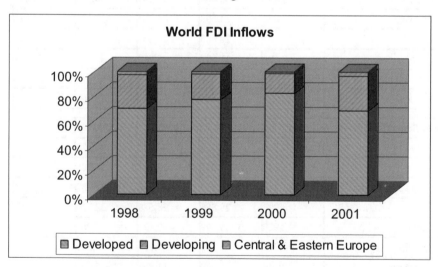

**Figure 16.1.** World FDI inflows in country groups 1998-2001

The top ten developed FDI host economies in 2001 are the US, the UK, France, Belgium & Luxembourg, the Netherlands, Germany, Canada, Spain, Italy and Sweden, according to the UNCTAD. FDI inflow figures for these economies

in the five years between 1997 and 2001 are provided in the top panel of Table
16.2. The top ten developing FDI host economies in 2001 are the PRC, Mexico,
the Hong Kong Special Administrative Region of the PRC, Brazil, Bermuda, Po-
land, Singapore, South Africa, Chile and the Czech Republic and FDI inflow figures for these economies in the five years between 1997 and 2001 are provided in
the lower panel of Table 16.2. If the two groups are mixed together, then the PRC
overtook the UK as the second largest FDI host country in 1997. While FDI inflows to the PRC have been stable in this period, FDI inflows to the UK in 2000
have more than tripled its 1997 figure, due to the increase in cross border mergers
and acquisitions that is particularly active in the west and the UK. Although then
the UK is the second largest FDI host country in the years up to 2001 when the
UNCTAD statistics end, the PRC once again overtook the UK in 2002.

**Table 16.2.** Top ten FDI host economies (US$ millions)

| Developed countries | 1997 | 1998 | 1999 | 2000 | 2001 |
|---|---|---|---|---|---|
| United States | 103,398 | 174,434 | 283,376 | 300,912 | 124,435 |
| United Kingdom | 33,229 | 74,324 | 87,973 | 116,552 | 53,799 |
| France | 23,174 | 30,984 | 47,070 | 42,930 | 52,623 |
| Belgium & Luxembourg | 11,998 | 22,691 | 133,059 | 245,561 | 50,996 |
| Netherlands | 11,132 | 36,964 | 41,289 | 52,453 | 50,471 |
| Germany | 12,244 | 24,593 | 54,754 | 195,122 | 31,833 |
| Canada | 11,527 | 22,809 | 24,435 | 66,617 | 27,465 |
| Spain | 7,697 | 11,797 | 15,758 | 37,523 | 21,781 |
| Italy | 3,700 | 2,635 | 6,911 | 13,377 | 14,873 |
| Sweden | 10,968 | 19,564 | 60,850 | 23,367 | 12,734 |

| Developing countries | 1997 | 1998 | 1999 | 2000 | 2001 |
|---|---|---|---|---|---|
| China | 44,237 | 43,751 | 40,319 | 40,772 | 46,846 |
| Mexico | 14,044 | 11,933 | 12,534 | 14,706 | 24,731 |
| Hong Kong, China | 11,368 | 14,770 | 24,596 | 61,938 | 22,834 |
| Brazil | 18,993 | 28,856 | 28,578 | 32,779 | 22,457 |
| Bermuda | 2,928 | 5,399 | 9,470 | 10,980 | 9,859 |
| Poland | 4,908 | 6,365 | 7,270 | 9,342 | 8,830 |
| Singapore | 10,746 | 6,389 | 11,803 | 5,407 | 8,609 |
| South Africa | 3,817 | 561 | 1,502 | 888 | 6,653 |
| Chile | 5,219 | 4,638 | 9,221 | 3,674 | 5,508 |
| Czech Republic | 1,300 | 3,718 | 6,324 | 4,986 | 4,916 |

Source: UNCTAD

While the US and the PRC appear to top the list of FDI host economies, their sizes of the economy are enormous. Therefore the ranking of inward FDI performance may take into account the size of the economy in concern. The inward FDI performance index has consequently been devised to remove the effect of the size of the economy. It is the inward FDI to an economy adjusted by its GDP – the ratio of an economy's share in global FDI inflows to its share in global GDP, namely:

$$FDIPI_i = \frac{FDI_i/FDI_w}{GDP_i/GDP_w} \qquad (16.1)$$

where $FDIPI_i$ is the inward FDI performance index of the $i^{th}$ country, $FDI_i$ is FDI inflows to the $i^{th}$ country, $FDI_w$ is world FDI inflows, $GDP_i$ is GDP produced in the $i^{th}$ country, and $GDP_w$ is world GDP.

However, size does matter in many cases and the size effect should not be removed completely. Moreover, there are other factors that affect the attractiveness of an economy to foreign investors and influence the location decision by MNCs. So, the UNCTAD has devised another index, the potentials index, with a multifactor model. 12 equally weighted factors are included. They are:

(a)     GDP per capita, an indicator of the sophistication and breadth of local demand and of several other factors, with the expectation that higher income economies attract relatively more FDI geared to innovative and differentiated products and services.

(b)     The rate of GDP growth over the previous 10 years, a proxy for expected economic growth.

(c)     The share of exports in GDP, to capture openness and competitiveness.

(d)     The average number of telephone lines per 1,000 inhabitants and mobile telephones per 1,000 inhabitants, as an indicator of modern information and communication infrastructure.

(e)     Commercial energy use per capita, for the availability of traditional infrastructure.

(f)     The share of R&D spending in GDP, to capture local technological capabilities.

(g)     The share of tertiary students in the population, indicating the availability of high-level skills.

**Table 16.3.** FDI Performance Index 1999-2001

| Rank | Economy | Score | Rank | Economy | Score |
|---|---|---|---|---|---|
| 1 | Belgium&Luxembourg | 10.955 | 71 | Venezuela | 0.902 |
| 2 | Angola | 6.455 | 72 | Mexico | 0.9 |
| 3 | Hong Kong, China | 6.387 | 73 | Costa Rica | 0.871 |
| 4 | Ireland | 5.861 | 74 | Austria | 0.855 |
| 5 | Malta | 4.465 | 75 | Romania | 0.81 |
| 6 | Singapore | 3.978 | 76 | Tunisia | 0.763 |
| 7 | Sweden | 3.857 | 77 | Ghana | 0.736 |
| 8 | Netherlands | 3.74 | 78 | Peru | 0.726 |
| 9 | Denmark | 3.485 | 79 | United States | 0.719 |
| 10 | Brunei Darussalam | 3.445 | 80 | Colombia | 0.7 |
| 11 | Czech Republic | 2.929 | 81 | South Africa | 0.696 |
| 12 | Gambia | 2.861 | 82 | Benin | 0.669 |
| 13 | Nicaragua | 2.81 | 83 | Nigeria | 0.639 |
| 14 | Bolivia | 2.735 | 84 | Uzbekistan | 0.634 |
| 15 | Kazakhstan | 2.714 | 85 | Myanmar | 0.63 |
| 16 | Congo, Rep. | 2.519 | 86 | Cote d'Ivoire | 0.627 |
| 17 | Guyana | 2.316 | 87 | Belarus | 0.532 |
| 18 | Moldova, Republic of | 2.314 | 88 | Ukraine | 0.524 |
| 19 | Chile | 2.273 | 89 | Madagascar | 0.514 |
| 20 | Cyprus | 2.227 | 90 | Philippines | 0.514 |
| 21 | Estonia | 2.211 | 91 | Australia | 0.495 |
| 22 | Croatia | 2.003 | 92 | Korea, Republic of | 0.483 |
| 23 | Jamaica | 2.001 | 93 | Tajikistan | 0.476 |
| 24 | Mozambique | 1.939 | 94 | Senegal | 0.475 |
| 25 | Bulgaria | 1.926 | 95 | El Salvador | 0.459 |
| 26 | Slovakia | 1.836 | 96 | Lebanon | 0.454 |
| 27 | Trinidad and Tobago | 1.811 | 97 | Iceland | 0.417 |
| 28 | United Kingdom | 1.806 | 98 | Qatar | 0.416 |
| 29 | TFYR Macedonia | 1.707 | 99 | Guatemala | 0.405 |
| 30 | Canada | 1.642 | 100 | Uruguay | 0.394 |
| 31 | Dominican Republic | 1.633 | 101 | Algeria | 0.386 |
| 32 | Panama | 1.581 | 102 | Taiwan, China | 0.385 |
| 33 | Azerbaijan | 1.573 | 103 | Syrian Arab Republic | 0.374 |
| 34 | Namibia | 1.535 | 104 | Paraguay | 0.372 |
| 35 | Ecuador | 1.523 | 105 | Slovenia | 0.36 |
| 36 | Switzerland | 1.511 | 106 | Ethiopia | 0.332 |
| 37 | Brazil | 1.443 | 107 | Kyrgyzstan | 0.321 |
| 38 | Armenia | 1.423 | 108 | Russian Federation | 0.314 |
| 39 | Germany | 1.419 | 109 | Italy | 0.297 |
| 40 | Tanzania | 1.373 | 110 | Egypt | 0.286 |
| 41 | Spain | 1.314 | 111 | Sri Lanka | 0.271 |
| 42 | Argentina | 1.311 | 112 | Turkey | 0.268 |
| 43 | Papua New Guinea | 1.293 | 113 | Greece | 0.258 |
| 44 | New Zealand | 1.279 | 114 | Guinea | 0.223 |
| 45 | Togo | 1.276 | 115 | Botswana | 0.222 |
| 46 | Morocco | 1.269 | 116 | Pakistan | 0.2 |
| 47 | Poland | 1.256 | 117 | Sierra Leone | 0.193 |
| 48 | Mongolia | 1.252 | 118 | Kenya | 0.192 |
| 49 | Finland | 1.246 | 119 | Burkina Faso | 0.182 |
| 50 | Viet Nam | 1.24 | 120 | India | 0.159 |
| 51 | Latvia | 1.21 | 121 | Niger | 0.156 |
| 52 | Portugal | 1.184 | 122 | Cameroon | 0.145 |
| 53 | Hungary | 1.168 | 123 | Haiti | 0.119 |
| 54 | Jordan | 1.163 | 124 | Zimbabwe | 0.112 |
| 55 | Honduras | 1.13 | 125 | Bangladesh | 0.111 |
| 56 | Bahrain | 1.126 | 126 | Rwanda | 0.072 |
| 57 | Sudan | 1.112 | 127 | Congo, Dem. Rep. | 0.065 |
| 58 | Uganda | 1.109 | 128 | Japan | 0.058 |
| 59 | China | 1.107 | 129 | Oman | 0.054 |
| 60 | Lithuania | 1.098 | 130 | Nepal | 0.044 |
| 61 | Thailand | 1.04 | 131 | Iran, Islamic Rep. | 0.011 |
| 62 | France | 1.01 | 132 | Kuwait | -0.016 |
| 63 | Georgia | 1.01 | 133 | Malawi | -0.034 |
| 64 | Zambia | 1.007 | 134 | Libya | -0.11 |
| 65 | Israel | 1.001 | 135 | Saudi Arabia | -0.144 |
| 66 | Bahamas | 0.987 | 136 | United Arab Emirates | -0.187 |
| 67 | Albania | 0.958 | 137 | Yemen | -0.203 |
| 68 | Mali | 0.923 | 138 | Indonesia | -0.68 |
| 69 | Norway | 0.918 | 139 | Gabon | -0.995 |
| 70 | Malaysia | 0.904 | 140 | Suriname | -1.613 |

Source: UNCTAD

**Table 16.4.** FDI Potentials Index 1999-2001

| Rank | Economy | Score | Rank | Economy | Score |
|------|---------|-------|------|---------|-------|
| 1 | United States | 0.689 | 71 | Brazil | 0.183 |
| 2 | Singapore | 0.49 | 72 | South Africa | 0.183 |
| 3 | Norway | 0.489 | 73 | Tunisia | 0.183 |
| 4 | United Kingdom | 0.489 | 74 | Iran, Islamic Rep. | 0.181 |
| 5 | Canada | 0.481 | 75 | Viet Nam | 0.179 |
| 6 | Germany | 0.457 | 76 | Suriname | 0.174 |
| 7 | Sweden | 0.455 | 77 | Gabon | 0.17 |
| 8 | Belgium&Luxembourg | 0.454 | 78 | Jamaica | 0.169 |
| 9 | Netherlands | 0.454 | 79 | Namibia | 0.168 |
| 10 | Finland | 0.445 | 80 | Peru | 0.167 |
| 11 | Ireland | 0.436 | 81 | Algeria | 0.166 |
| 12 | Japan | 0.428 | 82 | Bolivia | 0.163 |
| 13 | Hong Kong, China | 0.424 | 83 | Kazakhstan | 0.161 |
| 14 | France | 0.422 | 84 | India | 0.16 |
| 15 | Switzerland | 0.416 | 85 | Ukraine | 0.159 |
| 16 | Denmark | 0.411 | 86 | Turkey | 0.159 |
| 17 | Iceland | 0.41 | 87 | Gambia | 0.158 |
| 18 | Korea, Republic of | 0.408 | 88 | Yemen | 0.156 |
| 19 | Taiwan, China | 0.405 | 89 | Nigeria | 0.151 |
| 20 | Qatar | 0.404 | 90 | Syrian Arab Republic | 0.151 |
| 21 | Australia | 0.392 | 91 | Romania | 0.149 |
| 22 | Austria | 0.377 | 92 | Indonesia | 0.148 |
| 23 | Israel | 0.376 | 93 | Morocco | 0.148 |
| 24 | United Arab Emirates | 0.364 | 94 | Colombia | 0.147 |
| 25 | Spain | 0.354 | 95 | Uzbekistan | 0.144 |
| 26 | Italy | 0.35 | 96 | Honduras | 0.143 |
| 27 | New Zealand | 0.318 | 97 | Albania | 0.142 |
| 28 | Kuwait | 0.318 | 98 | Papua New Guinea | 0.142 |
| 29 | Slovenia | 0.315 | 99 | Uganda | 0.142 |
| 30 | Saudi Arabia | 0.304 | 100 | Myanmar | 0.139 |
| 31 | Bahrain | 0.301 | 101 | Guatemala | 0.138 |
| 32 | Brunei Darussalam | 0.297 | 102 | TFYR Macedonia | 0.137 |
| 33 | Malaysia | 0.295 | 103 | Ecuador | 0.136 |
| 34 | Portugal | 0.29 | 104 | Congo, Rep. | 0.135 |
| 35 | Russian Federation | 0.288 | 105 | Angola | 0.131 |
| 36 | Greece | 0.285 | 106 | Azerbaijan | 0.13 |
| 37 | Czech Republic | 0.271 | 107 | Paraguay | 0.128 |
| 38 | Estonia | 0.269 | 108 | Mozambique | 0.128 |
| 39 | Bahamas | 0.267 | 109 | Moldova, Republic of | 0.127 |
| 40 | China | 0.259 | 110 | Cote d´Ivoire | 0.126 |
| 41 | Hungary | 0.257 | 111 | Guinea | 0.126 |
| 42 | Cyprus | 0.255 | 112 | Nicaragua | 0.126 |
| 43 | Poland | 0.255 | 113 | Ghana | 0.123 |
| 44 | Malta | 0.254 | 114 | Madagascar | 0.122 |
| 45 | Chile | 0.245 | 115 | Cameroon | 0.119 |
| 46 | Croatia | 0.244 | 116 | Sri Lanka | 0.119 |
| 47 | Libya | 0.24 | 117 | Mali | 0.119 |
| 48 | Slovakia | 0.238 | 118 | Armenia | 0.119 |
| 49 | Mexico | 0.233 | 119 | Senegal | 0.118 |
| 50 | Oman | 0.222 | 120 | Malawi | 0.117 |
| 51 | Argentina | 0.22 | 121 | Bangladesh | 0.115 |
| 52 | Thailand | 0.214 | 122 | Togo | 0.112 |
| 53 | Panama | 0.214 | 123 | Sudan | 0.111 |
| 54 | El Salvador | 0.213 | 124 | Ethiopia | 0.11 |
| 55 | Latvia | 0.211 | 125 | Burkina Faso | 0.107 |
| 56 | Lithuania | 0.209 | 126 | Niger | 0.104 |
| 57 | Venezuela | 0.208 | 127 | Kenya | 0.104 |
| 58 | Lebanon | 0.206 | 128 | Kyrgyzstan | 0.102 |
| 59 | Botswana | 0.206 | 129 | Pakistan | 0.099 |
| 60 | Costa Rica | 0.205 | 130 | Tanzania | 0.096 |
| 61 | Trinidad and Tobago | 0.202 | 131 | Georgia | 0.096 |
| 62 | Guyana | 0.202 | 132 | Benin | 0.092 |
| 63 | Belarus | 0.201 | 133 | Nepal | 0.088 |
| 64 | Bulgaria | 0.201 | 134 | Zambia | 0.086 |
| 65 | Dominican Republic | 0.201 | 135 | Haiti | 0.076 |
| 66 | Philippines | 0.195 | 136 | Tajikistan | 0.075 |
| 67 | Uruguay | 0.192 | 137 | Zimbabwe | 0.075 |
| 68 | Jordan | 0.19 | 138 | Rwanda | 0.062 |
| 69 | Mongolia | 0.188 | 139 | Congo, Dem. Rep. | 0.047 |
| 70 | Egypt | 0.184 | 140 | Sierra Leone | 0.044 |

Source: UNCTAD

(h)    Country risk, a composite indicator capturing some macroeconomic and other factors that affect the risk perception of investors. The variable is measured in such a way that high values indicate less risk.

(i)    The world market share in exports of natural resources, to proxy for the availability of resources for extractive FDI.

(j)    The world market share of imports of parts and components for automobiles and electronic products, to capture participation in the leading MNC integrated production systems.

(k)    The world market share of exports of services, to seize the importance of FDI in the services sector that accounts for some two thirds of world FDI.

(l)    The share of world FDI inward stock, a broad indicator of the attractiveness and absorptive capacity for FDI, and the investment climate.

Table 16.3 ranks 140 economies according to their size adjusted FDI performance index based on 1999-2001 data. It obviously favours smaller economies and penalises larger ones. For example, the US and the PRC, the top two FDI host economies, are ranked $79^{th}$ and $59^{th}$ respectively; whereas Belgium & Luxembourg, Hong Kong, Malta and Singapore all remain or become top FDI performers. Comparatively, the potentials index in Table 16.4 presents a general picture about the relative attractiveness of 140 economies around the world. It can be observed that those on the top of the list are a mixture of small, medium and large economies, e.g., the US, Singapore, Norway, the UK and Canada. Therefore, the FDI potentials index in Table 16.4 may provide some helpful guidance in MNCs' location decision making processes. It is further advised by the UNCTAD to combine the use of the FDI performance index and the FDI potentials index with the following matrix.

|  | High FDI performance | Low FDI performance |
|---|---|---|
| High FDI potential | Front runners | Below potential |
| Low FDI potential | Above potential | Under performers |

Front runners are economies with high FDI potential and performance. Economies are considered to be above potential if they possess low FDI potential but strong FDI performance. Economies are regarded as being below potential if they possess high FDI potential but low FDI performance. Under performers are economies with both low FDI potential and performance. The first group, front runners, includes many industrial, newly industrialising and advanced transition economies. The last group, under performers, include mainly poor or unstable economies – all the South Asian economies and many poor and least developed countries, along with Turkey, with a weak record on risk and FDI stock. In 1999-2001, according to the UNCTAD, economies performing below potential include such major industrial countries as Australia, Italy, Japan and the US, and such newly industrialising economies as the Republic of Korea, the Philippines and Taiwan Province of China. The group also includes the Russian Federation, Saudi Arabia and United Arab Emirates, all countries with enormous resource bases that should be able to attract greater direct investment. Economies performing above potential include Brazil.

## 16.2 FDI Types and Strategies

FDI is one of the three major modes of foreign market entry as well as doing business in the foreign land. The other two modes are exporting and licensing. Exporting is the marketing and direct sale of domestically produced goods in a foreign country. Exporting is a traditional and well established method of reaching foreign markets. Since exporting does not require that the goods be produced in the target country, no investment in foreign production facilities is required. Most of the costs associated with exporting take the form of marketing expenses, which are usually higher than those in the domestic market, since the exporting firm need to acquire foreign sales information as well as knowledge in local custom and culture, among others. Licensing essentially permits a firm (licensee) in the foreign country to use the property of the licensor. Such property is usually intangible, e.g., trademarks, patents, and production techniques. The licensee pays a fee in exchange for the rights to use the intangible property with possible technical assistance. Because little investment on the part of the licensor is required, licensing has the potential to yield high returns. However, because the licensee produces and markets the product, potential returns from manufacturing and marketing activities may be lost.

Operating in a foreign country gives rise to additional tasks that incur additional human and monetary costs. These include logistics of co-ordinating activities across multiple sites, measures for dealing with legal, institutional and cultural issues, and efforts to acquire local knowledge. Therefore, a firm goes abroad must overcome the difficulties associated with doing business in a foreign land and successfully confront the challenges created in the due course. FDI is preferred to exporting or licensing under certain circumstances when the advantages of FDI can be materialised. Typically, FDI is perceived to have three major advantages: the ownership advantage, the location advantage and the internalisation advantage.

The ownership advantage suggests that business can be performed better within the firm than being negotiated between business partners with short-term financial interests. For example, there are following perceived benefits associated with the ownership of a subsidiary or a branch in the foreign country: (a) the potential of technology may be better exploited and cost saving in production and marketing processes may be better achieved when the activities are co-ordinated within the firm; (b) management and organisation skills of the parent firm may be readily transferred to the subsidiary to raise the efficiency in the subsidiary; (c) the good practice in the subsidiary may be transferred back to the parent firm or transferred to other subsidiaries, which has become increasingly important and imminent in recent years; (d) absorption of local knowledge is made easier under the same management team; (e) easy shifts of production between different sites or plants in response to changes in economic conditions, such as appreciation of the local currency in one of the host countries; and (f) institutional and cultural differences can be dealt with in a co-ordinated manner and the differences and diversities may serve as a propeller rather than an obstacle to the growth of the firm.

The location advantage means that there exist some benefits for the product to be made locally in the host country, including (a) lower factor prices such as labour costs and easy access to local finances; (b) higher transportation costs deterring trade and in favour of local production; (c) import restraints in the host country and other barriers to trade making exporting impossible or financially infeasible; (d) easy access to the host country's natural resources that are scarce in the home country; and (e) easy access to customers.

The internalisation advantage is derived to a certain extent from the ownership advantage. Market failure or market imperfections are one of the reasons to internalise business activities. The benefits of internalisation include (a) avoiding higher external transaction costs; (b) saving resources from writing excessively detailed contracts for every task and activity; (c) co-ordination activities in production and marketing can be effectively performed; (d) enforcement of various measures can be easily monitored; and (e) production lines can be rationally integrated.

FDI itself takes different forms and MNCs adopt different strategies in their FDI activities. There are three major forms of FDI – setting up a new firm or facility (Greenfield FDI); acquiring of, or merging with, an existing firm (M&A FDI); and expanding the existing firm or facility (Greenfield FDI). The first two forms of FDI are concerned with foreign entry or the start of a business in a foreign country, while the first and third forms of FDI together constitute Greenfield investment. An MNC's strategic considerations are always associated with the choice of FDI forms – to enter into a new market or expand in a market where the MNC has been operating already, and to acquire an existing company or establish a new one when entering into a new market? There are a number of factors that influence the choice of foreign entry modes – FDI versus exporting or licensing, the choice of FDI forms – Greenfield investments versus cross border mergers and acquisitions, and the choice of locations – the developed country versus the developing country or one developing country versus another developing country. These factors include, among others, the foreign exchange regime and arrangements of the host country, foreign exchange exposure arising from doing business in the host country, many factors covered by country risk analysis, and the rankings of the inward FDI, FDI performance and FDI potential of the host country.

According to the Foreign Direct Investment Survey 2002 by the Multilateral Investment Guarantee Agency (MIGA) of the World Bank Group, which received 643 responses to its questionnaires mailed to 3,000 companies including 100 top MNCs, 42 percent of the respondents indicate mergers and acquisitions as the mode of their FDI activities, the rest of 58 percent of the Greenfield investment mode is split between 43 percent of building/leasing a new facility and 15 percent of expanding an existing company facility. Figure 16.2 shows the profile of FDI modes considered by the respondents. Detailed analysis reveals that larger companies are somewhat more likely to pursue mergers and acquisitions than their smaller counterparts. There exist regional differences in FDI modes too – both North American and Asian companies rank build/lease, mergers and acquisitions, and expanding an existing facility – first, second and third. In contrast, more than half of the Western European companies point to mergers and acquisitions as their primary mode of FDI activities.

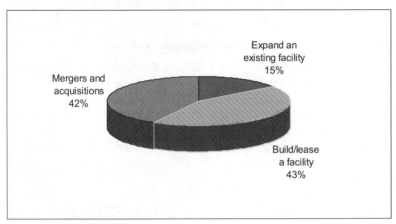

Source: MIGA/World Bank

**Figure 16.2.** FDI modes

With regard to the choice of FDI locations, it is found that access to customers is the leading consideration, followed by stable social and political environment, ease of doing business, reliability and quality of infrastructure and utilities, and ability to hire technical professionals. Furthermore, larger companies are less likely to identify labour relations and unionisation as critical location factors, and more likely to focus on labour cost. They are also more likely than smaller companies to select national taxes as a key factor. Smaller companies more often select the ability to hire skilled labourers, technical professionals, and management staff as very important issues. They are also more likely than larger companies to be concerned with the availability of fully serviced land as well as the reliability and quality of utilities. Figure 16.3 lists and ranks top 20 factors influencing MNCs' choice of locations. It is observed that most of these factors can be identified with the factors in country risk analysis undertaken by most of rating and risk analysis agencies. So the survey results may be helpful to decide the factor weightings in country risk analysis models.

(a) Top 10 factors

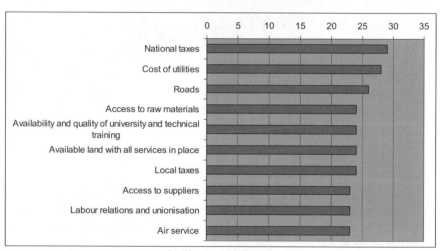

(b) The next 10 factors

Source: MIGA/World Bank

**Figure 16.3.** Factors influencing FDI location choice

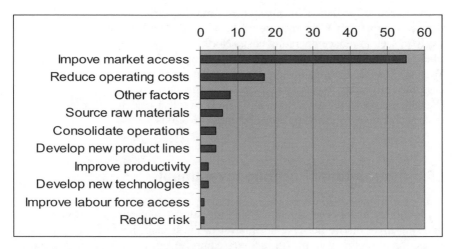

(a) Most important objectives

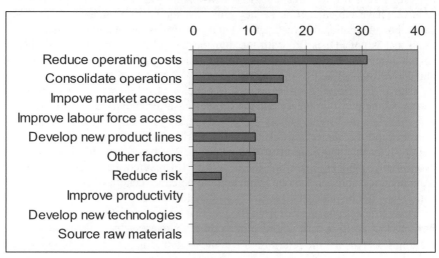

(b) Second most important objectives

Source: MIGA/World Bank

**Figure 16.4.** Objectives of FDI activities

Figure 16.4 lists and ranks the top 10 most important objectives and the top 10 second most important objectives of FDI engagements. Market access is the chief objective in establishing foreign operations. Overwhelmingly, improving market access is considered to be the most important objective in their foreign expansion strategies. The next primary objective is to reduce operating costs and a key second most important objective is to consolidate operations. It is further revealed that Most North American companies rank improving market access as their primary objective for their FDI engagement, but they are less likely to do so than their counterparts in Western Europe, Asia and Pacific Rim, and relatively more likely to seek to reduce operating costs. North American companies are also more likely than their counterparts to view improving productivity as a key objective. Western European companies are the most concerned with improving market access, but least likely to choose reducing operating costs as their primary objective. Western European companies are most likely to select reducing costs as their secondary objective, followed by consolidating operations.

## 16.3 International Portfolio Investment

IPI is another major type of international investment, alongside FDI. International portfolio investors do not take an interest in the management of the corporation located in a foreign country. IPI includes equity securities, debt securities, money market instruments, and financial derivatives. All of them, especially financial derivatives, have sub-categories, as they grow fast and become increasingly sophisticated. For international investment in equity securities that entail ownership, anything that is not FDI is IPI, with the division being decided by the thresholds of shareholdings. For international investment in non-equity securities, such as bonds and derivatives, all is IPI.

One of the primary motives as well as benefits of IPI is international diversification. While portfolio theory and the Capital Asset Pricing Model (CAPM) apply to a domestic market as well as the world market in principle, market imperfections beyond the domestic market, notably market segmentation in various forms, require relevant modifications to the single market based investment theory and asset pricing models. Therefore, the benefit of IPI may not be gained exclusively from diversification on the one hand, and the potential benefit of further diversification may not be realised through IPI on the other hand.

Diversification gains stem from the fact that returns on national markets do not have perfect positive correlations or they do not move exactly in the same way all the times. Let $R_h$ be the return on the home or domestic market portfolio, $R_{rw}$ be the return on the market portfolio in the rest of the world, $\sigma_h$ be the standard deviation of the return on the domestic market, $\sigma_{rw}$ be the standard deviation of the return on the market in the rest of the world, $\rho_{h,rw}$ be the correlation between the return on the domestic market and that on the rest of the world's market, then an international portfolio consisting of a weighting of $w_h$ in the domestic portfolio and $(1-w_h)$ in the market portfolio in the rest of the world would have a return of:

$$R_p = w_h R_h + (1-w_h)R_{rw} \qquad (16.2a)$$

and a standard deviation of:

$$\sigma_p = w_h^2 \sigma_h^2 + 2\rho_{h,rw} w_h (1-w_h)\sigma_h \sigma_{rw} + (1-w_h)^2 \sigma_{rw}^2 \qquad (16.2b)$$

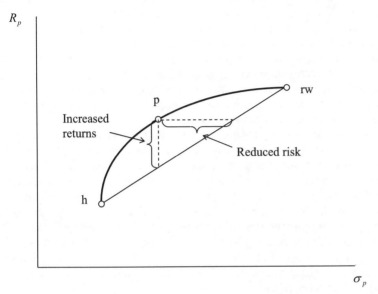

**Figure 16.5.** International diversification gains

There would be diversification gains as long as $\rho_{h,rw} < 1$, shown in Figure 16.5. All of the feasible international portfolios are plotted on the h-p-rw curve, with h representing investment in the domestic market, rw representing investment in the rest of the world, and p representing an international portfolio described by equation (16.2). The straight line h-rw shows the combinations of the portfolios h and rw as if there were no diversification, or $\rho_{h,rw} = 1$. Therefore, diversification can lead to increased return with the same risk, or diversification can lead to reduced risk with the same return, compared with the non-diversification case. Various statistics have suggested and confirmed that national markets do not have a perfect positive correlation, so international diversification may always be attempted and, indeed, has been practised by many institutional and individual investors around the world.

Nevertheless, there are barriers to international diversification, notably, (a) segmented markets, (b) illiquid foreign markets, (c) less developed foreign markets, (d) foreign exchange exposure, (e) foreign exchange control; and (f) obstacles to access to information and acquisition of knowledge. Other factors, mostly of them invisible, also hinder diversification into foreign lands, such as (a) utility bias towards the home country, (b) increased risk aversion against investment in foreign countries, and (c) differences in consumption baskets across countries. Consequently, international diversification may not as simple as being illustrated by Figure 16.5 and international diversification gains may not exist or may not materialise under various circumstances.

Besides international diversification gains, IPI may bring about other benefits, including (a) seizing greater opportunities in foreign lands, (b) catching the growth in foreign markets, (c) generating abnormal returns from market segmentation, and (d) time diversification with differed business cycles and business cycle timing. Market segmentation distorts returns to different investor groups, so it may generate abnormal returns for a certain group of investor at the expense of others on the one hand, and it may reduce the benefit of international diversification or even offset some of the domestic returns for another group of investors on the other hand. We discuss these benefits in the following.

Larger domains always provide greater opportunities. However, the size of the domain and the enormity of the opportunities need not to be proportional. Investment in a foreign country similar to the home country in character and in size does not double the opportunities. To some extent, opportunities are proportional to the dissimilarities between the home country and the foreign country and the economic growth in the foreign country. Therefore, investors in the west have been increasingly seeking opportunities in developing countries, especially those with fast economic growth and development, with IPI being one of the channels, since the benefits from these opportunities will eventually be passed onto the financial market. That is, IPI offers the benefit of higher returns indirectly through seizing opportunities in the foreign land.

High economic growth usually accompanies even higher growth in capital markets in developing countries. It is because capital markets came into existence only fairly recently in many developing countries. For the capital market to function properly to support rapid economic development, it must grow and expand more rapidly than the economy as a whole. Therefore, IPI offers the benefit of high growth in foreign capital markets directly.

When the markets are segmented, investors do not have free and equal access to all the markets. Under complete market segmentation, one group of investors (group A), can only access one market (market A) and the other group of investors (group B) can only access the other market (market B). Under such circumstances, no IPI can take place. Most market segmentation is milder than complete segmentation, involving restrictions imposed on a sub set of investors, or different restrictions imposed on different investors, through legal and/or financial means. Market segmentation distorts risk return profiles and shifts efficient frontiers, leading to positive abnormal returns as well as negative abnormal returns. Properly exploited, investing in segmented markets through IPI may yield positive abnormal returns. One of the most noted examples of great significant is the distinction between the A share and the B share traded on the Shanghai Stock Exchange and the Shenzhen Stock Exchange. A shares are traded in RMB and B shares are traded in US dollars on the Shanghai market and in HK dollars on the Shenzhen market. A shares can only be purchased by PRC residents and, until February 19, 2001, B shares could only be purchased by foreigners. From February 20, 2001, restrictions are no longer imposed on PRC residents to purchase B shares. So the PRC

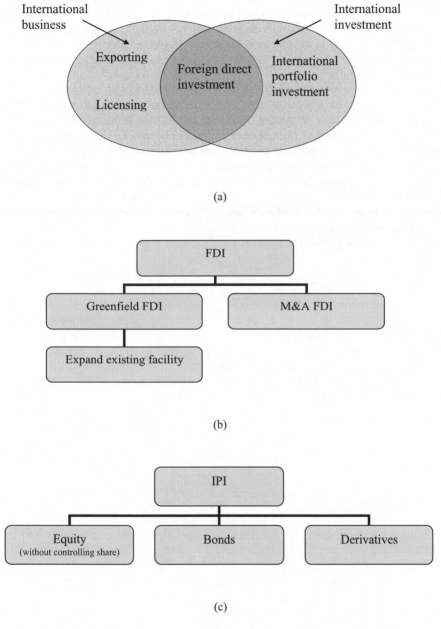

(a)

(b)

(c)

**Figure 16.6.** International economic activities

market is a typical segmented market, offering the opportunities to exploit abnormal returns.

IPI has another benefit – time diversification with differed business cycles and business cycle timing. Diversification within a national market may reduce risk but will not be able to prop up returns during economic recessions. Therefore, returns on well diversified domestic portfolios still exhibit cyclical movements in the medium to long term. International diversification with different business cycles and business cycle timing may further smooth such medium to long term cyclical fluctuations in returns.

Finally, we summarise international investment along with other major activities of doing business in the foreign land – international economic activities altogether, using diagrams. Exporting, licensing and FDI are doing business in foreign countries and are termed international business. FDI and IPI are investing in foreign countries and together constitute international investment. Therefore, FDI spans both the international business area and the international investment area. IPI, without significant interest in the running and control of the business, is confined to international investment exclusively. Panel (a) of Figure 16.6 demonstrates all major international economic activities – the area where international business and international investment overlap is FDI. Panel (b) of Figure 16.6 shows the forms of FDI and panel (c) of Figure 16.6 shows the three major types of IPI.

# References

Abuaf, N. and Jorion, P. (1990), Purchasing power parity in the long run, *Journal of Finance*, 45, 157-174.

Adler, M. and Lehmann, B. (1983), Deviations from purchasing power parity in the long run, *Journal of Finance*, 38, 1471-1487.

Akiba, H. (1996), Exchange-rate sensitive demand for money and overshooting, *International Economic Journal*, 10, 119-129.

Bahmani-Oskooee, M. (1995), The decline of the Iranian rial during the post-revolutionary period: the monetary approach and Johansen's cointegration analysis, *Canadian Journal of Development Studies*, 16, 277-289.

Baillie, R.T. and McMahon, P. (1989), *The Foreign Exchange Market: theory and econometric evidence*, Cambridge, England: Cambridge University press.

Boothe, P. and Glassman, D. (1987), Off the mark: lessons for exchange rate modelling, *Oxford Economic Papers*, 39, 443-457.

Burdekin, R.C.K. and Burkett, P. (1996), Hyperinflation, the exchange rate and endogenous money: post-World War I Germany revisited, *Journal of International Money and Finance*, 15, 599-621.

Campbell, J.Y. and Shiller, R.J. (1987), Cointegration and tests of present value models, *Journal of Political Economy*, 95, 1062-1088.

Cavaglia, S. (1991), Permanent and transitory components in the time series of real exchange rates, *Journal of International Financial Markets, Institutions and Money*, 1, 1-44.

Chang, W.Y. and Lai, C.C. (1997), The specification of money demand, fiscal policy, and exchange rate dynamics, *Journal of Macroeconomics*, 19, 79-102.

Chen, B. (1995), Long-run purchasing power parity: evidence from some European monetary system countries, *Applied Economics*, 27, 377-383.

Cheung, Y.W., Fung, H., Lai, K.S. and Lo, W.C. (1995), Purchasing power parity under the European monetary system, *Journal of International Money and Finance*, 14, 179-189.

Cheung, Y.W. and Lai, K.S. (1993), Long-run purchasing power parity during the recent float, *Journal of International Economics*, 34, 181-192.

Chowdhury, A.R. and Sdogati, F. (1993), Purchasing power parity in the major European Monetary System countries: the role of price and exchange rate adjustment, *Journal of Macroeconomics*, 15, 25-45.

Cochrane, S.J. and DeFina, R.H. (1995), Predictable components in exchange rates, *Quarterly Review of Economics and Finance*, 35, 1-14.

Cumby, R.E. and Obstfeld, M. (1984), International interest rate and price level linkage under flexible exchange rates: review of recent evidence, in J.F.O. Bilson and R.C. Marston (eds.), *Exchange Rate Theory and Practice*, Chicago: University of Chicago Press, pp. 121-151.

Cushman, D.O. (2000), The failure of the monetary exchange rate model for the Canadian-U.S. dollar, *Canadian Journal of Economics*, 33, 591-603.

Darby, M. (1983), Movements in purchasing power parity: the short and long runs, in M. Darby and J. Lothian (eds.), *The International Transmission of Inflation*, Chicago: University of Chicago Press.

Diamandis, P.F. and Kouretas, G.P. (1996), Exchange rate determination: empirical evidence for the Greek drachma, *Managerial and Decision Economics*, 17, 277-290.

Diebold, F.X., Husted, S. and Rush, M. (1991), Real exchange rates under the gold standard, *Journal of Political Economy*, 99, 1252-1271.

Dornbusch, R. (1976), Expectations and exchange rate dynamics, *Journal of Political Economy*, 84, 1161-1176.

Driskill, R. (1981), Exchange rate overshooting, the trade balance, and rational expectations, *Journal of International Economics*, 11, 361-377.

Dutt, S.D. and Ghosh, D. (1999), An empirical examination of the long run monetary (exchange rate) model, *Studies in Economics and Finance*, 19, 62-83.

Enders, W. (1988), ARIMA and cointegration tests of PPP under fixed and flexible exchange rate regimes, *Review of Economics and Statistics*, 70, 504-508.

Enders, W. (1989), Unit roots and the real exchange rate before World War I: the case of Britain and the USA, *Journal of International Money and Finance*, 8, 59-73.

Engle, R.F. and Granger, C.W.J. (1987), Co-integration and error correction: representation, estimation, and testing, *Econometrica*, 55, 251-267.

Engsted, T. (1996), The monetary model of the exchange rate under hyperinflation: new encouraging evidence, *Economics Letters*, 51, 37-44.

Fleming, J.M. (1962), Domestic financial policies under fixed and floating exchange rates, *IMF Staff Papers*, 9, 369–79.

Fleming, J.M. (1971), *Essays in International Economics*, London: Allen and Unwin.

Francis, B., Hasan, I. and Lothian, J.R. (2001), The monetary approach to exchange rates and the behaviour of the Canadian dollar over the long run, *Applied Financial Economics*, 11, 475-481.

Frankel, J.A. (1979), On the mark: a theory of floating exchange rates based on real interest differentials, *American Economic Review*, 69, 610-622.

Frankel, J.A. (1986), International capital mobility and crowding out in the US economy: imperfect integration of financial markets or of goods markets, In R.W. Hafer (ed.), *How Open Is the US Economy?* Lexington, Mass., and Toronto: Heath, Lexington Books, pp33-67.

Frankel, J.A. and Rose, A.K. (1996), A panel project on purchasing power parity: mean reversion within and between countries, *Journal of International Economics*, 40, 209-224.

Frenkel, J.A. (1976), A monetary approach to the exchange rate: doctrinal aspects and empirical evidence, *Scandinavian Journal of Economics*, 78, 200-224.

Frenkel, J.A. (1978), Purchasing power parity doctrinal perspective and evidence from the 1920s, *Journal of International Economics*, 8, 169-191.

Frenkel, J.A. (1981), The collapse of purchasing power parity during the 1970s, *European Economic Review*, 16, 145-165.

Froot, K.A. and Rogoff, K. (1994), Perspectives on PPP and long-run real exchange rates, *NBER Working Papers*, No. 4952.

Ghosh, M. (1998), Structural break and cointegration tests of the monetary exchange rate model, *Keio Economic Studies*, 35, 67-77.

Glen, J.D. (1992), Real exchange rates in the short, medium, and long run, *Journal of International Economics*, 33, 147-166.

Grilli, V. and Kaminsky, G. (1991), Nominal exchange rate regimes and the real exchange rates: evidence from the United Stated and Great Britain 1885-1986, *Journal of Monetary Economics*, 27, 191-212.

Groen, J.J. and Kleibergen, F. (2003), Likelihood-based cointegration analysis in panels of vector error-correction models, *Journal of Business and Economic Statistics*, 21, 295-318.

Groen, J.J. (2002), Cointegration and the monetary exchange rate model revisited, *Oxford Bulletin of Economics and Statistics*, 64, 361-380.

Hakkio, C.S. (1984) A Re-examination of purchasing power parity: a multicountry and multi-period study, *Journal of International Economics*, 17, 265-277.

Husted, S. and MacDonald, R. (1998), Monetary-based models of the exchange rate: a panel perspective, *Journal of International Financial Markets, Institutions and Money*, 8, 1-19.

Hwang, J.K. (2003), Dynamic forecasting of sticky-price monetary exchange rate model, *Atlantic Economic Journal*, 31, 103-114.

Johansen, S. (1988), Statistical analysis of cointegration vectors, *Journal of Economic Dynamics and Control*, 12, 231-254.

Johansen, S. (1991), Estimation and hypothesis testing of cointegration vectors in Gaussian vector autoregressive models, *Econometrica*, 59, 1551–1580.

Johansen, S. and Juselius, K. (1990), Maximum likelihood estimation and inference on cointegration - with applications to the demand for money, *Oxford Bulletin of Economics and Statistics*, 52, 169-210.

Jorion, P. and Sweeney, R. J. (1996), Mean reversion in real exchange rates: evidence and implications for forecasting, *Journal of International Money and Finance*, 15, 535-550.

Kiguel, M.A. and Dauhajre, A. (1988), A dynamic model of the open economy with sluggish output, *International Economic Review*, 29, 587-606.

Kim, S. (2001), International transmission of US monetary policy shocks: evidence from VAR's, *Journal of Monetary Economics*, 48, 339-372.

Kim, Y. (1990), Purchasing power parity: another look at the long-run data, *Economics Letters*, 32, 339-344.

Krugman, P. (1978), Purchasing power parity and exchange rates: another look at the evidence, *Journal of International Economics*, 8, 397-407.

Krugman, P. and Obstfeld, M. (1994), *International Economics Theory and Policy* 4th ed., New York: Harper Collins College Publishers.

Kugler, P. and Lenz, C. (1993), Multivariate cointegration analysis and the long-run validity of purchasing power parity, *Review of Economics and Statistics*, 75, 180-184.

Levin, J.H. (1989), On the dynamic effects of monetary and fiscal policy under floating exchange rates: simulations with an asset market model, *Weltwirtschaftliches Archiv*, 125, 665-680.

Levin, J.H. (1994), On sluggish output adjustment and exchange rate dynamics, *Journal of International Money and Finance*, 13, 447-458.

Lothian, J.R. (1997), Multi-country evidence on the behavior of purchasing power parity under the current float, *Journal of International Money and Finance*, 16, 19-35.

Lothian, J.R. (1998), Some new stylized facts of floating exchange rates, *Journal of International Money and Finance*, 17, 29-39.

Lothian, J.R. and Taylor, M.P. (1996), Real exchange rate behavior: the recent float from the perspective of the past two centuries, *Journal of Political Economy*, 104, 488-509.

MacDonald, R. (1993), Long-run purchasing power parity: is it for real? *Review of Economics and Statistics*, 75, 690-695.

MacDonald, R. and Taylor, M.P. (1991), The monetary approach to the exchange rate: long-run relationships and coefficient restrictions, *Economics Letters*, 37, 179-185.

MacDonald, R. and Taylor, M.P. (1993), The monetary approach to the exchange rate: rational expectations, long-run equilibrium, and forecasting, *IMF Staff Papers*, 40, 89-107.

MacDonald, R. and Taylor, M.P. (1994), The monetary model of the exchange rate: long-run relationships, short-run dynamics and how to beat a random walk, *Journal of International Money and Finance*, 13, 276-290.

Mahdavi, S. and Zhou, S. (1994), Purchasing power parity in high-inflation countries: further evidence, *Journal of Macroeconomics*, 16, 403-422.

Mark, N.C. (1990), Real and nominal exchange rates in the long run: an empirical investigation, *Journal of International Economics*, 28, 115-136.

Mark, N.C. (1995), Exchange rates and fundamentals: evidence on long-horizon predictability, *American Economic Review*, 85, 201-218.

McNown, R. and Wallace, M.S. (1989), National price levels, purchasing power parity and cointegration: a test for four high inflation economies, *Journal of International Money and Finance*, 8, 533-545.

McNown, R. and Wallace, M.S. (1994), Cointegration tests of the monetary exchange rate model for three high-inflation economies, *Journal of Money, Credit, and Banking*, 26, 396-411.

Meese, R. and Rogoff, K. (1988), Was it real? The exchange rate-interest differential relation over the modern floating-rate period, *Journal of Finance*, 43, 933-948.

Mundell, R.A. (1960), The monetary dynamics of international adjustment under fixed and flexible exchange rates, *Quarterly Journal of Economics*, 84, 227–257.

Mundell, R.A. (1961), The international disequilibrium system, *Kyklos*, 14, 154–172.

Mundell, R.A. (1962), The appropriate use of monetary and fiscal policy for internal and external stability, *IMF Staff Papers*, 9, 70–79.

Mundell, R.A. (1963), Capital mobility and stabilization policy under fixed and flexible exchange rates, *Canadian Journal of Economics and Political Science*, 29, 475–485.

Mundell, R.A. (1964), A reply: capital mobility and size, *Canadian Journal of Economics and Political Science*, 30, 421–431.

Mundell, R.A. (2001), On the history of the Mundell-Fleming model, *IMF Staff Papers*, 47 (special issue), 215-227.

Mussa, M. (1982), A model of exchange rate dynamics, *Journal of Political Economy*, 90, 74-104.

Mussa, M. (1986), Nominal exchange rate regimes and the behavior of real exchange rates: evidences and implications, in K. brunner and A. H. Melzer (eds.), *Real Business Cycles, Real Exchange Rates and Actual Polices*, Carnegie-Rochester Conference Series on Public Policy, 25, 117-214.

Natividad-Carlos, F.B. (1994), Monetary policy, fiscal policy and intervention in a model of exchange-rate and aggregate-demand dynamics, *Journal of Macroeconomics*, 16, 523-537.

O'Connell, P.G.J. (1998), The overvaluation of purchasing power parity, *Journal of International Economics*, 44, 1-19.

Obstfeld, M. (2001), International Macroeconomics: beyond the Mundell-Fleming Model, *IMF Staff Papers*, 47 (special issue), 1-39.

Obstfeld, M. and Rogoff, K. (1995), Exchange rate dynamics redux, *Journal of Political Economy*, 103, 624-660.

Oh, K.Y. (1996), Purchasing power parity and unit root tests using panel data, *Journal of International Money and Finance*, 15, 405-418.

Oh, K.Y. (1999), Are exchange rates cointegrated with monetary model in panel data? *International Journal of Finance and Economics*, 4, 147-154.

Papell, D.H. and Theodoridis, H. (1998), Increasing evidence of purchasing power parity over the current float, *Journal of International Money and Finance*, 17, 41-50.

Patel, J. (1990), Purchasing power parity as a long run relation, *Journal of Applied Econometrics*, 5, 367-379.

Pippenger, M.K. (1993), Cointegration tests of purchasing power parity: the case of Swiss exchange rates, *Journal of International Money and Finance*, 12, 46-61.

Rapach, D.E. and Wohar, M.E. (2002), Testing the monetary model of exchange rate determination: new evidence from a century of data, *Journal of International Economics*, 58, 359-385.

Rogoff, K. (1996), The purchasing power parity puzzle, *Journal of Economic Literature*, 34, 647-668.

Rogoff, K. (2002), Dornbusch's overshooting model after twenty-five years, *IMF Staff Papers*, 49 (Special Issue), 1-35.

Smith, G.W. (1995), Exchange-rate discounting, *Journal of International Money and Finance*, 14, 659-666.

Taylor, M.P. (1988), An empirical examination of long-run purchasing power parity using cointegration techniques, *Applied Economics*, 20, 1369-1381.

Taylor, M.P. and Sarno, L. (1998), The behavior of real exchange rates during the post-Bretton Woods period, *Journal of International Economics*, 46, 281-312.

Verschoor, W.F.C. and Wolff, C.C.P. (2001), Exchange risk premia, expectations formation and "news" in the Mexican peso/US dollar forward exchange rate market, *International Review of Financial Analysis*, 10, 157-174.

Wu, Y. (1996), Are real exchange rates nonstationary? Evidence from a panel data test, *Journal of Money, Credit and Banking*, 28, 54-63.

# Index